MW00388643

A TALMUD IN EXILE

Program in Judaic Studies
Brown University
Box 1826
Providence, RI 02912

BROWN JUDAIC STUDIES

Edited by

David C. Jacobson
Ross S. Kraemer
Saul M. Olyan
Michael L. Satlow

Number 342

A TALMUD IN EXILE
The Influence of Yerushalmi Avodah Zarah
on the Formation of Bavli Avodah Zarah

by
Alyssa M. Gray

A Talmud in Exile

The Influence of Yerushalmi Avodah Zarah on the Formation of Bavli Avodah Zarah

Alyssa M. Gray

Brown Judaic Studies
Providence, Rhode Island

Copyediting: Jordan D. Rosenblum and Abe Hendin
Design and typesetting: Abe Hendin / AH Prepress (http://ahprepress.com)
Indexing: Nancy Zibman

Library of Congress Cataloging-in-Publication Data
Gray, Alyssa M.
    A Talmud in exile : the influence of Yerushalmi Avodah zarah on the formation of Bavli Avodah zarah / Alyssa M. Gray.
        p. cm. — (Brown Judaic studies ; no. 342)
    Includes bibliographical references and index.
    ISBN-13: 978-1-930675-23-0 (cloth binding : alk. paper)
    ISBN-10: 1-930675-23-2 (cloth binding : alk. paper)
    1. Talmud Yerushalmi. Avodah zarah—Comparative studies. 2. Talmud. Avodah zarah—Comparative studies.   I. Title. II. Series.

    BM506.A17G75 2005
    296.1'244—dc22
                                                            2005017041

Printed in the United States of America
on acid-free paper

To my parents, Robert and Miriam Gray

Contents

Acknowledgments

I have been privileged over the years to study with a number of important scholars, whose courses, seminars, encouragement, and critiques helped me develop and refine my interest in the comparative study of the Talmuds, resulting in the book you hold in your hands. I owe a special debt of gratitude to Professor Richard Kalmin of the Jewish Theological Seminary of America. It was in Dr. Kalmin's doctoral seminar on the Talmud Yerushalmi that I first conceived the idea for the present book and took preliminary steps in this direction. As a doctoral advisor and colleague he sets the standard for methodological rigor and careful analysis to which I aspire in my own scholarship, and he is always more than generous with his time and attention. I am grateful for the opportunity to thank him publicly.

I am also pleased to thank Professor Christine Hayes of Yale University, who took an interest in this project from early on and whose keen comments and questions have been valuable in the preparation of this book. I am also grateful to her for inviting me to present some of this research to her graduate seminar in rabbinic literature.

I benefited greatly from my interactions with Professor Michael Fishbane, Professor Joel L. Kraemer, and graduate students in Judaic Studies at the University of Chicago, who invited me to present some of this research at their Judaic Studies Workshop. Professor Kraemer also read the manuscript in its entirety and provided probing and helpful comments, for which I am thankful. I am also grateful for invitations to present some of this research at a Talmud Department Seminar at the Jewish Theological Seminary and at the Seminary's "Revson 25 Academic Conference and Celebration," and for the eagerness of my HUC-JIR colleagues to comment on some of this work at a faculty seminar here. Professor Matthew Kraus of Williams College also invited me to present a paper related to this research at a conference there, and I remain grateful for that opportunity and its stimulus to my thinking. As always, I am grateful to Professor Gwynn Kessler for her friendship, for hours of stimulating conversation, and for always challenging points I thought were settled. I would also like to thank Professor Judith Hauptman for her support of this project, and for graciously sharing with me her as-yet unpublished introduction to her newest work, which has points of contact with my own.

I would also like to publicly thank our Provost, Dr. Norman J. Cohen, and our Dean, Dr. Aaron D. Panken, for allowing me a course reduction in Spring 2004 so that I could complete the revisions of this manuscript.

It is also my pleasure to publicly thank the editors at Brown Judaic Studies, especially Professor Saul M. Olyan, for accepting this volume into the Brown Judaic Studies series. I also wish to express my deepest thanks to the anonymous readers, one of whom in particular helped me refine and sharpen my thinking and presentation of key arguments.

On a personal note, I would also like to acknowledge the constant support and encouragement of Robert and Miriam Gray, Michael and Stephanie Gray, Erica Gray, Skylar Gray, Ann Gray, and Robin Riback. This book is lovingly dedicated to my parents, Robert and Miriam Gray, lifelong educators, who had to have foreseen that their eldest daughter would someday write a book. Robin has generously rejoiced in this book's coming to fruition and for this and much else she deserves thanks. Finally, I hope that Erica and Skylar will pick this book up someday and see what their aunt was doing during their earliest years.

Conventions and Abbreviations

Hebrew transliteration is phonetic. Throughout this book, ' = א, ' = ע (except where pronunciation is sufficiently indicated by the vowel), "kh" = כ, "ts" = צ, and "q" = ק. The letter "h" is used to transliterate both ה and ח, while "s" is used to transliterate both ס and שׂ. The *dagesh* is not represented. Foreign words will be italicized, except for commonly-used terms such as "sugya," "tanna(im)," "amora(im)," "geon(im)," "rishon(im)," "midrash(im)," and "saboraim." In all translations in this book, tannaitic materials will be presented in **bold**, the anonymous voice in *italics*, and amoraic traditions in regular Roman type.

1 Sam	1 Samuel
2 Chr	2 Chronicles
AZ	Avodah Zarah
ARN	Avot de-Rabbi Natan
AJSR	*Association for Jewish Studies Review*
Arakh	Arakhin
B./b.	Bavli (Babylonian Talmud)
b.	*ben* or *bar* or *bereh*
BB	Bava Batra
BM	Bava Metzia
BQ	Bava Qamma
Bekh	Bekhorot
Ber	Berakhot
Betz	Betzah
Bik	Bikkurim
ca.	circa
CJ	*Codex Justinianus*
CTh	*Codex Theodosianus*

d.	died
Dan	Daniel
Dem	Demai
Deut	Deuteronomy
DS	*Diqduqei Soferim*
Eccl	Ecclesiastes
Eduy	Eduyyot
Eruv	Eruvin
ed.	editor(s); edited by
Exod	Exodus
Gen	Genesis
GenR	Genesis Rabbah
Git	Gittin
Hag	Hagigah
Hal	Hallah
Hor	Horayot
HTR	*Harvard Theological Review*
HUCA	*Hebrew Union College Annual*
Hul	Hullin
Isa	Isaiah
JJS	*Journal of Jewish Studies*
JQR	*Jewish Quarterly Review*
Kel	Kelim
Ker	Keritot
Ket	Ketubbot
Kil	Kilayim
Lev	Leviticus
M./m.	Mishnah
ms.	manuscript
Maas	Maaserot
MSh	Maaser Sheni
Mak	Makkot
Makh	Makhshirin
Meg	Megillah
Meil	Meilah
Men	Menahot
Mid	Middot
MQ	Moed Qatan
Naz	Nazir
Ned	Nedarim
Nid	Niddah
Num	Numbers
Ohal	Ohalot

Orl	Orlah
PAAJR	*Proceedings of the American Academy for Jewish Research*
Par	Parah
Peah	Peah
Pes	Pesahim
pl.	plural
Ps/Pss	Psalms
Qid	Qiddushin
R.	Rabbi or Rav
REJ	*Revue des études juives*
RH	Rosh Hashanah
Sanh	Sanhedrin
Sem	Semahot
sg.	singular
Sirm	*Constitutiones Sirmondianae*
Shab	Shabbat
Sheq	Sheqalim
Shevi	Sheviit
Shevu	Shevuot
Sof	Soferim
Sot	Sotah
ST	Sefer Torah
Suk	Sukkah
T./t.	Tosefta
Taan	Taanit
Tam	Tamid
Teh	Teharot
Tem	Temurah
Ter	Terumot
TY	Tevul Yom
Tzitz	Tzitzit
Y./y.	Yerushalmi (Palestinian Talmud)
Yad	Yadayim
Yev	Yevamot
Yoma	Yoma
Zav	Zavim
Zev	Zevahim
Zeph	Zephaniah

1

Introduction

I
The Question

As a matter of both historical fact and rabbinic tradition, the Land of Israel was the birthplace of Rabbinic Judaism and the scene of most of its literary production between the second and seventh centuries CE. Rabbinic tradition points to Yavneh as R. Yohanan b. Zakkai's chosen site for the reconstitution of Torah learning after the destruction of 70. The scholars of the Mishnah, Tosefta, and so-called tannaitic midrashim (the tannaim, who flourished between 70 and 220 CE) were overwhelmingly, although not exclusively, Palestinian,[1] and most of the classic rabbinic compilations—those already noted as well as the Talmud of the Land of Israel (Yerushalmi), Genesis Rabbah, Leviticus Rabbah, and Pesiqta de-Rav Kahana—were produced in Palestine.

But that is not the entire story. Further to the east, the rabbinic enterprise took root in Babylonia. Although the Babylonian contribution to the tannaitic enterprise was small, the productive amoraic period (the post-tannaitic period of scholars known as amoraim; sing. amora) in Babylonia began with the third-century arrival there of the Mishnah (ca. 220 CE). Rabbinic tradition credits Rav, said to be a student of the Patriarch R. Yehudah ha-Nasi, with the introduction of the Mishnah to Babylonia. Rav, together with his contemporary Shmuel, were the pivotal figures of the first of seven generations of Babylonian amoraim.

---

1. Aside from the famous and myth-shrouded example of Hillel, who allegedly came to Palestine from Babylonia, tannaitic sources mention some others, notably Nathan "the Babylonian," R. Yehudah b. Beteira (of Nisibis), Mattyah ben Heresh (of Rome) and Nahum "the Mede."

The amoraic periods in Palestine and Babylonia were not of equal duration. The Palestinian amoraic period ended in approximately 360–370 CE,[2] while that of Babylonia ended in approximately 500–501.[3] The Talmud Yerushalmi came to a close shortly after the end of the Palestinian amoraic period, around 400,[4] while the final editing of the Babylonian Talmud (Bavli) most likely occurred in the seventh century.

Both Talmuds represent that scholarly exchanges took place between the Palestinian and Babylonian rabbinic communities throughout their shared portion of the amoraic period.[5] Babylonian scholars are quoted by

---

2. On the basis of internal evidence in the Yerushalmi, Jacob N. Epstein asserted that the Talmud Yerushalmi was "sealed" during the years 410–420 CE, during the time of R. Ashi (the sixth generation of Babylonian amoraim) in Babylonia. Yaacov Sussman revisited the issue of the Yerushalmi's dating in "Ve-shuv le-Yerushalmi Neziqin," and concluded that the Yerushalmi was completed with the close of its amoraic period during the period 360–370. Sussman explicitly rejected Epstein's calculation of the duration of the amoraic period in Palestine, arguing that the five Palestinian amoraic generations were actually much more compressed in time than Epstein had allowed. See J. N. Epstein, *Introduction to Amoraitic Literature: Babylonian Talmud and Yerushalmi* (Tel-Aviv: Dvir, 1962), 273–276 (Heb.); Yaacov Sussman, "Ve-shuv le-Yerushalmi Neziqin," in *Mehqerei Talmud: Talmudic Studies* (ed. Yaacov Sussman and David Rosenthal; Jerusalem: Magnes, 1990), 1:132n187.

3. See, e.g., Richard Kalmin, *The Redaction of the Babylonian Talmud: Amoraic or Saboraic?* (Cincinnati: Hebrew Union College Press, 1989).

4. Both Epstein and Sussman implicitly assumed that the close of the Palestinian amoraic period was also the close of the Yerushalmi itself. But for this to be so, then the (or at least some) late Palestinian amoraim must have functioned as editors/redactors as well as amoraim. Neither Epstein nor Sussman provide any evidence of this. Second, as Baruch Bokser noted earlier in his study of y. Pesahim, the Yerushalmi's sequences of topics and sugyot are clearly the products of a post-amoraic hand; no individual amora is aware of the larger context in which he is now found. This observation suggests that although the Palestinian amoraic period may well have ended in 360–370, there was a post-amoraic period of Talmud formation in Palestine. Thus, it remains reasonable to posit an early fifth-century date for the completed Yerushalmi. See Baruch Bokser, *Yerushalmi Pesachim* (ed. Lawrence Schiffman; vol. 13 of *The Talmud of the Land of Israel: A Preliminary Translation and Explanation,* ed. Jacob Neusner; Chicago: University of Chicago Press, 1994).

5. Although both Talmuds utilize the teachings of amoraim in both rabbinic centers, neither draws on the same set of amoraim; moreover, the Bavli includes the teachings of Palestinian post-amoraic scholars who lived and worked during the career of R. Ashi (d. 427 CE), after the completion of the Yerushalmi. Among the early Palestinian amoraim mentioned only in the Yerushalmi are R. Abba b. Tablai (e.g., y. AZ 1:1, 39b) and R. Shimon b. R. Yannai (y. Shab 13:7, 14b; y. MQ 2:2, 81a). Among the early Palestinian amoraim mentioned only in the Bavli are R. Yoshiah

name in the Yerushalmi, which also contains Babylonian *sugyot* (sing. *sugya*).[6] Palestinian amoraim are ubiquitous in the Bavli, as are Palestinian sugyot and clusters of sugyot. Most of the aggadah (non-legal material) in the Bavli is of Palestinian provenance, despite the clear evidence of its having been reworked by later Babylonian editors.[7] Indeed, the remarkable abundance of Palestinian materials in what is, after all, the *Babylonian* Talmud prompted one medieval commentator to declare that "most of the Babylonian Talmud is from them (i.e., Palestinian scholars such as R. Yohanan and Resh Laqish)."[8] The ubiquity of Palestinian sources in the Bavli and the interactions between the rabbinic communities during the amoraic period are a given. This being so, is it possible that the redactors of a particular Bavli tractate relied on the earlier parallel Yerushalmi tractate, or not?

II
Factors Complicating Resolution of the Question

This question is deceptively simple and the obstacles to arriving at an answer rather complex. Both Talmuds are composed of sources from different time periods that underwent a lengthy process of transmission and reworking. While we can be fairly certain that many, or even most, sugyot are not identical to what they looked like when first formulated, we cannot always be sure we can precisely reconstruct their textual history—

---

de-min Usha (b. Men 39a; b. Bekh 28b and 38b; b. Git 33b) and R. Mani b. Patish (b. Pes 66b, 80b; b. BQ 55b; b. BB 89b; b. Hul 48b, 85a, 102a, 135a; and b. Ker 7b). The Palestinian post-amoraic scholars mentioned in the Bavli include R. Abba (b. Shab 107a), as well as the anonymous scholars who "sent [an answer to a halakhic question] from there [Palestine]" mentioned at b. Hul 59b. Similarly, the Babylonian amoraim beginning with the fourth generation are not mentioned in the Yerushalmi, with the notable exception of a solitary reference to Rava at y. Betz 1:3, 60b. Their absence from the Yerushalmi is most likely due to their having lived and worked while the earlier Talmud was being brought to a close.

6. For some studies of the Babylonian materials in the Yerushalmi, see, e.g., Epstein, *Introduction*, 312–314; Joel Florsheim, "Sugyot Bavliot be-Yerushalmi Nezikin," *Sinai* 120:2 (1997): 53–85; 120:3 (1998): 161–181.

7. See, e.g., Shamma Friedman, "La-aggadah ha-historit ba-Talmud ha-Bavli," in *Saul Lieberman Memorial Volume* (ed. Shamma Friedman; New York: Jewish Theological Seminary, 1993), 119–164 (Heb.); Jeffrey Rubenstein, *Talmudic Stories: Narrative Art, Composition, and Culture* (Baltimore: Johns Hopkins University Press, 1999); Richard Kalmin, *The Sage in Jewish Society of Late Antiquity* (London: Routledge, 1999).

8. R. Yonatan, quoted in *Shittah Mequbetset* to b. BM 65a.

contra the self-confidence of some earlier source criticism practitioners. While we know—because we have Talmudic tractates—that sugyot were linked to each other and that tractates of "Talmud" eventually emerged, our knowledge about the process by which sugyot, or even chains of sugyot, became a Talmud tractate is only partial. This undercuts the confidence of the redaction critics. Not only is our understanding of the formation of the Bavli partial, but there seems to be evidence that supports different, even conflicting, theories.

Concerns such as these have led some scholars either to abandon research into the formation of the Bavli entirely, or to focus research on the redacted Bavli alone, eschewing the older critical methods.[9] Limiting research on the Bavli to the level of its final redaction is reminiscent of the recent literary turn to the study of the poetics and rhetoric of biblical narrative in biblical studies.[10] But as Christine Hayes has pointed out,[11] the Bible gives unmistakable evidence of wishing to be read synchronically, at the level of its final redaction. The Bible attempts to smooth over its prior sources by various narrative devices. The Bavli, on the other hand, gives unmistakable evidence of the opposite tendency: it wishes to be read diachronically, by constantly pointing the student to its diverse sources— diverse in both provenance and time period. The Bavli attributes source materials to various scholars in different amoraic generations, it calls attention to its citation of tannaitic or amoraic sources, and it provides multiple versions of individual traditions or sugyot.[12] The Bavli's call for attention to the diversity of its sources has caught the eye of recent critical Talmudic scholarship, which shows us that source and redaction criticism can still tell us a great deal about the Bavli and the scholars responsible for it.[13] While we can never know for certain what happened between the

---

9. See, e.g., David Kraemer, *Reading the Rabbis: The Talmud as Literature* (New York: Oxford University Press, 1996); idem, *The Meanings of Death in Rabbinic Judaism* (London: Routledge, 2000).

10. See, e.g., Meir Sternberg, *The Poetics of Biblical Narrative: Ideological Literature and the Drama of Reading* (Bloomington, IN: Indiana University Press, 1987).

11. Christine Elizabeth Hayes, *Between the Babylonian and Palestinian Talmuds: Accounting for Halakhic Difference in Selected Sugyot From Tractate Avodah Zarah* (New York: Oxford University Press, 1997), 13.

12. This is not to say that the Bavli redactors never touch earlier source materials at all. Indeed, as we will see throughout this book they do rework them, sometimes extensively. But the point is that even in reworking prior sources, the Bavli redactors do not completely smooth over these sources' diversity.

13. See, e.g., Shamma Friedman, "A Critical Study of *Yevamot X* With a Methodological Introduction," in *Texts and Studies: Analecta Judaica* (ed. H. Z. Dimitrovsky; vol. 1; New York: Jewish Theological Seminary, 1978), 275–441 (Heb.); idem, "La-aggadah ha-historit"; Richard Kalmin, *Sages, Stories, Authors, and Editors in Rab-*

completion of the Yerushalmi and the redaction of the Bavli, critical scholarship gives us a justified confidence that judicious use of the appropriate critical methods, attention to detail as well as to the form and organization of whole tractates, and attentiveness to the non-literary remains of Late Antique Jewish culture will (as we will see in the course of this book) change our perception of the development of the Bavli.[14]

In preparing to answer the question of the relationship between the Talmuds, then, we must begin by distinguishing between different types of identifiable Palestinian materials in the Bavli: discrete traditions attributed to particular amoraim (called *memrot*), sugyot, clusters of two or more sugyot, aggadah, and any macro-level orderings of sugyot and topics attached to each mishnah (pl. *mishnayot*) that are common to the two Talmuds. It is this last category that is of the most significance as we probe the relationship of a Bavli tractate to its Yerushalmi parallel. Distinguishing between these categories of Palestinian materials is important because a satisfactory explanation of why one particular type of Palestinian source made its way into the Bavli is not necessarily an adequate explanation of another, let alone of all the others. As an example, the Bavli itself draws attention to the amoraim known as the *nahote* (נחותי, "those who descended") who traveled between Palestine and Babylonia carrying rabbinic traditions.[15] Earlier scholars who examined the *nahote*, especially Isaac Halevy and Ze'ev Wolf Jawitz, assumed that the *nahote* were responsible for the large Palestinian content of the Bavli. But the Talmuds' portrayals of their activity do not permit us to infer that the *nahote* were responsible for *all* the Palestinian sugyot,[16] clusters of sugyot, and Palestinian aggadah

---

binic Babylonia (Atlanta: Scholars Press, 1994); Christine Hayes, *Between the Babylonian and Palestinian Talmuds.*

14. I hasten to point out that this book will focus on *one* Bavli tractate (Avodah Zarah) and its Yerushalmi parallel, and that the book's conclusions are limited to that tractate alone. Further research is needed to determine whether or not this book's conclusions are generalizable to the Bavli as a whole.

15. The principal *nahote* are R. Dimi, R. Yitshaq b. Yosef, R. Shmuel b. Yehudah, Rabin, and Ulla. The *nahote* are mentioned as a group at b. Suk 43b, b. Hul 101b and 124a, and b. Nid 10b and 39b, although in some of these places we find the variant reading "nahote yama" ("those who descend to the sea," meaning "sailors"). Interestingly, at b. Ber 38b, Ulla is referred to as "raboteinu ha-yordim me-erets Yisra'el," or "our master(s) who descended from the land of Israel." There is as yet no comprehensive study of the *nahote*. Such a study is a desideratum that would help us understand the diachronic dimensions of the penetration of Palestinian learning into Babylonia.

16. Earlier scholars, working from the evidence of the *nahote*'s activity in the Bavli as well as from R. Sherira Gaon's reference to them in his famous *Iggeret*, assumed that the *nahote* were the principal sources for the arrival of Palestinian

we see in the Bavli. The Talmudic evidence certainly does not at all permit the inference that the *nahote* were responsible for the macro-level ordering of sugyot and topics attached to each mishnah by the Bavli. An examination of all the materials attributed to R. Dimi, the *nahota* who looms largest in the Bavli, enables us to paint the portrait of a scholar whose primary role was carrying individual legal traditions.[17] Sometimes he conveyed stories, and sometimes whole sugyot or discrete aggadic traditions,[18] although the transmission of these types of learning is clearly portrayed as being of secondary importance in his work. Moving beyond R. Dimi, the handful of references to the *nahote* as a group (in which the Bavli refers to "Rabin and all the *nahote*"—or "nahote yama") also portrays this anonymous collectivity as transmitting discrete (legal) traditions—not the collected legal wisdom of the Palestinian rabbinic community. Further, the hypothesis that the *nahote* were responsible for the massive presence of Palestinian materials in the Bavli cannot explain an interesting pattern in the Palestinian materials in the Bavli. The fourth Babylonian amoraic generation is one in which the influence of Palestinian halakhah, literary forms, and/or terminology is more pronounced than in others.[19] If *nahote*

---

learning in Babylonia. See, e.g., Isaac Halevy, *Dorot ha-Rishonim* (6 vols.; Berlin: n.p., 1897–1939; repr. 6 vols. in 8, Israel: Mifalei Sefarim le-Yitso), 7:455–473; Ze'ev Wolf Jawitz, *Sefer Toldot Yisra'el* (10 vols.; Tel-Aviv: Ahiever, 1935), 7:159–164.

17. This aspect of R. Dimi's activity looms largest, so I will only provide a few examples from each tractate in which he is mentioned. See b. Ber 6b, 44b; b. Shab 52a, 134b; b. Eruv 3b, 77a, 87a; b. Pes 110b; b. Yoma 55a, 88a; b. Suk 10a, 11b; b. Hag 15b; b. MQ 13b; b. Yev 78a, 84b; b. Ket 17a, 100a; b. Ned 40a; b. Sot 43b (three occurrences); b. Git 59a; b. Qid 75a; b. BQ 76a; b. BM 105b; b. BB 73b, 80b; b. Sanh 7b, 57a, 69a; b. Shevu 20b; b. AZ 11b, 27a, 47a, 70b; b. Zev 20a, 115a; b. Men 26b, 55a; b. Hul 53a (two occurrences); b. Bekh 8a; b. Tem 12b–13a; b. Ker 25b; b. Nid 25a.

18. Stories: b. Ber 44a; b. Shab 13b (R. Dimi comments on a story, which implies that he knows it); b. Shab 50a, 74a, 125b, 147a; b. Eruv 86b; b. Suk 16b; b. Yev 59b; b. Qid 31a; and b. AZ 8b, 35b.

Sugyot: b. Shab 76a; b. MQ 10a; b. Ket 34b–35a, 57a, 104b, 107b; b. BB 27b, 129a, 152b; b. Sanh 70a; b. Zev 10a; b. Men 71b; b. Hul 103b, 134a; b. Meil 21b. A particularly interesting subset of these sugyot are those in which R. Dimi is represented as engaging with Abaye, and those in which Abaye and Rava use R. Dimi's sugyot as the basis for their own argumentation. Examples such as these require further research; could it be that Palestinian learning such as that of R. Dimi—introduced during the fourth Babylonian amoraic generation—helps account for the "spike" in Palestinian influence that we see in that generation?

Aggadic traditions: b. Ber 31b; b. Hag 14a; b. Ket 105b, 111b; b. BB 74b–75a, 79a; b. Sanh 100a, 108a; b. AZ 8b, 35a; and b. Zev 118b.

19. See Zwi Moshe Dor, *The Teachings of Eretz Israel in Babylon* (Tel-Aviv: Dvir, 1971) (Heb.); Richard Kalmin, *Sages, Stories, Authors and Editors*. Unfortunately,

had been moving back and forth between the rabbinic centers throughout the amoraic period, why is it that Palestinian learning is particularly prominent then?

When we extricate ourselves from the *nahote* hypothesis and look at the Talmuds as whole compilations, we see that despite the noticeable and unquestionable differences between them,[20] the Talmuds do indeed seem sufficiently alike for us to raise the question: were the redactors responsible for the later Talmud aware of, and influenced by, the work of the redactors of the earlier Talmud? The two Talmuds are the only compilations of their genre ("talmud")[21] produced by the rabbis in Late Antiquity, and stand out as the only compilations produced during this period arranged in the form of sustained commentaries on the Mishnah. The Talmuds utilize similar terminology and share structures of argumentation.[22] The

---

despite David Kraemer's fine analyses of the fourth generation's noticeably greater tendency to preserve argumentation than earlier or later amoraic generations, he did not investigate the possibility of a connection between this tendency and the Palestinian influence on that generation. See David Kraemer, "Stylistic Characteristics of Amoraic Literature" (Ph.D. diss., Jewish Theological Seminary, 1984); idem, *The Mind of the Talmud* (New York: Oxford University Press, 1991); and the review essay by Yaakov Elman, "Argument for the Sake of Heaven: *The Mind of the Talmud*," *JQR* 84:2–3 (1993–1994): 261–282. Elman's fine essay calls attention to key lacunae in Kraemer's arguments, but does not note his failure to consider the Palestinian connection.

20. The differences between the Talmuds have been, and continue to be, extensively studied. For some of the more recent studies of the differences in their respective rhetorics and argumentation, see Jacob Neusner, *Judaism: The Classical Statement* (Chicago: University of Chicago Press, 1986); idem, *The Bavli and its Sources: The Question of Tradition in the Case of Tractate Sukkah* (Atlanta: Scholars Press, 1987); idem, *The Bavli's Unique Voice: A Systematic Comparison of the Talmud of Babylonia and the Talmud of the Land of Israel* (7 vols.; Atlanta: Scholars Press, 1993); idem, *Are the Talmuds Interchangeable?* (Atlanta: Scholars Press, 1995); Jeffrey L. Rubenstein, *Talmudic Stories: Narrative Art, Composition, and Culture*. For a study of selected halakhic differences, see Christine Elizabeth Hayes, *Between the Babylonian and Palestinian Talmuds*. For a study of Babylonian/Palestinian cultural differences as reflected in their respective literatures (both the Yerushalmi and Palestinian sources preserved in the Bavli), see Richard Kalmin, *Sage in Jewish Society*.

21. For the notion of "talmud" as its own genre, see Jacob Neusner, *The Bavli's Unique Voice*, 1:2; David Kraemer, *Reading the Rabbis*, 7–8.

22. On similar terminology, see Zechariah Fraenkel, *Mavo ha-Yerushalmi* (Breslau: n.p., 1870; repr., Jerusalem: n.p., 1967), 8–18, where Fraenkel explains a number of Yerushalmi terms, often giving their Bavli equivalents. An example Fraenkel did not discuss is the Yerushalmi's *niha* ("it is well," or colloquially, "it makes sense") and the Bavli's equivalent *be-shelama*. An example of shared structures is the common *tserihah* construction in the Bavli, whereby the Talmud explains the

Talmuds share sugyot and have even been observed to order their parallel mishnah commentaries in structurally similar ways.[23] Moreover the Talmuds—the *only two* of their genre—were not created by two rabbinic communities working alone, innocent of each others' scholarly activities, but by communities with an historical, scholarly, and religious relationship that spanned over 150 years. The completed Talmuds themselves are separated by about two hundred years; certainly enough time for the Babylonian rabbinic community to have become aware of (at least part of) the Palestinian rabbis' magnum opus. So, once again the question: can we find any evidence that the redacted Yerushalmi influenced the formation of the redacted Bavli?

This book answers, simply, "yes." The argument of this book is that the redactors of tractate Avodah Zarah of the Babylonian Talmud were indeed aware of, and influenced by, elements of the structure and content of tractate Avodah Zarah of the Palestinian Talmud. They did not passively incorporate parts of the earlier Talmud, but selected, rejected, and reworked the portions they adopted in ways calculated to make them conform to Babylonian rabbinic linguistic, cultural, and religious norms.[24]

III
Prior Research on the
Relationship between the Talmuds

There is a large body of scholarship that bears in one way or another on the issue of the relationship between the Bavli and Yerushalmi. For heuristic purposes, we can categorize this scholarship under three headings: (1) scholars who argue that the redactors of the Bavli knew and relied upon the Yerushalmi and those who argue the diametrically opposing view;

---

necessity of seemingly redundant clauses in a mishnah or baraita. This construction is also found in the Yerushalmi.

23. Martin Jaffee, "The Babylonian Appropriation of the Talmud Yerushalmi: Redactional Studies in the Horayot Tractates," in *The Literature of Early Rabbinic Judaism: Issues in Talmudic Redaction and Interpretation* (ed. Alan J. Avery-Peck; vol. 4 of *New Perspectives On Ancient Judaism*; Lanham, MD: University Press, 1989), 3–27.

24. In chapter 6 we will examine some external evidence that buttresses this textually derived conclusion. Specifically, we will see that it is reasonable to assume that y. AZ was brought to Babylonia by a small coterie of Palestinian scholars who, in conformity with the precedent of the *nahote* and with the traveling habits of upper-class Romans, Christian clergy, and pagan philosophers, traveled with this learning to Babylonia in the sixth or seventh centuries.

(2) scholars who contend that what we see as the Palestinian contribution to the Bavli came to Babylonia incrementally throughout the amoraic period; and (3) scholars who study the edited Palestinian materials in the Bavli without pondering what, if any, implications their presence has for the redaction of the Bavli. All three bodies of scholarship are valuable sources of findings and methodological insights and I have drawn upon them all. But I will limit this survey to the scholars in groups (1) and (2), whose work has the most direct bearing on this book.[25] And, since the scholars in group (2) are, in essence, proposing an alternative theory to the one offered in this book, I will subject their arguments to closer scrutiny than those of the scholars in group (1).

III.a. *The Bavli Knew/Did Not Know the Yerushalmi*

Although the current scholarly consensus is that the Bavli redactors did not know the Yerushalmi,[26] a review of the research does reveal the existence of several contrary views and thus the potential for a reconsideration of the consensus. Although the validity of this book's argument does not depend on the existence of such contrarians, they show that the issue is not as cut-and-dried as it has been made to appear.

A well-known statement by R. Isaac Alfasi (the "Rif"; Morocco and Spain, 1013–1103) at the end of his codification of tractate Eruvin has traditionally been used as the starting-point for discussion of whether or not the Bavli was aware of the Yerushalmi.[27] There, the Rif writes:

---

25. Scholars who fall into what I have described as "group (3)" include Yaacov Sussman, "Babylonian Sugyot to the Orders Zera'im and Toharot" (Ph.D. diss., Hebrew University, 1969) (Heb.); Zwi Moshe Dor, *Teachings of Eretz Israel*; David Rosenthal, "Arikhot qedumot ha-meshuqa'ot ba-Talmud ha-Bavli," in *Mehqerei Talmud*, 1:155–204; Shamma Friedman, "La-aggadah ha-historit"; Richard Kalmin, *Sages, Stories, Authors, and Editors*; idem, *Sage in Jewish Society*; Jeffrey L. Rubenstein, *Talmudic Stories*; and Alon Goshen-Gottstein, *The Sinner and the Amnesiac: The Rabbinic Invention of Elisha ben Abuya and Eleazar ben Arach* (Stanford: Stanford University Press, 2000).

26. For the most recent reiterations of this consensus, see Jeffrey L. Rubenstein, *The Culture of the Babylonian Talmud* (Baltimore: Johns Hopkins University Press, 2003), 159; Leib Moscovitz, "Designation is Significant: An Analysis of the Conceptual *Sugya* in bSan 47b–48b," *AJSR* 27:2 (Nov 2003): 248n100. Moscovitz seems to leave the ultimate resolution of the question open.

27. See b. Eruv 35b (in the pages of the Rif). Louis Ginzberg and Leopold Greenwald both argued that the Rif was not actually claiming that the Bavli knew the Yerushalmi, and that his only concern was to argue that the Bavli was the halakhic *batra* of the Yerushalmi (and hence more halakhically reliable) in keeping with the geonic principle that *hilkheta ke-batrai* (the law follows the latest [scholars]). See

And we have seen that a few rabbis hold like Ulla and rely on the *gemara* of the Westerners[28] [the Yerushalmi] ... but we do not hold thus, for since our discussion in our gemara [inclines toward] permissiveness, it does not matter to us what they prohibit in the gemara of the Westerners. For we rely on our gemara, for it is the later. And they [presumably the sages of "our" gemara] were more expert than we in the gemara of the Westerners. And were it not for the fact that they held that this statement [of prohibition] of the Westerners was not authoritative, they would not have permitted it to us.

At first glance, it appears as if the Rif is indeed saying that the Bavli knew the Yerushalmi.[29] Yet the term "gemara" may not mean a finished Talmud.[30] The Rif may thus actually be saying that the sages of "our" gemara (the Bavli) were more expert "than we" in the traditional (Chanoch Albeck) or concise and "apodictic" (David Halivni) learning of the Palestinian sages, a claim which is certainly credible and also certainly not

---

Louis Ginzberg, *A Commentary on the Palestinian Talmud* (4 vols.; New York: Jewish Theological Seminary, 1941), 1:83–90 (Heb.); Greenwald, *Ha-ra'u mesadrei ha-Bavli et ha-Yerushalmi?* (Jerusalem: ha-Makhon le-Mehqar u-le-Madda ha-Yerushalmi, 1954), 70–71.

28. In the Bavli, the people residing in the Land of Israel are customarily referred to as the "Westerners," since Palestine lies to the west of Iran and Iraq, the home of the Babylonian amoraim.

29. Interestingly, this statement of the Rif does not appear to have been cited by anyone prior to the nineteenth century, so we are at a loss to know how medieval scholars understood it. But see Rabbenu Yonatan, *Shittah Mequbetset* to b. BM 45: "for those latter scholars who arranged the Babylonian Talmud for us, brought us all of those rationales which are [of] legal [validity] in the Talmud Yerushalmi, and most of the Babylonian Talmud is from them [the Palestinian scholars of the Yerushalmi] such as the words of R. Yohanan and R. Shimon b. Laqish, and all those who are called by the name 'Rabbi.'" An interesting variation of the Rif's statement appears in a responsum attributed to R. Hai Gaon, found in Zvi Benjamin Auerbach's edition of the medieval legal compendium *Sefer ha-Eshkol* (R. Abraham of Narbonne, 1110–1179). We shall discuss that responsum later in the Appendix to chapter 6. All we need note now is that the attribution of that responsum to R. Hai is doubtful, and it remains unclear who wrote the responsum and what the writer's agenda was.

30. See Chanoch Albeck, *Introduction to the Talmud, Babli and Yerushalmi* (Tel-Aviv: Dvir, 1969), 4 (Heb.) ("the word 'gemara' ... means ... that which was passed down and received from previous generations"). See also David Halivni, *Sources and Traditions*: Erubin-Pesahim (New York: Jewish Theological Seminary, 1982), 92–94 (Heb.) ("therefore it appears that 'gemara' has the meaning as well of an apodictic formulation").

equivalent to the claim that the Bavli was aware of the Yerushalmi. Without a thorough analysis of the various terms by which the Rif refers to the Yerushalmi in his "Halakhot" and his understanding of "gemara," it cannot be said with certainty that the Rif believed the redactors of the Bavli to have been aware of, and influenced by, the Yerushalmi. And even if we do adopt that understanding of his statement, the Rif's obvious anti-Yerushalmi polemic undercuts the value of his statement as an historical source—even though, as Martin Jaffee has pointed out, a polemical statement need not be presumed false.[31]

The first major investigations of the relationship between the Talmuds date to the nineteenth century. Shlomo Yehudah Rappaport (known as "Shir," 1790–1867) and Zvi Hirsch Chajes (1805–1855) conducted investigations into the relationship between the Talmuds that yielded the result that the Bavli *was* aware of the Yerushalmi. Rappaport compared the similar structures of the Talmuds' commentaries to the same mishnah, while Chajes focused on cases that seemed to show a Bavli sugya picking up on a concluding point in the Yerushalmi parallel or supplying information missing from the Yerushalmi parallel.[32] Zechariah Fraenkel (1801–1875) was familiar with the work of Rappaport and Chajes, and vigorously attacked some of their examples. First, he rejected Chajes' argument that the Bavli's incomplete presentation of a Palestinian *memra* more completely presented in the Yerushalmi is an intentional intertextual reference. Many Palestinian *memrot* are found in the Bavli, Fraenkel argued, and so all Chajes has shown is that a given Palestinian *memra* found in the Yerushalmi is also found in another form in the Bavli. This phenomenon is unremarkable and not dispositive of the larger issue of the relationship between the Talmuds. Turning his attention to Rappaport's work, Fraenkel points out that in many cases "the order [of sugyot and topics attached to the same mishnah in both the Bavli and Yerushalmi] cannot be any other way"—meaning, presumably, that if a given mishnah contains issues A, B, and C, one should not be surprised that both Talmuds present discussions of the mishnah in the order A, B, C.

Like Rappaport and Chajes, Isaac Halevy (1847–1914) argued in favor of the Bavli's awareness of the Yerushalmi. Taking a different tack, he purported to demonstrate that the anonymous, redactional voice of the Bavli

31. See Jaffee, "The Babylonian Appropriation of the Talmud Yerushalmi," 5.

32. Shlomo Yehudah Rappaport, "Toldot Rabbenu Nissim," *Bikkurei ha-Ittim* (1831): 90–92n16; Zvi H. Chajes, *Imrei Binah,* in idem, *Responsa of Mohara"ts* (Heb.) (1849–1850; repr., *Kol Sifrei Mohara"ts Chajot* [2 vols.; Jerusalem: Divrei Hakhamim, 1959]), 2:495–497.

was aware of its anonymous Yerushalmi counterpart, and that it incorporated conclusions from Yerushalmi sugyot into the Bavli parallels.[33]

Louis Ginzberg (1873–1953) briefly treated the issue of the relationship between the Talmuds in his *A Commentary on the Palestinian Talmud*.[34] He rejected the notion that the Rif's statement in Eruvin means that the Bavli knew the Yerushalmi, and also criticized Isaac Halevy's argumentation.[35] Yet Ginzberg did not present his *own* case for the view he obviously preferred—that the Bavli did not know the Yerushalmi.[36] In the 1950's, the independent scholar Yequtiel Yehudah (Leopold) Greenwald reached a similar conclusion through his analysis of the many differences between the Talmuds as to attributions of amoraic statements and versions thereof, as well as of materials present in the one Talmud but missing from the other.[37]

Jacob Nahum Epstein's (1878–1952) views on the relationship between the Talmuds were published after his death in the book *Introduction to Amoraitic Literature*.[38] Epstein's comments display a sense of the complexity of the issue not seen in his predecessors. He opened his discussion of the relationship between the Talmuds with a telling emphasis: "it is an old dispute as to whether the Bavli knew the Yerushalmi—*our* Yerushalmi—or did not know it."[39] After presenting the major geonic and rishonic viewpoints on the subject, Epstein concluded "but anyone who compares the Bavli with the Yerushalmi in even a cursory way will see immediately that the Bavli did not know *our Talmud Yerushalmi*, nor did the Yerushalmi know *our Talmud Bavli*" (emphasis in original).[40] What the Bavli *did* know, however (according to Epstein), was "not *our Talmud*, but in many, many places [it was] a Talmud in another edition—the edition of another yeshiva in another place in the Land of Israel, or a Talmud of a generation prior or *subsequent* to the editing of our Yerushalmi. Everything is according to the dating of the Bavli sugya and according to its lay-

---

33. Isaac Halevy, *Dorot ha-Rishonim*, 8:128–130. We will take up the issue of the anonymous Bavli and its (possible) role in the appropriation of Palestinian learning in chapter 5.

34. Ginzberg, *A Commentary*, 1:83–88.

35. Ibid., 1:87.

36. Some hint of what that case may have been may be found on page 87, where Ginzberg discusses the existence of material found in the one Talmud but not in the other, a phenomenon that could be made to support an argument that the Bavli did not know the Yerushalmi.

37. Greenwald, *Ha-ra'u mesadrei ha-Bavli et ha-Yerushalmi?*, 56–70.

38. J. N. Epstein, *Introduction*, 290–292.

39. Ibid., 290.

40. Ibid., 291.

ers" (emphasis in original).[41] Epstein thus believed that the Bavli did not know "our" Yerushalmi, but did not entirely rule out that it did know "a" Yerushalmi. Ultimately, Epstein suggested that for those wishing to understand *the relationship between the Bavli and the Yerushalmi* (emphasis in the original), the best course is to compare statements cited in the Bavli with the term *ma'arava* (the "West," meaning Palestine) with their parallels in the Yerushalmi, and to compare Babylonian statements introduced by *taman* ("there," which for the Yerushalmi is Babylonia) in the Yerushalmi with their parallels in the Bavli.[42]

In the 1960's, M. A. Tennenblatt unequivocally concluded that "'the Talmud of the Land of Israel' or the 'gemara of the Westerners' or the 'Yerushalmi' as it was named afterwards as an edited work, was certainly known to those in Babylonia and even if [it was] not in the form [in which it is now] before us, then at least [the Babylonians had it as] scrolls [containing] sugyot or chapters, and certainly whole tractates."[43] Tennenblatt asserted even more forcefully a little later that "it makes sense that a fully edited 'Yerushalmi' arrived in Babylonia already at the end of R. Ashi's life."[44] Tennenblatt provided the following rationale for this conclusion:

> For it cannot be imagined that their [the Babylonians'] Talmud was based solely on what [traditions] the "travelers" brought to them or on the responses [to legal queries] that they received from the Land of Israel . . . it is more correct—and also easier—to build a Babylonian structure that completes what is missing [from the Palestinian] in time and in place . . .[45]

Of course, such a statement—logical though it is—requires proof, which Tennenblatt rather incompletely provided.[46] Of most interest in the context of this book are the proofs he draws from y. and b. Avodah Zarah. In the text, he presents a comparison of y. AZ 3:2, 41d and b. AZ 41b–42b. Tennenblatt notes that both Talmuds present the same R. Yohanan/Resh Laqish dispute in connection with the same mishnah, and also points out the Palestinian provenance of many of the materials the Bavli uses to turn the original, rather simple dispute into a complex sugya. In a footnote to this discussion, he points as well to a similarity in the selection and sequence of topics between y. AZ 2:3, 41a and b. AZ 30a.[47]

---

41. Ibid., 292.
42. Ibid.
43. M. A. Tennenblatt, *Peraqim hadashim le-toldot Erets Yisra'el u-Bavel bi-tequfat ha-Talmud* (Tel-Aviv: Dvir, 1966), 224.
44. Ibid., 240.
45. Ibid., 224.
46. Ibid., 263–270.
47. Ibid., 267n56.

Martin Jaffee's pioneering comparison of y. and b. Horayot was a major turning-point in the scholarship on our question. He proposed to "argue that the appropriation of the Palestinian Talmud by the Bavli's editors becomes clear, not at the level of individual textual parallels, but rather at the level of literary craft and organization, as large sequences of discourse are redacted in each gemara around the core of the same Mishnaic tractate."[48] Jaffee thus proposed—similar to S. Y. Rappaport in 1831 and M. A. Tennenblatt—to examine our question entirely from the macro perspective of comparing the Talmuds' parallel commentaries on the same mishnah. His examination revealed three types of what he called "structural correspondences": similar lengths of discussions of a given mishnah in both Talmuds, common placements of themes extraneous to the mishnah at similar points in the discussion, and, finally, use of the same mishnayot as opportunities for placement of aggadah.[49] Jaffee ultimately concluded that "the post-Amoraic editors of the [Bavli] had something much like the extant version of the [Yerushalmi] before them and reflected upon the logic of its construction as they composed their own commentary."[50]

Jacob Neusner has devoted a great deal of attention to the relationship between the Talmuds, concluding that the Bavli does not at all know the Yerushalmi.[51] Neusner's work on the Talmuds is animated in part by a justified opposition to a traditional mode of study that views the entire vast corpus of rabbinic literature as representative of one uniform rabbinic point of view. He sets this view in opposition to his own "documentary hypothesis" according to which each rabbinic compilation (or "document") exhibits particular and distinct characteristics that set it apart from the others.[52] Neusner's many studies of the Talmuds have led him to the view that the Bavli is completely independent of the Yerushalmi, notwithstanding some materials that the two can be observed to have in common. The Bavli has its own agenda, pursues its own rhetorical and topical program, uses Scripture as the basis of large units of discourse, and in general is not in any way dependent upon the Yerushalmi.[53]

---

48. Jaffee, "The Babylonian Appropriation of the Talmud Yerushalmi," 6–7.

49. Ibid., 18–23.

50. Ibid., 23–24.

51. See particularly Neusner's seven-volume study *The Bavli's Unique Voice* and his subsequent *The Two Talmuds Compared* (13 vols.; Atlanta: Scholars Press, 1996). See also his *Judaism: The Classical Statement,* 222–234, wherein he summarizes what he terms "the literary and redactional distinction" between the two Talmuds.

52. See Neusner, *Are the Talmuds Interchangeable?,* v-xxix for a discussion of, and bibliography for, the documentary hypothesis.

53. It is interesting to note that although Neusner ultimately bases his conclusion on the macro-level differences he catalogues between the Talmuds, he is not

The key distinction between those scholars who do see a relationship between the Talmuds and those who do not is whether they are more engaged by the similarities between the Talmuds or by the differences between them. Rappaport, Chajes, Halevy, Tennenblatt, and Jaffee seemed to be drawn by a focus on similarity toward the acceptance of a possible relationship between the Talmuds, while Fraenkel, Ginzberg, Epstein, Greenwald, and Neusner focused on the differences between the Talmuds, and came to the opposite conclusion. This dichotomy informs the methodological approach of this book: we will pay close attention to the similarities between y. and b. Avodah Zarah *and* to the causes of the many differences between them. To the extent that these differences can be explained, the conclusion that b. Avodah Zarah knew and relied on y. Avodah Zarah is not undermined.

III.b. The Palestinian Contribution to the Bavli Was Made Incrementally Throughout the Amoraic Period: The Theorists of "Early Talmud"

Noah Aminoah, Yaacov Sussman, and Shamma Friedman point to the existence of a layer of "early talmud" (Aminoah and Friedman), "early arrangement" (Aminoah), or "early basic amoraic material" (Sussman) shared by both Talmuds.[54] None of these scholars presents early talmud as a hypothesis which *might* explain some inter-Talmudic similarities; rather, each presents his analyses of sugyot as if early talmud is an established fact. In what follows, my goal is to evaluate early talmud as the hypothesis it is, assessing its utility as an explanation of inter-Talmudic similarities in discrete cases and its overall strengths and weaknesses. At appropriate points throughout the book, we will consider our findings in light of the early talmud hypothesis.

Let us begin with a relatively simple illustrative example.[55] At b. Sanh 5b, the Bavli presents two sugyot in the same order in which they are

---

at all unaware of the similarities between them. It is just that he does not subject the similarities to the same rigorous analysis to which he subjects the differences. Apropos of this point, Neusner is the only scholar of whom I am aware who raises the issue of whether the existing similarities between the Talmuds can be explained along the lines of a Q hypothesis analogous to that current in New Testament studies. We will return to this issue shortly.

54. Despite the differences in terminology between these scholars (and in approach), I will refer throughout this discussion to "early talmud."

55. Shamma Friedman, *Talmud Arukh: BT Bava Mezi'a VI* (2 vols.; New York: Jewish Theological Seminary, 1993 and 1996), 2:16n62.

found at y. Shevi 6:1, 36a–b (‖ y. Git 1:2, 43c). Now, does this mean that the redactors of b. Sanhedrin knew y. Sheviit (and/or y. Gittin)? Friedman approvingly quotes Yisrael Levy's 1870 review of Zechariah Fraenkel's *Mavo ha-Yerushalmi,* in which he said, "There were already [in the amoraic period] complete sugyot taught in the Land of Israel which came from there to Babylonia—just as there were already sugyot taught in Babylonia prior to the compiling of the Bavli—[but] the edited Yerushalmi was not before the later Babylonian sages."[56] Levy and Friedman correctly conclude that this example does not prove that the Yerushalmi was available to the Bavli redactors. But my agreement with their conclusion is based on a different point. This example should be studied together with *all* other Sheviit sugyot found in the Bavli. Only on the basis of such a macro-level study should any conclusions be drawn about the relationship between Sheviit and the Bavli—and even then, one should confine one's conclusions to Sheviit and the Bavli and not claim to be opining about the relationship of the *entire* Yerushalmi to the Bavli. After such a study is done, it may indeed turn out to be the case that this example is part of a larger pattern of the Bavli's incorporation of sequences of Sheviit sugyot, or it may not. But on the basis of this one example, it is unreasonable to conclude one way or the other about the relationship between the two Talmuds.

But there is more. In the Yerushalmi passage, R. Aha b. Yaaqov in the name of R. Imi explicitly introduces the connection between the two sugyot by saying "From two cases [involving] Rabbi, we learn that Akko has characteristics of the Land of Israel and characteristics of the Diaspora." When we examine the lengthy sequence of materials that follows this introduction, we do indeed find two stories about Rabbi and the status of Akko. There is therefore no question that these two juxtaposed stories likely circulated in the two rabbinic communities during the amoraic period. But these stories are separated by a good deal of material about the (im)propriety of a student's issuing halakhic rulings in the vicinity of his master. Is this material also a part of what R. Aha b. Yaaqov is transmitting or not?

In order to answer this question, we must pay careful attention to the literary structure of the entire sequence. Immediately following R. Aha b. Yaaqov's first story about Rabbi and Akko, R. Yaaqov b. Idi comments on the story "from that moment they decreed that no student should issue rulings." R. Yaaqov b. Idi is thus aware of the first story, although it is unclear whether he knows it through R. Aha b. Yaaqov or not. (Alternatively, it is possible from a chronological standpoint for R. Aha b. Yaaqov to have quoted R. Yaaqov b. Idi, but it is unlikely that he did so, since the Yeru-

---

56. Ibid.

shalmi never portrays him as doing so.[57]) And if R. Aha b. Yaaqov did not quote R. Yaaqov b. Idi, we cannot assume that he nevertheless transmitted the other sources about students' halakhic rulings that follow (and assume the quotation of) R. Yaaqov b. Idi and separate the first Rabbi/Akko story from the second. Also, R. Aha b. Yaaqov explicitly introduced his tradition as being two stories about Rabbi and Akko. Why would he say this and then transmit a good deal of other (irrelevant) material besides? It is far more likely that the Yerushalmi editors themselves introduced R. Yaaqov b. Idi and the other sources that follow about students' halakhic rulings.

The real significance of this analysis becomes apparent when we look again at b. Sanh 5b. Although the Bavli editors have reworked R. Aha b. Yaaqov's two stories (most notably by eliminating any reference to Akko), we can still see versions of the stories there. Not only that, but the Bavli has reworked the first story to be about students' halakhic rulings, and the subject of students' rulings separates the Bavli's versions of the first and second stories. The point is that we have identified the hands of the Yerushalmi redactors at y. Shevi 6:1, 36a–b, and the Bavli's version of this material includes the work of the earlier Talmuds' redactors. Thus it is incorrect to attribute the readily identifiable similarities in the Talmuds' presentations of these stories to early talmud. While some of the similarity is unquestionably early, as I have shown, the structure of the Bavli material as it now appears includes material that can only have been placed there by the Yerushalmi redactors—not by transmitters of early talmud.[58] Although this isolated example does not prove that the Bavli knew y. Sheviit as a whole, let alone the entire Yerushalmi, it does show that the hypothesis of early talmud must be approached more critically and that the whole issue requires careful consideration on a case-by-case basis.[59]

Friedman discusses early talmud more generally in the introduction to the text volume of *Talmud Arukh*.[60] He presents a sugya found at b. Yev 9a with a parallel at y. Yev 1:1, 2c and incisively analyzes how the Bavli recast the older Palestinian expressions in its own uniquely Babylonian idiom. Following this analysis, he comments:

> From the lengthy continuation [of the Talmudic discussion] in the two Talmuds we see that the two sugyot are parallels in their entirety, both in

---

57. See y. Ber 5:5, 9d; y. Orl 3:1, 63a; y. Shab 1:1, 2d; y. Suk 1:1, 51d.

58. We will soon address the questions surrounding how this transmission may have occurred.

59. Cf. Jeffrey Rubenstein, "Some Structural Patterns of Yerushalmi Sugyot," in *The Talmud Yerushalmi and Graeco-Roman Culture* (ed. Peter Schäfer; Tübingen: Mohr Siebeck, 2003), 3:309.

60. Friedman, *Talmud Arukh*, 2:7–23.

the language of the [amoraic] *memrot* and in the words of the Talmud (as
we have seen in many places) . . . . the give-and-take of the *stam ha-Talmud*
here [in the Bavli] is parallel to the stam of the Yerushalmi there. And it is
clear that it came along with the *memrot* from the early talmud that the
sages of Babylonia received from the sages of the Land of Israel (for the
two Talmuds before us draw from those same early traditions, to which
the Yerushalmi is generally still closer in its expression).[61]

Friedman is thus saying that in the case of b. Yev 9a, the Babylonian
sages received from Palestine the amoraic *memrot* together with anonymous material. Moreover, there existed in Palestine a pool of early traditions, from which both rabbinic communities drew. This early material, as
presented in the Yerushalmi, is closer to the form it had when it was part
of these "early traditions." So, to the extent that b. Yev 9a and y. Yev 1:1, 2c
are similar, this similarity is due to the transmission from Palestine to Babylonia of this early talmud at some point prior to the redaction of the
Bavli.

A bit later, Friedman expands this observation beyond the isolated
case of Yevamot and points out that, in many cases, the structure of a
given sugya is common to both the Yerushalmi and the Bavli.[62] The existence of "frameworks of *memrot* and stam in the Bavli, just as they are
found in parallel in the earlier traditions reflected in the Yerushalmi," is a
"foundational principle."[63] Now we must ask: what assumptions under-
lay this theory of early talmud? What burdens of proof must be met in order for the theory of early talmud to be ultimately persuasive? What questions can it help/not help answer?

The major assumption here is that there existed in Palestine early traditions from which both rabbinic communities drew, and which account
for the similarities in structure of parallel sugyot (the early talmud). The
original form of these early traditions is unrecoverable, although the early
talmud found in the Yerushalmi is closest to them. Friedman's suggestion
sounds intriguingly like a Q-style hypothesis.[64]

---

61. Ibid., 15.

62. Ibid., 16.

63. Ibid., 17. Interestingly, Friedman did hint in earlier work that the Bavli may
use Yerushalmi sugyot. See *"Yevamot X,"* 340–343, where he analyzes the striking
similarity between b. Yev 88b–89a and its Yerushalmi parallel using language such
as "our sugya is exactly like the Yerushalmi sugya," " . . . the expansions and additions of the Bavli to the Yerushalmi sugya," and "from the fact that the redactor
did not change the structure in the Yerushalmi . . ."

64. Interestingly, Friedman has argued against a Q hypothesis in other work. In
his recent studies of Toseftan baraitot and their Bavli parallels, Friedman has argued that compelling evidence suggests that the differences between the Toseftan

It is rare to encounter a Q hypothesis in studies of rabbinic literature. The only scholar who has explicitly pondered the existence of a rabbinic Q is Jacob Neusner.[65] The Q hypothesis is well known in New Testament studies, where it still enjoys the status of the consensus view on the formation of the Synoptic Gospels (despite its recent detractors).[66] Despite the differences between the New Testament Q hypothesis and early talmud and the resulting fact that the arguments for and against Q are not transferable in their entirety to this analysis of early talmud, some of the arguments recently advanced against Q are suggestive.

In the New Testament context, Q was a heuristic construct devised to explain a puzzle: the Gospels of Matthew and Luke share approximately two hundred verses that are not found in the Gospel of Mark, which is presumed to be chronologically prior to both. These shared verses came to be seen as a *Quelle* ("source," hence Q) of Matthew and Luke, along with Mark and other materials particular to those two Gospels. As Mark Goodacre has recently pointed out, this classic formulation of Q assumes that Matthew and Luke used Mark independently and had no contact with each other.[67] If that assumption is persuasively challenged, then Q

baraitot and their Bavli parallels may be accounted for by conscious Babylonian reworking of the Toseftan baraitot. He prefers this hypothesis to the traditional view that the different versions of the Toseftan baraitot are due to their origins in different collections. The rationale of the traditional view is that later scholars would not have consciously emended earlier material. Friedman rejects this rationale, insisting that evidence suggests that later scholars would have, and did, engage in such reworking. There is a similarity between the traditional view that he rejects in the context of Toseftan studies and the view that he suggests in the context of Bavli-Yerushalmi studies. Now, I do not deny that there may be compelling reasons for Friedman to hold opposing views in the two contexts. But nowhere, to my knowledge, does he articulate clearly why he sees the two cases as different; nor does he establish any other proofs for early talmud as an explanation for the similarities between the Talmuds. See Shamma Friedman, "Ha-baraitot she-be-Talmud ha-Bavli ve-yahasan le-Tosefta," in *Atara L'Haim: Studies in the Talmud and Medieval Rabbinic Literature in Honor of Professor Haim Zalman Dimitrovsky* (Jerusalem: Magnes, 2000), 103–201 (Heb.); idem, "Uncovering Literary Dependencies in the Talmudic Corpus," in *The Synoptic Problem in Rabbinic Literature* (ed. Shaye J. D. Cohen; Providence, RI: Brown Judaic Studies, 2000), 35–57.

65. See Jacob Neusner, *Are There Really Tannaitic Parallels to the Gospels?* (Atlanta: Scholars Press, 1993).

66. See, e.g., Donald Harmon Akenson, *Saint Saul: A Skeleton Key to the Historical Jesus* (New York: Oxford University Press, 2000), 108–116; Mark Goodacre, *The Case Against Q* (Harrisburg, PA: Trinity Press International, 2002).

67. Goodacre, *The Case Against Q*, 47. Parenthetical references in the list below refer to this work.

may not be necessary. Goodacre aims right for this assumption, and advances a number of arguments to establish that Matthew knew Mark, and Luke knew Matthew as well as Mark. Goodacre's arguments that have methodological implications for this study include:

1. Arguments for Q tend to stress differences between Matthew and Luke on the micro level and ignore their "striking" similarity at the macro level (47);

2. On the issue of dating, the greater the distance in time between Matthew and Luke, the less likely it is that Luke was unaware of Matthew (48);

3. Scholars have paid insufficient attention to the characteristically Matthean character of Matthew's additions to Mark, and the characteristically Lukan character of his additions (51–61);

4. Instead of focusing on the obvious differences between Matthew and Luke, scholars might instead ask whether the points of contact between them are sufficiently strong as to suggest that Luke might have known Matthew (56);

5. Q's workability as a theory and the fine scholarship behind it are not an argument against questioning it (76);

6. Occam's Razor (the simpler interpretation is more likely to be true) militates against Q (77);

7. Without Q, scholars are in a better position to appreciate the literary creativity deployed by Luke in crafting his Gospel (117, 145);[68]

8. If Q is right, then the common Matthew/Luke material will not resemble its surrounding Gospel context (since it is a separate source), but if Luke derived that material from Matthew, the common material may still bear the imprints of its Matthean context (182)—which it does.

---

68. Goodacre also notes that

a narrow redaction-critical model in which it is regarded as inevitable for the evangelists to have taken over every congenial word, phrase, or theme from their sources . . . without consideration of broader narrative context . . . and the literary agenda of the evangelists is, in the end, a blunted instrument that can only detract from our appreciation of the Gospels and their writers. (145)

It is interesting to compare this observation to Friedman's own observations about the relationships between Toseftan baraitot and their Bavli parallels.

Goodacre's methodological points make a good deal of sense in the context of this study. To begin with, his emphasis on the importance of macro analysis is right on the mark; in our case, by studying y. and b. Avodah Zarah first as whole compilations (examples of the results of that study are presented in chapter 2) and following up that study with micro analyses of specific textual parallels (chapters 3–4), we will be better able to appreciate how the inter-Talmudic similarities we will observe are more likely the results of b. Avodah Zarah's reworking of y. Avodah Zarah than of early talmud. Second, applying Goodacre I would say that it is not enough to focus on the differences between the tractates (although we will), but that we must pay careful attention to whether the points of contact between the tractates are sufficiently strong as to suggest that b. Avodah Zarah knew y. Avodah Zarah. As we will see in chapters 2–4, b. Avodah Zarah sugyot with multiple parallels in rabbinic literature tend to resemble y. Avodah Zarah sugyot more closely, b. Avodah Zarah has characteristic ways of reworking y. Avodah Zarah materials, and b. Avodah Zarah even exhibits the tendency to pick up on issues where y. Avodah Zarah left off. Third, many differences between the tractates can be explained on the basis of the differing intellectual, religious, and other agendas of the two Talmuds, which is sometimes glossed over by scholars' focus on the mere fact of difference. Fourth, the first three points implicate Occam's Razor—since we can explain the similarities and differences between y. and b. Avodah Zarah without early talmud, we do not need it as a global explanation. In a related vein Friedman himself has pointed out the tendency of older scholars such as Chanoch Albeck and J. N. Epstein to hypothesize the existence of now non-extant compilations in order to explain differences among our existing literatures because of the earlier (now outdated) assumption that the redactors of later compilations could not, *would* not, have intentionally changed the earlier. But, as Friedman has incisively demonstrated recently, this older assumption is flawed.[69] There is thus little reason to hypothesize a pool of shared rabbinic traditions in order to explain similarities between y. and b. Avodah Zarah, when these similarities (and differences) can be well-explained by reference to the creativity of the Babylonian redactors, whose contributions in reworking their prior sources has been, and continues to be, amply demonstrated.[70] Finally, Goodacre's point about the chronological gaps between compilations is also on target. The Bavli (and hence b. Avodah Zarah) is at least two hundred years the Yerushalmi's junior. That being so, it is not reasonable to assert without proof that b. Avodah

---

69. See the sources cited in n. 64, above.

70. See, e.g., Rubenstein, *Talmudic Stories*; idem, *Culture of the Babylonian Talmud.*

Zarah's redactors had no knowledge of y. Avodah Zarah, and that any similarities between the two are due to early talmud which *pre-dated* y. Avodah Zarah. The closer the Talmuds are to each other in time, the more sense early talmud makes as a global explanation of the similarities; the more separated in time, the more sense it makes to test the theory that a given Bavli tractate knew its Yerushalmi parallel.

To be sure, the Q hypothesis in New Testament studies and the early talmud hypothesis result from the intellectual creativity of superb scholars, and merit careful consideration. Friedman's work in particular sets a high standard of erudition and methodological rigor. Moreover, early talmud does at times adequately explain certain similarities between the Talmuds. But none of this should preclude a re-examination of evidence. The evidence itself should decide whether the early talmud hypothesis or the hypothesis that b. Avodah Zarah knew y. Avodah Zarah is the more reasonable explanation for the similarities we see between the tractates.

Friedman is also unclear about the process by which early talmud was transmitted to Babylonia. The *nahote,* as we discussed earlier, do not suffice as an explanation for this transmission. Aminoah's and Sussman's work on early talmud is equally unclear on this point. Without an explanation of exactly how all these parallel materials went from Palestine to Babylonia, these scholars leave us to assume that the materials somehow "circulated" there. But what exactly does it mean that Palestinian material "circulated" until given final form in the Bavli? The issue is more complex than it seems. Palestinian materials traveled a geographical distance between the rabbinic centers, away from the living community of learners and interpreters in which they had originated and were a staple of study. Such conditions are not ideal for the preservation and transmission of literary productions, especially if their primary mode of transmission is oral. The reason for this is that when these literary productions are removed from the communities of those who studied them, an important check on variability in their content—the scholarly community itself—is also removed. Thus, these literary productions may come to change, perhaps significantly.[71] A scholarly theory about the presence of Palestinian materials in the Bavli must take this into account and do more than merely assume that these materials "circulated" from one place to the other. It is far more reasonable to claim that—in the case of *this* pair of tractates— most of the Palestinian material came to Babylonia attached to mishnayot (as "Talmud Yerushalmi" to m. Avodah Zarah), whereupon it was then reworked and eventually incorporated into what became b. Avodah Zarah.

---

71. I will discuss this issue in greater depth in chapter 6 as part of my analysis of the impact of orality studies on the thesis of this book.

Lastly, if early talmud was being transmitted to Babylonia throughout the amoraic period, we should not see what, in fact, we do see: the preservation of argumentation noticeably increases with the fourth generation, along with Palestinian influence. The theory of early talmud would lead us to expect that Babylonian amoraic activity would be more uniform if early talmud was steadily arriving from Palestine. This being so, the hypothesis of early talmud is insufficiently grounded, despite its other merits.

Noah Aminoah studied the redactions of tractates Qiddushin, Betzah, Rosh Hashanah, Taanit, Sukkah, and Moed Qatan.[72] He carefully studied the sugyot shared by the Talmuds on a case-by-case basis and broadly distinguished two types of shared Palestinian sugyot: sugyot edited early in Palestine that the Talmuds share, but which they differently interpret and expand, and completed Yerushalmi sugyot that form the core of sugyot that the Bavli subsequently edited in its own way. Within these broad categories, Aminoah isolated the following types:

1. Bavli sugyot that were Palestinian in their foundation;

2. Sugyot whose subject is a Palestinian source;

3. Palestinian sugyot in the Bavli that are essentially similar to Yerushalmi sugyot, except that the parallel Yerushalmi sugyot contain different attributions, or reversed positions;

4. Babylonian parallels to Yerushalmi materials that contain different attributions or reversed positions; and

5. Babylonian sources in the Yerushalmi.[73]

Aminoah's close attention to detail and heuristic classifications of the parallel materials are helpful. But although his individual analyses indicate his conviction that Palestinian sugyot came to Babylonia throughout the amoraic period, he, like Friedman and Sussman, fails to explain just how that might have happened.

---

72. Noah Aminoah, *The Redaction of the Tractate Qiddushin in the Babilonian Talmud* (*sic*) (Tel-Aviv: Tel Aviv University, 1977) (Heb.); idem, *The Redaction of the Tractate Betza, Rosh-Hashana, and Ta'anit in the Babilonian Talmud* (*sic*) (Tel-Aviv: Tel Aviv University, 1986) (Heb.), idem, *The Redaction of the Tractate Sukkah and Moed-Katan in the Babilonian Talmud* (*sic*) (Tel-Aviv: Tel Aviv University, 1989) (Heb.), idem, "Qit'ei talmud mi-siddur qadum be-massekhet Rosh Hashanah," in *Studies in Rabbinic Literature, Bible, and Jewish History* (ed. Yitshaq D. Gilat; Ramat-Gan: Bar-Ilan University Press, 1982), 185–197.
73. See Aminoah, *The Redaction of the Tractate Qiddushin*, 328–365.

Aminoah is also commendably sensitive to the issue of which Babylonian amoraim seem to be aware of the Palestinian sugyot *qua* sugyot (which has implications for when those Palestinian materials might have become known in Babylonia).[74] But while he recognizes that the presence of, say, Abaye in a Palestinian sugya could be an example of Babylonian reworking, he assumes—and never questions his own assumption—that Abaye's presence points to him as the Babylonian editor of the Palestinian material. But without a theory as to how the Palestinian material came to Babylonia (or even with such a theory), the assumption that Abaye was the editor of the material is not necessarily more logical than the assumption that later editors came into possession of the Palestinian material and deployed Abaye in the sugya themselves. Aminoah himself recognizes (following Chanoch Albeck) that the Talmudic editors did at times deploy amoraic statements themselves, in contexts of their own choosing,[75] which makes it all the more curious that he does not seriously consider this possibility. Another significant lacuna is Aminoah's failure to employ the macro perspective of looking at the Yerushalmi and Bavli parallel tractates as whole tractates; had he done so, he may have noticed large-scale similarities in the selection and ordering of sugyot and topics in the two Talmuds. The micro perspective of sugya analysis is vital, but lacking the macro perspective, it is insufficient.

Aminoah illustrated his understanding of early talmud in an interesting paper entitled "Qit'ei talmud mi-siddur qadum be-massekhet Rosh Hashanah." In that paper, he studied a lengthy series of sugyot at b. RH 9b–15b which is similar in substance, form, style, and juxtaposition of sugyot to series of sugyot found at y. RH 1:2, 57a, y. Bik 2:5, 65a, y. Shevi 5:1, 35d, y. Shevi 2:7, 34a, and y. Shevi 4:1, 35d. Aminoah arrived at the conclusion that a common *siddur qadum* (early arrangement) of sugyot was shared by the Talmuds because "when we remove from the arrangement before us anonymous sugyot whose signs are obviously Babylonian and late and sugyot that are not [related] to excerpts from the mishnah of Rosh Hashanah . . . we obtain one continuous arrangement to the excerpts of mishnah Rosh Hashanah in both the Bavli and Yerushalmi."[76] Aminoah acknowledges again and again that Babylonian "later editor(s)"[77] rearranged materials and introduced uniquely Babylonian argumentation and language into the "early arrangement." If that is so, then we may well

---

74. See Aminoah, *The Redaction of the Tractate Qiddushin,* 332 and idem, "Qit'ei talmud," 188 (noting the Bavli's addition of Abaye to a Palestinian sugya, which Aminoah interprets as evidence that Abaye edited the material).

75. Aminoah, "Qit'ei talmud," 189.

76. Ibid., 187.

77. Aminoah, "Qit'ei talmud," 186, 187, 188, 189.

wonder why it is more reasonable to assume that the common arrangement of shared sugyot came to both rabbinic communities during the amoraic period rather than during the post-amoraic period of redaction. Aminoah does not adequately explain why the common sequence of sugyot in the Talmuds need not necessarily be viewed as a product of the amoraic period.

Aminoah does point to the presence of third-generation Babylonian amoraim in three of the parallel sugyot in the sequences in both Talmuds, and to the presence of Abaye and Ravina in two sequences in the Bavli alone. From this he concluded that Abaye's school already had the earlier arrangement of sugyot before it, which it edited—as shown by the addition of Abaye. Aminoah asks rhetorically: "For if the sequence had been arranged . . . for the first time in the school of Abaye, how is it that neither follow-up to his words nor argumentation [about them] is found in the Yerushalmi? It may be inferred that their [Abaye's and Ravina's] words were added to the early arrangement."[78] Now, Aminoah's question assumes an important point that requires proof, namely, that the "early arrangement" is in fact early. Only one who assumes that the shared sequence of sugyot is early would find the challenge of the rhetorical question compelling. But the sequence could very well have originated in the Yerushalmi and become known to the Bavli redactors, who edited it by adding Babylonian materials, terminology, and argumentation—including teachings of Abaye and Ravina. Aminoah's argument from the names and generations of quoted amoraim does not suffice as a proof of "early arrangement."

Moreover, we may make another observation about the shared sequence of sugyot studied by Aminoah that also casts doubt on his hypothesis of "early arrangement." Aminoah himself points out that the sequences of sugyot from y. Rosh Hashanah, y. Bikkurim and y. Sheviit, when juxtaposed in that order, make up the sequence found at b. RH 9b–15b. In other words, whoever put together b. RH 9b–15b combined materials found in those three places in the Yerushalmi. Of even greater interest is the fact that b. RH 9b–15b utilizes Sheviit material in an order different from that found in the Yerushalmi (as Aminoah points out in his appendix *bet*). We thus have two levels of arrangement of the sugyot: the order in y. Rosh Hashanah, y. Bikkurim, and y. Sheviit, and then the order in b. Rosh Hashanah, which utilizes and alters them. Is it reasonable to assume (as Aminoah does) that the Bavli's appropriation and adaptation of the Yerushalmi's sequences of sugyot happened during the early to mid-amoraic period in Babylonia? This question must be answered with another question: can

---

78. Ibid., 188.

amoraim be demonstrated to have created and reworked this sequence of sugyot, attaching it to the respective mishnayot by which it is found? In order for amoraim to have been the ones responsible for creating and attaching the sequence of sugyot to mishnayot, *they must be demonstrated to be aware of the sequence of sugyot qua sequence and to be aware of its attachment to the mishnayot by which it is found.* If the amoraim cannot be demonstrated to have such an awareness, then it is more reasonable to assume that the sequence of sugyot and its linkage to certain mishnayot is the work of the redactors.

We find that no amora at b. RH 9b–15b is aware of the sequence of sugyot *qua* sequence of sugyot, or that it is now found as a sequence of sugyot attached to m. RH 1:1. Similarly, no amora at y. RH 1:2, 57a, y. Bik 2:5, 65a, or y. Shevi 5:1, 35d; 2:7, 34a; or 4:1, 35d is aware of those sequences of sugyot or that they are attached to the mishnayot to which they are attached. The work of forging the Yerushalmi sequences of sugyot was the work of the Yerushalmi redactors. The Bavli redactors took these sequences of sugyot, added to them, rearranged them, and edited them to conform to Babylonian norms of language and argumentation.

But what about the fact that the y. Bikkurim sugyot are Babylonian in origin and that early- to middle-generation amoraim are mentioned throughout the sequence of sugyot? This fact is undeniable, but must be appreciated for what it does and does not show. The amoraim in both rabbinic centers studied mishnayot and other sources, and created sugyot. It is an overstatement to claim—as some scholars do—that the Bavli is entirely, or largely, pseudepigraphic and that all sugyot, with all names of amoraim, are the creations of post-amoraic editors and redactors. But while amoraim created sugyot, it cannot be satisfactorily demonstrated that they linked sugyot into lengthy sequences, passed these sequences back and forth between the two rabbinic centers, and attached those sequences to particular mishnayot. I will say more about amoraic awareness and activity later in this chapter.

Yaacov Sussman also dealt with the issue of early talmud in his important article "Ve-shuv le-Yerushalmi Neziqin."[79] Sussman pointed out that despite the many striking differences between the Bavli and Yerushalmi Neziqin, the two share all the amoraic material relating directly to the mishnayot and topics of the tractate, which stems from the "first amoraic period" (the amoraic period from 220 CE until the end of the

---

79. According to rabbinic tradition, the three tractates Bava Qamma, Bava Metzia, and Bava Batra once constituted a large tractate called simply "Neziqin" (b. AZ 7a). These tractates were the focus of Saul Lieberman's work on the so-called "Talmud of Caesarea," which, in turn, was the subject of Sussman's article.

amoraic period in Palestine, which Sussman dates to 360/370).[80] Although
the two Talmuds share this material, they differ radically in how they
present it: y. Neziqin presents this early amoraic material as short traditions, without much of a dialectical context, while the Bavli—as is its
way—embeds this material in complex dialectical constructions. Sussman
refers to this shared material as "early basic amoraic material" (חומר
אמוראי בסיסי קדום), and stresses that owing to an extended process of development that the Bavli underwent for hundreds of years after the close
of the Yerushalmi, it is the immense and different rabbinic compilation
that it is, essentially the product of the "school of the last geonim."[81]

As with Friedman and Aminoah, Sussman's interpretation of the role
of "early basic amoraic material" in the making of the Bavli assumes without adequate argumentation that it somehow made its way from Palestine
to Babylonia *during* the amoraic period. Once again, it bears noting that
the temptation to attribute this transmission to the *nahote* must be resisted.
Not all of the "early basic amoraic layer" is transmitted in the names of
nahote, and it is methodologically unsound to assume that because many
traditions were so transmitted, *all* the Palestinian amoraic material in the
Bavli reached Babylonia through that channel.

But Sussman squarely confronts a more serious problem with the assumption of an amoraic-era transmission to Babylonia of an early amoraic
layer. He acknowledges that it is often unclear in the Bavli where the
"early basic amoraic material" ends and the dialectical elaboration of it
begins. The early amoraic layer underwent editing and reworking by later
amoraim, saboraim, and geonim over a long period of time,[82] and the contributions of these other scholars "necessarily affected the formulation of
the [early amoraic] teachings themselves. And just as it is not possible to
distinguish between earlier and later, between 'rationale' and 'addition,'
so also the boundaries between the form of the sugya and the body of the
teaching, *between the interpretation of the teaching and its formulation*—are
progressively blurred"[83] (emphasis added). Although Sussman fails to
consider the impact of this key admission on the assumption of an "early
basic amoraic" layer, the impact is clear—it is difficult if not impossible in
many cases to even know how the "early basic amoraic material" had
originally been formulated, not to mention the impossibility of distinguishing it from the dialectical construct in which it is now embedded.
And, once it is acknowledged that these distinctions cannot be made, then

---

80. Sussman, "Ve-shuv le-Yerushalmi Neziqin," 98.
81. Ibid., 99–106.
82. Ibid., 109–110.
83. Ibid., 110.

it might be the case that the "early" amoraic material reached Babylonia late in the amoraic period or even later as a fully-integrated component of already-formulated sugyot. In light of these problems, Sussman's assertion of "early basic amoraic material" shared by both Talmuds cannot be accepted as formulated.

As with Aminoah, an example (although somewhat technical in this case) will illustrate the problems attendant upon Sussman's admission that early amoraic material cannot always be distinguished from later amoraic or even redactional emendation. M. Avodah Zarah 3:4 records an alleged dialogue between "Proclus b. Philosophus" and Rabban Gamliel. Proclus asks Rabban Gamliel how the rabbi can bathe in Aphrodite's bathhouse in light of Deut 13:18's prohibition against deriving benefit from any forbidden idolatrous items. The rabbi declines to answer Proclus in the bathhouse but once outside, offers a number of alternative responses: he did not enter Aphrodite's domain, she entered his; people build statues of Aphrodite for bathhouses, not bathhouses for Aphrodite (which shows that the statues are decorative rather than cultic); men behave disrespectfully in front of Aphrodite (standing around naked, urinating), which they would presumably not do if the statue were meant for worship. At y. AZ 3:4, 42d, R. Hama b. Yose is part of a chain of tradition reporting that "[R. Gamliel] responded to him [Proclus b. Philosophus] with an evasive answer. For if it [the answer] were not so [evasive], [Proclus] should have [further] responded to him from [the case of] Baal Peor, the worship of which is only by means of uncovering [one's body]." The Yerushalmi's anonymous voice then provides a way that R. Gamliel's response can be responsive to Proclus' question, and yet not provoke a further response: "What is the result? That [deity] as to which a person behaves [disrespectfully] because of divinity [like Peor], it is forbidden. And that [deity] as to which a person does not behave [disrespectfully] because of divinity [like Aphrodite], it is permitted." Thus R. Gamliel's response to Proclus was responsive, since he established that he was permitted to go into Aphrodite's bathhouse, and Proclus could not respond to R. Gamliel from the case of Peor, which is in a different worship category than Aphrodite.

At b. AZ 44b, R. Hama b. Yosef—the very same amora—reports, "R. Gamliel responded to the general [Proclus] with a deceptive answer, but I say it was not deceptive." The Bavli then presents four suggestions of the possible deceptiveness of the answer, and how that deceptiveness is more apparent than real. Each of these four suggestions ends with a suggested continuation of R. Hama b. Yosef's *memra*, picking up from his words "but I say it was not deceptive . . . ." and then giving the reason the answer was not deceptive. The first suggestion presented includes mention of the name of Rava, while the other three are clearly presented in the names of Abaye, R. Shimi b. Hiyya, and Rabbah b. Ulla. The first solution (mentioning Rava although not in his name) most closely resembles that of the Yerushalmi, and the suggested ending to the *memra* is "and I say it was not deceptive. This one's [Peor's] worship is in this fashion, and this one's [Aphrodite's] worship is not in this fashion." This suggested ending to the *memra* closely resembles the resolution attributed to the Yerushalmi's anonymous voice.

Now, what is the "early basic amoraic material"? The likely response to this question is that it is R. Hama b. Yose(f)'s *memra*. If only the *memra* is the early amoraic material, then there is a problem. What did it look like in its form as "early basic amoraic material"? In the Yerushalmi, the *memra* includes mention of Peor, but in the Bavli it does not—which gives the Bavli the opening to suggest four possibilities for how to interpret it. (An alternative explanation of the difference in the Talmuds' presentation of the *memra* will be discussed shortly). The Bavli's first suggested interpretation, which is closest to the Yerushalmi, includes a mention of Peor by Rava. But as the Tosafot point out (s.v. *veha-amar*), Rava's mention of Peor is introduced by "but did not Rava say . . .?," which indicates to them that "Rava made his statement in another place." Rava is thus unaware that he is being deployed to interpret R. Hama b. Yosef's *memra*. It is not Rava who is proposing a solution similar to that of the Yerushalmi; it is the Bavli redactors, whose first interpretation of R. Hama b. Yosef demonstrates awareness not only of his *memra*, but of the Yerushalmi's own interpretation of that *memra*. The similarity between the Yerushalmi's and Bavli's (initial) interpretation of R. Hama b. Yose(f) is thus more likely due to the Bavli's appropriation of the Yerushalmi's interpretation of the *memra* along with the *memra* than to a hypothesis of "early basic amoraic material."

Alternatively, the difference between the Talmuds' presentations of R. Hama b. Yosef's *memra* could be due to conscious Bavli reworking of the *memra*. In other words, the Bavli could have received the *memra* from Palestine during the amoraic period as we find it in the Yerushalmi (which includes the mention of Peor) but deliberately shortened it so as to allow for the formation of the complex sugya we now find at b. AZ 44b. But if this is so, then the formulation of the *memra* as it appears in the Bavli is the product of editorial reworking that postdates R. Hama b. Yosef. We cannot then say with any confidence that the *memra* or any portion of it is convincingly identifiable as early talmud. The fact that both these possibilities for understanding the differences between the *memra*'s versions are equally plausible casts reasonable doubt on the facile assumption that the *memra* is early talmud.

Moreover, the Bavli's deployment of the fourth-generation Rava in its first interpretation of the *memra* could only be by scholars who come *later* than Rava. "Later" can conceivably include fifth-, sixth-, or seventh-generation amoraim, and/or the post-amoraic redactors. It is more reasonable, however, to maintain that Rava was deployed by post-amoraic redactors. Looking at the Bavli sugya at b. AZ 44b as a whole, we see that it is a complex sugya organized in a tight, recurring literary pattern and including anonymous argumentation. If we argue that Rava was deployed by later amoraim, then we must demonstrate that fifth- to seventh-generation amoraim created sugyot of this sort. Now, scholarship has demonstrated both that middle-generation amoraim may have functioned as editors[84] and that the later amoraic generations are characterized by greater and greater preservation of argumentation.[85] But it does not seem to be the case that later Babylonian amoraim produced sugyot of this sort. This sort of work is more characteristic of the post-amoraic redactors.

The theory of early talmud is a cousin of the "historical kernel," the search for which many scholars of rabbinics today eschew. Scholars once assiduously studied rabbinic stories for the historical kernels they contained about rabbinic sages and historical events, although the current scholarly consensus has moved in the direction of arguing that the stories themselves are hermeneutically and ideologically generated literary and cultural artifacts that likely do not contain historical kernels. Although the search for the historical kernel is out of scholarly fashion in the world of aggadah, it persists in the study of halakhic sugyot. Although the scholars whose work I have discussed in this section do not frame the issue in these terms, it is apparent that they see the halakhic sugya's parallel to the aggadic "historical kernel" in the shared material found in parallel Bavli and Yerushalmi sugyot. Stripping parallel sugyot down to their shared skeletons (as Noah Aminoah did with his Rosh Hashanah example) is thought to reveal the "amoraic halakhic kernel." Unlike the earlier investigators of the aggadic historical kernel, however, Yaacov Sussman is aware of the difficulty of separating the amoraic halakhic kernel from the argumentational matrix in which it is embedded. As I have demonstrated, his caution is well placed. Although the search for the "amoraic halakhic kernel" has much merit and may explain some inter-Talmudic similarities, its utility as a hypothesis must be explored carefully on a case-by-case basis. And, as this book will demonstrate, the theory of the amoraic halakhic kernel does not explain all of the similarities we see between b. and y. Avodah Zarah. The work of Friedman, Aminoah, and Sussman, as well as that of Jaffee, shows that bolder conclusions are justified.

---

84. See Kalmin, *Sages, Stories, Authors, and Editors*, 172n9.
85. See David Kraemer, "Stylistic Characteristics of Amoraic Literature"; idem, *Mind of the Talmud*.

To be clear, I am not denying that the Talmuds share material, or that some, or even much shared material may be the result of scholarly exchanges during the amoraic period. This cannot be denied in the face of the Talmuds' portrayals of *nahota* activity. Scholars certainly moved back and forth between the rabbinic centers throughout the Talmudic period, diligently pursuing their studies. But I *am* questioning whether these scholarly exchanges alone can account for the structural similarities we observe. An argument that they do account for all the structural similarities must be based on the following assumptions (or better still, the argument must prove these points):

1. When we find similar sequences of "uncalled-for"[86] topics and/or sugyot attached to a mishnah, this is the work of the amoraim;

2. When the Bavli juxtaposes a complex sugya (defined for this purpose as one with three or more steps in its argumentation) to a mishnah with the same (sizable) number of argumentational steps and/or a similar argumentational content as the parallel Yerushalmi sugya, this is the work of the amoraim;

3. Amoraim functioned as editors and original creators of all kinds of sugyot—simple as well as complex.

The scholar who assents to all three propositions is making large claims for the amoraim, essentially arguing that they functioned as sugya-editors and even redactors throughout the amoraic period. These claims are not reasonable in light of what we know at this point about amoraic activity. Amoraim certainly created and transmitted sugyot, and Richard Kalmin has even suggested that middle-generation amoraim may have functioned as editors.[87] But when we examine sugyot actually transmitted by amoraim, these appear to be relatively simple affairs.[88] As an example, let us look at b. AZ 24a. There, the Bavli presents R. Papa's and R. Zevid's versions of a sugya that consists of a teaching of the tanna R. Eliezer and the discussion of that teaching by the amoraim R. Yosef and Abaye. R. Papa and R. Zevid are represented as "reciting" or "teaching" (*matnei*)

---

86. I will explain the meaning and significance of this phrase later in this chapter. Briefly, this refers to sugyot and topics that are present in the Bavli's or Yerushalmi's commentaries on a particular mishnah, but which are not necessary for a complete explication of that mishnah.

87. See Richard Kalmin, *Sages, Stories, Authors, and Editors,* 169–173.

88. The amoraic sugyot I am discussing are those that can be clearly seen from context to be known to the amoraim as sugyot. This issue of what the amoraim were and were not aware of is critical in an assessment of amoraic activity.

that sugya. This sugya is striking in its brevity and non-analytic quality; it *collects* rather than *analyzes* teachings of the previous amoraic generation. A similar example is found at b. Git 3a. There, a small sugya begins with an anonymous question, to which R. Yohanan and R. Hanina are represented as supplying answers. Once again, this brief sugya is simply a short compilation rather than an analytic composition. An especially interesting example is found at b. Ket 57a. There, R. Dimi and Rabin both transmit different versions of the same sugya. The sugya consists of a statement by R. Shimon b. Pazi in the name of R. Yehoshua b. Levi in the name of Bar Qappara, a rather opaque comment on that statement by R. Yohanan, and then an interpretation by R. Abbahu of the initial statement in light of R. Yohanan. Once again, the amoraic sugya is rather simple. And even though R. Papa is portrayed as being aware of both R. Dimi's and Rabin's versions of the sugya (although they are not represented as being aware of each other's!) and attempting to understand the difference between them, even R. Papa is not portrayed as being aware that these sugyot, and his comments upon them, are part of a larger context that ranges beyond these sugyot.

Although three sugyot are (admittedly) hardly a statistically significant sample, they suggest three significant points. The first is that although more research remains to be done to identify and study amoraic sugyot, it is not correct to assume—as proponents of early talmud implicitly do—that any and all types of sugyot traveled back and forth between the rabbinic centers during the amoraic period. Some types of sugyot did circulate, but the lengthier and more argumentational the sugya, the less likely it was created or transmitted by amoraim.[89] Second, amoraic sugyot are not likely to display the multiple steps of argumentation and casuistic virtuosity characteristic of later sugyot. If the Talmuds are found to share sugyot of this variety, the sharing likely occurred later than the amoraic period. Third, these three sugyot suggest that the issue of amoraic awareness of context is an important factor. Amoraim were certainly aware of mishnayot, and it is certainly possible (although the matter requires demonstration, not mere assertion) that they may have attached baraitot, *memrot,* or simple amoraic sugyot to mishnayot. But we cannot proceed on the basis of unproven assumptions about amoraic activity. Many times amoraim are not portrayed as being aware of a dialectical context larger than their own quoted *memra,* or at best, larger than the short sugya in which they are found. Amoraim are not portrayed as being aware of a lengthy chain of topics attached to a mishnah, let alone of what sugyot are

---

89. But see b. Sanh 87a–88a, which appears to be a lengthy sugya taught by R. Papa at Rava's request. This example requires further investigation.

included in that chain and what topics they cover. As the example of R. Papa (b. Ket 57a) demonstrates, even an amora who is portrayed as being aware of two sugyot does not seem aware of the larger context of those sugyot. The point of this is that proponents of early talmud are not on firm ground when they simply assert (or imply) that chains of topics and sugyot could have become attached to mishnayot in the amoraic period. Although it is certainly not impossible that this could have happened in some cases, an assessment of *amoraic awareness* militates against it.

Early talmud works best as a theory explaining similarities between the Talmuds when a simple amoraic *memra*—or perhaps a *memra* with a brief interpretative comment or short sugya following—is what is present in the one Talmud, while the other uses that *memra* (and/or comment or sugya) as the basis of a longer sugya. The lengthier and more complex the parallel materials are in *both* Talmuds, the less well early talmud works as an explanation of the similarities.

Although the work of Aminoah, Sussman, and Friedman does not fully settle the issue of the similarities between the Talmuds, their sensitivity to the development of Talmudic literature and the complexity of sugya-formation raises another question: might it not be the case that *Babylonian* sugyot influenced *Palestinian* sugyot, as well as the reverse? We know that the Yerushalmi contains Babylonian sugyot; it has also been demonstrated that the rabbinic movement in Babylonia was extremely decentralized in comparison with Palestine.[90] Taking these two data together, we may well ask whether a given sugya was originally formulated in Babylonia, transmitted to Palestine, and then re-introduced into Babylonia at another time and place. I will consider this possibility as it arises in specific cases in the course of the detailed textual work in chapters 2–4.

IV
The Method of This Book

In demonstrating that the b. Avodah Zarah redactors were influenced by y. Avodah Zarah, I employ two levels of analysis: "macro" and "micro." Chapter 2 is a report of the findings of the macro analysis.

The point of the macro analysis of the Avodah Zarah tractates is to compare them as *wholes*—not to look simply at this or that parallel sugya, but to study the tractates as whole compilations. Macro analysis is the methodological result of taking seriously the notion that the redacted tractates as whole compilations are the only meaningful level at which re-

---

90. See, e.g., Richard Kalmin, *Sage in Jewish Society.*

search into whether or not b. Avodah Zarah relied on y. Avodah Zarah must proceed. In practice, this involves comparing each Talmud's *entire* treatment of a given mishnah to the other's. As Jacob Neusner has shown in numerous contexts (and as Shlomo Yehudah Rappaport and Martin Jaffee have shown in the context of Bavli-Yerushalmi studies), macro analysis is an important tool for uncovering major patterns in Talmudic phenomena.[91] Analyses of isolated sugyot are important, but are not dispositive of large issues such as the relationship between the Talmuds. In elucidating such a large and complex issue, macro analysis is absolutely indispensable.

In examining y. and b. Avodah Zarah's parallel mishnah treatments, I begin by noting what on a basic level looks similar in the two Talmuds' treatments of the same mishnah. I then test these similarities to determine if they are "called for by the mishnah." A topic is "called for by the mishnah" when the mishnah cannot be adequately explained without discussion of this topic. For example, in m. AZ 1:1, the mishnah rules that Israelites must abstain from various commercial activities with Gentiles during the three days prior to an idolatrous festival. This three-day period is an essential element of the mishnah, and it is therefore unremarkable that both Talmuds discuss it. That is, the mere *fact* that both Talmuds discuss the three-day period is "called for by the mishnah" since the mishnah cannot be adequately explicated without some consideration of that period. Nevertheless, closer examination of *how* the Talmuds go about discussing that three-day period is necessary in order to establish whether each Talmud independently dealt with it or whether the later Talmud's discussion of it is in some way beholden to that of the earlier Talmud.[92]

If a particular topic is called for by the mishnah, what determines whether or not the Bavli's treatment of that topic was or was not influ-

---

91. Mention should also be made of other studies of literary dependency between rabbinic compilations that have influenced the method employed in this book. See Chanoch Albeck's introduction to GenR in Juda Theodor and Chanoch Albeck, eds., *Midrash Bereschit Rabba* (3 vols.; Berlin: Akademie für die Wissenschaft des Judentums, 1903–1936; repr., Jerusalem: Shalem, 1996), 3:1–138; Hans-Jürgen Becker, *Die grössen rabbinischen Sammelwerke Palästinas* (Tübingen: Mohr Siebeck, 1999); Yaakov Elman, *Authority and Tradition: Toseftan Baraitot in Amoraic Babylonia* (New York: Ktav, 1994), and idem, "Orality and the Transmission of Tosefta Pisha in Talmudic Literature," in *Introducing Tosefta: Textual, Intratextual, and Intertextual Studies* (ed. Harry Fox and Tirzah Meacham; Hoboken, NJ: Ktav, 1999), 123–180.

92. See my discussion of the Talmuds' explications of this mishnah at pp. 89–101 and 189–193. In fact, on the basis of such a closer examination, it is indeed possible to establish that a structural similarity exists between the Talmuds' discussions of the three-day period, although the topic itself is called for by the mishnah.

enced by the Yerushalmi? If both Talmuds take up a particular topic and deal with it in different ways, a good argument exists that at least as to that term of the mishnah, the Bavli was not influenced by the Yerushalmi. On the other hand, m. AZ 5:1 and its explication by both Talmuds is a good example of the Yerushalmi's influence on the Bavli's discussion of a topic that *is* called for by the mishnah. While both Talmuds take up the is-sue of the hired "worker" (פועל) mentioned in m. AZ 5:1 (which renders such a discussion "called for by the mishnah"), each Talmud's treatment of the issue follows a nearly-identical five-step progression of argumenta-tion. Given the largely similar nature of the discussion, an argument can be made that, in this instance, the later Talmud was influenced by a ver-sion of the earlier.[93]

Implicit in what I have been saying is a distinction between each Tal-mud's decision to discuss a given topic, which may be "called for by the mishnah," and the way it goes about developing that discussion, which is "not called for by the mishnah." The mishnah neither contains instruc-tions for how its constituent parts are to be explicated, nor for whether the Talmuds should explicate some, and not others. The decisions about what amoraic statements, sugyot, and aggadic materials to weave together into the discussion of a mishnah are the decisions of the *Talmudic*, not the mishnaic, editors. Dissimilarity in the selection and sequence of these amoraic statements, sugyot, and aggadic materials in each Talmud may indicate that the later Talmud was most likely not influenced by the ear-lier. The *more* similarity we see between the selection and sequence of these constituent materials in the two Talmuds, the more likely it is that the redactors of the Bavli tractate under study were influenced by the Yerushalmi.

A topic is "not called for by the mishnah" if the mishnah can be ade-quately explicated without discussion of that topic. For an example, let us return to m. AZ 1:1. That mishnah contains neither aggadic materials nor scriptural verses, and yet both Talmuds' discussions of that mishnah in-clude lengthy aggadic materials. Such aggadah is "not called for by the mishnah." Another example from m. AZ 1:1 of a similarity between the Talmuds "not called for by the mishnah" is more subtle, and teaches us that we must be careful not to confuse what is *required* for an adequate ex-plication of the mishnah with what we know (or sense) to be "typical" Tal-mudic give-and-take. The mishnah sets out normative behavior regarding Jewish commercial activity during the three days preceding a pagan festi-val which the mishnah's editors presumably expected (or hoped) would be obeyed. Yet both the Yerushalmi at y. AZ 1:1, 39b and the Bavli at b. AZ

---

93. For detailed discussion of this example, see pp. 62–68.

6b utilize, *inter alia*, a tradition of R. Yohanan in order to explore the issue of the legal consequences of *violating* the mishnah's prohibitions. Such a discussion is "not called for by the mishnah," because the *mishnah itself* does not call for the Talmudic tendency to juxtapose baraitot or other sources to the mishnah which *contradict* its halakhic stance. The decision to do this is post-mishnaic, and cannot be assumed to be called for by the mishnah itself.

Finally, the Talmuds' discussions of m. AZ 3:2 provide another good example of a discussion "not called for by the mishnah." That mishnah rules that shards of (Gentile) vessels are permitted (per the Yerushalmi's version of the mishnah), or that shards of (Gentile, non-idolatrous) images are permitted (per the Bavli's version). Both Talmuds use that mishnah as the opportunity to discuss a R. Yohanan/Resh Laqish dispute about "an idol that was broken (y. Avodah Zarah) by itself" (b. Avodah Zarah). Even if one were to argue that a dispute about broken idols should be considered "called for" by a mishnah that talks about shards of vessels or images, the fact that the Bavli deals with the issue by taking over and expanding upon the same sugya as that found in the Yerushalmi is suggestive of its editorial reliance upon that Talmud.[94]

This initial step of the research allows me to exclude from further consideration materials that, being entirely "called for by the mishnah," are not dispositive of the question of the relationship between the Talmuds. If both Talmuds discuss a topic that is called for by the mishnah, and their discussions of it differ sufficiently that they are appropriately judged independent, then there is no further point in looking for evidence of the Bavli's reliance on the Yerushalmi in these cases. These materials may be excluded from further analysis.

Once I determine, on the contrary, that a given similarity between the Talmuds' discussion of a mishnah is "not called for by the mishnah," I examine this similarity against the other tannaitic materials (baraitot and other mishnayot) cited in the course of the Talmuds' discussions of the

---

94. The alert reader may further contend that the presence in both Talmuds of a R. Yohanan/Resh Laqish dispute is attributable to early talmud. While that suggestion makes a certain intuitive sense, it must be dismissed in this case. The Bavli sugya expands the amoraic dispute by drawing on, among other sources, other materials found in the Yerushalmi that were explicitly marked by the Yerushalmi editors as being relevant to this R. Yohanan/Resh Laqish dispute. So, whether or not the amoraic dispute itself is early talmud found in b. AZ, the latter's expansion of it draws on Yerushalmi editing. And, once we see the influence on the Bavli of the materials marked as relevant to the dispute by the Yerushalmi editors, we cannot be certain that what looks like early talmud did not in fact also come to the Bavli by way of the Yerushalmi.

mishnah. The reason for this second analytical step is identical to the first. If the observable similarity between the Talmuds is determined to be due to independent reliance on these tannaitic sources, the similarity is considered "called for by the other tannaitic sources" and is not dispositive of the question about whether the later Talmud was influenced by the earlier. And, since these materials are not dispositive of the question, they are excluded from consideration in this book. For example, t. AZ 2:6[95] is cited at both y. AZ 1:7, 40a and b. AZ 18b in relation to m. AZ 1:7. But each Talmud uses the Toseftan material in a radically different way. The Yerushalmi uses it to help explicate the mishnah, while the Bavli uses it as the starting-point of discussions having nothing at all to do with the mishnah. We may therefore conclude that each Talmud independently cited the Toseftan material for its own purposes.[96] On the other hand, when tannaitic materials are found integrated within discussions shared by the Talmuds, the likely conclusion is that the common citation of these tannaitic materials is the *result* rather than the *cause* of the similarity of the overall discussion. In such a case, the similarity is "not called for by the other tannaitic sources." For example, t. Shevi 6:26[97] is cited at both y. AZ 5:1, 44c and b. AZ 62a in relation to m. AZ 5:1. Yet each Talmud's anonymous voice integrates the Toseftan baraita into its own version of the same sugya; that is, it cites the baraita as part of a sugya explicating the mishnah rather than using the baraita as the starting-point for the formation of a sugya explicating it.

These two examples point to a key difference that is central to the question of whether a given similarity between the Talmuds is due to independent reliance on tannaitic materials or not. If one or both Talmuds use the baraita as the starting-point of new and dissimilar sugyot that explicate *it* rather than the mishnah, it is most likely that they cited it independently. On the other hand, if the Talmuds integrate the baraita in a sugya that explicates the mishnah, the common citation of the baraita is

---

95. *Tosephta: Based On the Erfurt and Vienna Codices, With Parallels and Variants* (ed. M. S. Zuckermandel; Jerusalem: Wahrmann, 1975), 462. Hereinafter this work will be referred to as "Zuckermandel."

96. Or, following Judith Hauptman, t. AZ 2:6 was part of a selection and sequence of baraitot that became attached to m. AZ 1:7 at an early stage, forming the earliest layer of "talmud" to that mishnah. See Judith Hauptman, *The Development of the Talmudic Sugya: Relationship Between Tannaitic and Amoraic Sources* (Lanham, MD: University Press of America, 1988).

97. *The Tosefta: According to Codex Vienna, With Variants From Codex Erfurt, Genizah Mss. And Editio Princeps (Venice 1521), Together With References to Parallel Passages in Talmudic Literature and a Brief Commentary: The Order of Zera'im* (ed. Saul Lieberman; New York: Jewish Theological Seminary, 1955), 194.

more likely the *result* of the similarity between the Talmuds than its *cause*. Thus, if a Yerushalmi sugya appears in the Bavli, and the parallel Bavli sugya demonstrates evidence of consciously reworking the *whole* Yerushalmi sugya—amoraic and anonymous material as well as tannaitic—then it seems more likely that the Bavli received the sequence of baraitot as part of that sugya rather than prior to the formation of the sugya.

If a given similarity between y. and b. Avodah Zarah is neither called for by the mishnah nor by other tannaitic sources, and is not reasonably identifiable as early talmud, then it is what I call a "structural similarity" between the Talmuds. That is, the similarity is a similarity in the selection and sequence of topics and sugyot in relation to a given mishnah that is likely due to nothing other than b. Avodah Zarah's reliance on y. Avodah Zarah. As a result of my macro analysis of the tractates, I identified nearly fifty structural similarities. Space considerations preclude the presentation of all these passages in this book, but in chapter 2 I present key examples of structural similarities that illustrate noteworthy patterns in b. Avodah Zarah's appropriation of y. Avodah Zarah materials.[98]

As important as this macro analysis of structural similarities is, it is not enough to support the conclusion that the b. Avodah Zarah redactors were aware of the work of the y. Avodah Zarah redactors. These macro similarities must themselves be carefully studied in order to probe the key differences between the Talmuds. We must see whether and how b. Avodah Zarah made changes to the older y. Avodah Zarah sugyot and how it adapted them to their new Bavli context. This close analysis of particular textual parallels is what I call the "micro" analysis. Chapter 3 will present these results, offering the first systematic analysis of what may be termed the Bavli's characteristic ways of reworking Yerushalmi materials. This work will continue in chapter 4, which will focus more pointedly on cases in which b. Avodah Zarah begins its treatment of an issue at the point at which y. Avodah Zarah ended its own, or takes up an issue that y. Avodah Zarah left unresolved.

Chapter 5 takes up the question of whether, and to what extent, b. Avodah Zarah's anonymous (stam) voice offers clues about b. Avodah Zarah's appropriation of y. Avodah Zarah materials. Finally, chapter 6 asks whether the hypothesis that b. Avodah Zarah was aware of y. Avodah Zarah is reasonable in light of literary, historical, and archaeological evidence from outside the Talmuds. The Talmuds did not emerge in an

98. The interested reader should turn to the Appendix (pp. 243–245) for a complete listing of all the parallel passages studied as part of the macro analysis. This listing is the source from which the textual examples were drawn for close analysis in this book.

intellectual vacuum, and any hypothesis about their relationship—no matter how plausible on the basis of textual analysis alone—that cannot be supported by a reasonable reading of the historical record beyond their pages is simply not well supported.

This book's thesis departs from the reigning scholarly consensus about the relationship between the Talmuds. I am hopeful that skeptical readers will come away from this book persuaded that the interpretation offered here is the most reasonable reading of the evidence. But this book even has value for readers who remain skeptical because it demonstrates (at the least) that b. Avodah Zarah appropriated and reworked sizable portions of y. Avodah Zarah, and thus gives us insight into the activities of the Bavli redactors. Skeptical readers will have to articulate another hypothesis to explain this evidence that does justice to its richness and complexity.

2

B. Avodah Zarah Drew Sequences of Sugyot and Topics from Y. Avodah Zarah (Macro Analysis)

The necessary beginning of our inquiry as to whether or not b. Avodah Zarah knew and relied on y. Avodah Zarah is to identify structurally and substantively similar parallels between the tractates that are neither "called for by the [local] mishnah" nor "called for by other tannaitic sources." Once we have identified such parallels we must examine them further to see whether they should be eliminated from further consideration as evidence for b. Avodah Zarah's reliance on y. Avodah Zarah on the grounds of early talmud. This "macro" analysis of the tractates—so called because the analysis encompasses both tractates *in toto* as well as each Talmud's total treatment of a given mishnah—is a vital first step that enables us to identify the pool of Bavli sugyot that merit further "micro" scrutiny of their literary relationship to their Yerushalmi parallels.

Macro analysis of the Avodah Zarah tractates yields approximately fifty parallel passages that b. Avodah Zarah most likely appropriated from y. Avodah Zarah.[1] Some of these passages are lengthy, ranging over a full Bavli folio (or even more), while others are much shorter. Some consist of lines of continuous text, while in others one or the other Talmud

---

1. For a complete listing of these parallel passages, see the Appendix, pp. 243–245.

suddenly digresses from the parallel materials, resuming the parallels at some point after the interruption. Despite the number and variety of these parallels, we can discern some interesting types and tendencies in b. Avodah Zarah's appropriation of y. Avodah Zarah that are worth examining in more depth both on account of their inherent interest and because of the possibility that these types will recur in macro analyses of other Bavli-Yerushalmi pairs. These types of appropriation are:

1. B. Avodah Zarah tends to appropriate y. Avodah Zarah sugyot (or sequences of two or more y. Avodah Zarah sugyot in the same order as y. Avodah Zarah) attached to the same mishnah;

2. In one case b. Avodah Zarah builds a simple sugya into a complex one using some materials that the y. Avodah Zarah editors had explicitly marked as relevant to the amoraic dispute that was the kernel of the original y. Avodah Zarah sugya;

3. In some cases in which b. Avodah Zarah material has a parallel not only in y. Avodah Zarah but also in other rabbinic compilations, b. Avodah Zarah tends to more closely resemble y. Avodah Zarah;

4. There is a case in which both Talmuds place parallel materials at similar points in the tractate although not attached to the same mishnah; and

5. B. Avodah Zarah sometimes uses the same mishnah as y. Avodah Zarah to explore the same legal issue (one that is not called for by the mishnah) or to present similar genres of material (such as aggadah or stories about sages).

It is important to stress that these types of appropriation are tendencies, not immutable rules. There may exist passages in a given pair of tractates that "should" fit into one of these categories but do not. But the significance of these types of appropriation and the examples that do exist to illustrate them is that they point to a literary dependency between b. and y. Avodah Zarah, not between Babylonian and Palestinian sugyot generally.[2]

---

2. Because the agenda of this chapter is to illustrate the macro analysis of the tractates, the following analyses all focus on the similarities between the Talmuds and pay little, if any, attention to the differences between them. These differences will be extensively analyzed in chapters 3 and 4.

I

B. Avodah Zarah Tends to Appropriate Y. Avodah Zarah Sugyot (or Sequences of Two or More Y. Avodah Zarah Sugyot in the Same Order as Y. Avodah Zarah) Attached to the Same Mishnah

This type of appropriation is the most common that we see in b. Avodah Zarah, accounting for most of the fifty passages that are neither "called for by the mishnah" nor "called for by other tannaitic sources." We will begin with an example from the beginning of the tractates (b. AZ 8a ‖ y. AZ 1:2, 39c) which, although lengthy, well illustrates this sort of structural similarity and how the macro analysis helps us to understand that the similarity is due to b. Avodah Zarah's reliance on y. Avodah Zarah and not some other cause.[3]

I.a. B. Avodah Zarah 8a ‖ Y. Avodah Zarah 1:2, 39c

Y. Avodah Zarah 1:2, 39c

A. Rav said: "Kalends—the First Man (Adam) established it. When he saw the long nights [of winter] he said, 'Woe is me! Lest he [the serpent] of whom it is written (Gen 3:15): 'he will crush your head, and you will strike his heel,' come to bite me! If I say (Ps 139:11–12) 'surely the darkness will surround me [and thus I will be protected, that will not be because] . . . even the darkness will not be dark to you.'

B. "Once he saw the days getting longer, he said: 'Kalends!—*kalon deo*! What a beautiful (*kalon*) day (*diem*)!'"[4]

---

3. In all translations in this book the following conventions will be observed regarding typeface: tannaitic materials will be presented in bold, the anonymous voice in italics, and amoraic traditions in regular Roman type.

4. *Kalon* is Greek for "good," while *deo* is apparently a corruption of the Latin *diem*, meaning "day." Although this translation of the expression assumes a "barbarous" original because of its blending of Greek and Latin, this interpretation is the most likely meaning of the phrase. The alternative is to understand the exclamation as entirely Greek, but then Adam would be saying *Kalon Dia!*, or "Zeus is good!," which the Yerushalmi is highly unlikely to attribute to him. Peter Schäfer also proposes this translation in his "Jews and Gentiles in Yerushalmi Avodah Zarah," in *The Talmud Yerushalmi and Graeco-Roman Culture* (ed. Peter Schäfer; Tübingen: Mohr Siebeck, 2003), 3:339n13. See also P'nei Moshe, s.v. אמר קלנדס קלון דיאו, who offers an interpretation of the phrase that is similar to the translation above. My thanks to Prof. Seth Schwartz for assisting me with this translation.

C. *And* [this story] *goes well according to the one who says that the world was created in Tishrei* [because then Adam would not yet have had the experience
of the days getting longer]. *But according to the one who says the world was
created in Nisan* [i.e., spring], *he* [Adam] *knew!* [If the world had been created in spring, then Adam would have been aware that the natural order
is to have long days and short nights, followed later by short days and
long nights.]

D. R. Yose b. R. Bun said: "Who is it who holds that the world was created at
the New Year [in Tishrei]? Rav; as it was taught in the [verses recited with
the] shofar blasts of the house of Rav: 'This is the day of the beginning of
Your activity; a remembrance of the first day.' So it was at New Year's
that the world was created."

E. R. Yohanan did not say thus [he did not agree with this account of the origin of Kalends]. Rather, the kingdom of Egypt and the kingdom of Rome
were at war with each other. They said: "How long will we be killing
[each other] in this controversy? Come, let us establish that whichever
kingdom says to its commanding general 'Fall on your sword' and he
obeys it, [that kingdom] will seize hold of [world] empire ahead [of the
other]." [The commanding general of] Egypt did not listen to them. [The
commanding general] of Rome—there was there one old man whose
name was Yanobris,[5] and he had twelve sons. They said to him: "Listen to
us [to kill yourself] and we will make your sons *duces*[6] and *eparchoi* and
strateletai." He listened to them. For this reason, they shouted [about him]
"Qalendas Yanobris!" ["Yanobris is free!"—that is, the members of his
house are now rulers in Rome, which is now ruler of the world. Thus, in
remembrance of this event, Rome made the days of early January—
named for Yanobris—the holiday "Kalends"]. On the day following
[Kalends], they [Rome] mourned for him, "Oh, the black [unfortunate]
day!"

F. R. Yudan Antodria said: "One who plants lentils on that day, they will
not flourish."

G. Rav said: "Kalends is forbidden for everyone [that is, Israelites are forbidden to transact business with any Gentiles at Kalends time, whether
or not they are observing the holiday]."

H. R. Yohanan said: "Kalends is only forbidden for those who worship on it
[that is, on Kalends Israelites must avoid only Gentiles observing the fes-
tival]."

---

5. "Yanobris" is "Januarius," and this sugya is an allusion to the Roman myth
about the origins of the January Kalends. See, e.g., Peter Schäfer, "Jews and Gentiles in Yerushalmi Avodah Zarah," 340 and sources cited.

6. See Michael Sokoloff, *A Dictionary of Jewish Palestinian Aramaic of the Byzantine
Period* (Ramat-Gan: Bar-Ilan University Press, 1990), 142, who reads דוכסין cautiously as "princes." Prof. Seth Schwartz pointed out to me (personal communication) that these three Greek titles were high ranks in the late imperial administra-
tion, as well as topoi in the Yerushalmi and Palestinian midrash compilations.

I.   [Rav presumably continues]: "Saturnalia is forbidden for everyone."

J.   R. Yohanan said: "Whether Kalends or Saturnalia, it is only forbidden for those who worship on it."

K.   The Scholars[7] asked: "Are the wives of worshipers [considered to be like] worshipers [themselves]?"

L.   R. Abbahu asked: "And this office of the civil governor[8] in Caesarea?" [Is it off-limits to commerce?]

M.   *Since there are many Samaritans there, it is* [implicitly as if] *they are worshiping* [the idol of the place].

N.   *This office of the civil governor of Duqim?* [It is still] *necessary* [to answer this question, since the status of that office remains unclear].

O.   R. Bibi sent [a message to] R. Zeirah to buy him a small web of yarn at the Saturnalia of Bashan. [R. Bibi came before R. Yose. He thought that he would rule "permitted" for him in accordance with the view of R. Yehoshua b. Levi, but he ruled "forbidden" for him in accordance with the view of R. Yohanan.

P.   Rav said: "Kalends is eight days before the solstice, and Saturnalia is eight days after the solstice."

Q.   R. Yohanan said: "*Tropiqe*[9]—[Saturnalia is] the beginning of the midwinter solstice."

B. Avodah Zarah 8a

A.   R. Hanan b. Rava said: "Kalends is eight days after the solstice, Saturnalia is eight days before the solstice. And your sign [for remembering this order]: 'You created me after and before' (Ps 139:5)." [Since the mishnah refers to Kalends first, the term "Kalends" goes with the scriptural word "after," and "Saturnalia" goes with "before."]

---

7. Sokoloff, *Dictionary*, 185 offers "friend" and "colleague" as possible meanings, but also points to Palestinian sources in which the term also means "scholar" or "student."

8. Sokoloff reads טקסיס as "regiment" at *Dictionary*, 230, while Jastrow renders it as "garrison" at *Dictionary of the Targumim, the Talmud Bavli and Yerushalmi, and the Midrashic Literature* (New York: Pardes, 1950), 535. P'nei Moshe, on the other hand, interprets טקסיס as a place *within* Caesarea. Taking these interpretations together it seems that the טקסיס is a not necessarily permanent gathering of persons within a city. On this interpretation R. Abbahu's question is sensible within its context as a question analogous to that about wives and other legal dependents. Most recently, Kenneth G. Holum has defined טקסיס as "office . . . of the civil governor," which is the translation I have adopted. See Kenneth G. Holum, "Identity and the Late Antique City: The Case of Caesarea," in *Religious and Ethnic Communities in Later Roman Palestine* (ed. Hayim Lapin; Bethesda, MD: University Press of Maryland, 1998), 157–177.

9. See Jastrow, *Dictionary*, 1222, who emends the Yerushalmi's term פרוקטו to טרופיקי, which he defines as "the day of the midwinter solstice."

B.   *Our Rabbis taught:* **Since the First Man saw the day growing progressively shorter, he said, "Woe is me! Since I sinned, the world is getting dark because of me and is returning to primordial chaos. And this is the death that was imposed on me from Heaven."** He undertook to sit for eight days in fasting and prayer. When he saw the winter solstice, and saw the day growing progressively longer, he said: "This is the way of the world." He went ahead and established eight festive days. The next year he made both these [the eight days prior to the solstice, which he had spent in fasting] **and these** [the eight days he had established as a festival] **as festive days** [the first set of eight became Saturnalia, the second Kalends]. [Adam] **established them for the sake of Heaven; they** [the idolaters] **established them for the sake of idolatry.**

C.   *This works well according to the one who says that the world was created in Tishrei. [Thus] he saw short days, [but] he still had not seen long days. But according to the one who says that the world was created in Nisan, he saw short days and long days!*

D.   [Yet] *he still had not seen days that were especially short.*

E.   *Our Rabbis taught:* **On the day in which Adam was created, once he saw the sun setting over him, he said: "Woe is me! Since I sinned, the world is getting dark on me, and will return to the primordial chaos, and this is the death that is imposed on me from Heaven." He sat in fasting and cried all night, and Eve cried alongside him. Once the dawn star rose, he said: "It is the way of the world." He got up and offered a bull whose horns stretched out beyond its hooves, as it is said: "This will please the Lord more than an ox, more than a bull with its horns and hooves"** (Ps 69:32).

F.   And R. Yehudah said in the name of Shmuel: "The bull that Adam offered had one horn on its forehead, as it is said, 'with its horns' (Ps 69:32)."

G.   *This* [מקרין] *implies two* [horns]!

H.   R. Nahman b. Yitshaq said: "'With its horns' is written [defectively] as 'מקרן' [which implies only one horn]."

I.   R. Matana asked:[10] "Rome makes a Kalends celebration, are all the cities subjugated to her forbidden or permitted?" [Since the cities are subject to

---

10. Following *Tractate Avodah Zarah of the Babylonian Talmud: MS Jewish Theological Seminary of America* (ed. Shraga Abramson; New York: Jewish Theological Seminary, 1957) (hereinafter "JTS ms."), I have translated בעי רב מתנה rather than אמר רב מתנה, which is the reading of the printed edition. This reading (which is confirmed by Rif and Rosh) makes more sense since R. Matana is, after all, asking a question and not simply making a statement. Nevertheless, there is still a chronological problem, for how could R. Yehoshua b. Levi and R. Yohanan respond to a question asked by R. Matana? Albeck notes two amoraim of this name: one of

Rome, are they off-limits to Israelite commerce because the mother city is observing the idolatrous holiday, even if they are not?]

J.   R. Yehoshua b. Levi said: "Kalends is forbidden to everyone." [That is, Israelites are forbidden to interact commercially with any Gentiles at Kalends time, whether or not the latter are observing.]

K.   R. Yohanan said: "It is only forbidden for its worshippers alone."

L.   *There is a baraita in support of R. Yohanan*: **Even though they said that if Rome makes a Kalends, all the neighboring cities are subject to her, it itself** [the period of Kalends] **is forbidden in respect of its celebrants alone. Saturnalia and Kratesis and the birthdays of their emperors, and the coronation day of the emperor—before, it is forbidden** [for the Israelite to engage in commerce with the Gentiles]; **afterwards, it is permitted. And an idolater who made a wedding for his son—only that day and that very man are forbidden.**

M.   R. Ashi said: "Even we can derive this principle from our mishnah, as it is taught: **The day of the shaving of his beard and forelock, and the day that he returns from the sea, and the day he left prison—only that very day and that very man are forbidden.**"

N.   *It works well* [to understand the phrase] *"that very day" as excluding the one before and after it. But* [as to the phrase] *"that very man," what?* [What can it come to tell us? Is it not obvious that Israelites should only be forbidden to do business with that particular person alone?] *Is it not to exclude those people subject to him?* [This is not so obvious, since I might have thought that I could not do business with the family or servants of the particular Gentile who had returned from the sea, etc. Thus,] *hear from this* [that even though commerce with the Gentile himself is forbidden, commerce is not forbidden with those subject to him].

As always, we must begin with the mishnah. Both Talmuds attach this parallel sequence of sugyot to m. AZ 1:3. The mishnah begins by listing in the name of R. Meir those idolatrous festivals on which, and three days before which, an Israelite must be careful to abstain from commercial interactions with Gentiles (per m. AZ 1:1–2): Kalends, Saturnalia, Kratesis, the coronation days of emperors, their birthdays, and the anniversaries of their deaths. The Sages then point out that deaths of emperors that are accompanied by "burning" (property of the dead emperor) will have some idolatrous worship as part of the commemoration, unlike those not marked by burning. Finally m. AZ 1:3 lists certain private holidays as to

whom was a second-generation Babylonian amora who studied with Shmuel, and the other of whom lived in the fourth generation. Yet, even if we assume that the R. Matana mentioned here is the earlier, R. Yehoshua b. Levi still could not have answered one of his questions. See Albeck, *Introduction to the Talmud,* 204, 370.

which m. AZ 1:1–2's three-day period of commercial abstention does not apply. These are the days of shaving the beard and forelock,[11] the day of returning from the sea, the day of release from prison, and the wedding prepared by a Gentile for his son. As to these private holidays, Israelites must abstain from commercial dealings only with the celebrating Gentile and only on the day of the celebration.

The first notable structural similarity between the Talmuds is the presence of versions of the same aggadah—the etiology of Kalends as the biblical Adam's response to the winter solstice—very early in each Talmud's discussion of the mishnah (y. AZ 1:2, 39c at §§A–C; b. AZ 8a at §§A–H). The mishnah contains neither aggadah nor scriptural verses (which could serve as a "hook" for aggadah) and thus does not call for aggadah to be presented by either Talmud, let alone versions of the *same* aggadah. Moreover nothing in the mishnah requires both Talmuds to locate their versions of the aggadah within the same larger contexts, as they clearly do. To begin with, both Talmuds incorporate similar anonymous discussion of the aggadah in their respective §§C, according to which the Adam story makes sense according to the view that the world was created in the month of Tishrei, but not according to the view that it was created in Nisan. Second, both Talmuds present two versions of the origin of Kalends. R. Yohanan's second, and different, version of the origin of Kalends is found at y. AZ 1:2, 39c (§§E–F), while the Bavli presents a second version of the Adam story at b. AZ 8a (§§E–H). Third, both Talmuds juxtapose these aggadot to discussions about whether Israelites are forbidden to do business during Kalends and Saturnalia only with Gentiles observing those festivals, or even with the legal dependents of the observant and the non-observant (y. AZ 1:2, 39c at §§G–K; b. AZ 8a at §§I–N). Nothing in the mishnah requires both Talmuds to juxtapose these similar materials to each other in this order.

Moving beyond the mishnah to other tannaitic sources, we see that only b. Avodah Zarah quotes baraitot in its sequence of sugyot, so that we cannot speak of a common set of other tannaitic sources on which both Talmuds may have independently relied. But when we look closer we see that b. Avodah Zarah presents some material in the form of baraitot that y. Avodah Zarah attributes to amoraim. This raises the possibility that this allegedly amoraic material in y. Avodah Zarah was originally baraita-material quoted by amoraim that over time came to be attributed to

---

11. See Hayes, *Between the Babylonian and Palestinian Talmuds*, 88–91 for a discussion of the Greco-Roman sources concerning rituals surrounding the shaving of the beard and forelock.

amoraim directly.[12] And if that is so, then perhaps we *can* speak of a shared tannaitic layer in both Talmuds' sequences of sugyot. But even if this reconstruction is correct it does not prove that a shared set of tannaitic materials accounts for all the structural similarities between b. and y. Avodah Zarah. This hypothesized shared set of tannaitic sources accounts neither for the fact that both Talmuds open their considerations of this mishnah with versions of the same aggadah, nor for the fact that both Talmuds include similar anonymous discussions of the aggadah, as well as two versions of the origin of Kalends.

Early talmud is also inadequate as an explanation of these similarities. First, the lengthy sequence of sugyot in both Talmuds is clearly the product of an editorial hand. No y. Avodah Zarah amora is demonstrably aware of the shifts in topic from Adam to the month in which the world was created and then on to the second etiology of Kalends and a discussion about whether an Israelite is forbidden to interact commercially with the legal dependents of Gentiles observing the festivals. These topical shifts—which show y. Avodah Zarah's discussion of the mishnah opening with aggadah and then moving on to halakhah—are more likely the work of redactors, who reproduce here a literary pattern that we can observe elsewhere in that tractate. For example, at y. AZ 1:1, 39a–b the Yerushalmi presents a lengthy aggadic composition dealing with the biblical king Jeroboam b. Nebat and his surrender to the temptations of idolatry, followed by halakhic consideration of m. AZ 1:1.[13] We can observe a similar transition from aggadah to halakhah at y. AZ 3:1–2, 42b–c, which discusses whether or not an Israelite can derive benefit from images and broken pieces of images he happens to find. Putting this all together, we may reasonably conclude that since no amora is demonstrably aware of the orchestration of sources in y. AZ 1:2, 39c and since that orchestration of sources displays a pattern we see elsewhere in the editing of y. Avodah Zarah, y. AZ 1:2, 39c is more likely the product of the Yerushalmi redactors than an example of early talmud.

Turning to b. AZ 8a, we also fail to see amoraic awareness of the sequence of sugyot *qua* sequence of sugyot. The more reasonable explanation

---

12. See Avraham Weiss, *Le-heqer ha-Talmud* (New York: Feldheim, 1954), 59. Judith Hauptman subsequently revisited these and other conclusions of Weiss (and others) on the subject of baraitot and amoraic *memrot* that seem to repeat them in her *Development of the Talmudic Sugya*.

13. We will examine y. AZ's halakhic consideration of m. AZ 1:1 in detail at the beginning of chapter 3.

of the inter-Talmudic similarities is that b. AZ 8a has relied on the editorial choices made in the earlier Talmud.[14]

I.b. B. Avodah Zarah 53a ‖ Y. Avodah Zarah 4:5, 44a

Y. Avodah Zarah 4:5, 44a

A.   R. Zeirah said: "That which it [the mishnah] says [in quoting the opinion of the Sages, according to whom selling or pawning an idol does not invalidate it], [applies to a situation] in which he [the worshiper] sold it out of [a feeling of] calm [that is, he did not sell it because of negative feelings toward the idol]. But if he sold it out of anger, everyone [the Sages and Rabbi] agrees that it is invalidated."

B.   "And it shall be that when he is hungry, he will become angry and curse his king and his god. . . . (Isa 8:21). [And thus, since the worshiper cursed the god in anger, it must be invalidated]."[15]

C.   Zeorah b. Hinena in the name of R. Hananiah: "[Rabbi and the Sages] are disputing [about a situation] in which he sold it to a smelter.[16] But all agree that if he sold it to a [fellow-]worshiper, it is not invalidated." R. Yirmiyah in the name of Rav: "They are disputing [about a situation] in which he sold it to its [the idol's] worshipers. But if he sold it to a smelter, all agree that it is invalidated."

---

14. More detailed consideration will be given to issues of early talmud in the micro analyses to be undertaken in chapters 3 ("B. Avodah Zarah Sugyot as Secondary Reworkings of Y. Avodah Zarah Sugyot") and 4 ("B. Avodah Zarah's Awareness of Y. Avodah Zarah's Editing").

15. P'nei Moshe, s.v. והיה כי ירעב וגו׳, reads into this verse the interpretation given it by the Bavli at 53a, to wit, that the verse is quoted to explain the mishnah's counterintuitive ruling that spitting or urinating in the face of the idol does not invalidate it. The problem with his interpretation is that it seems imposed on the Yerushalmi rather than explicative of it. Moreover, P'nei Moshe's interpretation implies that the Yerushalmi is interpreting the clauses of the mishnah out of order, since the mishnah discussed "spitting" and "urinating" prior to the "selling" and "pawning" discussed in §A. On the other hand, nothing in the text indicates that R. Zeirah himself cited the verse as a proof text for his position as to selling and pawning. Nevertheless, it is more reasonable to assume that either R. Zeirah himself—or the Yerushalmi on his behalf—cited the verse as support for his position than to assume that it is to be interpreted as the P'nei Moshe does. Consequently I have appended commentary to the verse which connects it to R. Zeirah.

16. The Venice and Kratoschin editions read "for need" (לצורך) instead of "to a smelter" (לצורף) in each of the places in which the latter word appears. The Leiden ms. reads "to a smelter," as we have translated. Interestingly the Bavli's version of the sugya also reads "to a smelter," demonstrating that the Bavli is preserving a more accurate version of the y. AZ sugya than what we currently find in printed editions of the Yerushalmi.

D. R. Yaaqov b. Aha in the name of R. Yohanan: "All agree." R. Hila in the name of R. Shimon b. Laqish: "It is a matter of disagreement" [the Yerushalmi does not yet specify what these observations mean]. *And that which R. Hanina* [=Hananiah] *said* [that Rabbi and the Sages were disputing about a worshiper who sold the idol to a smelter, but that if he sold it to a worshiper, all agree it is not invalid] *is consistent with R. Yohanan, and that* [statement] *of R. Yirmiyah* [that Rabbi and the Sages were disputing about a sale to a worshiper, but that both agree that a sale to a smelter renders the idol invalid] *is like* [the statement of] *Resh Laqish. What is the result? They* [Rabbi and the Sages] *were disputing* [about a situation] *in which he sold it to a smelter, but if he sold it to its worshipers, all agree that it is not invalidated.*

B. Avodah Zarah 53a

A. [The mishnah rules that] **If he smashed it** [the idol], **even though he did not diminish it** [none of the idol itself was lost in the process], **he has invalidated it.** [Now the anonymous voice asks:] *If he did not diminish it, how has he invalidated it?* R. Zera said: "In that he smashed it in its face" [and thus ruined its features. Even though all of the pieces of the idol may be recoverable, smashing the idol's face certainly should be seen as invalidation].

B. [Citing the mishnah:] **If he spit in its face, or urinated in its face** [it is not invalidated]. *From where do these words* [that such behavior does not invalidate the idol] *derive?* Hezekiah said: "The verse says: 'And it shall be that when he is hungry, he will become angry and curse his king and his god, and turn upward' (Isa 8:21–22). [Out of his anger and frustration, the idolater will reject his idol and turn upward toward God.] And it is written after that: 'And he [the idolater] will look toward the ground, and behold, it is narrow and dark.' [That is, even though initially the idolater rejected his god out of anger, he will once again "look to the ground," turn away from God, and return to the worship of the idol. Thus, cursing the idol, or in the mishnah's terms "spitting" or "urinating" on it, does not signify complete rejection.] For even though he cursed his king and his god and faced upward—he will look toward the ground."

C. Zeiri said in the name of R. Yohanan, and R. Yirmiyah b. Abba said in the name of Rav. One said: "The dispute [between Rabbi and the Sages] is about an idolatrous smelter. But all agree [that if we are dealing with the sale of the idol to an Israelite] that with respect to an Israelite smelter, he has invalidated it." And one said: "The dispute is about an Israelite smelter." *They asked* [about this last statement]: "Is there a dispute about an Israelite smelter, but all agree that as to an idolatrous smelter he did not invalidate it; or perhaps is there a dispute in both situations?" [The Bavli goes on to discuss this question, but the issue is unresolved.]

M. Avodah Zarah 4:5 discusses how an idol is invalidated. Among the behaviors that indisputably invalidate the idol is smashing its face. Spitting at it, urinating in its presence, and rolling it around in dung do *not* invalidate it. The latter part of the mishnah is a dispute between Rabbi and the Sages about whether selling or pawning an idol is sufficiently disrespectful behavior so that the idol is thereby invalidated. Rabbi claims that it is, while the Sages disagree.

The commonality between the Talmuds is the citation of Isa 8:21 (y. AZ 4:5, 44a at §B) or 8:21–22 (b. AZ 53a at §B), followed by the dispute between similarly-named sets of amoraim about selling to a "smelter" (לצורף). Nothing in the mishnah calls for the citation of the verse or for the juxtaposition of the amoraic dispute and the verse. Nor are any other tannaitic sources cited which may have led to this similarity in selection and sequence of topics. Moreover, no amora in either Talmud is demonstrably aware of the orchestration of topics and sugyot in this way. The reasonable conclusion is that the Bavli was influenced in its selection and sequence of topics by the earlier arrangement of these materials in y. Avodah Zarah.

I.c. B. Avodah Zarah 24a–b ‖ Y. Avodah Zarah 2:1, 40c

Before leaving section I, we should mention one other lengthy and noteworthy example of b. Avodah Zarah's tendency to appropriate from y. Avodah Zarah sugyot or sequences of y. Avodah Zarah sugyot attached to the same mishnah. It opens (in the Bavli) with R. Ami and R. Yitshaq Napha discussing R. Eliezer's view about purchasing animals from Gentiles (m. Par 2:1) in light of Isa 60:7. The Bavli then moves on to a related discussion of this topic by R. Yosef and Abaye (based on Zeph 3:9), followed by a mini-review of biblical precedents for purchasing or accepting sacrificial animals from Gentiles. This review begins with Moses and Jethro, and moves on to Saul and then David's interaction with Aravnah the Jebusite. Objections based on 1 Sam 6:15 are then raised and reconciled.

This sugya opens in y. Avodah Zarah with anonymous discussion of R. Liezer's (=Eliezer) view in light of Isa 60:7, followed by further discussion along this line by R. Hoshaya and R. Abin. Y. Avodah Zarah then represents R. Yitshaq and R. Ami as the scholars engaged in the mini-review of biblical history, beginning with 2 Chr 15:11, moving back to 1 Sam 6:15, Saul, David and Aravnah, and then relevant verses from Leviticus.

M. Avodah Zarah 2:1 does not call for this similar developmental path, and there are no other tannaitic sources cited which could account for it either. Early talmud is an appealing explanation because the biblical history review is attributed to amoraim in y. Avodah Zarah, and hence might be thought of as early talmud in b. Avodah Zarah. But this material is part of a larger structural similarity that undermines this explanation: in both Talmuds, the biblical history review is placed after a sugya (b. AZ 22b–23a ‖ y. AZ 2:1, 40c) which, as we will show in chapter 3, b. Avodah Zarah appropriated from y. Avodah Zarah and improved upon. This structurally similar macro-ordering of the material in both Talmuds—of which no amora is represented as being aware—is therefore more likely the work of redactors reflecting upon the work of redactors than early talmud.[17]

II

B. Avodah Zarah Builds a Complex Sugya Using Some Materials Marked as Relevant by the Y. Avodah Zarah Redactors

We find only one example of this type of b. Avodah Zarah appropriation of y. Avodah Zarah, and it deserves careful scrutiny because it shows the editors of b. Avodah Zarah creating a complex sugya from a simpler early amoraic one by utilizing (in part) materials explicitly marked by the y. Avodah Zarah redactors as relevant to the early amoraic dispute.[18] These other relevant materials are found elsewhere in y. Avodah Zarah, although not necessarily in connection with m. AZ 3:2, to which this Yerushalmi sugya and its Bavli embellishment are linked.

Y. Avodah Zarah 3:2, 42d

A.   *An idol that was broken:* R. Yohanan said: "[The broken pieces of the idol are] forbidden"; R. Shimon b. Laqish said: "[The broken pieces of the idol are] permitted." *With what sort of situation are we dealing? If he* [the idol's owner] *will in the future return them* [the broken pieces] *to their* [state of] *wholeness, all agree* [that the broken pieces are] *forbidden. If he will not in the future return them to their* [state of] *wholeness, all agree* [that the broken pieces are] *permitted. Rather, we are dealing with a situation* [in] *which* [the owner's intention] *is undefined.* R. Yohanan said that *"undefined"* [intentions are] *like the* [intentions of one] *who will in the future return them* [the broken pieces] *to their* [wholeness]. R. Shimon b. Laqish said that *"unde-*

---

17. For yet another example (b. AZ 30a–31a ‖ y. AZ 2:3, 41a–b), see chapter 6, pp. 214–215.

18. The only material marked as relevant by the y. AZ editors that does not appear in the Bavli sugya is at y. AZ 3:8, 43b (the relationship of the R. Yohanan/Resh Laqish dispute to the case of a person whose house, located next to an idolatrous temple, fell apart. Such a person is not permitted to rebuild).

fined" [intentions are] *like the* [intentions of one] *who will not in the future return them* [the broken pieces] *to* [their state of] *wholeness.*

B.   R. Yudan the father of R. Matanya said: "If they [the broken pieces] were resting in their places [where they had fallen upon breaking]—this is like [the situation of] one who will in the future return them to their wholeness." [By having left the pieces where they fell, the owner is indicating his intention to re-assemble them at some point.]

C.   Resh Laqish raised an objection to Rabbi [=R. Yohanan]: "And is it not written, 'For this reason, the priests of Dagon do not step on the threshold of Dagon' (1 Sam 5:5)." [That the priests paid honor only to the smashed Dagon's threshold and not to his broken pieces shows that the broken pieces were no longer considered holy and thus should be permitted.]

D.   [R. Yohanan] said to him: "This [verse] teaches that they paid the threshold more honor than Dagon [himself]." [Since the priests were paying more honor to the threshold, they obviously had no intention of rebuilding Dagon on that spot. Thus, this was a case of "one who will not in the future return them to their wholeness," as to which even R. Yohanan agrees that the pieces are permitted.]

E.   R. Yirmiyah in the name of R. Hiyya b. Ba said: "The nations of the world made one threshold [that of Dagon, which was as much of an object of worship as Dagon himself] and Israel made a number of thresholds [one for each idol they worshiped. Like other nations, Israel turned these thresholds into objects of worship]. The reason [i.e., the verse on which this observation is based]: 'I will punish all who avoid stepping on the threshold'" (Zeph 1:9).

The following sugya is the first one marked by y. Avodah Zarah's redactors as relevant to the R. Yohanan/Resh Laqish dispute:

Y. Avodah Zarah 4:1, 43d

F.   [From m. AZ 4:1:] **And the Sages say, "That which appears with [near] it [the Mercurius[19]] is forbidden; and that which does not appear with it is permitted."**

G.   **And that which appears with it is forbidden**?! *Does that not conflict with* [the view of] *Resh Laqish? For Resh Laqish said:* "An idol that broke is permitted." *No—thus do we hold: if* [the owner] *will not in the future return them* [the broken idols] *to their* [state of] *wholeness, then everyone* [R. Yohanan and Resh Laqish] *says that* [they are] *permitted.*[20] [Thus, since the object or

---

19. Piles of stones personified this god of travelers, and these piles marked out boundaries and protected doors and gates. See, e.g., Ramsay MacMullen, *Paganism in the Roman Empire* (New Haven: Yale University Press, 1981) at 52, 141n2, 170n11; Peter Schäfer, "Jews and Gentiles in Yerushalmi Avodah Zarah," 348.

20. The text reads: "If he is in future to return them to their state of wholeness, everyone agrees that they are permitted," which makes no sense since if the idol is

stone is found with the Mercurius, Resh Laqish would agree that the owner probably intends to put it together with the idol, and the object or stone should therefore be forbidden.]

The following is the next sugya marked by y. Avodah Zarah's redactors as relevant to this amoraic dispute:

Y. Avodah Zarah 3:13, 43b–c

H. *And does this* [R. Yose's statement in m. AZ 3:13 that one should not plant vegetables in the shade of a sacred tree even in winter because the rain will cause foliage to drop on them and serve as fertilizer] *not even conflict with* [the view of] *R. Yohanan* [who agreed that if an owner was not going to return a broken idol to its state of wholeness, the pieces would be permitted]*? Did we not hold that if the owner would not return* [the idol] *to its* [state of] *wholeness in the future, everyone* [R. Yohanan and Resh Laqish] *agrees that it is permitted?* [And so, since the foliage of the sacred tree will not be returned to the tree once it falls off, even R. Yohanan would have ruled that the foliage is permitted. Yet in m. AZ 3:13, R. Yose nevertheless declares it forbidden!][21]

I. *Resolve* [that m. AZ 3:13 is dealing] *with an Israelite's idolatry* [which can never be invalidated].

J. *And does this* [R. Yose's view in m. AZ 3:13] *not disagree with* [the view of] *Rav? For Rav said:* "[If the sacred tree was groomed] for its need [in order to help the plant grow, but not in order to beautify it for idolatrous worship, then] it is forbidden and its trimmings are permitted." [Thus, Rav would also hold that if rain caused foliage to fall from the sacred tree, that foliage would be permitted since it was not deliberately removed in order to beautify the tree for idolatrous worship. Rav thus disagrees with R. Yose's view in m. AZ 3:13.]

K. *Once again resolve* [the contradiction by saying that m. AZ 3:13 deals] *with an Israelite's idolatrous object* [which can never be invalidated].

With all of this material in view, we now proceed to b. Avodah Zarah.

---

returned to a state of wholeness it should be forbidden. The glosses to the Kratoschin edition of the Yerushalmi actually suggest emending "permitted" to "forbidden," but adding "will not" (לא) to the text is a less intrusive emendation.

21. This text is difficult, because R. Yose's ruling is actually consistent with R. Yohanan's view as it appears in the Leiden ms. and in the printed editions. R. Yohanan's view is that the broken idol is forbidden, while R. Yose is, in effect, saying the same thing. Therefore P'nei Moshe (s.v. פליגא על ר׳ יוחנן) interprets as follows: "That which [the Yerushalmi] says [that the difficulty is a difficulty as to R. Yohanan's view] really means that [m. AZ 3:13] conflicts *even* with R. Yohanan's view." P'nei Moshe's reading is a reasonable way to make sense of a difficult text, and I have translated accordingly.

B. Avodah Zarah 41b

A. *It was said: An idol that broke by itself*—R. Yohanan said: "Forbidden." R. Shimon b. Laqish said: "Permitted." *R. Yohanan said "Forbidden" for behold, he* [the owner] *did not invalidate it.* [Since it broke by itself, R. Yohanan assumes that the owner still religiously values it.] *R. Shimon b. Laqish said "Permitted" for it is implied that he would invalidate it.* [The owner] *would surely say: "It* [the idol] *could not save itself, how can it save that man* [me]*?"*

B. R. Yohanan raised an objection to R. Shimon b. Laqish: "'His [Dagon's] head and hands were broken off and were lying on the threshold' (1 Sam 5:4), and it is written, 'For this reason, the priests of Dagon do not step on the threshold' (1 Sam 5:5)." [That the priests would not step on the threshold on which Dagon's pieces were lying shows that they still revered the pieces. Thus, the pieces should be forbidden.]

C. He [Resh Laqish] said to him: "Is there proof [for your position] from there? There [in the two verses] they abandoned Dagon and worshiped the threshold. For they [the priests] said thus: 'Thus divine power has left Dagon and has settled in the threshold.'"[22]

B. Avodah Zarah 42a–b

D. *He* [R. Yohanan] *raised an objection to* [Resh Laqish]: "[If] **an idolater took stones from a Mercurius and used them to cover roads and theatres, they are forbidden.**" *Why* [should the stones be forbidden according to you, Resh Laqish]? *Let them be like the "idol that broke by itself"* [which Resh Laqish held was permitted]*! Here also* [the reason that the stones are forbidden despite Resh Laqish's view that they ought to be permitted is because we take account of a concern] *like that of Rava* [who voiced a particular concern about an Israelite's holding an idol that was improperly invalidated and so remained "an idol in the hands of an Israelite"].

E. *He* [R. Yohanan] *raised an objection to* [Resh Laqish]: **R. Yose says: "Not even vegetables in winter, because the foliage** [of the sacred tree] **drops on them."** *Why* [should R. Yose rule this way in light of your opinion, Resh Laqish]? *Let it* [the sacred tree] *be like the "idol that broke by itself"* [which you, Resh Laqish, hold is permitted]*!*

F. [The situation is] *different there* [m. AZ 3:13] *because the main part of the idol* [the tree itself] *is standing* [and thus the idol is really not considered broken].

G. [But the solution in §F leads to this:] *And what about the* [tree] *trimmings?! For* [as to them] *the main part of the idol* [the tree] *is standing, and it was taught:* [If the sacred tree was groomed] **for its need** [to help it grow] **it is forbidden and its trimmings are permitted!** [Since the main part of the

22. The Bavli includes eight more challenges from R. Yohanan to Resh Laqish, and one from Resh Laqish to R. Yohanan. We will resume with the challenges that reflect borrowings from y. AZ.

idol—the tree—is still standing, then the trimmings should be forbidden!]

H. R. Huna b. de-R. Yehoshua said: "[The distinction between the resolution in §F and the new problem in §G is] because an idol is not invalidated through normal growth" [thus R. Yose is correct that the foliage of the sacred tree is forbidden, but since a tree naturally sheds leaves and branches all the time, the Gentile's intention in trimming those branches must have been to invalidate them].

According to y. AZ 3:2, 42d, the "broken shards of vessels" of the mishnah are those that come from objects that were *not* idols. Thus, in y. Avodah Zarah, the mishnah does not call for its presentation of the dispute between R. Yohanan and Resh Laqish about the "idol that was broken," with its attendant discussion of the idol owner's intentions regarding its repair and the proof adduced by Resh Laqish from the biblical case of the fallen Philistine idol Dagon. By contrast, both Shmuel and the Bavli's anonymous voice understand the "images" mentioned in the Bavli's version of the mishnah to include idols.

Although the Bavli's mishnah—unlike the Yerushalmi's—thus calls for discussion of broken idols, it does *not* call for the Bavli to take over the R. Yohanan/Resh Laqish dispute with their discussion of the issue in terms of the Philistine idol Dagon.[23] But even if this particular similarity is attributed to early talmud, early talmud cannot explain why, in building this dispute into a complex sugya that extends from 41b through 42b, the Bavli draws in relevant materials from elsewhere in y. Avodah Zarah and creates a much smoother sugya around the R. Yohanan/Resh Laqish dispute than we find in y. Avodah Zarah itself. At 42a, the Bavli includes a question and answer that relate to the Mercurius statue discussed later in m. AZ 4:1 (b. §D). The y. Avodah Zarah editors explicitly considered the Mercurius in light of the R. Yohanan/Resh Laqish dispute at y. AZ 4:1,

---

23. Moreover, Shamma Friedman points out that the Bavli's addition of an explanatory note to R. Yohanan's position ("R. Yohanan said 'Forbidden' for behold, he [the owner] did not invalidate [מבטל] it") is consistent with its tendency to use the term "invalidation" (ביטול) to refer to how it is that an idol can become permitted to an Israelite. The Yerushalmi, by contrast, thinks of the permissiveness as stemming from the idol's owners' desire (or lack thereof) to return to and repair the broken idol. Friedman finds support for his contention that the two Talmuds have different perspectives on the permissiveness of idols in his comparison of t. AZ 5:5 and the parallel at b. AZ 53a–b. This comparison shows that the Bavli adds the verb root ב-ט-ל to its version of the Toseftan baraita, which originally had declared the idol permitted to an Israelite only if its owners fail to return to it. See Shamma Friedman, "Ha-baraitot she-be-Talmud ha-Bavli ve-yahasan le-Tosefta," 174–175.

43d (y. §§F–G). Similarly, toward the end of 42b, the Bavli includes a question and answer pertaining to m. AZ 3:8 that the Yerushalmi editors at y. AZ 3:13, 43b–c had explicitly considered in light of this R. Yohanan/Resh Laqish dispute (b. §§E–H).

By collecting these relevant materials from elsewhere in y. Avodah Zarah and placing them all within one large sugya, the Bavli has improved on the Yerushalmi's presentation of the R. Yohanan/Resh Laqish dispute, which was scattered about in three different places. Moreover, even within its large sugya, the Bavli's arrangement of these materials follows a logical order that is missing from the Yerushalmi. After opening the dispute with reference to Dagon (as in y. Avodah Zarah), the Bavli presents the Mercurius challenge as the fifth challenge from R. Yohanan to Resh Laqish. This is a turning point in the sugya since the idols that were the subjects of the first four challenges were solid objects (whether whole statues or images of hands and feet), while the Mercurius is a statue made of a pile of stones. The Bavli follows this challenge with another switch, moving in the sixth through the ninth challenges (with the exception of the eighth) to discussing ever more unrecognizable pieces of worshiped objects. The Bavli presents the challenge based on the dripping foliage of a sacred tree (an *asherah*) as the ninth challenge from R. Yohanan to Resh Laqish since the separation of drippings from the idolatrous tree is an extreme example of a separated and otherwise-unrecognizable piece of a worshiped object. The Bavli has thus improved upon the presentation of these materials in the Yerushalmi, in which there was no such logical progression at all.[24]

No other cited tannaitic materials require both Talmuds to take up the R. Yohanan/Resh Laqish dispute and the discussion based on Dagon. Nor do any tannaitic materials require the Bavli to incorporate other materials thought relevant by the y. Avodah Zarah editors into its discussion of this dispute.

Early talmud also fails to persuade because it is not a y. Avodah Zarah amora who calls attention to other halakhic materials relevant to the R. Yohanan/Resh Laqish dispute, but y. Avodah Zarah's anonymous voice, which cannot be demonstrated in these cases to have an amoraic provenance.[25] Y. Avodah Zarah's anonymous voice here more likely represents the voice of the tractate's redactors. Moreover, in utilizing the materials marked by the editors in building its own sugya, the Bavli is obviously do-

---

24. For detailed analyses of the phenomenon of the Bavli improving upon the Yerushalmi's order of presentation of materials, see chapter 3, pp. 125–136.

25. For a closer look at the Yerushalmi's anonymous voice and the question of whether or not it has an amoraic provenance, see chapter 5.

ing more than simply sharing sugyot equally available to both rabbinic communities: it is relying on y. Avodah Zarah's redactors' reflections on their own halakhic argumentation.[26]

III
When Material in B. Avodah Zarah
Has a Parallel in Y. Avodah Zarah and in Some Other
Rabbinic Compilation, B. Avodah Zarah Tends to
More Closely Resemble Y. Avodah Zarah

Examples of this type are important because they clearly undermine the notion that all observable similarities between y. and b. Avodah Zarah are due simply to the Talmuds' shared reliance on a common pool of rabbinic traditions. These examples show that there are cases of multiple parallels in which b. Avodah Zarah more closely resembles y. Avodah Zarah in some specific way(s), thus strongly suggesting that the similarity between them is due not to the hypothesized common pool, but to Bavli appropriation of the Yerushalmi material. We will begin with a fairly simple example, and then move on to one of greater complexity.

III.a. *T. Hullin 2:22–23 ‖ B. Avodah Zarah 27b ‖*
Y. Avodah Zarah 2:2, 40d–41a

T. Hullin 2:22–23

> It once happened that a snake bit R. Eleazar b. Dama, and Yaaqov of Kefar Sama came to heal him in the name of Yeshua b. Pantera, but R. Yishmael would not allow it. He said, "You are not permitted [to accept healing from Yaaqov], Ben Dama." He said to him, "I will bring you a proof that he can heal me." But [Eleazar b. Dama] did not manage to bring the proof before he died.

---

26. The Talmuds' sharing of this Palestinian sugya has been noticed by other scholars. M. A. Tennenblatt pointed to the attachment of this R. Yohanan/Resh Laqish dispute to the same mishnah in both Talmuds, and to the Bavli's use of other Palestinian materials in building its complex sugya, as a key proof for his own conviction that the Bavli (in *toto*) relied on the Yerushalmi. See Tennenblatt, *Peraqim hadashim*, 265–268. While David Kraemer convincingly pointed out that the Bavli's expansion of the originally small, shared Palestinian sugya was probably late, he failed to take into account that the Bavli's expansion was done using other y. AZ materials marked by the y. AZ editors as relevant to the dispute. See his "Stylistic Characteristics of Amoraic Literature," 190–192.

R. Yishmael said, "Happy are you, Ben Dama, for you exited [the world] in peace and did not break the fence[27] of the Sages, for afflictions will eventually come upon anyone who breaks the fence of the Sages, as it is said, 'A snake bites the one who breaks the fence'" (Eccl 10:8).[28]

Y. Avodah Zarah 2:2, 40d–41a

A. **It once happened that a snake bit Eleazar b. Dama, and Yaaqov of Kefar Sama came to heal him. [Yaaqov] said to him: "Let us say to you [=heal you] in the name of Jesus b. Pandera." R. Yishmael said to him: "Ben Dama, you are not permitted** [to be healed by Yaaqov]." **He said to him: "I will bring a proof that he may heal me," but he did not succeed in bringing the proof before he died. R. Yishmael said to him: "Happy are you, Ben Dama, for you left the world in peace and did not break the fence of the Sages** [that they erected around the Torah], **as it is said, 'A snake will bite the one who breaks the fence'"** (Eccl 10:8).

B. *But did not a snake bite him?* [And so how did Ben Dama escape the fate the verse predicted for one who disobeys the Sages?] *Rather* [his adherence to the Sages' fence ensures that a "snake"] *will not bite him in the coming future* [the afterlife].

C. *And what would he have said* [to R. Yishmael to defend his right to treatment]*?* [He would have cited Lev 18:5:] *"That a man may do them* [the commandments] *and live by them"* [the implicit point being that a person is supposed to live by, and not die by, the commandments. Thus Ben Dama would have reasoned that he should be permitted to relax the prohibition of idolatry in order to continue to live].

B. Avodah Zarah 27b

A. **It once happened that a snake bit Ben Dama the nephew of R. Yishmael, and Yaaqov of Kefar Sakanya came to heal him but R. Yishmael did not allow him. He [Ben Dama] said to him: "R. Yishmael my brother, leave him [Yaaqov] be** [to treat me] **and let me be healed by him, and I will bring you a verse from the Torah** [to prove that] **it is permitted." He did not manage to complete the matter** [of quoting the verse] **before his soul departed and he died. R. Yishmael recited concerning him: "Happy are you, Ben Dama, for your body is pure and your soul departed in purity. And you did not transgress the words of**

---

27. The correct reading should be "fence" (גדירן) rather than "decree" (גזירן) as appears in the text, especially since another reference to "fence" immediately follows and Eccl 10:8 itself refers to a "fence."

28. Zuckermandel, 503.

your colleagues, who say: 'A snake bites the one who breaks the fence.'" (Eccl 10:8).

B. *Heresy* [*minut*] *is different* [from other transgressions] *because it pulls, and he* [the one who falls in with heresy] *will come to be pulled after them* [the heretics].[29]

C. The Master said: **"You did not transgress the words of your colleagues . . ."** *He* [Ben Dama] *was bitten by a snake anyway!* [And so how did he escape the punishment decreed by the verse for one who transgresses a fence erected by the Sages, as R. Yishmael said he did? Rather, Ben Dama escaped being bitten by the] *"snake of the Rabbis," for* [the bite of] *which there is no cure at all. And what could he* [Ben Dama] *have said? "And he shall live by them"—and not that he should die by them* (Lev 18:5).

D. *And to R. Yishmael, these words* [Lev 18:5] *apply in private* [a person may choose transgression over death if the transgression will take place in private], *but in public, no. As it was taught in a baraita:* **R. Yishmael would say: "From where do we know that if they say to a person 'Serve idols and do not be killed' that he may serve and not be killed? The verse teaches 'And he shall live by them'—and not die by them. Is that true even in public? The verse teaches: 'And do not desecrate My holy Name** [in public]'" (Lev 22:32) (Sifra to Leviticus, *Aharei Mot, pereq* 13).

The story of the hapless Eleazar b. Dama holds immense fascination for the window it opens into the relationship of the Rabbis to the world of the *minim* (heretics; sing. *min*), who may have been Jewish-Christians.[30] From a literary perspective, the different versions of the story are also valuable for the light they shed on the Bavli redactors' characteristic methods of reworking and revising older sources, especially materials appropriated from the Yerushalmi.[31] But at the moment our concern is to point out that b. Avodah Zarah's version of the Eleazar b. Dama story is indeed

---

29. This statement actually resolves an implicit objection, for was Ben Dama not bitten by a snake? The answer is that heresy is a different sort of "breaching of the fence," one which will result in the heretic's being "bitten by a snake," or pulled after heresy. We will say more about §B in chapter 3, when we focus on the differences between y. and b. AZ.

30. For readings of this story that focus on just that aspect, see, e.g. Richard Kalmin, *Sage in Jewish Society,* 69; Daniel Boyarin, *Dying for God: Martyrdom and the Making of Christianity and Judaism* (Stanford: Stanford University Press, 1999), 34–36; and my "A Contribution to the Study of Martyrdom and Identity in the Palestinian Talmud," *JJS* 54:2 (Autumn 2003): 242–272.

31. As noted, we will analyze how the Bavli redactors introduce Babylonian cultural and halakhic perspectives into the y. AZ version of this story below in chapter 3, pp. 134–136.

an appropriation of y. Avodah Zarah's version, not an independent appropriation of either the Toseftan story or some other tannaitic version of the story now lost to us.

Both Talmuds attach their versions of the Eleazar b. Dama story to m. AZ 2:2, which provides that Jews may accept medical services from Gentiles that fall into the category of "healing of money" (ריפוי ממון) but not of "healing of lives" (ריפוי נפשות). Although there is a clear link between ריפוי נפשות and the story of Eleazar b. Dama, who died rather than accept healing from a *min*, the mishnah does not call for such a story and could certainly have been fully explicated without it. The more interesting question is: Is t. Hul 2:22–23 responsible for the Talmuds' versions of the story, or did b. Avodah Zarah derive its version from y. Avodah Zarah?

In the Toseftan version, no anonymous editorial voice intervenes to ask what proof Eleazar could have offered R. Yishmael, let alone to suggest one. Nor does the Tosefta ask the rather obvious question of how Eleazar—who was dying of snake-bite—had avoided the fate predicted by Eccl 10:8 ("A snake bites the one who breaches the fence") for one who breaches the "fence of the Sages." By contrast, both y. Avodah Zarah (§B) and b. Avodah Zarah (§C) ask the latter question and offer resolutions. Both Talmuds (y. Avodah Zarah at §C and b. Avodah Zarah at §§C–D) then move on to inquire about the scriptural verse that Eleazar could have cited to R. Yishmael to establish his right to treatment, and both Talmuds point to Lev 18:5—"and he shall live by them"—as understood through the lens of the rabbinic midrash "and not die by them." Far from being an independent interpretation of t. Hul 2:22–23, then, b. Avodah Zarah was clearly drawing its version of the Eleazar b. Dama story from y. Avodah Zarah. Moreover, given the close relationship between y. and b. Avodah Zarah's versions of the story, it is more logical to conclude that b. Avodah Zarah drew its version from y. Avodah Zarah than that it drew its version from a now-missing rabbinic text that formed part of the hypothesized "pool" of rabbinic materials shared by the rabbinic communities.

III.b. *Y. Sheviit 8:6, 38b* ‖ *B. Avodah Zarah 62a–b* ‖ *Y. Avodah Zarah 5:1, 44c*

Let us begin by comparing the two Yerushalmi versions of this sugya to each other:

Y. Sheviit 8:6, 38b

A. *It was taught:* **The donkey-drivers and the shoulder-bearers and all those who work with Sabbatical year produce—their wage is שביעית** (t.

Shevi 6:26). [There is an ambiguity in this baraita. Does "their wage is שביעית" mean that it is forbidden to the workers, since it is unlawful to do business with Sabbatical year produce? Or does it mean that their wage will somehow be paid from Sabbatical year produce?]

B.   R. Zeirah said: "Our baraita is dealing with permitted fruits. What is 'their wage is שביעית'? That they should take [their pay] from what they were working with [that is, they should take their produce in kind from whatever they were working with].

C.   "And let that which R. Yohanan ruled for those of the house of R. Yannai—that they should take their payment in hand not as oil, but as money—be considered in accordance with R. Yudan and R. Nehemiah."[32]

D.   R. Hila said: "Our baraita is dealing with those who carry fruits of transgression. And what does 'their wage is שביעית' mean? [It is interpreted] in accordance with what R. Abbahu said in the name of R. Yohanan: '[As to] libation wine, [the Sages] penalized him [the person who unlawfully transacts business in libation wine] with a penalty [in that he cannot retain his wage].'" [Thus the meaning of "their wage is שביעית" is that the donkey-drivers, shoulder-bearers, and all who work with Sabbatical year produce may not retain their wage as a penalty for their unlawful conduct].

Y. Avodah Zarah 5:1, 44c

A.   *And is it not his* [the worker's] *wage he* [the master] *is giving him?* [So why should the wage be forbidden?]

B.   R. Abbahu in the name of R. Yohanan: "[The Sages] penalized him with a penalty [for working with an item, libation wine, that is forbidden in benefit]."

---

32. The reference to R. Yudan and R. Nehemiah is a reference to an earlier sugya at y. Shevi 8:4, 38a. There, a baraita (t. Shevi 6:21) was quoted according to which R. Yudan and R. Nehemiah forbade a person to accept a loaf of bread worth a *dupondium* from a bakery in the Sabbatical year on the condition that he would pay for it with the "[ownerless] vegetables of the field." Their concern was that since many people were scrambling to gather and eat the ownerless produce, the bakery would not rely on the buyer's word (since he might not be able to acquire any ownerless produce), but would instead consider that the buyer owed them a debt for the bread. If this was the bakery's thought process, reasoned R. Yudan and R. Nehemiah, then it would be forbidden for the buyer subsequently to bring them produce in exchange for the bread, since he would be considered to be one who is paying his debts with Sabbatical year produce. In our sugya, R. Zeirah has distinguished his position from R. Yohanan's by claiming that the latter—like R. Yudan and R. Nehemiah—holds that payment in kind during the Sabbatical year is forbidden, while payment in money is not.

C. *It was taught*: **The donkey-drivers and the shoulder-bearers, and all those who work with Sabbatical year produce—their wage is שביעית.**

D. R. Zeirah said: "The baraita is dealing with permitted fruits. And as to that which R. Yohanan ruled for the house of R. Yannai—that they should not take [their] wage into their hands [in the form of] wine but rather [as money]—he ruled for them in accordance with R. Yehudah and R. Nehemiah."

E. R. Yeli said: "The baraita is dealing with fruits of transgression.[33] As R. Abbahu said in the name of R. Yohanan concerning libation wine: '[The Sages] penalized [the worker] with a penalty.'"

The sugyot are largely similar, with one critical difference. The similarity and difference are illustrated in this outline:

> y. AZ → The anonymous voice asks the opening question of the sugya (§A).
>
> y. AZ → There is a statement by R. Abbahu in the name of R. Yohanan (§B).
>
> y. Shevi ‖ y. AZ → The Talmud cites t. Shevi 6:26.
>
> y. Shevi ‖ y. AZ → R. Zeirah initially attempts to read t. Shevi 6:26 permissively.
>
> y. Shevi ‖ y. AZ → R. Zeirah deals with a potential challenge to his reading by interpreting t. Shevi 6:26 as referring to R. Yohanan's conflicting ruling for the house of R. Yannai. He answers the potential challenge by claiming that R. Yohanan ruled for them in accordance with two particular tannaim.
>
> y. Shevi ‖ y. AZ → The sugya ends with R. Hila's (=Yeli's) restrictive reading of the baraita, which is confirmed by R. Abbahu's statement.

The clear differences between the two sugyot are that y. Avodah Zarah links its version of the sugya to its local mishnah (m. AZ 5:1) and places R. Abbahu's statement (that the Sages penalized the laborer who works with libation wine) early in the sugya. The pertinent part of the mishnah rules that if an employer hires a worker to work with libation wine, the worker's wage is forbidden to him. Y. Avodah Zarah's consideration of the mishnah begins in §A with a logical question: Is it not the worker's wage the mishnah is talking about? Why is the worker not entitled to his wage? R. Abbahu in the name of R. Yohanan provides the answer: the worker is not entitled to his wage because the Sages (in m. AZ

---

33. We have translated according to the parallel at y. Shevi 8:6, 38b because y. AZ here reads "fruits of idols," which makes no sense.

5:1) penalized him for working with libation wine, from which an Israelite is forbidden to derive benefit, presumably including the benefit of a wage.

The odd point about y. Avodah Zarah is why it requires §§C–E at all. Does not R. Abbahu's response in §B adequately answer the opening question? The answer is that it does, and that y. Avodah Zarah §§C–E originated in y. Sheviit as the argumentation leading up to R. Abbahu's statement. In y. Sheviit (as in y. Avodah Zarah) R. Hila (=Yeli) cites what R. Abbahu in the name of R. Yohanan said about libation wine in connection with his restrictive reading of t. Shevi 6:26 *at the end of the sugya*. As it is R. Hila's statement (including that of R. Abbahu) that ends the y. Sheviit sugya, the y. Avodah Zarah redactors understood it as the conclusion. They therefore lifted out R. Abbahu's statement about a penalty on a wage earned from working with libation wine, formulated a rhetorical question to which it would be an appropriate answer, *and only then* incorporated the rest of the y. Sheviit sugya which had originally led up to that result. Y. Avodah Zarah is thus an editorial construction built upon the more original y. Shevi 8:6, 38b. Y. Sheviit and y. Avodah Zarah are not simply contemporaneous alternative versions of the same sugya; y. Avodah Zarah is a reworking of y. Sheviit. Now let us turn to the Bavli.

B. Avodah Zarah 62a–b

A. *What is the reason his* [the worker's] *wage is forbidden? If it is said, since libation wine is forbidden in benefit its wage should likewise be forbidden*—behold [the cases of] orlah[34] *and mixed seeds of a vineyard,*[35] *which are forbidden in benefit and* [concerning which] *it is taught in a mishnah:* **If he sold** [them] **and betrothed** [a woman] **with their monetary value, she is betrothed** (m. Qid 2:9). [Thus, just because an item is forbidden in benefit does not mean that monies obtained through it are also forbidden in benefit. So too the wages of a worker who worked with libation wine should not be forbidden in benefit].

B. *Rather,* [the reason the wage of the worker is forbidden is that] *since it* [libation wine] *"holds its monies like idolatry"* [that is, just as monies obtained through selling an idol never lose their status as idols, so do monies obtained through selling libation wine never lose their status as libation wine].

C. *But behold Sabbatical year produce, which "holds its monies" and* [concerning which] *it is taught in a mishnah:* **One who says to a worker: "Here is this dinar, gather a vegetable for me today with it"**—**his wage is forbidden;**

---

34. Lev 19:23 states that the fruit a tree produces during its first three years of life is to be considered ערלים, or "uncircumcised," and hence forbidden.

35. Deut 22:9 forbids planting seeds of different species of plants in the same vineyard.

[if he says instead,] **"Gather a vegetable for me today"—his wage is permitted** (m. Shevi 8:4)? [Thus, there is a case in which a worker's wage is permitted as to something which "holds its monies." So too should the worker's wage in m. AZ 5:1 be permitted].

D. R. Abbahu said in the name of R. Yohanan: "It is a penalty that the Sages imposed with respect to donkey-drivers and libation wine."

E. [The penalty as to] *libation wine: as we have stated.* [The penalty as to] *donkey-drivers, what is it? As it was taught in a baraita:* **The donkey-drivers who were working with Sabbatical year fruits—their wage is שביעית** (t. Shevi 6:26).

F. *What does* **"their wage is שביעית"** *mean? If it is said that we give them a wage from Sabbatical year fruits, it turns out that this one* [the master] *is paying his debt from Sabbatical year fruits, and the Torah said: "to eat it"* (Lev 25:22)—*and not* [to use the fruits of the Sabbatical year] *for commerce.*

G. *But rather,* [the reason there is a penalty on wages earned through working with Sabbatical year produce] *is that their wage is sanctified with the holiness of the Sabbatical year.*

H. *And is it sanctified? Was it not taught in a mishnah:* **One who says to a worker: "Here is this *dinar*, gather a vegetable for me today"—his wage is permitted;** [if he says instead,] **"Gather a vegetable with it for me today"—his wage is forbidden** (m. Shevi 8:4)?

I. Abaye said: "Really, [the meaning of 'their wage is שביעית' in t. Shevi 6:26] is that we give him a wage from Sabbatical year fruits. . . ."[36]

J. And Rava said: "Really, [the meaning of t. Shevi 6:26] is that [the wage] is sanctified with the holiness of the Sabbatical year." *And concerning your difficulty with* [m. Shevi 8:4's ruling that] *the worker* [can at times be paid with Sabbatical year produce], *the Sages did not penalize the worker* [of m. Shevi 8:4] *whose fee is not great; the Sages did penalize the donkey-drivers* [of t. Shevi 6:26] *whose fee is great.*

K. *And as to our mishnah* [m. AZ 5:1]—*the stringency of libation wine is different* [thus, even though our mishnah also deals with a worker like that in m. Shevi 8:4, the law is stricter and the worker penalized because our mishnah deals with libation wine].

The pertinent part of m. AZ 5:1 (to which both Avodah Zarah tractates attach these sugyot), provides as noted that if a master[37] hires a worker to work with him in transporting libation wine, the worker's wage for this activity is forbidden. On the other hand, if the worker was hired to do other work, then he is permitted to retain his wage even if the master also incidentally asked him to move a jug of libation wine from one place to another.

---

36. Abaye engages in a harmonization that temporarily digresses from the forward progress of the underlying argument.

37. The mishnah does not specify that the master must be a Gentile, but that certainly must be assumed because how could one Israelite hire another to assist in

Both y. and b. Avodah Zarah present variations of the same sugya in which they examine the issue of the worker's wage. The sugyot follow the same basic five-step pattern:

1. The anonymous voice asks the opening question of the sugya (y. and b. Avodah Zarah at §A);

2. There is a statement by R. Abbahu in the name of R. Yohanan (y. Avodah Zarah at §B and b. Avodah Zarah at §D);

3. T. Sheviit 6:26 (y. Avodah Zarah at §C and b. Avodah Zarah at §E);

4. There is an attempt to read the Toseftan phrase "their wage is שביעית" permissively (y. Avodah Zarah at §D and b. Avodah Zarah at §I); and

5. The sugya ends with a restrictive reading of the phrase (y. Avodah Zarah at §E and b. Avodah Zarah at §J).

While the mishnah unquestionably calls for discussion of the worker's wage, nothing there requires both Talmuds to present sugyot that unfold in such a strikingly similar way. Further, no other tannaitic sources provide for this similarity either. The Bavli cites m. Qid 2:9, t. Shevi 6:26, and m. Shevi 8:4. The only one of these sources the Talmuds hold in common—t. Shevi 6:26—is integrated into both Talmuds' sugyot at an equivalent place in the discussion, and both Talmuds use it in the same way. It therefore does not generate the similarity between the sugyot, but is a result of it.

Moreover, the Bavli redactors were working with a sugya that more closely resembled y. Avodah Zarah than y. Sheviit. As we established, the y. Avodah Zarah editors lifted R. Abbahu's statement about the penalty on workers who work with libation wine out of R. Hila's statement, and deployed it as the answer to a rhetorical question with which they opened their sugya. They then reinserted the rest of the y. Sheviit sugya, which in y. Sheviit had originally led up to R. Abbahu's statement. When we examine the Bavli, we see that b. Avodah Zarah opens as well with a rhetorical question (albeit one that is considerably more expansive than that in y. Avodah Zarah), and then proceeds to R. Abbahu's statement. B. and y. Avodah Zarah's shared early placement of R. Abbahu's statement in their shared sugya demonstrates b. Avodah Zarah's greater reliance on y. Avodah Zarah than on y. Sheviit.

the libation wine trade? See Rashi to b. AZ 62a, s.v. השוכר, and the Ran's commentary to the Rif on Avodah Zarah, s.v. השוכר (p. 30a in the pages of the Rif).

Since we have traveled a long way in studying this example, let us summarize. We began by comparing two versions of the same sugya found in y. Sheviit and y. Avodah Zarah, and noted the key differences between them. In comparing these sugyot to the parallel in b. Avodah Zarah, we saw that b. Avodah Zarah was clearly more similar to y. Avodah Zarah's version and can even be seen to be a version that takes the conclusion of the y. Avodah Zarah sugya into account. The importance of this example, like the previous one, is that it shows that b. Avodah Zarah does not simply utilize Palestinian sugyot generally (as per early talmud); it can be demonstrated to bear a greater similarity to y. Avodah Zarah specifically.

III.c. B. Avodah Zarah 15a, 16a–b ‖ Y. Avodah Zarah 1:6, 39d–40a ‖ Y. Avodah Zarah 1:7, 40a ‖ Y. Pesahim 4:3, 30d–31a

At y. AZ 1:6, 39d–40a the Yerushalmi presents a sugya about an Israelite's selling a beast to a Gentile. The sugya closes with some consideration of a non-final sale of the animal to the Gentile for testing purposes as compared to a final sale. At y. AZ 1:6, 40a the Yerushalmi continues with Rabbi's teaching that Israelites may not sell horses to Gentiles and a brief discussion of that based on a baraita that equates a large wild animal to a large domesticated animal. Y. Avodah Zarah then moves seamlessly to 1:7, 40a, which opens with the anonymous voice's observation that "Behold, it is permitted [to sell to Gentiles] something in which there is no danger to the public," and the quotation of t. AZ 2:6.

Y. Pesahim 4:3, 30d–31a is a parallel to this material. There is a parallel to the discussion of a non-final sale of a beast for testing at 30d that is followed (after a digression into other matters) at 31a by the discussion of Rabbi's view on selling horses to Gentiles. The discussion of Rabbi's view also raises the issue of the equation of large wild animals to large domesticated ones, or to small domesticated animals.

Like these Yerushalmi sources, the Bavli moves first (at 15a) into a sugya about selling beasts, including non-final sales for testing as well as other impermanent transfers of ownership (such as leasing). After an interruption for other issues, the Bavli returns at 16a to Rabbi's views on selling horses to Gentiles, and then after some discussion of the large wild animal in relation to the small domesticated one, b. Avodah Zarah's anonymous voice declares, "The reason [for not selling bears or lions to Gentiles] is that there is in them [the possibility of] danger to the public. Behold, if there is no danger to the public, it is permitted [to sell them such items]." The point is that b. Avodah Zarah—like y. Avodah Zarah and unlike y. Pesahim—includes the anonymous observation about there being no legal obstacle to selling non-dangerous items to Gentiles. Although the three tractates share this large selection and ordering of materials, y. and b. Avodah Zarah share a similar feature that is missing from y. Pesahim.

Although m. AZ 1:6 does call for discussion of "small beasts," "large beasts," and "horses," it does not call for the precise selection of topics we see, especially the treatment of non-permanent sales of animals followed by the comparison of large wild animals to large domesticated ones. No other tannaitic sources cited can reasonably be construed as calling for the material, either. And the fact that y. and b. Avodah Zarah share a similarity that is missing from the third parallel at y. Pesahim militates against the conclusion that b. Avodah Zarah's similarity to y. Avodah Zarah is due simply to the two Talmuds' shared reliance on a common pool of rabbinic traditions. B. Avodah Zarah is more similar to y. Avodah Zarah—once again suggesting that the b. Avodah Zarah redactors were relying on that Yerushalmi tractate specifically.

Another example of the Bavli's greater similarity to a y. Avodah Zarah parallel than to a parallel found elsewhere may be found at y. AZ 2:9, 41d ‖ b. AZ 35b–36a (the prohibition of Gentile oil). This example is a particularly rich illustration of how the Bavli redactors reworked their prior sources, and we will defer a detailed discussion of it to chapter 3.

IV

Y. Avodah Zarah And B. Avodah Zarah Place Similar Material at a Similar Point in the Tractate, Although Not Attached to the Same Mishnaic Passage

IV.a. B. Avodah Zarah 19b–20a ‖ y. Avodah Zarah 1:9, 40a–b

This example illustrates a structural similarity between y. and b. Avodah Zarah that would be missed were we to adhere too closely to the divisions of mishnayot that we find in our printed editions of the Talmuds. These divisions are late conventions, and by no means should they be allowed to obscure structural similarities visible around them. In b. Avodah Zarah, m. AZ 1:8 is divided into two. The first part consists of the prohibition against an Israelite's fashioning of ornaments for idols and a dispute about selling a Gentile plants that are attached to the ground (b. AZ 19b). The second part of the mishnah (a discussion about renting houses and fields to Gentiles in the Land of Israel, Syria, and the Diaspora) is found at 20b–21a. Y. Avodah Zarah does not include the mishnaic material on fashioning ornaments for idols, although it does include the dispute about selling attached plants. All this is significant because the Bavli attaches its version of y. AZ 1:9, 40a–b to the portion of m. AZ 1:8 that deals with selling a Gentile attached plants, while y. Avodah Zarah attaches its own version to the portion of m. AZ 1:8 that discusses renting houses and fields to Gentiles. The similarity we will observe between the Talmuds is thus not called for by the mishnah because *no one* mishnaic passage calls for it.[38] After presenting the text, we will give further consideration to the causes of the similarity.

Y. Avodah Zarah 1:9, 40a–b

A.   R. Zeirah in the name of R. Yose b. Hanina; R. Abba, R. Hiyya in the name of R. Yohanan: "'Do not show them mercy' (לא תחנם, Deut 7:2) [means] do not give them grace (חן). לא תחנם—do not give them a free gift (חנם). לא תחנם—do not give them settlement (חניה) in the Land [of Israel]."

[· · · · · · · · · · · · · · · · · · ·]³⁹

B.   לא תחנם—do not give them a free gift. *But was it not taught in a baraita* [t. Pes 2:15⁴⁰]:

C.   **It once happened that R. Gamliel was traveling along the way, and he saw a loaf of fine bread (קלוסקין) cast aside on the road. He said to his slave Tavi: "Pick up this loaf." He [R. Gamliel] saw a Gentile coming towards him. He said: "Mabgai [presumably the name of that Gentile], take this loaf." R. Ilai ran after him [the Gentile Mabgai]. He said to him: "What is your name?" He said to him: "Mabgai." "And from where are you?" He said to him: "I am one of the station-guards** [of the stations leading to royal vineyards]. **"And had you ever met R. Gamliel before?" He said to him: "No."** R. Gamliel had discerned this [that the Gentile's name was Mabgai] **with the holy spirit. And we learned from him three things: We learned that we do not pass by** [abandoned] **foods, and that the leaven of a Gentile is permitted immediately after Passover, and that we assume that most passers-by are Gentile."**

[· · · · · · · · · · · · · · · · · · ·]⁴¹

---

38. And hence, this lengthy sugya is not necessary to fully explicate any particular part of the mishnah.

39. The intervening material—R. Yose's view that houses may be rented to Gentiles in Palestine and R. Yose b. R. Bun's view that Gentiles may not be buried there—is omitted because it has no Bavli parallel.

40. *The Tosefta: According to Codex Vienna, With Variants From Codex Erfurt, Genizah Mss. And Editio Princeps (Venice 1521), Together With References to Parallel Passages in Talmudic Literature and a Brief Commentary: The Order of Mo'ed* (ed. Saul Lieberman; New York: Jewish Theological Seminary, 1962), 146–147.

41. Further discussion of this Toseftan passage, as well as more Toseftan material about R. Gamliel's release of a vow, has been omitted because it has no parallel in the Bavli.

D. "'Do not show them mercy'– do not give them 'grace.'" *But was it not taught:* **It once happened that R. Gamliel was strolling on the Temple Mount and saw a Gentile woman there, and blessed her.** *And was it R. Gamliel's practice to look at women? Rather, it was an extremely crooked path* [on which he encountered her], *like Pesaurus, and he looked at her unwittingly.* **"And he blessed her"**?—*and did not R. Zeirah say in the name of R. Yose b. Hanina, and R. Ba in the name of R. Hiyya in the name of R. Yohanan:* "'Do not show them mercy'—do not give them 'grace'"?

E. *What did he say? He did not say "abascanta,"*[42] *but rather, "Blessed is He Who has such beautiful creatures in His world." For similarly, even if one saw a nice donkey, camel, or horse, one would say, "Blessed is He Who has such beautiful creatures in His world."*

B. Avodah Zarah 19b–20a

A. *From where are these words* [of the mishnah] *derived?* R. Yose b. Hanina said: "For the verse [Deut 7:2] says: 'Do not show them mercy'—do not give them 'settlement' in the Land."

B. *This "לא תחנם" is required for that which the Merciful says: "Do not give them 'grace.'"*

C. *If that is so, then let the verse read "לא תחונם." What is* [the significance of the fact that the verse reads] *"לא תחנם"? Learn both from it* [no "settlement" and no "grace"].

D. *But now [Deut 7:2] is needed for that which the Merciful One said: "Do not give them a free gift."*

E. *If that is so, let the verse read לא תחינם. What is לא תחינם? Learn from it all three of them* [all three interpretations].

F. *It is also taught thus in a baraita . . .*[43]

G. *And the* [prohibition against giving a free gift to a Gentile is] *a tannaitic dispute. As we learn in a baraita:*

H. **Do not eat anything that dies by itself. Give it to the stranger (גר)** [i.e., the Gentile who adheres to the Noahide laws] **in your gates and he will eat it, or sell it to the Gentile (נכרי)** (Deut 14:21). **This teaches only that** [the animal that dies by itself] **is to be "given" to the stranger and "sold" to the Gentile** [idolater]. **From where do we know that it can be "sold" to the stranger?—Scripture says, "Give it" or "sell." From where do we know that it can be "given" to the Gentile?—Scripture says, "Give it and he will eat it," or "sell to the Gentile." It turns out that you can say**

---

42. "May you be 'unbewitched,'" or "may no harm befall you." See Jastrow, *Dictionary*, 8; Jacob Levy, *Neuhebräisches und Chaldäisches Wörterbuch über die Talmudim und Midraschim* (rev. Lazarus Goldschmidt; 2nd ed.; Berlin: Benjamin Harz, 1924), 1:13 ("unberufen," that is, "touch wood," or in American parlance, "knock on wood"); see also Alexander Kohut, *Arukh ha-Shalem* (8 vols.; 1878–1892; repr., Vienna: Menorah, 1926), 1:15 ("unberufen").

43. Repeating the three definitions of לא תחינם.

that the stranger and the Gentile are the same in that both "giving" and "selling" apply to each—the words of R. Meir. R. Yehudah says: "The matters are as written. To the stranger by 'giving,' and to the idolater by 'selling.'"

[·]⁴⁴

I. *Another interpretation:* "Do not show them mercy"—do not give them "grace." *This* [tannaitic teaching] *assists Rav, for Rav said:* "It is forbidden for a man to say: 'How beautiful is this Gentile [woman].'"

J. *They raised an objection:* **It once happened that R. Shimon b. Gamliel was on a step on the Temple Mount and he saw one particularly beautiful idolatress. He said: "How many are Your works, Lord!"**

K. **And even R. Aqiva** [gave grace to a beautiful Gentile woman, for he] **saw the wife of the evil Turnus Rufus** [and] **spat, laughed, and wept. He spat—because she came from a putrid drop. He laughed—because in the future she would convert and he would marry her. He wept—that this beauty would be buried in the dust.**

L. *And Rav certainly agrees* [that one can praise God upon seeing a beautiful Gentile], *for the Master said:* **"One who sees beautiful creations says: 'Blessed is He Who created such in His world.'"**

B. Avodah Zarah 19b–20a offers a series of interpretations of the command "Do not show them [Gentiles] mercy" (Deut 7:2). At §§A–F, the Bavli interprets "Do not show them mercy" in three ways: as a prohibition against giving Gentiles settlement (חנייה; a play on חן) in the Land; not giving them grace (חן); and not giving them free gifts (חינם). The Bavli points out in §H that the "no free gifts" interpretation is actually a matter of tannaitic dispute. Finally, at §§I–L, the Bavli points out that the "no grace" interpretation supports a view of Rav, and presents two stories of Sages (R. Shimon b. Gamliel and R. Aqiva) encountering Gentile women. It closes with the blessing of God "Who created such [beautiful people] in His world."

The thematic link between this material and the portion of m. AZ 1:8 to which the Bavli attaches it (the mishnaic discussion of selling a Gentile plants that are attached to the ground) is the interpretation of Deut 7:2 as prohibiting Gentiles from settling in the Land of Israel. But the Bavli clearly goes far beyond what that mishnah calls for in presenting a lengthy discussion of Deut 7:2, most of which does not concern Gentile settlement in the Land at all.

---

44. Further discussion of the dispute between R. Meir and R. Yehudah is omitted because there is no parallel in the Yerushalmi.

Y. Avodah Zarah places a very similar sequence of interpretations of Deut 7:2 in relation to the portion of m. AZ 1:8 that deals with selling and/ or leasing houses or fields in the Land of Israel, Syria, or the Diaspora. Once again, we see a clear thematic link between the mishnaic material and the interpretation of Deut 7:2 as a prohibition against Gentile settlement in the Land. But y. Avodah Zarah's discussion of Deut 7:2 ranges far beyond its portion of m. AZ 1:8, and is largely similar to b. Avodah Zarah's: the same three understandings of Deut 7:2, a tannaitic discussion of "no free gifts," a story about R. Gamliel's encounter with a Gentile woman, and the blessing of God for creating "such beautiful creatures in His world."

Since y. and b. Avodah Zarah have attached these similar sugyot to different parts of m. AZ 1:8, there is no particular mishnaic language that can be said to call for the sugyot. Nor can the similarity be attributed to other tannaitic materials: the other tannaitic materials cited in the sugyot are well integrated into the unfolding discussion, and their presence is more likely the result, rather than the cause, of the overall similarity between the sugyot. Early talmud also does not suffice as an explanation of the similarities. Y. Avodah Zarah 1:9, 40a–b and b. AZ 19b–20a are the *only* two places in which all these elements—the discussion of Deut 7:2, the stories about R. (Shimon b.) Gamliel, the dispute about "no free gifts," and the blessing over beauty—appear together in this order. Although y. Avodah Zarah's story about R. Gamliel (§§D–E) is also found at y. Ber 9:2, 13b–c, the story lacks the overall redactional context there that we see here. It is not reasonable, therefore, to attribute this lengthy structural similarity to early talmud when we can more reasonably conclude that it is due to b. Avodah Zarah's reliance on y. Avodah Zarah. Moreover, the fact that b. Avodah Zarah placed this similar material at a similar point in the tractate despite the difference in the mishnaic language used as the "hook" for the material strongly suggests that the redactors of b. Avodah Zarah made this editorial choice after reflecting upon the overall editing and arrangement of materials in the earlier tractate.

V

Y. Avodah Zarah and B. Avodah Zarah Use the Same Mishnah as the Occasion to Explore the Same Legal Issue (Or Present Similar Genres of Materials)

Shlomo Yehudah Rappaport and Martin Jaffee noted the Bavli's tendency to use the same mishnayot as the Yerushalmi as opportunities for the presentation of aggadah.[45] We find two examples of this in the Avodah Zarah tractates. The first is the Talmuds' presentations of lengthy aggadic sequences attached to m. AZ 1:1 (b. AZ 2a–5b ‖ y. AZ 1:1, 39a–b), which itself contains neither aggadah nor scriptural verses and thus does not call for aggadah. The second example, which we studied earlier, is the Talmuds' common use of versions of the story of the biblical Adam's institution of the days that come to be known as Kalends and Saturnalia (b. AZ 8a ‖ y. AZ 1:2, 39c).

We can also observe a related phenomenon: the Talmuds' tendency to use the same mishnayot as the opportunity to present stories about sages. At b. AZ 48b ‖ y. AZ 3:13, 43b both Talmuds conclude their discussions about the permissibility or not of walking in front of, or under, idols and/ or sacred trees with stories about sages' conduct in those situations. In both Talmuds, the sages conclude that they are permitted to pass in front of images or under the branches of a sacred tree that extend into the public domain. At b. AZ 58b–59a ‖ y. AZ 4:10, 44b both Talmuds use m. AZ 4:9 as the opportunity to present stories about Palestinian amoraim who observe and respond to perceived popular violations of rabbinic law.[46] In neither case does the local mishnah call for these stories, since both mishnayot can be explicated without resort to the genre of sage-stories. Moreover, as to the second case, the apparent violations of law the rabbis remark upon go far beyond the subject matter of m. AZ 4:9. Nor are these stories called for by any other tannaitic source.

We will now look more closely at an example in which both Talmuds use the same mishnah as the opportunity to explore the same legal issues using a similar selection and sequence of topics. The significant point here is less the presence of specific shared materials by both Talmuds than the presence in both of a shared selection and sequence of topics. Thus our presentation will be in the form of a summary of the Talmuds' sequences of topics rather than translations of texts.

V.a. B. Avodah Zarah 46a–47a ‖ Y. Avodah Zarah 3:6, 42d–43a

Y. Avodah Zarah 3:6, 42d–43a

A.   Dispute about whether a person can render only his own property forbidden if he uses it in the religious service of an idol (rendering the object

---

45. See Rappaport, "Toldot Rabbenu Nissim," 90–92n16; Jaffee, "The Babylonian Appropriation of the Talmud Yerushalmi," 18–23.
46. For more on this see Richard Kalmin, *Sages, Stories, Authors, and Editors,* 87–91.

"worshiped" [נעבד]), or whether he can also render someone else's property forbidden by that means.

B.   Dispute between Hezekiah and R. Yohanan about whether one who bows to a "בצה" renders it forbidden. R. Zeirah claims that they are arguing about an egg (ביצה), while the Scholars say that they are arguing about the rocks found on both sides of a swamp (בצה). This dispute clearly is a more specific illustration of the dispute in §A as to whether the act of worship renders the בצה forbidden as a worshiped object.

C.   At this point, y. Avodah Zarah moves from consideration of נעבד to the related but distinct issue of whether or not a change to the worshiped object will result in a change in its legal status. Since the physical change makes the object into a different object, should what was forbidden now be permitted? Y. Avodah Zarah opens its consideration of this issue with the question of the "idolatrous egg" that hatched and therefore became (literally, "was made") a young bird. Is the bird permitted or not?

D.   Y. Avodah Zarah considers the same issue with respect to the "*orlah* nut" that was planted (thus yielding fruit that will eventually be permitted after three years), and the "consecrated egg" (belonging to the Temple) that hatched, yielding a young bird.

B. Avodah Zarah 46a–47a

A.   Dispute between the sons of R. Hiyya and R. Yohanan about whether the detached stones of a worshiped mountain are permitted or forbidden. The Talmud is initially unable to decide who holds what.

B.   The Talmud uses Hezekiah's question about one who sets up an egg (ביצה) to bow to it, in an attempt to resolve the unanswered question in §A.

C.   Rami b. Hama asks whether the detached stones of a worshiped mountain may be used for the altar of the Jerusalem Temple. He specifically wonders whether something that was worshiped when attached to the ground is disqualified from divine service or not.

D.   Rami b. Hama asks whether a sheaf of wheat to which someone had bowed (thus rendering it "worshiped") can be used for meal offerings in the Temple. He asks whether or not the legal doctrine of "change" applies to worshiped objects or not (that is, whether a physical change to the idolatrous object can render it fit for Temple use).

E.   Resh Laqish asks whether one may use a palm branch on Sukkot that is taken from a palm tree to which someone had bowed.

F.   R. Papa asks whether one can fashion the thread of blue required by the Torah in the ritual fringes attached to four-cornered garments[47] from the wool of an animal that had been worshiped.

---

47. Num 15:38–41 requires the placement of fringes (ציצית) at the corners of four-cornered garments.

G.   Rabbah asks whether water libations in the Temple may be poured using water from a spring that had been worshiped.

[§§E–G are, in essence, questions about whether a change to a worshiped object can render the item permissible for Israelite sacred use.]

M. Avodah Zarah 3:5's basic concern is to distinguish between the legal effect of worship of a fixed, natural object untouched by human hands—such as mountains and hills—and that of objects that have either been created or embellished by human beings. Worship renders the latter forbidden, but not the former.

The mishnah employs the Hebrew root ע-ב-ד, which means "worship." Thus it is unsurprising that both Talmuds take up the issue of worshiped objects, which they refer to as "נעבד" (worshiped). What is *not* called for by the mishnah is the similar selection and sequence of topics the Talmuds use to discuss the נעבד, especially the transition that both make from discussing the נעבד to discussing the case of שינוי (a change to a worshiped object) and how, if at all, a change to a worshiped object will or will not alter its prohibited status.

Y. Avodah Zarah §B is a dispute between Hezekiah and R. Yohanan about the legal effect of bowing to a בצה, the meaning of which is itself a disputed matter. Similarly, b. Avodah Zarah §B refers to Hezekiah's question about a ביצה (egg). The Bavli has clearly chosen one of the two alternative interpretations of בצה offered in the Yerushalmi, while the latter keeps the matter in dispute. In y. Avodah Zarah §§C–D and b. Avodah Zarah §§C–G, both Talmuds move from this discussion of a worshiped object to discussion of the possible legal effect of a change (שינוי) to it. Y. Avodah Zarah considers the issue of change with reference to three cases: the egg dedicated to an idol which then hatched, the *orlah* nut, and the egg dedicated to the Temple which subsequently hatched. B. Avodah Zarah deals with the issue of change by presenting a series of five questions: whether the detached stones of a worshiped mountain can be used for God's altar, whether a worshiped sheaf of wheat can be used for meal offerings in the Temple, whether a worshiped palm branch can be used to fulfill the commandment of waving the palm branch on Sukkot, whether a worshiped animal's wool can be used to make the ritual thread of blue required in ritual fringes, and whether water from a worshiped stream can be used for water libations in the Temple.

Although the mishnah rules that human crafting of a natural object to make it suitable for worship renders the object itself forbidden, nothing in the mishnah requires the precise sort of "change" discussion we see in both Talmuds. In the mishnah, the effect of human intervention is to make a natural object that would be permitted (although it had been worshiped) forbidden, while the underlying issue in most of the Talmuds' examples of "change" is whether the change—which may not even be due to human intervention—can render an otherwise forbidden object permitted. Nor do any other tannaitic sources cause the Talmuds to move along this path from נעבד to שינוי, since there is nearly total dissimilarity in the mix of mishnayot and baraitot cited in both Talmuds. The hypothesis of early talmud is undermined in this case because it is not necessarily the texts themselves which are similar in the two Talmuds, but rather the selection and sequence of topics. Unless one wishes to argue that the Babylonian and Palestinian rabbinic communities drew from a common pool of topics appropriate to various mishnayot (a sort of sharing of protocols of mishnaic exegesis, as it were)—for which there is no proof—the more reasonable conclusion is that b. Avodah Zarah followed the lead of y. Avodah Zarah in choosing to use this mishnah as the opportunity for an exploration of the legal effect of a change to a forbidden object.

VI
Did Y. Avodah Zarah Rely on Babylonian Sugyot in B. Avodah Zarah?

Before concluding our review of the results of the macro analysis of the Avodah Zarah tractates, it is appropriate for us to consider the possibility that perhaps the similarities we have observed are due not to b. Avodah Zarah's appropriation of y. Avodah Zarah, but rather to y. Avodah Zarah's appropriation of edited Babylonian sugyot now found in b. Avodah Zarah. There are two pairs of parallel passages that appear more susceptible than others to such an interpretation: b. AZ 15a ‖ y. AZ 1:6, 39d–40a and b. AZ 48b ‖ y. AZ 3:13, 43b.

VI.a. *B. Avodah Zarah 15a* ‖ *Y. Avodah Zarah 1:6, 39d–40a*

Y. Avodah Zarah 1:6, 39d–40a

A. *In any case, we do not sell them a large beast* (בהמה גסה).

B. *A large beast—why* [not]*?*

C. *A large beast—it has* [can generate for its previous Israelite owner] *the obligation of a sin-offering.* [If the Israelite sells the animal to a Gentile who works with it on the Sabbath, the Israelite will be obligated to bring a sin-offering in atonement. By working the animal on the Sabbath, the Gentile has caused the Israelite to violate the Torah's command that animals also be given Sabbath rest.]

D. *And a small beast* (בהמה דקה) *does not have the obligation of a sin-offering?* [By selling a small animal to a Gentile, would not the Israelite once again run the risk of violating the Torah's law that animals must be allowed to rest?] *Does he not milk it? Does he not shear it?*

E.   *They said: "There* [in the case of the large beast] *it is obligated* [that is, the beast is said to "bear the obligation of a sin-offering" since it itself does the work that causes its Israelite owner to owe an expiatory sacrifice]. *But here* [in the case of a small beast] *he is obligated* [because when a small beast is milked or sheared, the beast itself does not act, but is acted upon. Thus it is the human actor who generates his own obligation to bring the sin-offering]."

F.   *Once he* [the Israelite] *sells it, is it not like the Gentile's beast?* [And even with a large beast, why should the Israelite even be liable at all?]

G.   R. Ami the Babylonian said in the name of the "Rabbis of There" [=Babylonia]: "At times, he [the Israelite] will sell it to the [Gentile] for testing [just for a limited time to see if the Gentile wants to buy it], and he will return it to him after three days, and it turns out that [the Gentile] did work with an Israelite's animal [on the Sabbath]."

H.   *From here* [based on this view] *let sales for "testing" be forbidden but permanent sales be permitted!*

I.   *This* [permanent sales were forbidden] *because of this* [the possibility that people would move from permanent sales to forbidden temporary sales for "testing"].

J.   *If he transgressed and sold* [permanently], *we penalize him* [despite the fact that such sales are only forbidden as a "fence against transgression"]. *Just as we penalize for* [violations of] *law, so do we penalize for* [violations of] *custom.*

B. Avodah Zarah 15a

A.   *What is the reason* [that Israelites should not sell large beasts to Gentiles]? [Although] *we are not concerned about bestiality, we are concerned that* [the Gentile] *will do work with the beast* [on the Sabbath].

B.   *And let him do work!* [on the Sabbath]. *Since* [the Israelite] *has sold it* [to the Gentile, the Gentile] *has acquired it!*

C.   *There is a decree* [against the Israelite's selling the animal] *because of* [the possibility that Israelites will then become accustomed to] *renting* [their animals to Gentiles, who will then work with them on the Sabbath].

D.   *Borrowing acquires it* [the borrowed item becomes the property of the borrower], *renting acquires it. Rather,*

E.   Rami b. de-R. Yeba said: "There is a decree [forbidding the sale of large beasts to Gentiles] because of [the possibility that an Israelite will give his animal to a Gentile for] testing [prior to an anticipated final sale]." *For sometimes* [the Israelite] *will sell it to* [the Gentile for testing purposes] *close to sunset on Friday evening. And* [the Israelite] *will say to him: "Come, test it," and the beast will hear* [the Israelite's] *voice and come, which will be acceptable to the Israelite,* [who will turn out to] *be directing his beast on the Sabbath. And one who directs his beast on the Sabbath is liable for a sin-offering.*

[·]⁴⁸

F. [After discussion of rental]: *But hear from this that renting does not acquire* [the rented item to the renter]. *And now that you have said renting does not acquire,* [the prohibition against selling a large beast to a Gentile is a] *decree on account of renting, a decree on account of borrowing, and a decree on account of "testing"* [that is, the prohibition against selling a large beast to Gentiles is a decree designed to prevent an Israelite from renting, lending, or allowing a Gentile to "test" the animal in anticipation of a possible sale].

M. Avodah Zarah 1:6 deals generally with the sorts of animals Israelites may or may not sell to Gentiles. The mishnah permits the sale of a "small beast" (בהמה דקה) in a place in which people are accustomed to do so, and forbids it in places in which the practice is not to sell them. The sale of a "large beast" (בהמה גסה) is categorically forbidden in all places, as is the sale of heifers and foals, whether healthy or not. R. Yehudah disagrees and permits the sales of damaged heifers and foals, while Ben Beteira goes even further and permits sales of horses.

Both Talmuds (y. Avodah Zarah at §§A–J; b. Avodah Zarah at §§A–F) take up the issue of exactly why it is that sales of large beasts are forbidden. While such an inquiry is itself called for by the mishnah, the similarities between the Talmuds' treatments of the issue make it unlikely that they took it up independently. §C of y. Avodah Zarah's sugya and §A of the Bavli's make it clear that the mishnah's prohibition is due to the concern that the Gentile will work the beast on the Sabbath. Although y. Avodah Zarah digresses in §§D and E to take up the issue of a small beast, it returns in §F to ask why the Sabbath is a concern at all: once the sale takes place the beast is no longer the property of an Israelite and hence is not required to be given Sabbath rest. B. Avodah Zarah, which does not digress on the subject of a small beast, asks the same question in §B. Y. Avodah Zarah answers its own question in §G with the Babylonian tradition about selling the beast for "testing," and finally concludes in §I that permanent sales to Gentiles were forbidden as a "decree" (גזירה) to safeguard against non-permanent "sales" to Gentiles for testing purposes. Similarly, b. Avodah Zarah raises the "testing" rationale in §E, ultimately concluding in §F that the mishnah's prohibition against selling a large beast to Gentiles was in part intended as a "decree" to prevent non-permanent sales to Gentiles for "testing." Once again, although the question about the reason for the prohibition could have occurred to both Talmuds independently, their structurally similar development of the issue strongly suggests dependence

---

48. The Bavli's extended discussion of whether or not "rental" effects a legally valid acquisition of an object to the renter is omitted.

of the one upon the other. Tannaitic sources other than the mishnah do not account for the similarity, since none are cited in the sugyot themselves.

The early talmud hypothesis draws strength in this case from R. Ami the Babylonian's quotation of "the Rabbis of There" (=Babylonia) in y. Avodah Zarah §G. This suggests that perhaps the undeniable similarities between the Talmuds are due to y. Avodah Zarah's appropriation of edited Babylonian material rather than b. Avodah Zarah's appropriation of y. Avodah Zarah material. But this suggestion is without merit. First, while y. Avodah Zarah presents the Babylonian tradition in the name of "R. Ami the Babylonian" (ר' אמי בבליא), b. Avodah Zarah does so in the orthographically similar name of "Rami b. de-R. Yeba" (רמי בריה דר' ייבא).[49] Whether or not the tradent is the same, the tradition itself is, and when we compare the versions we see that neither tradent is aware of the larger context in which his tradition appears. Neither tradent seems aware of the local mishnah under discussion, and neither is aware of the (identical) anonymous questions to which his tradition is the alleged response. That is, while the Palestinians represent themselves as having received this particular tradition from the Babylonians, they most likely did not receive it in this dialectical context. It is more likely that the dialectical context was created in Palestine and subsequently re-appropriated by the Babylonians.[50]

This argument from context draws further support from the intra-Yerushalmi parallel at y. Pes 4:3, 30d–31a. We discussed earlier how y. Pesahim presents a parallel to the "testing" material at 30d followed (after a digression) by a parallel to the discussion found at y. AZ 1:6, 40a of Rabbi's views on the legal equivalence of large wild animals and large domesticated beasts. B. Avodah Zarah presents the "testing" material at 15a, while Rabbi's tradition appears at 16a. We thus see a broadly similar macro-ordering of material which is far larger than any selection of ma-

---

49. Albeck, in *Introduction to the Talmud*, assumes Rami b. de-R. Yeba to be a third-generation Babylonian amora, but does not provide any specific information. This amora also appears at b. Betz 8b (where Rabbenu Hananel reads the name as "Yemar") and b. Arakh 11b. Moreover, the JTS ms. records the amora's name as "Rami b. R. Yeba," while b. AZ 15a (*DS*) records no variation of that name. The orthographic similarity between this name and that of "R. Ami the Babylonian" makes it tempting to see "Rami b. de-R. Yeba" as a corruption of it, or to see "R. Ami the Babylonian" as an attempt to replace an unfamiliar with a familiar name. This issue requires further investigation.

50. Given the highly decentralized nature of the rabbinic movement in Babylonia, it is not at all impossible that a given tradition—such as this "testing" tradition—was known in some places in Babylonia but not in others, became known in Palestine, and eventually returned to Babylonia later as part of a sugya. On Baby-

terial that amoraim were likely to have passed back and forth between Palestine and Babylonia, judging by what we see of their transmission activity.[51]

In a related vein, it is unlikely that the Palestinians received the entire "testing" sugya from Babylonia in essentially the form in which we now have it. That would mean that the sugya had to be formulated this way and transmitted to Palestine within the amoraic period. But as we noted in chapter 1, amoraic sugyot are typically short[52] and typified by amoraic awareness of these sugyot as sugyot.[53] This sugya, by contrast, is lengthy, cites only one amora, and neither he nor anyone else preceding or following the sugya is aware of this sugya as an edited sugya. The more plausible conclusion is that b. Avodah Zarah drew this sugya from y. Avodah Zarah.

VI.b. B. Avodah Zarah 48b ‖ Y. Avodah Zarah 3:13, 43b

Y. Avodah Zarah 3:13, 43b

A. There [in Babylonia] they said in the name of R. Hisda: "Its [the sacred tree's] shade is forbidden; the shade of its shade is permitted."

B. *Which is the shade of its shade and which is its shade? There* [in Babylonia], *they said:* "Every [point such that] if [the tree] falls, [the top of the tree] touches that [point]—that is 'its shade.' And every [point such that] if [the tree] falls, [the top of the tree] does not touch [that point]—that is 'the shade of its shade.'"

C. *Why is* [the tree's] *shade forbidden? Because* [the tree] *is forbidden in benefit.*

D. *Behold the grave is forbidden in benefit and its shade is permitted! Behold the Sanctuary* [the Temple] *is forbidden in benefit and R. Yohanan b. Zakkai used to sit and repeat* [traditions] *in the shadow of the Sanctuary! Let it be that the reason* [the shadow of the sacred tree is forbidden] *is not because* [the sacred tree] *is forbidden in benefit,* [but because of the stringency of all matters pertaining to idolatry].

E. R. Abin in the name of the "Rabbis of There" [=Babylonia]: "This [the mishnah's ruling that if the sacred tree was bending over into the public domain and a person passed under it in the public domain, the person is

---

lonian decentralization see David Goodblatt, *Rabbinic Instruction in Sassanian Babylonia* (Leiden: E. J. Brill, 1975), 267–272; Kalmin, *Sages, Stories, Authors, and Editors,* 15, 175–212.

51. See our earlier discussion in chapter 1, pp. 31–33.

52. For a summary of the stages in the literary formation of Talmudic literature and the progression of that literature from the simple (in the early amoraic period) to the highly complex (during the post-amoraic period), see Sussman, "Ve-shuv le-Yerushalmi Neziqin," 90–114.

53. See, e.g., the different versions of Abaye's dispute with R. Yosef at b. AZ 24a.

ritually clean] means that the ritual impurity of the dead [that is, the reach of the impurity generated by the grave] is not clearly established [from Scripture]. For if it were not so [that is, if the extent of the reach of the impurity generated by the grave were established in Scripture, how could it be that case that] a person who passed under a grave that extended into the public domain is ritually clean?" [R. Abin is implicitly assuming an analogy between the ritual impurities of graves and idols.]

F.   Gamliel Zuga was leaning upon R. Shimon b. Laqish, and they came upon an image. [Gamliel Zuga] said to him: "What about passing in front of it?" [Is it permitted or not?] [Resh Laqish] said to him: "Pass in front of it and blind its eyes [treat it disrespectfully by passing before it without showing honor]." R. Yitshaq b. Matana was leaning on R. Yohanan, and they came upon a statue [standing in front] of the public assembly building. [R. Yitshaq b. Matana] said to him: "What about passing in front of it?" [R. Yohanan] said to him: "Pass before it and blind its eyes." R. Yaaqov b. Idi was leaning upon R. Yehoshua b. Levi, and they came upon a procession in which an idol was being carried. [R. Yehoshua b. Levi] said: "Nahum the man of the Holy of Holies passed [before an idol in such a situation] and you will not pass? Pass before it and blind its eyes."

B. Avodah Zarah 48b

A.   [From the mishnah:] **He shall not sit in its** [the sacred tree's] **shade.** *This is obvious!* Rabbah b. Bar Hana said in the name of R. Yohanan: "This is only needed [with reference] to the shade of its shade." *From this* [amoraic teaching] *may it be inferred that if he sat in the shadow of its trunk, he is unclean? No, for even* [if he sat] *in the shadow of its trunk, he is ritually clean. And this* [clause of the mishnah] *comes to teach us that he must not sit in the shade of its shade* [ideally, in the first instance, but if he nevertheless did so, the second clause of the mishnah provides that he is ritually clean after the fact].

B.   *There are those who teach this* [sugya that was just set out] *in relation to the latter* [clause of the mishnah, which reads: **If he sat, he is clean.** This version of the sugya reads as follows:] *This is obvious!* Rabbah b. Bar Hana said in the name of R. Yohanan: "This [**"If he sat, he is clean"**] is only needed with reference to the shade of its trunk." *From this may it be inferred that he may sit in the shade of its shade even in the first instance? No, this* [**"If he sat, he is clean"**] *comes to teach us that even if he sat in the shade of its trunk, he is ritually clean.*

C.   *What is the reason* [for the mishnah's ruling that a person should not pass under a sacred tree, and that if he did so he is unclean]? *It is impossible that there not be any offerings to idols* [under the tree].

D.   *Whose* [teaching is reflected in the mishnaic ruling discussed in §C]? *It is R. Yehudah b. Beteira, as it was taught in a baraita:* **R. Yehudah b. Beteira says: "From where do we know that an offering to an idol conveys tent impurity** [like a corpse]? **As it is said, 'They yoked themselves to Baal**

Peor, and ate the sacrifices of the dead (Ps 106:28).' **Just as a corpse conveys tent impurity, so does a sacrifice offered to an idol convey tent impurity."**

E.   *They asked* [concerning the clause of the mishnah which states that a person is clean if he passed under a sacred tree that was bending over into the public domain: Should the mishnah read] "עבר" [*if* he passed, after the fact], *or* "עובר" [he may pass under it even in the first instance]? R. Yitshaq b. Eleazar in the name of Hezekiah said: "עובר," and R. Yohanan said: "אם עבר" [if he passed—after the fact], *and they do not dispute. This one,* [R. Yohanan, states his view for a situation in which] *there is another way* [and thus in the first instance he must not go that way, but after the fact, it is alright]; *this one,* [Hezekiah, states his view for a situation in which] *there is no other way* [and thus, having no choice, he may pass under the tree even in the first instance].

F.   R. Sheshet [who was blind] said to his attendant: "When you get there [to the point in the journey at which they will be passing under a sacred tree that extends into the public domain], cause me to run." *What is the situation? If there is no other way,* [why does he need to say] "Cause me to run"? *It is permissible* [as per Hezekiah]! *And if there is another way* [by saying "Cause me to run"], *does that make it permitted* [even in the first instance]? *Really,* [the situation is one in which] *there is no other way,* [but R. Sheshet wanted to be hurried along, although that was not legally required, because] *an important man is different* [and must not appear to be walking in a leisurely manner under a sacred tree that was hanging over into the public domain].

The pertinent part of m. AZ 3:8 rules that although ideally an Israelite should not sit in the shade of a sacred tree, he nevertheless remains ritually pure if he does so. The opposite applies to walking under the tree: once again the Israelite must ideally not walk under it, and doing so renders him unclean. The one exception is that an Israelite will remain ritually pure if he unavoidably walks under a sacred tree that extends into the public domain.

Y. Avodah Zarah's discussion of this mishnah (§§A–F) is divisible into three parts. In §A the Yerushalmi cites a tradition it identifies as Babylonian according to which the shade of the sacred tree is forbidden while the "shade of its shade" is permitted. Y. Avodah Zarah discusses this tradition in §§B–D. In §E, R. Abin cites another Babylonian tradition that draws an analogy between the uncleanness caused by the sacred tree and that of the grave. §F presents three stories about Palestinian rabbis passing in front of idols.

B. Avodah Zarah 48b (§§A–F) is similarly divisible into three parts. At §A, a tradition of Rabbah b. Bar Hana in the name of R. Yohanan is cited in response to an objection. That tradition establishes that the forbidden "shade" of the mishnah under which an Israelite must not sit is, in reality, the "shade of its shade." B. Avodah Zarah discusses this tradition further in §§B–C. At the end of §C, the anonymous voice suggests that walking under the sacred tree renders an Israelite impure because of the likely presence under the tree of offerings made to idols. This observation provides the segue to §D, where the anonymous voice—assuming that its own suggestion about offerings to idols represents the plain sense of the mishnah—attributes its own rationale to R. Yehudah b. Beteira, who equates offerings to idols with corpse-uncleanness. In §§E–F the Bavli discusses walking under a sacred tree that extends into the public domain. Finally, in §F, the Bavli presents a story about R. Sheshet's concern about walking under a sacred tree that is similar to the stories found in y. Avodah Zarah §F.

Both Talmuds thus follow a similar developmental path. Although the mishnah mentions "shade," nothing there requires either Talmud to define that forbidden shade as the "shade of its shade," let alone to move similarly to the other common topics. Nor do tannaitic sources other than the local mishnah require it; y. Avodah Zarah quotes none and the one baraita quoted in b. Avodah Zarah §D is well-integrated into the sugya.

Nevertheless one might argue on the basis of the Babylonian traditions cited in y. Avodah Zarah §§A–B and E that there was indeed inter-Talmudic influence, but that it was y. Avodah Zarah that was influenced by edited Babylonian sugyot now found in b. Avodah Zarah. In order to make a convincing case for this, one would have to show that these Babylonian traditions themselves are the cause of the similarity in the Talmuds' parallel sugyot. If the traditions are not themselves the cause, but rather are *integrated into* a dialectical context that was likely created by editors, then one would have to demonstrate (through comparison to other amoraic sugyot) that such a dialectical construction can reasonably be attributed to the amoraic period.

Of the three traditions y. Avodah Zarah attributes to "the Rabbis of There" (=Babylonia), two are also found in b. Avodah Zarah. These traditions, by themselves, are clearly not responsible for the three-step development of the parallel sugya found in both Talmuds. Nothing in y. Avodah Zarah §§A–B would lead us to predict that we would eventually encounter a comparison of the "shade of its shade" to the uncleanness of the grave. Nothing in R. Abin's Babylonian tradition in §E would lead us to expect that it would be followed by stories of sages passing before idols. Moreover, y. Avodah Zarah's anonymous editorial voice set the stage for the presentation of R. Abin's tradition in §E by raising the specter of the grave itself in §D. Thus these Babylonian traditions do not themselves generate the context in which we find them in y. Avodah Zarah; they are embedded in a dialectical context created by y. Avodah Zarah's redactors.

Nor do these same traditions generate the context in which we find them at b. AZ 48b. The "shade of its shade" tradition at b. Avodah Zarah §A is presented as the answer to an observation made by the anonymous voice. In §D, the anonymous voice quotes a baraita about corpse-uncleanness in order to support the context it created itself at the end of §C. And once again, nothing about these materials requires the story of R. Sheshet in §F.

Since in both Talmuds these "Babylonian" (for the Palestinians, that is) traditions are embedded within their sugya contexts, the question remains whether it is reasonable to assert that such a complex construction was likely transmitted from Babylonia to Palestine during the amoraic period. While there is evidence that editorial activity may have begun in Babylonia during the middle amoraic generations,[54] the editorial activity characteristic of the amoraim is not consistent with the large-scale orchestration of traditions and dialectical context we see here.

VII
Conclusion

Assessing the literary relationship (if any) between a Bavli tractate and its Yerushalmi counterpart requires the first step of "macro" analysis. Macro analysis, as I described it in chapter 1, requires a close study of both Talmuds' entire treatments of all the mishnayot of the tractate. The purpose

---

54. See Kalmin, *Sages, Stories, Authors, and Editors,* 169–173 and the other sources cited there at 170n4. Nevertheless, evidence that the amount of argumentation in Babylonian amoraic material increases toward the middle of the amoraic period does not reasonably support the claim that amoraim are responsible for the sort of three-step sugya under discussion here. Nor does Avraham Weiss's suggestive theory that R. Yohanan and Resh Laqish originated the amoraic dispute-format that was subsequently adopted in Babylonia support such a claim. Let us take R. Yohanan's and Resh Laqish's dispute about "the idol that was broken" (y. AZ 3:2, 42d ‖ b. AZ 41b) as an illustration. Even if Weiss is correct to point to examples like this as proof that the dispute format was a Palestinian innovation exported to Babylonia, we see that this sugya is brief and *does not generate a context* into which other issues and sugyot will be placed. On the other hand, the example under discussion here from y. AZ 3:13, 43b ‖ b. AZ 48b is a more complex orchestration of attributed and anonymous materials that is unlikely to be anything other than a product of post-amoraic editors. Unless one wishes to argue for an extremely late date for y. AZ by arguing that it could have appropriated post-amoraic editing of b. AZ, the more reasonable conclusion is that it was post-amoraic activity in y. AZ which was appropriated by b. AZ. See Avraham Weiss, *'Al ha-yetsirah ha-sifrutit shel ha-amoraim* (New York: Horeb, 1962), 10–23.

of macro analysis is to identify similarities in the selection and sequence of topics and sugyot in each Talmud's treatment of the mishnah, and to eliminate those similarities that can reasonably be considered "called for by the [local] mishnah" or "called for by other tannaitic sources." Similarities which remain must be further analyzed to see if they can be accounted for by the early talmud hypothesis more reasonably than by the hypothesis that they are due to the later Talmud's reliance on the earlier.

Applying this method to y. and b. Avodah Zarah, I identified nearly fifty passages that are likely examples of b. Avodah Zarah's appropriation of materials from y. Avodah Zarah. These passages yielded interesting patterns, which we illustrated in this chapter:

1. The largest number of parallel passages are due to b. Avodah Zarah's appropriation of sugyot from y. Avodah Zarah in the same order and attached to the same mishnah;

2. There is one example of b. Avodah Zarah turning a simple y. Avodah Zarah sugya into a complex sugya by using materials the y. Avodah Zarah editors had marked as relevant to the original, simple amoraic dispute;

3. In some cases in which b. Avodah Zarah has a parallel in y. Avodah Zarah and in some other rabbinic compilation, b. Avodah Zarah tends to more closely resemble y. Avodah Zarah;

4. There is one example of b. and y. Avodah Zarah placing a similar selection and sequence of materials at a similar place in the tractate, although not attached to the same mishnah (which suggests that b. Avodah Zarah was aware of the overall editing and arrangement of y. Avodah Zarah); and

5. B. and y. Avodah Zarah sometimes use the same mishnah as the opportunity to explore a particular legal issue (that is not called for by that mishnah) or to present the same genres of material (such as aggadah or stories about sages).

Now that we have identified the passages that b. Avodah Zarah likely appropriated from y. Avodah Zarah, we must move on to the next analytical step: the micro analysis of just how it is that b. Avodah Zarah reworks its y. Avodah Zarah sources. Whereas our focus in this chapter was the *similarities* between the Talmuds, our focus in chapters 3 and 4 will be the *differences* and how these differences demonstrate conscious and careful Babylonian appropriation of y. Avodah Zarah sugyot.

3

B. Avodah Zarah Sugyot as Secondary Reworkings of Y. Avodah Zarah Sugyot (Micro Analysis I)

Not *every* sugya in b. Avodah Zarah has a Yerushalmi parallel, but examining those that do yields a pattern: b. Avodah Zarah sugyot tend to be secondary reworkings of their Yerushalmi parallels that take the Yerushalmi sugyot into account and rework them in characteristic ways. Studying this pattern is important because we cannot consider the question of y. Avodah Zarah's influence on b. Avodah Zarah settled until we understand not only that b. Avodah Zarah appropriated materials from y. Avodah Zarah (chapter 2), but also how and why there are so many differences between the b. and y. Avodah Zarah sugyot. When we understand how the b. Avodah Zarah redactors went about their work of adapting and altering Yerushalmi sugyot to fit their new Babylonian context, the theory that the redactors of b. Avodah Zarah were aware of, and guided by, the example of y. Avodah Zarah will be considerably strengthened.

Our examination of how b. Avodah Zarah sugyot rework their Yerushalmi parallels will be divided between chapters 3, 4, and 5. In this chapter we will study five ways in which b. Avodah Zarah may be observed to rework its Palestinian parallels:

1. B. Avodah Zarah tends to add a Babylonian cultural, linguistic, or halakhic feature to a y. Avodah Zarah sugya;

2. In a related vein, b. Avodah Zarah tends to eliminate materials that are of particular and specific relevance to the Land of Israel;

3. B. Avodah Zarah tends to re-arrange y. Avodah Zarah materials in a more sensible order;[1]

4. B. Avodah Zarah evaluates a source in connection with an amoraic concern that y. Avodah Zarah had viewed in connection with a tannaitic concern;[2] and

5. B. Avodah Zarah revises y. Avodah Zarah sugyot so as to raise a legal issue in the sugyot to a higher level of abstraction.

Our work on the mechanics of b. Avodah Zarah's reworking of Yerushalmi sugyot will continue in chapter 4 with a sharper focus on examples that show that the b. Avodah Zarah redactors were cognizant at times of how y. Avodah Zarah had been edited. In those examples the b. Avodah Zarah redactors are aware of how y. Avodah Zarah ended its discussion of a particular point or how it left an issue unresolved; they, in turn, commence their discussion at that point or begin by taking up the unresolved issue. Finally, in chapter 5 we will consider b. Avodah Zarah's anonymous (stam) voice and what part it plays in b. Avodah Zarah's appropriation of y. Avodah Zarah.

We will begin with a particularly rich example from the beginning of the Avodah Zarah tractates: b. AZ 6b ‖ y. AZ 1:1, 39b. This example is a useful starting-point because it illustrates all five of the characteristic ways in which b. Avodah Zarah reworks its Palestinian parallels. Due to the length of the texts, the reader is advised to skim them quickly before reading the analysis and to refer back later to the particular sections under discussion.

---

1. What constitutes "a more sensible order" is admittedly subjective. See the analysis at pp. 125–136.

2. The point is that if b. AZ, which is the later compilation, used a particular source in connection with an amoraic dispute which y. AZ had used in connection with a tannaitic dispute, b. AZ's use is likely a secondary development beyond y. AZ. For an analysis of this argument in relation to parallel sugyot in y. Ber and GenR, see Baruch Bokser, "A Minor for *Zimmun* (y. Ber. 7:2, 11c) and Recensions of Yerushalmi," *AJSR* 4 (1979): 1–25; and my "A Bavli Sugya and Its Two Yerushalmi Parallels: Issues of Literary Relationship and Redaction," to be included in *New Methods in Reading Rabbinic Literature: Hermeneutical Limits and Possibilities* (ed. Matthew A. Kraus; Piscataway, NJ: Gorgias, forthcoming).

Y. Avodah Zarah 1:1, 39b

A. *It was taught:* **If he transgressed and transacted** [business with a Gentile in the three days before an idolatrous festival, the profits are] **permitted.**

B. R. Yaaqov b. Aha, R. Yose in the name of R. Yohanan: "And even on the day of his festival."

C. *And so it was taught:* **With respect to which situations** [is it the case that an Israelite is forbidden to benefit from a transaction with a Gentile before or on his festival]? [If the transaction was] **with a Gentile that** [the Israelite] **does not know. But** [if the transaction was] **with a Gentile that** [the Israelite] **knows, it is permitted, because** [the Israelite] **is like one who is deceptively flattering him.**

D. *It was taught:* **If** [an Israelite] **entered a city** [during an idolatrous festival] **and found them rejoicing, he may rejoice with them, because he is simply like one who is deceptively flattering them.**

E. A certain *ducenarius*[3] honored R. Yudan Nesiah with one pouch full of *denarii.* He accepted one of them and sent the rest back [to the *ducenarius*]. [R. Yudan Nesiah] asked R. Shimon b. Laqish [whether he could accept even the one *denarius*]. [Resh Laqish] said: "He [the Patriarch] must bring the benefit [obtained from the *ducenarius*] to the Dead Sea [thus he could not accept even the one coin]." *Behold* [the case concerns a Gentile] *whom* [the Israelite] *knows, behold* [the case concerns a gift made] *after the fact, and Resh Laqish says:* "He must bring the benefit to the Dead Sea"*?!*

F. R. Abbahu said: "And as for me, did not R. Gamliel the son of Rabbi ask me: 'What about [my] going down to an [idolatrous] fair,' and I forbade him? [I forbade him despite the fact that] it was taught: [Israelites] **may go to an** [idolatrous] **fair and buy male and female slaves from there.**" Resh Laqish said: "Not just Israelite slaves, but even Gentile [slaves], because [the Israelite who buys them] brings them near under the wings of the Divine Presence."

G. *What is the reason*[4] [that Resh Laqish forbade R. Yudan Nesiah to accept the *denarius* despite his general leniency on the subject of idolatrous fairs]? *R. Gamliel was a minor and R. Abbahu wished to set a limit for him. But R. Yudan Nesiah was a grown man!* [What, therefore, could justify Resh Laqish's stringency?]

H. [Even so,] *Resh Laqish wished to set a limit on the matter* [so as not to have people see the Patriarch accepting gifts from idolaters].

---

3. The word דוקינר is rendered as "commander" or "procurator" by Jastrow, *Dictionary,* 288, and more recently by Sokoloff, *Dictionary,* 142. The term is better rendered as *ducenarius,* meaning "an official who receives a salary of 200 *sesterces* per annum." See *Paulys Real-Encyclopädie der Classischen Altertum Wissenschaft* (ed. Georg Wissowa; 24 vols.; Stuttgart: J. B. Metzler Buchhandlung, 1905), 5:1571. My thanks to Prof. Seth Schwartz for assisting me with this translation.

4. I have translated the term מאי כדון as "what is the reason?" per the comment of P'nei Moshe, s.v. מאי כדון.

I. *It is understandable* [that there be a prohibition] *against lending* [items to Gentiles three days before their festivals].

J. *But not to borrow* [items] *from them?*

K. [The prohibition of borrowing makes sense] *because* [the Israelite] *is like one who raises up a name for* [the Gentile. By borrowing from him, the Israelite shows him honor in which the Gentile will rejoice on his festival].

L. *It is understandable* [that there be a prohibition] *against lending him money* [three days before his idolatrous festival].

M. *But not to borrow* [money] *from them?*

N. *Because* [the Israelite] *is like one who raises up a name for him.*

O. *It is understandable* [that there be a prohibition] *against repaying them* [three days prior to their festivals].

P. *But not to be repaid by them* [for a loan]?

Q. *It is in order that* [the Gentile] *not say that his idolatry assisted it* [the repayment].

R. R. Ba b. Tablai said in the name of Rav: "If it was a lost [unsecured] loan, it is permitted [to receive repayment three days prior to, or on, the Gentile's festival]."

S. *And so it was taught:* **A lost** [unsecured] **loan** [is one made] **with witnesses; a loan is not lost** [if made] **with a document. Even a loan with a document may be lost, since a person does not always merit** [being able] **to pay off his debt.**

T. *What is the result?* [What is the definition of a "lost," or unsecured, loan?]

U. *An unsecured loan is a loan without collateral; a loan is not unsecured with collateral.*

V. *Then he found it* [the meaning of "lost loan"] *taught as in the first* [baraita in §S]: **A loan is lost if made with witnesses, a loan is not lost with a document.**

W. *It was taught there in a mishnah:* **R. Yehudah says: "A woman should not put on cosmetic paint, because it is a disgrace for her"** (m. MQ 1:7). [While she has the paint on, she looks unattractive; the cosmetic benefits of the paint will only be apparent when she removes it. Thus R. Yehudah holds that she should not put it on during the intermediate days of a Festival, since she will look unattractive during the Festival.]

X. R. Hanina and R. Mana [disagreed about what R. Yehudah and his opponents, the Sages, really meant]. One said: "They were arguing about a cosmetic paint that she removes during the Festival, but a cosmetic paint that she removes after the Festival is forbidden." [As to the first, since she will obtain some of the cosmetic benefit during the Festival, the Sages permit it. Yet the Sages and R. Yehudah both agree that if she will in no way benefit from the paint during the Festival, she is forbidden to apply it.] And the other said: "They were arguing about a cosmetic paint that she removes after the Festival, but a cosmetic paint that she removes during the Festival is permitted."

Y. *And they did not know which said which and which said which* [unnamed sages did not know which statement was attributable to R. Hanina and which to R. Mana].

Z. *From what R. Hanina said in the name of R. Yose in the name of R. Yohanan:* "R. Yehudah is consistent with his own opinion. Just as he said there [m. MQ 1:7] that temporary disgrace is considered disgrace, so he says here [m. AZ 1:1] that temporary pain is pain." *So it is* [R. Hanina] *who says that they were arguing about a cosmetic paint that she removes during the Festival, but a cosmetic paint that she removes after the Festival is forbidden.*

Before presenting the parallel material at b. AZ 6b, let us pause to consider the structure of y. AZ 1:1, 39b. This lengthy sugya is divisible into five parts:

1. A dispute about the legal consequences of violating the mishnah's prohibitions (§§A–D)

2. The story of R. Yudan Nesiah's hesitation about accepting a gift from a Gentile and Resh Laqish's advice (§§E–H);

3. Y. Avodah Zarah's wonderment at the mishnah's prohibition of pairs of transactions such as lending and borrowing (§§I–Q);

4. The clarification of the type of loan that is considered "lost" (§§R–V); and

5. The discussion from tractate Moed Qatan about the application of cosmetic paint during the intermediate days of an Israelite festival and the relation between that and loan repayment by a Gentile prior to his own festival (§§W–Z).

Let us keep this structure in mind as we examine b. AZ 6b.

B. Avodah Zarah 6b

A. *They asked:*[5] [If an Israelite] *transacted* [business with a Gentile prior to the latter's festival], *what* [is the law as to whether the Israelite can profit from the transaction]?

B. R. Yohanan said: "If he transacted—[the resulting profit is] forbidden."

---

5. The issue of whether the anonymous question "They asked" (איביעא להו) is of amoraic provenance or is the work of the Bavli's anonymous voice is a thorny one that remains unresolved. David Halivni maintains that the question is amoraic; see his *Sources and Traditions:* Erubin-Pesahim, 249n3**. On the other hand, Shamma Friedman has indicated both that it may be amoraic (*Talmud Arukh,* 1:237) and that it may be anonymous (ibid., 257). Throughout this book I have considered the איביעא להו question to be anonymous except in those cases in which there is clear evidence that it is, in fact, amoraic.

C.   Resh Laqish said: "If he transacted—[the resulting profit is] permitted."

D.   *R. Yohanan raised an objection to Resh Laqish:* "**As to the festivals of idola-ters**—[if an Israelite went ahead and impermissibly] **transacted,** [the re-sulting profit is] **forbidden.** What, does this [baraita] not apply [to the three day period] before their festivals?" *No,* [runs the answer on behalf of Resh Laqish,] *it applies to the exact day of their festival itself.* [Thus, R. Yo-hanan's challenge fails.]

E.   *There are those who say: R. Shimon b. Laqish raised an objection to R. Yohanan:* "**As to the festivals of idolaters**—[if an Israelite went ahead and imper-missibly] **transacted,** [the resulting profit is] **forbidden.** On their festi-vals—yes [the profit is forbidden]; before their festivals—no."

F.   [The response to §E on behalf of R. Yohanan:] [As for the] tanna [who taught the baraita **As to the festivals of idolaters—transacted, forbid-den**]—*he calls both these* [the days before the festival] *and these* [the days of the festival] *"their festivals"* [and thus an Israelite is forbidden to keep the profits of commerce he conducts either prior to or on the idolatrous festi-val].

G.   *There is a baraita supporting Resh Laqish:* **When** [the Sages] **said that it is forbidden to transact business** [with Gentiles] **they only forbade** [trans-actions in] **durable goods. But as to** [transactions in] **perishable goods, no** [there is no prohibition]. **And even as to durable goods,** [if the Israel-ite went ahead and impermissibly] **transacted,** [the profit is] **permitted.**

H.   R. Zevid taught a baraita of the house of R. Hoshaya:[6] [Israelites may] **sell to them, but not buy from them, perishable goods.**

I.   There was a certain *min* who sent a Caesarean[7] *denarius* to R. Yehudah Nesiah on the day of [the *min*'s] festival. Resh Laqish happened to be sit-ting before him. [The Patriarch] said: "What should I do? If I take it from him, he will go and thank [his god that the Patriarch showed him such honor]. If I do not take it from him, there will be enmity." Resh Laqish said to him: "Take it and throw it into a pit in front of him." He said: "How much more so will there then be enmity!" [Resh Laqish replied:] "I meant [throw it into a pit] 'off the back of the hand'[8] [i.e., in an unusual way such that the *min* would not realize that the act was deliberate]."

J.   *It is understandable* [that it be forbidden] *to lend* [items] *to them, since* [then the Israelite] *is enriching them.*

K.   *But by borrowing from them he is diminishing them!* [so why the prohibi-tion?]

L.   Abaye said: "There was a decree [prohibiting] borrowing from them lest he lend to them."

M.   Rava said: "All of [the prohibitions of m. AZ 1:1] are on the grounds that [the Gentile] will 'go and thank' [his god]."

---

6. Cf. *DS* note מ here, where the reading is "R. Zevid son of R. Oshaya."

7. *DS* (note נ) reads "of Caesar."

8. Missing from *DS.*

N. *It is understandable* [that it be forbidden] *to lend them money, since* [the Israelite] *is then enriching them.*

O. *But borrowing* [money] *from them, why* [should it be forbidden]?

P. Abaye said: "There was a decree [prohibiting] borrowing money from them lest he lend to them."

Q. Rava said: "All of it is on the grounds that he will 'go and thank.'"

R. *It is understandable* [that it be forbidden] *to repay them, since he is then enriching them.*

S. *But by being repaid by them* [the Israelite] *is diminishing them!*

T. Abaye said: "There was a decree [prohibiting] being repaid by them lest he repay [a loan he borrowed from] them."

U. Rava said: "All of it is on the grounds that he will 'go and thank.'"

V. *And they* [the prohibitions of m. AZ 1:1] *are all necessary. For had the tanna taught only* [that it was forbidden] *to transact business with them on the grounds that he would be enriching* [the Gentile, who would then] *go and give thanks, one then would have thought that* [he is permitted to] *borrow from them, since he thereby diminishes them!*

W. *And had the tanna taught* [the prohibition against] *borrowing from them,* [that would have been on the grounds that borrowing from the Gentile] *is important to him* [it makes the Gentile feel important], *and he would "go and thank." But borrowing money from them should be permitted since it would be a cause of sorrow. He would say: "The money will not return to me."*

X. *And had the tanna taught that it was forbidden to borrow* [money] *from them because he would say: "Against his* [the Israelite borrower's] *will I will exact repayment," and nevertheless now go and thank, but* [then I might have thought that it would be permitted] *to be repaid by them, since the money would not return to them. I would say: "He is in pain, and will not go and thank"*—[so all the statements in m. AZ 1:1 are] *necessary.*

Y. *And R. Yehudah disagrees* [with the principle that] *"even though* [the Gentile] *is upset now, he will be happy later"?* [In m. AZ 1:1 R. Yehudah permits an Israelite to accept repayment from a Gentile prior to the festival because this will upset the Gentile prior to the festival. The Sages forbid the repayment because even though the Gentile is "upset now," he will be "happy later."]

Z. *And was it not taught in a baraita:* **R. Yehudah says: "A woman should not put on cosmetics during the Festival, since it is a disgrace for her." And R. Yehudah agrees that she can apply a cosmetic paint during the Festival that she can remove during the Festival; even though she is upset now, she will be happy later.**

AA. R. Nahman b. Yitshaq said: "Leave aside the laws of the intermediate days of a Festival, for all of them [are based on the principle of] 'upset now, happy later' [thus, they are not to be compared to the laws against doing business with idolaters]."

AB. Ravina said: "When it comes to loan repayment, an idolater is always upset."

AC. *Our mishnah* [which prohibits accepting repayment from a Gentile in every case] *is inconsistent with R. Yehoshua b. Qorha. For it was taught in a baraita:* **R. Yehoshua b. Qorha said: "We do not collect from them a loan evidenced by a document, but we do collect from them a loan made orally, because** [the Israelite collecting] **is like 'one who saves** [Israelite property] **from their hands'"** (t. AZ 1:1[9]).

The structure of this lengthy sugya at b. AZ 6b strongly resembles y. Avodah Zarah, but with one critical difference. Once again, we see a five-step structure:

1. A dispute about the legal consequences of violating the mishnah's prohibitions (§§A–H);

2. The story of R. Yehudah Nesiah's hesitation about accepting a gift from a *min* and Resh Laqish's advice (§I);

3. B. Avodah Zarah 6b's wonderment at the mishnah's prohibition of pairs of transactions such as lending *and* borrowing (§§J–X);

4. The discussion from Moed Qatan about the application of cosmetic paint during the intermediate days of a festival and the relation between that and loan repayment prior to an idolater's festival (§§Y–AB); and

5. Clarification of what sort of loan is, or is not, "lost" (§AC).

The critical difference between the order of topics in the two Talmuds is that y. Avodah Zarah discusses "lost loans" prior to the sugya from Moed Qatan, while b. Avodah Zarah, as we see immediately above, does the opposite. We will have much to say about this switched order presently, but we must first perform a macro analysis of this parallel sequence of sugyot in order to ascertain that the strong similarities between them are likely due to b. Avodah Zarah's having appropriated this sequence from y. Avodah Zarah, and not some other cause.

A. Macro Analysis of B. Avodah Zarah 6b ‖ Y. Avodah Zarah 1:1, 39b

M. Avodah Zarah 1:1 includes three basic elements: the three-day period of commercial abstention prior to a Gentile festival,[10] a list of prohibited

---

9. Zuckermandel, 460.

10. See Hayes, *Between the Babylonian and Palestinian Talmuds*, 118–119 for discussion of the ambiguity in the mishnah: is the three-day period inclusive or exclusive of the festival day itself?

activities, and then a view of R. Yishmael that a three-day period of abstention is required after the festival as well. Nothing in the mishnah calls for a topic like (1), above, which discusses the violations of the mishnah's prohibitions, since presumably the authors of the mishnah expected its strictures to be obeyed. Nor does m. AZ 1:1 call for the story of R. Yudan (=Yehudah) Nesiah. Similarly, nothing calls for the juxtaposition of a discussion about the application of cosmetic paint during an Israelite festival to a discussion about the types of loans exempted from the repayment prohibition of the mishnah. Of the five topics in this sequence, only (3) is arguably called for by m. AZ 1:1—the Talmuds' discussion of the pairing of prohibitions such as borrowing *and* lending. But even if the Talmuds separately chose to pursue topic (3), this one similarity could not have generated all the rest. The close linguistic and rhetorical similarity between y. AZ §§I–Q and b. AZ §§J–X makes it unlikely that b. Avodah Zarah independently formulated this sugya, and far more likely that it worked with a version of y. Avodah Zarah Moreover, the "sandwiching" of this sugya in both Talmuds among the same set of topics that are clearly not called for by the mishnah makes it even less likely that y. and b. Avodah Zarah independently chose to pursue topic (3).

Nor do other tannaitic materials call for this shared sequence of sugyot. The baraitot and m. MQ 1:7 are well-integrated into the Talmuds' discussions of these topics. The similarities between the Talmuds are clearly the *cause*, rather than the *result*, of the tannaitic commonalities.[11]

Now that we have established that b. Avodah Zarah likely drew this sugya from y. Avodah Zarah, we must probe further and perform micro analyses of the constituent topics in the sugya in order to understand just what the b. Avodah Zarah redactors were doing as they adapted the y. Avodah Zarah sugya for their own Talmud. Let us begin by looking at topics (1) and (2) as a unit: the legal consequences of violating m. AZ 1:1's prohibitions and the story of R. Yudan (=Yehudah) Nesiah. Upon completion of the micro analysis, we will be better able to assess the hypothesis of early talmud in relation to this pair of sugyot.

B. B. Avodah Zarah 6b §§A–I ‖ Y. Avodah Zarah 1:1, 39b §§A–H

M. Avodah Zarah 1:1 prohibits commercial interactions between Israelites and Gentiles in the three days prior to an idolatrous festival. Y. Avodah Zarah opens its consideration of the legal consequences of violating that prohibition with *"It was taught."* B. Avodah Zarah, on the other hand,

---

11. We will defer our consideration of the early talmud hypothesis until the conclusion of the micro analysis.

opens with *"They asked."* The significance of this change is that, by opening with *"They asked,"* the b. Avodah Zarah redactors fit this opening
passage (as well as the entire sugya which it heads) neatly into the material preceding it at 6a, which consists of two sugyot each beginning *"They
asked."* Whereas y. Avodah Zarah saw this entire sugya as a new unit of
material unconnected to what preceded it, b. Avodah Zarah made a clear
effort to fit this inherited sugya into the natural flow of its own gemara.

Moving from structure to substance, the law that emerges from
y. Avodah Zarah's consideration of the legal consequences of violating
that prohibition (y. AZ §§A–D) is that an Israelite may retain the ill-gotten
gains of a transaction with a Gentile that took place either during the three
days prior to, or even on, the festival day itself as long as the Israelite was
acquainted with the Gentile (presumably meaning that the Gentile is
known not to be an idolater). Profit earned from a transaction with a Gentile not known to the Israelite may not be retained, whether earned before
or on the holiday. To y. Avodah Zarah, the key is not *when* the unlawful
transaction occurred, but *with whom*. Y. Avodah Zarah carries this halakhic perspective over into its version of the story of R. Yudan (=Yehudah)
Nesiah in §§E–H. In §E, the story does not specify whether the *ducenarius*
sent the gift before or on the festival, which is an unimportant detail relative to the all-important detail of whether or not the Patriarch knew the
ducenarius. And, consequently, the anonymous voice is puzzled over Resh
Laqish's insistence that the Patriarch divest himself of the gift because he
knows the *ducenarius* (the gift should therefore be permitted whether before or on the festival) and the situation is after the fact (that is, the gift has
already been sent). Resh Laqish's stance is ultimately explained as a
"fence" around the Patriarch's conduct.

B. Avodah Zarah's recasting of this material in its §§A–F must be seen
in light of the first-generation Babylonian amora Shmuel's teaching that
"only their festival day itself is prohibited" (b. AZ 7b, 11b). Shmuel's teaching renders the three-day period of m. AZ 1:1 a dead letter, and also makes
it clear that (*contra* y. Avodah Zarah) what is important is *when* the transaction occurs, *not* whether or not the Israelite knows the Gentile. Examining
the R. Yohanan/Resh Laqish dispute in §§A–F, we see that despite their disagreement, both implicitly *agree* that an Israelite may not retain profit
earned on the festival day itself—as Shmuel directs—and nowhere in these
paragraphs is the issue of knowing the Gentile seen as significant. Moreover, b. Avodah Zarah in §I specifically points out that the *min* sent his gift
to the Patriarch *on the festival day*. Whereas y. Avodah Zarah could leave this
issue vague, b. Avodah Zarah cannot do so. To b. Avodah Zarah, if the gift
was sent prior to the festival, the Patriarch can keep it whether or not he
knows the *min*. B. Avodah Zarah must specify that the gift was sent on the
festival or else the story presents no issue worth discussing.

The story of R. Yudan Nesiah and Resh Laqish shows other evidence of Bavli reworking. Y. Avodah Zarah's *"ducenarius"* becomes b. Avodah Zarah's *"min"*[12] and y. Avodah Zarah's *"disqus"* (pouch) disappears completely from b. Avodah Zarah. It is hardly surprising that the Bavli would do away with the unfamiliar Greek terms, especially *"ducenarius,"* which refers to a political post unfamiliar to it.[13] Moreover, y. Avodah Zarah related that the *ducenarius* sent the Patriarch this *disqus* of coins from which he took one and returned the rest. By eliminating the *disqus,* b. Avodah Zarah also eliminated this prolix detail, and simply recounts that the *min* sent the Patriarch one *dinar.*

Y. Avodah Zarah's Patriarch is represented as simply "asking" Resh Laqish; we are not given the content of his question, and must assume (no doubt correctly) that he asked what he should do with the gift. B. Avodah Zarah's Patriarch is represented as asking a complex question in which he proposes alternative courses of action, each unsatisfactory for some reason. This sort of question, beginning "What should I do?" and followed by the presentation of undesirable alternatives, is found only in the Bavli: here at b. AZ 6b, later at 10b, and at b. Taan 5b.[14] Moreover, this sort of question—in which the Patriarch ponders and rejects alternatives—is

---

12. The terms מין (in Hebrew, or מינאה here in Aramaic), מינים, or מינות are found at b. AZ 4a, 4b, 6b, 16b (two occurrences), 17a (nine occurrences), 26b (four occurrences), 27b (two occurrences), 28a, and 65a. These terms are completely absent from y. AZ. This lopsided finding is interesting in light of Richard Kalmin's study of the importance of *minut* to the Palestinian rabbis; see his *Sage in Jewish Society*, 68–74. Even when we eliminate the Palestinian sources in which the terms are used from the Bavli, we still see cases—such as this one at 6b—in which the b. AZ redactors themselves added the term to a y. AZ source that did not employ it. Moreover, even though many of the occurrences of the terms in b. AZ are Palestinian, it is interesting that it was b. AZ, and not y. AZ, that elected to present those sources as part of the Talmud. This question calls for further research. We may perhaps understand why b. AZ substituted *min* here when we examine y. AZ's entire gemara to m. AZ 1:1 from the beginning to this parallel point. Y. AZ's opening aggadah consists of three distinct traditions about the biblical king Jeroboam and his introduction of idolatry to the Land of Israel. Although y. AZ does not use the term, Jeroboam—an Israelite—is clearly portrayed as a *min*, or "heretic." In adapting this material for inclusion in b. AZ, the redactors may have taken over the older Palestinian implicit introduction of *minut* and used it in their revision of this sugya as a replacement for the unfamiliar Greek term.

13. Nevertheless, there are cases in which Greek terms do appear in the Bavli. See, e.g., GenR 68:12 and b. Ber 56b (the story about Cappadocia).

14. For more on this, especially b. AZ's casting of the halakhic story of 6b and the aggadic story of 10b as intertexts of each other, see my "The Power Conferred by Distance from Power: Redaction and Meaning bAZ 10a–11a." To be included in

reminiscent of the increased turn to argumentation characteristic of the fourth Babylonian amoraic generation and later.[15] B. Avodah Zarah has re-invented the Palestinian Patriarch as a proto-fourth-generation amora. B. Avodah Zarah's Patriarch also conceptualizes the issue at stake in the acceptance or rejection of the gift at a higher level of abstraction than y. Avodah Zarah's Patriarch did. B. Avodah Zarah's Patriarch refers to "enmity" (איבה), which recurs as a factor to be considered in Jewish-Gentile relations at b. AZ 26a. This conceptual tag for the legal issue at stake is missing from y. Avodah Zarah.

Finally, y. Avodah Zarah's Resh Laqish advises R. Yudan Nesiah to dispose of the coin in the Dead Sea. B. Avodah Zarah logically alters this advice, since there is no Dead Sea in Babylonia. Instead, b. Avodah Zarah's Resh Laqish advises R. Yehudah Nesiah to toss the coin into a pit "as if off the back of the hand" (כלאחר יד). This term is found fifteen times, all in the Bavli,[16] and is thus a term that could only reasonably have been added to the sugya in Babylonia.

C. B. Avodah Zarah 6b §§J–AC ‖ Y. Avodah Zarah 1:1, 39b §§I–Z

Y. Avodah Zarah moves abruptly and without any transition from a discussion of unsecured loans (y. AZ §§R–V) to a discussion based on m. MQ 1:7 about a woman's application of cosmetic face paint during the intermediate days of a Jewish festival (y. AZ §§W–Z).[17] The redactors of b. Avodah Zarah effected a smooth transition to their version of the Moed Qatan material by adding the unattributed material we find in b. AZ §§V–Y, which does not exist in y. Avodah Zarah. While b. AZ §§V and W deal with issues that were not taken up in y. Avodah Zarah, §X seems repetitious, the issues at stake there having been satisfactorily resolved in b. AZ §§O–Q and S–U. The key is that while §§V and W build upon the older y. Avodah Zarah sugya, taking up issues not treated there, the redundant §X is designed to lead up to the idea of the Gentile's being "in pain now,"

Creation and Composition: The Contribution of the Bavli Redactors (Stammaim) to the Aggadah (ed. Jeffrey L. Rubenstein; Tübingen: Mohr Siebeck, forthcoming [2005]).

15. See, e.g., David Kraemer, *Mind of the Talmud*.

16. The term is found at b. Shab 40b, 62a, 81a, 153b; b. Pes 47b, 66b (three occurrences); b. Yev 114a; b. Ket 60a (two occurrences); b. AZ 6b; b. Zev 85b; b. Hul 141b; and b. Bekh 25a.

17. Y. AZ's Moed Qatan sugya originated at y. MQ 1:7, 80d. It was only brought over into y. AZ because of its use of R. Yehudah's view in m. AZ 1:1 to explain m. MQ 1:7.

which in turn paves the way for R. Yehudah's view about being "in pain now, but happy later" in §Y and then on to Moed Qatan. B. Avodah Zarah's introduction of the redundant §X shows that it had to have known y. AZ §§I–Q (which it supplemented with its own §§V and W), as well as the already-existing juxtaposition of that material to the Moed Qatan material—to which b. Avodah Zarah created a much-needed segue by means of b. AZ §X. B. Avodah Zarah's work here in creating this segue by means of §X caused a difference to appear in its order of materials as compared with y. Avodah Zarah's: whereas in y. Avodah Zarah the discussion of re-payment of unsecured loans *precedes* the Moed Qatan material, the order in b. Avodah Zarah had to be, of necessity, reversed.

When we understand how b. Avodah Zarah worked to create this segue to the Moed Qatan material, we see once again that the hypothesis of early talmud is flawed as an explanation of this case. There is no reason to assume that amoraim knew the y. Avodah Zarah sugya, or that amoraim composed the transitional §X. A proponent of early talmud may further object that the y. Avodah Zarah sugya may have become known in Babylonia during the amoraic period and revised there later in the post-amoraic period. But this hypothesis is too complicated because it requires us to posit two steps in the Babylonians' reception of this sugya: first, the amoraim knew it—for which we have no clear-cut evidence—and second, they passed it on to post-amoraic redactors. It is much simpler to posit a one-step reception: the sugya was created in Palestine by redactors there, and the results of their work became known to Babylonian post-amoraic redactors, who appropriated and reworked it.

The b. Avodah Zarah redactors also reworked the Moed Qatan material itself. Y. Avodah Zarah presents it (beginning "*It was taught there in a mishnah*") at §§W–Z. The connection between this material and m. AZ 1:1 is made only at the end, in §Z. The Moed Qatan material is obviously not directly relevant to m. AZ 1:1, and is largely taken up with the elucidation of which amora held which understanding of the dispute between R. Ye-hudah and the Sages in m. MQ 1:7. At b. Avodah Zarah §§Y–AA, by con-trast, the Bavli eliminates those parts of y. Avodah Zarah's Moed Qatan materials that are irrelevant to tractate Avodah Zarah, and introduces Moed Qatan in response to the anonymous question about whether R. Ye-hudah disagrees with the principle that "even though he is upset now, he will be happy later" (b. AZ §Y). Moreover, the interrogative formulation of R. Yehudah's position in §Y ("*And R. Yehudah disagrees* [with the princi-ple that] '*even though [the Gentile] is upset now, he will be happy later'?*") is due to the position of this question in the sugya. In §X, a position identical to R. Yehudah's view in m. AZ 1:1 was presented anonymously. Once "reminded" of R. Yehudah's position, the anonymous voice logically went on to ask in §Y whether R. Yehudah—the holder of the anonymous view rebutted in §X—disagrees with the "upset-happy" principle.[18]

Having reached the end of the micro analysis, we may summarize how the theory of early talmud fails to persuade. First, no amora in either Talmud is represented as being aware of the entire sugya *qua* sugya. There is thus no solid basis on which to claim that it was amoraim rather than post-amoraic scholars who transmitted it from Palestine to Babylonia. Second, one who wishes to argue that this shared sugya is early talmud must establish that amoraim did, in fact, transmit sugyot of this length, but current research does not promote confidence that they did so. Third, y. and b. Avodah Zarah are the *only two* rabbinic compilations in which this sugya is found. It is unclear what we gain by hypothesizing that both Talmuds drew this sequence from a hypothesized pool of shared rabbinic traditions when we can reach a conclusion based on the extant tractates we have, to wit, that b. Avodah Zarah drew the sequence of sugyot from y. Avodah Zarah.[19]

The micro analysis itself, in addition to the positive evidence it yields of how b. Avodah Zarah reworked y. Avodah Zarah, also yields evidence that constitutes the strongest argument against early talmud. As a result of the micro analysis, we see that b. Avodah Zarah carefully reworked y. Avodah Zarah's handling of the tannaitic dispute from Moed Qatan not only by streamlining that dispute itself, but also by reworking anonymous material it shared with y. Avodah Zarah in order to lay a groundwork for its change to the Moed Qatan material. It did this reworking in the context of a lengthy shared sugya in which it made other substantive changes. B. Avodah Zarah was thus not simply reworking and redeploying Palestinian rabbinic traditions also found in y. Avodah Zarah, it was reworking and re-presenting a sugya it appropriated from y. Avodah Zarah.

Having reached the end of a lengthy analysis, let us summarize. B. Avodah Zarah 6b ‖ y. AZ 1:1, 39b is a rich example that nicely illustrates all five of the ways b. Avodah Zarah characteristically reworked its y. Avodah Zarah sources: It

---

18. Before leaving b. AZ 6b ‖ y. AZ 1:1, 39b, there is one final revision of y. AZ by b. AZ that we should note: b. AZ's deployment of Abaye and Rava in its §§L–M, P–Q, and T–U. We find another example of this in the tractate at b. AZ 62a–b ‖ y. AZ 5:1, 44c and elsewhere in the Bavli at b. Ber 48a (‖ y. Ber 7:1, 11b and GenR 91:4) and b. Sanh 74a–75a (‖ y. Shevi 4:2, 35b). There are many more examples of the Bavli's addition of Abaye and Rava to its version of a given Palestinian sugya, and I intend to pursue this interesting issue in further research.

19. For a similar argument as it pertains to the relationship between Toseftan baraitot in the Bavli and the Tosefta, see Shamma Friedman, "Ha-baraitot she-be-Talmud ha-Bavli ve-yahasan le-Tosefta."

1. Introduces a Babylonian cultural or halakhic perspective or linguistic feature;

2. Eliminates materials that are too specific to the Palestinian context;

3. Re-arranges y. Avodah Zarah material in a more sensible order;

4. Combines and streamlines materials that y. Avodah Zarah had left distinct (such as the Moed Qatan and unsecured loans materials); and

5. Conceptualizes a legal issue at a higher level of abstraction.

Let us move on to consider these methods of reworking in relation to other examples in the tractates.

I
B. Avodah Zarah Reworks Y. Avodah Zarah to Introduce a Babylonian Cultural or Halakhic Perspective or Linguistic Feature

I.a. B. Avodah Zarah 8a ‖ Y. Avodah Zarah 1:2, 39c— The Primeval Origin of Kalends and Saturnalia

As we pointed out in Chapter 2, both Talmuds use an aggadic source about Adam—versions of the *same* aggadic source about Adam—as part of their treatments of the first clause of m. AZ 1:3: "And these are the festive-days of idolaters: Kalends and Saturnalia . . ." This example is a good illustration of how the different religious and cultural contexts in Palestine and Babylonia influenced the Talmuds' presentations of the Adam stories.

Y. Avodah Zarah 1:2, 39c

A. Rav said: "Kalends—the First Man (Adam) established it. When he saw the long nights [of winter] he said, 'Woe is me! Lest he [the serpent] of whom it is written (Gen 3:15): 'he will crush your head, and you will strike his heel,' come to bite me! If I say (Ps 139:11–12) 'surely the darkness will surround me [and thus I will be protected, that will not be because] . . . even the darkness will not be dark to you.'

B. "Once he saw the days getting longer, he said: 'Kalends!—*kalon deo*! What a beautiful (*kalon*) day (*diem*)!'"

C. *And* [this story] *goes well according to the one who says that the world was cre-ated in Tishrei* [because then Adam would not yet have had the experience of the days getting longer]. *But according to the one who says the world was created in Nisan* [i.e., spring], *he* [Adam] *knew!* [If the world had been cre-ated in spring, then Adam would have been aware that the natural order is to have long days and short nights, followed later by short days and long nights.]

D. R. Yose b. R. Bun said: "Who is it who holds that the world was created at the New Year [in Tishrei]? Rav; as it was taught in the [verses recited with the] shofar blasts of the house of Rav: 'This is the day of the beginning of Your activity; a remembrance of the first day.' So it was at New Year's that the world was created."

The Yerushalmi also uses this story at y. Ber 8:6, 12b to explain why a blessing must be recited over fire at the conclusion of the Sabbath. Al-though the context is clearly different, y. Berakhot is clearly working with y. Avodah Zarah's version of the story:

Y. Berakhot 8:6, 12b

A. And the First Man (Adam) would gaze with it [the primordial light cre-ated on the first day of creation] from one end of the earth to the other. Since the light did not cease, the entire world began to sing [in praise] . . .

B. When the week departed [and the Sabbath began], the darkness began to roll in. And Adam was afraid and said, "Lest the one of whom it is writ-ten (Gen 3:15), 'He will crush your head, and you will strike his heel,' come to bite me!" If I say, 'Surely the darkness will surround me' (Ps 139:11) [to protect me, the darkness will not protect me because 'even the darkness will not be dark' (Ps 139:12)]."

C. R. Levi said: "At that hour, God prepared two flints which he struck against each other and produced fire. It is that which is written 'And the night is lighted up for me' (Ps 139:11). And [Adam] blessed over it [the blessing] 'Who created the lights of fire.'"

D. Shmuel said: "Therefore we bless over fire at the ends of Sabbaths, for that was the beginning of its [fire's] creation."

Despite the different uses to which the two Yerushalmi tractates have put the story, the version with which both are working is the same. In both stories, Adam is frightened by the approaching darkness because of his concern that the serpent will bite him, and he expresses his fear by citing Gen 3:15 and Ps 139:11. Yet he is cheered by the coming of light—longer days in y. Avodah Zarah or God's fire in y. Berakhot—and his renewed spirit causes him to exclaim in joy. In y. Avodah Zarah, that exclamation takes the form of a Greek outburst proclaiming the beauty of the day, while in y. Berakhot he recites a blessing over the fire. Interestingly, in both stories his joyous outburst is considered to be the establishment of a human institution: Kalends in y. Avodah Zarah and the blessing over fire at the end of the Sabbath in y. Berakhot.

Let us now examine the Adam stories in the Bavli.

B. Avodah Zarah 8a

A. *Our Rabbis taught*: **Since the First Man saw the day growing progressively shorter, he said, "Woe is me! Since I sinned, the world is getting dark because of me and is returning to primordial chaos. And this is the death that was imposed on me from Heaven." He undertook to sit for eight days in fasting and prayer. When he saw the winter solstice, and saw the day growing progressively longer, he said: "This is the way of the world." He went ahead and established eight festive days. The next year he made both these** [the eight days prior to the solstice, which he had spent in fasting] **and these** [the eight days he had established as a festival] **as festive days** [the first set of eight became Saturnalia, the second Kalends]. [Adam] **established them for the sake of Heaven; they** [the idolaters] **established them for the sake of idolatry.**

B. *This works well according to the one who says that the world was created in Tishrei.* [Thus] *he saw short days,* [but] *he still had not seen long days. But according to the one who says that the world was created in Nisan, he saw short days and long days!*

C. [Yet] *he still had not seen days that were especially short.*

D. *Our Rabbis taught*: **On the day in which Adam was created, once he saw the sun setting over him, he said: "Woe is me! Since I sinned, the world is getting dark on me, and will return to the primordial chaos, and this is the death that is imposed on me from Heaven." He sat in fasting and cried all night, and Eve cried alongside him. Once the dawn star rose, he said: "It is the way of the world." He got up and offered a bull whose horns stretched out beyond its hooves, as it is said: "This will please the Lord more than an ox, more than a bull with its horns and hooves."** (Ps 69:32).

Sections A and D in b. Avodah Zarah are Adam stories which differ from each other, as well as from y. Avodah Zarah's Adam stories. The story in §A fits well into the context of the mishnah as an explication of the origins of Kalends and Saturnalia. The story in §D is related to §A—since both are stories about Adam's reaction to the approach of darkness—but not to the mishnah, since it does not provide an etiology of Kalends and Saturnalia. A version of §D also exists in version A of Avot de-Rabbi Natan (ARNA)[20] as part of a collection of Adam legends, and the story's

---

20. *Avot de-Rabbi Natan* (ed. Shneur Zalman Schechter; New York: Jewish Theological Seminary, 1967; repr., New York: Jewish Theological Seminary, 1997), 4.

picturesque reference to the bull whose "horns stretch out farther than its hooves" is also found at b. Hul 60a and b. Shab 28b.

Avot de-Rabbi Natan A 1

> Toward evening, the First Man saw the world leaning toward the west. He said: "Woe is me! Since I sinned, God is darkening the world over me"—and he did not know that this is the way of the world. Toward morning, when he saw the world getting lighter and inclining east, he rejoiced with a great joy. He got up and built altars and offered a bull whose horns stretched out farther than its hooves as a burnt-offering [citing Ps 69:32].

There are, then, three versions of this Adam story: the Yerushalmi version, the version of b. AZ 8a §A, and the version of §D, which in turn has a parallel at ARNA 1, and partial parallels at b. Hul 60a and b. Shab 28b. Interestingly, the version that b. Avodah Zarah used to explain the origin of Kalends was not the more widespread (at least judging by its frequency of appearance in the Bavli and Avot de-Rabbi Natan) version of §D, but rather, the version of §A. This may provide a clue as to why b. Avodah Zarah presented the version of §D at all. Examination of §D and its parallels shows that the issue of the sacrificial animal's *horns*—whether unnaturally long or unnaturally located—is a key and picturesque feature of that version, not to mention the climax of the story. A story meant to end with the sacrifice of such an unusual animal is not the best story to adapt as an illustration of a totally different concept—the establishment of Saturnalia and Kalends. Nevertheless, the story could not be omitted; its presence in three Bavli tractates as well as ARNA shows that it had some currency. Thus the Bavli redactors, *after* presenting a version of the Adam story that establishes the origins of the pagan holidays, appends what was probably a better-known version of the Adam story.

Yet even the version of the story that the Bavli utilized to explicate the mishnah in Avodah Zarah differs from that found in y. Avodah Zarah, which again raises the question of whether b. Avodah Zarah's editorial decision to use a version of the story derived from y. Avodah Zarah at all. The answer to this implicit question is a likely "yes." Earlier, in chapter 2, we noted that both Talmuds integrate their Adam stories in very similar redactional contexts. Both Talmuds follow the stories with anonymous gemara that establishes that the story works well if one assumes that the world was created in Tishrei, but not if the assumption is that the creation took place in Nisan (y. AZ §C, b. AZ §§B–C). The placement of this shared anonymous material after the story used to establish the origin of Kalends (and Saturnalia, in b. Avodah Zarah) is found only in the Avodah Zarah tractates and in no other place in which the story appears. Moreover, both Talmuds follow the story with accounts of a dispute between R. Yohanan and Rav (y. Avodah Zarah) or R. Matana (b. Avodah Zarah) about whether commercial transactions prohibited during Kalends and Saturnalia are prohibited with *all* Gentiles (whether or not they are celebrating) or only with those in the particular place observing the festivities. Finally, nothing in m. AZ 1:3 calls for aggadah at all. The common decision to place aggadic material here—which, although not identical, deals in both Talmuds with Adam's fear of the approaching darkness and his establishment of Kalends and Saturnalia—is more likely to have been the result of b. Avodah Zarah's editorial reflection on the path taken by y. Avodah Zarah.

Why then did b. Avodah Zarah not use y. Avodah Zarah's version? From a cultural perspective, the Bavli editors would have been unlikely to take over Adam's alleged Greek exclamation, which argues in favor of conscious Babylonian reworking of the Adam source. Looking more carefully at the two Talmuds' stories, we can see more evidence of likely Bavli reworking. Y. Avodah Zarah's Adam establishes the holidays *prior* to his disobedience of the divine commandment, while b. Avodah Zarah's Adam did so *after* his disobedience ("since I sinned"). B. Avodah Zarah's sequence of events is more sensible: only after his sin, when he must leave Eden and establish human society, would Adam be likely to establish human institutions such as holidays. Also, given that Adam is establishing (albeit unintentionally) what ultimately becomes a Roman holiday, b. Avodah Zarah's attribution of this establishment to a sinful Adam is more sensible than y. Avodah Zarah's attribution of it to a sinless Adam. Moreover, once Adam's establishment of Kalends and Saturnalia is placed *after* his sin, the nature of his fears and how he expresses them must change. While the quotation of scriptural verses attributed to Adam in y. Avodah Zarah expresses his (pre-disobedience) fear of the serpent and the darkness, Adam's (post-disobedience) fear in b. Avodah Zarah is less the serpent and darkness, and more the cosmic consequences of his awful sin. As a result, b. Avodah Zarah's Adam need not—and does not—quote the scriptural verses quoted by his Yerushalmi predecessor.

Yet, interesting as these differences are, they nevertheless do not (by themselves) prove that the b. Avodah Zarah redactors deliberately introduced these changes into y. Avodah Zarah. We must look for additional evidence that demonstrates the reasonableness of the assumption that y. Avodah Zarah is more likely than b. Avodah Zarah to present the image of a pre-disobedience Adam. When we examine the extant references in the Yerushalmi to אדם הראשון,[21] we find that none of the stories discusses a sinful Adam. The closest the Yerushalmi comes to a sinning Adam is the

---

21. Y. Ber 8:5, 12b; 9:1, 12d; 9:1, 13c (two occurrences); y. Shab 2:6, 5b (three occurrences); and y. Naz 7:2, 56b (three occurrences).

tradition at y. Naz 7:2, 56b that Adam was created from the dust of the site of the future Temple altar, which gives him the hope of "standing" (עמידה). In the Bavli, by contrast, seven[22] of the forty-two references to Adam[23] refer either to his disobedience, his punishment, or, interestingly, his heresy(!). This distinction between the Talmuds suggests that y. Avodah Zarah is indeed more likely to present the image of a sinless Adam, while b. Avodah Zarah may be more inclined to discuss his sinfulness. This distinction between the rabbinic centers may have much to do with the Palestinians' encounter with Christianity, which takes the primordial sin of Adam to be the sinful blot on humanity that only Christ can efface. By de-emphasizing his sin, the Palestinian rabbis protect themselves from the attacks of those (Jews and Bible-reading non-Jews) who would emphasize the sinfulness of Adam and draw Christological conclusions from it.[24] This concern is not as much of an issue for the Babylonians, whose contacts with Christianity appear to have been much more limited and infrequent.[25]

I.b.   B. Avodah Zarah 35b–36a, 37a ‖ Y. Avodah Zarah 2:9, 41d ‖ Y. Shabbat 1:6, 3c–d—Gentile Oil

Both Talmuds place this sugya in connection with m. AZ 2:6. The pertinent part of this mishnah reads as follows:

> And these are the items of idolaters which are forbidden, but their prohibition is not a prohibition of benefit: the milk that an idolater milked without a Jew seeing him, and their bread and oil. Rabbi and his court permitted oil.[26]

---

22. B. Ber 40a; b. Shab 55b; b. Eruv 18b; b. BB 75b; b. Sanh 38b, 70a, and 70b.

23. The other references are: b. Ber 31a (two occurrences), 34b, 58a (two occurrences); b. Shab 28b; b. Eruv 18b; b. Pes 54b; b. Hag 12a (two occurrences); b. Sot 46b (three occurrences); b. BB 14b, 75a; b. Sanh 37a, 38a (three occurrences), 38b (three occurrences in addition to the one mentioned), 56b, 59b (two occurrences), 70a, 100a; b. AZ 8a (three occurrences), 11b; b. Hul 60a (two occurrences), 60b; and b. Nid 45b.

24. My finding about the Yerushalmi's "sinless" Adam versus the Bavli's "sinful" Adam is consistent with Richard Kalmin's findings that the Bavli and Palestinian sources often take different positions on whether various biblical figures are to be viewed positively or negatively. See his *Sage in Jewish Society*, 83–109.

25. See Kalmin, *Sage in Jewish Society*, 70; idem, "Christians and Heretics in Rabbinic Literature of Late Antiquity," *HTR* 87:2 (1994): 155–169.

26. Medieval scholars held that the mishnaic phrase "Rabbi and his court permitted oil" is not an authentic part of the mishnah. Rashi (b. AZ 35b, s.v. רבי ובית דינו התירו בשמן) argues against the authenticity of the phrase on the ground that the lifting of the prohibition against Gentile oil is attributed at 37a to Rabbi's grand-

Let us begin with a comparison of y. Avodah Zarah to its y. Shabbat parallel.

Y. Avodah Zarah 2:9, 41d

A. *Who prohibited oil?*

B. R. Yehudah said: "Daniel prohibited it—[as it says in Dan 1:8,] 'And Daniel took it to heart not to be defiled with the portion of the king's bread nor with the wine of his drinking . . .'"

C. *And who permitted it?*

D. *Rabbi and his court permitted it. In three places R. Yehudah ha-Nasi is called "רבותינו" (our Rabbis): [with regard to] bills of divorce, and oil, and sandals. And they called him "the court that permitted [Gentile] oil." Every court that permits three things is called a "permissive court."*

E. R. Yudan said: "[R. Yehudah ha-Nasi's] court disagreed with him with respect to bills of divorce."

[The Talmud goes on to illustrate R. Yudan's contention that R. Yehudah ha-Nasi's court disagreed with him about bills of divorce].

F. "Shall she be permitted to marry [immediately upon learning of her husband's death, or must she wait until 12 months had expired]?"

G. R. Haggai said: "She is permitted to marry [immediately]."

H. R. Yose said: "She is forbidden to marry [immediately]."

I. R. Aha, R. Tanhum b. Hiyya in the name of R. Hanina, and some say it in the name of R. Yehoshua b. Levi: "[Daniel refused to eat the king's oil because he saw that] they [people sentenced to death by the king] would go up to the king's mountain and be killed upon it." [Consequently, Daniel refused to eat oil made from olives that had grown on such a place of bloodshed].

J. Yitshaq b. Shmuel b. Marta went down to Netsivin. He found Simlai the Southerner sitting and expounding: "Rabbi and his court permitted [Gentile] oil."

---

son, R. Yehudah Nesiah; the Tosafot (b. AZ 36a, s.v. אשר) make a similar argument. The Rashba, in his *novellae* to b. AZ 36a, made an interesting argument that Shmuel's failure to recite that mishnaic phrase to Rav (in support of his view that Gentile oil is permitted) is a telling proof of the inauthenticity of the attribution of the permission to Rabbi. The instincts of these rishonim are borne out by the JTS ms., which does not include the phrase in the mishnah, although it does appear in the mishnah of the Leiden ms. of the Yerushalmi. See also David Rosenthal, "*Mishna Aboda Zara*: A Critical Edition (with Introduction)" (Ph.D. diss., Hebrew University, 1971), 34 (Heb.). For a weak argument that the phrase is indeed an authentic part of the mishnah, see Martin Goodman, "Kosher Olive Oil in Antiquity," in *A Tribute to Geza Vermes: Essays on Jewish and Christian Literature and History* (ed. Philip R. Davies and Richard T. White; Sheffield, UK: JSOT, 1990), 227–245. My thanks to Dr. Lisa Grushcow for providing me with this reference.

K. [So] said Shmuel [=Simlai recited his learning before Shmuel, who accepted it], but Rav did not accept upon himself to eat [Gentile oil].[27]

L. Shmuel said to him [Rav]: "Eat, for if not, I will proclaim you to be a זקן ממרא (rebellious elder)."

M. He [Rav] said to him: "While I was there [in Palestine], I knew that it was Simlai the Southerner who was objecting to it [the prohibition on Gentile oil]." [Rav is saying that Simlai's objections to the prohibition are of no account.]

N. [Shmuel] said to him: "Did the master [Simlai] state it in his own name? No, in the name of R. Yudan Nesiah." [Thus, Rav cannot be more pious in this matter than the Patriarch.] He prevailed upon him and he ate.

O. R. Yohanan asked: "Did we not learn in the mishnah [m. Eduy 1:5]: **A court cannot invalidate the words of another court unless it be greater than it in wisdom and number?** And [nevertheless] Rabbi and his court permit what Daniel and his companions prohibited?"

P. *R. Yohanan is consistent with his own opinion. R. Yohanan said:* "I have received from R. Lazar b. R. Tsadoq that every decree that a court decrees and that most of the community do not accept upon themselves is not a [valid] decree." *They investigated and found with regard to his* [Daniel's] *decree about* [Gentile] *oil and did not find that most of the community accepted it upon themselves.*

Y. Shabbat 1:6, 3c–d

In y. Shabbat, this sugya is attached to m. Shab 1:4:

And these are among the laws that were stated in the upper-chamber of Hananiah b. Hezekiah b. Gurion when they went up to visit him. The House of Shammai outvoted the House of Hillel, and they decreed eighteen matters on that very day.

Among the items about which "they decreed" were Gentile bread, cheese, oil, and daughters, Gentile seminal emissions and urine, the laws of בעל קרי ([Jewish] seminal emissions), and the laws of the lands of the [Gentile] nations. The Yerushalmi then proceeds to take up these items in order.

Y. Shabbat 1:6, 3d

[Bold paragraph-designations show the order of these materials within y. AZ 2:9, 41d]

A. *Who prohibited oil?*

---

27. The first half of this sentence is not found in the parallel in y. Shab 1:6, 3d. Its presence here in y. AZ is almost certainly a scribal error. The sentence should read as it does in y. Shab.

B.   R. Yehudah said: "Daniel prohibited oil—[as it says in Dan 1:8,] 'And Daniel took it to heart not to be defiled with the portion of the king's bread nor with the wine of his drinking . . .'"

I.   R. Aha, R. Tanhum b. Hiyya in the name of R. Hanina, and some say it in the name of R. Yehoshua b. Levi: "[Daniel refused to eat the king's oil because he saw that] they [people sentenced to death by the king] would go up with him to the king's mountain and be killed upon it." [Consequently, Daniel refused to eat oil made from olives that had grown in such a place of bloodshed.]

C.   *And who permitted it?*

D.   *Rabbi and his court permitted oil. In three places R. Yehudah ha-Nasi is called "רבותינו" (our Rabbis):* [with regard to] *bills of divorce, and oil, and sandals. And they called him "the court that permitted* [Gentile] *oil." Every court that nullifies three things is called a "permissive court."*

E.   R. Yudan said: "[R. Yehudah ha-Nasi's] court disagreed with him with respect to bills of divorce."

O.   R. Yohanan asked: "Did we not learn in the mishnah [m. Eduy 1:5]: **A court cannot invalidate the words of another court unless it be greater than it in wisdom and number**? And [nevertheless] Rabbi and his court permit what Daniel and his association prohibited?"

P.   *Rather, R. Yohanan is consistent with his own opinion. And R. Yohanan said in the name of R. Lazar b. R. Tsadoq:* "I have received [the tradition] that every decree that a court decrees on the community and that most of the community do not accept upon themselves is not a [valid] decree."

Q.   *They investigated and found with regard to the decree about* [Gentile] *oil that most of the community had not accepted it upon themselves.*

J.   Yitshaq b. Shmuel b. Marta went down to Netsivin. He found Simlai the Southerner sitting and expounding: "Rabbi and his court permitted [Gentile] oil."

K.   Shmuel accepted it upon himself and ate [the Gentile oil], but Rav did not eat [the Gentile oil].

L.   Shmuel said to him [Rav]: "Eat, for if not, I will proclaim you to be a זקן ממרא (rebellious elder)."

M.   He [Rav] said to him: "While I was there [in Palestine], I knew that it was R. Simlai the Southerner who was objecting to it [the prohibition on Gentile oil]." [Rav is saying that Simlai's objections to the prohibition are of no account.]

N.   [Shmuel said to him]: "What, did he [Simlai] state it in his own name? No, in the name of Rabbi and his court." [Thus, Rav cannot be more pious in this matter than the Patriarch.] He prevailed upon him and he ate.

When we compare the two Yerushalmi versions of this sugya, we see that it is composed of distinct sources about Gentile oil that have been skillfully combined into one lengthy sequence. Y. Shabbat is clearly the better-organized of the two. Y. Avodah Zarah leaps back and forth in §§A–I between the original prohibitor of Gentile oil (Daniel in §§A–B), the one who permitted it (Rabbi in §§C–D), a digression from Gentile oil (§§E–H), and a return to Daniel's reason for the prohibition (§I). Y. Avodah Zarah also appends R. Yohanan's discussion of m. Eduy 1:5 (which also relates to the weighing of the relative authorities of Daniel and Rabbi) to the Rav and Shmuel conflict, to which it is unrelated. Y. Shabbat, by contrast, groups together all the materials that discuss Daniel's prohibition of the oil *before* moving on to discuss Rabbi's lifting of the prohibition. In addition, y. Shabbat minimizes the digression from Gentile oil (§D), and places R. Yohanan's discussion of m. Eduy 1:5 where it belongs—at the spot in the sugya at which we see the conflict between the authority of Daniel and that of Rabbi.

Using the better-organized y. Shabbat version, we can discern four sources within this lengthy sugya:

1. §§A, B, and I (Daniel is the original prohibitor of Gentile oil);

2. §§C–E (R. Yehudah ha-Nasi permitted Gentile oil and was called the "court that had permitted oil");

3. §§O–Q (R. Yohanan wondered on the basis of m. Eduy 1:5 how the Patriarch could have overturned Daniel's decree; investigation revealed that the decree about oil had not spread); and

4. §§J–N (the Rav and Shmuel dispute about Gentile oil).

Y. Avodah Zarah §§F–H is a fifth source explaining more about the dispute between Rabbi and his court about divorces. As was pointed out, y. Shabbat logically omitted this since it is not at all relevant to the main subject, Gentile oil.

Looking beyond its constituent parts to its overall message, y. Shab 1:6, 3d presents conflicting views about Patriarchal authority, with the abrogation of the prohibition of Gentile oil being merely the issue through which the conflict is expressed. Although the prohibition is traced back to biblical times, the Patriarch overturns it, which argues *for* his authority. Yet the sugya also claims that the Patriarch's rescission of the prohibition causes him to be tagged as the "court that permitted oil," which is not a positive appellation. Moreover, the sugya undercuts Patriarchal authority by pointing out that the permissive ruling is ultimately grounded not in any action of his, but in the people's refusal to accept the prohibition of Gentile oil. Yet the sugya ends on the note that one major Babylonian sage accepted the Patriarch's ruling and even compelled another to do so by threatening him with "rebellious elder" status—which again strongly reasserts Patriarchal authority. From a literary point of view, the sugya ends at exactly the opposite point from which it began: it opened with the exiled Daniel in Persia prohibiting Gentile oil, and ends with the Babylonian sages living under Persian hegemony accepting the Patriarch's reversal of that prohibition.

Which (if either) is the original version of the sugya: y. Shabbat or y. Avodah Zarah? Y. Avodah Zarah's inferior organization is a convincing argument in favor of its being the original version. An editor would have had little to gain by incorporating the y. Shabbat version into y. Avodah Zarah and rearranging it so as to make it flow *less* smoothly; on the other hand, an editor would have had much to gain by incorporating the y. Avodah Zarah version into y. Shabbat and rearranging it so as to make it flow *more* smoothly.

B. Avodah Zarah 35b–36b

A. Oil—Rav said: "Daniel decreed about it," and Shmuel said, "The oozing [into the oil] of [residues of] unclean [liquids from the] vessels [into the oil] made it forbidden."

B. *As to the whole world—are they eaters of purities? Rather,* [Shmuel said]: "The oozing of [residues of] forbidden [liquids from oil] vessels made it [oil] forbidden."

C. Shmuel said to Rav: "It works out well according to me, who says that the oozing of [residues of] forbidden vessels made it [oil] forbidden. That is [consistent with] when R. Yitshaq b. Shmuel b. Marta came and said: 'R. Simlai expounded in Netsivin [concerning Gentile oil], 'Oil—R. Yehudah and his court voted on it and permitted it.' He [R. Yehudah and his court] holds 'נותן טעם לפגם מותר' [taste imparted by a forbidden food item which does not improve the dish into which the taste was imparted is permitted].

D. "But according to you [Shmuel continues], who said that Daniel decreed about it [Gentile oil]—Daniel decreed and R. Yehudah the Prince and his court came and invalidated it? Is it not taught in a mishnah [m. Eduy 1:5]: **One court cannot invalidate the words of another court unless it be greater than it in wisdom and in number?**"

E. He [Rav] said to him: "Simlai the Loddite, you said? The Loddites are different, for they make light [of rabbinic prohibitions]."

F. He [Shmuel] said to him: "I will send for him" [i.e., Simlai; presumably to tell him what Rav had said].

G. He [Rav] was embarrassed. He said: "If they [R. Yehudah ha-Nasi and his court] did not expound [a scriptural verse in order to permit Gentile oil], shall we not expound [a scriptural verse in order to support the prohibition of Gentile oil]? And was it not written [Dan 1:8]: 'And Daniel set it on his heart not to pollute himself with the portion of the king's bread nor with the wine of his drinking'? The verse is talking about two 'drinkings' [משתאות, which is in the plural]; one is a משתה of wine, and one a משתה of oil.'"

H. *Rav holds that* [Daniel] *"placed"* [שם, from the verse] *on his heart, and ruled for all Israel* [that Gentile oil is prohibited]. *And Shmuel holds that* [Daniel] *"placed" on his heart, but did not rule for all Israel.*

[The Bavli now questions whether Daniel was really the source of the prohibition, and posits that perhaps Gentile oil was among the eighteen items forbidden by the students of Hillel and Shammai. It resolves that Daniel forbade Gentile oil in the city, while the students of Hillel and Shammai forbade it even outside. The Bavli then questions how R. Yehudah ha-Nasi could have permitted something forbidden by these students in light of m. Eduy 1:5 and in light of a tradition of R. Yohanan that the eighteen prohibited items can under no circumstances be permitted. We now continue.]

I. R. Mesharshya said: "What is the reason [that the eighteen items forbidden by the students of Hillel and Shammai can never be permitted]? Because their prohibition spread throughout [i.e., was accepted by] most of Israel. The prohibition of [Gentile] oil did not spread throughout most of Israel."

J. As R. Shmuel b. Abba said in the name of R. Yohanan: "Our Rabbis sat and checked concerning [Gentile] oil that its prohibition had not spread throughout most of Israel. And our Rabbis relied on the words of R. Shimon b. Gamliel and on R. Eleazar b. Tsadoq who said: **'We do not decree a decree on the community unless most of the community can abide by it.'**"

[A scriptural derivation of this principle in the name of R. Ada b. Ahavah follows.]

We will first compare b. Avodah Zarah to y. Avodah Zarah to note the similarities, beginning with overall structural similarities in the way the constituent parts of the sugya are arranged. B. Avodah Zarah opens with a Rav/Shmuel dispute about the origin of the prohibition, with Rav taking the position attributed in y. Avodah Zarah to his disciple, R. Yehudah; to wit, that Daniel is the source of the prohibition. What is interesting is that b. Avodah Zarah has taken over y. Avodah Zarah's editorial decision to juxtapose m. Eduy 1:5 *to* the Rav/Shmuel dispute, rather than place it *prior* to it, as y. Shabbat did. B. Avodah Zarah also resembles y. Avodah Zarah in placing R. Eleazar b. Tsadoq's (=R. Lazar b. R. Tsadoq) teaching that a decree that does not gain acceptance is not a valid decree *after* the Rav/Shmuel dispute, rather than before it, as y. Shabbat did.

Yet we must also analyze some similarities between b. Avodah Zarah and y. Shabbat. As in y. Shabbat, b. Avodah Zarah has excised the extraneous discussion about Rabbi's disagreement with his colleagues about divorce, dealing with that at b. AZ 37a. But it is just as likely that the y. Shabbat and b. Avodah Zarah redactors independently decided to excise this material in the interest of creating a smooth sugya. This alone does not demonstrate b. Avodah Zarah's reliance on y. Shabbat—there is a stronger potential link between the two: b. Avodah Zarah demonstrates awareness of the connection between Gentile oil and the "eighteen matters" of m. Shab 1:4. This is clear not merely from the fact that b. Avodah Zarah considers the issue of the "eighteen matters" right after its conclusion to the Rav/Shmuel dispute, but also from the fact that most of b. AZ 36b is taken up with the issue of who prohibited sexual relations with Gentile women on what basis, which y. Shab 1:6, 3d takes up right after the conclusion of the Rav/Shmuel dispute.

B. Avodah Zarah's similarity to both y. Avodah Zarah and y. Shabbat would seem to militate in favor of a theory that b. Avodah Zarah was influenced neither by y. Avodah Zarah nor by y. Shabbat, but by a sugya now unavailable to us that was similar to and yet distinct from both. However, b. Avodah Zarah's interest in the "eighteen matters" could have come from within itself, and need not have come from a (now non-existent) version of the Palestinian sugya on Gentile oil that was set within the "eighteen matters" context. At b. AZ 36a the Bavli places the scholar Bali's tradition about the eighteen matters after the Rav and Shmuel dispute. Bali's tradition is found at b. Shab 17b—and, significantly, *not* at y. Shab 1:4, 3d—where it is part of a larger sugya about the "eighteen matters" attached to m. Shab 1:4. Bali's tradition and the sugya of which it is a part build directly on m. Shab 1:4, and thus are called for by that mishnah. From there, b. Avodah Zarah could easily have imported the tradition into b. AZ 36a, utilized it in a larger "eighteen matters" discussion, and then re-quoted it for use as the basis of a large sugya on intermarriage at 36b–37a. Thus b. AZ 35b–36b's similarity to y. Shabbat in respect of the "eighteen matters" can reasonably be construed as the result of the work of b. Avodah Zarah's redactors within their own Talmud.

B. Avodah Zarah differs from both y. Avodah Zarah and y. Shabbat as well. First, it defers to 37a not only its consideration of Rabbi's argument with his colleagues about divorce, but also the notion that Rabbi was called "רבותינו," that his court was the one that had "permitted oil," and that a court that permits three things is "permissive." Whereas y. Shabbat and y. Avodah Zarah had placed their considerations of these matters within the sugya on Gentile oil, directly before the Simlai tradition (y. AZ §§D–H and y. Shab §§C–D), b. Avodah Zarah improved on this arrangement by moving these issues out of the sugya completely, thus allowing for an uninterrupted treatment of the subject of Gentile oil.

The other major difference between b. AZ 35b–36a and y. AZ 2:9, 41d is the differences in the Rav/Shmuel dispute. The version in b. Avodah Zarah differs in five ways from y. Avodah Zarah's version of this dispute.

First, Shmuel's relaxation of the prohibition against Gentile oil in y. Avodah Zarah is based solely on R. Yehudah ha-Nasi's having permitted it, as related by Simlai. By contrast, Shmuel's opinion in b. Avodah Zarah is that the oil should be permitted because the prohibition was due only to the rabbinic prohibition of "the oozing of [residues of] forbidden [liquids from oil] vessels," and that, moreover, R. Yehudah ha-Nasi had held נותן טעם לפגם מותר (as demonstrated by his relaxation of the prohibition as per the Simlai tradition). By recasting Shmuel's opinion in this way, b. Avodah Zarah has implicated him (and R. Yehudah ha-Nasi) in the thorny issue of נותן טעם לפגם מותר או אסור, a major issue of concern later at b. AZ 67a–b. Moreover, b. Avodah Zarah has attributed to them the view it seems to prefer at 67b—נותן טעם לפגם מותר.

Second, the anonymous voice challenges the initial presentation of Shmuel's view (§B) by asking: "As to the whole world—are they eaters of purities?" The expression I have translated as "as to the whole world" is אטו כולי עלמא. This expression appears six times in the Bavli,[28] but neither it nor an equivalent appear in the Yerushalmi. B. Avodah Zarah has thus added a uniquely Babylonian expression to y. Avodah Zarah, which of course makes b. Avodah Zarah look different from its predecessor.[29]

Third, Shmuel discomfits Rav in y. Avodah Zarah, y. Shabbat, and b. Avodah Zarah. In y. Avodah Zarah he threatens to have him declared a "rebellious elder," while in b. Avodah Zarah Rav ends his encounter with Shmuel feeling "embarrassed" (איכסיף). Interestingly (if unsurprisingly), both Talmuds have expressed Rav's discomfiture in culturally specific ways.[30] Of seven occurrences of the term זקן ממרא in the Bavli,[31] none involve one sage using the term against another, while of six occurrences of the phrase in the Yerushalmi[32] there are four occurrences (two stories and their parallels) in which one sage uses the term against another. As to Rav's "embarrassment" in b. Avodah Zarah, Jeffrey Rubenstein has recently discussed the importance of honor and shame among the post-amoraic Bavli redactors.[33] In reworking the Palestinian "oven of Hakhinai"

28. In addition to b. AZ 36a, it also appears at b. Ber 18b, b. Shab 85a, b. BB 88b, b. Mak 5b, and b. Hul 15a.

29. See Jeffrey Rubenstein's discussion of this phenomenon in *Talmudic Stories,* 196.

30. Recent studies exploring the culturally specific nature of portrayals of rabbis in the Talmuds are Kalmin's *Sage in Jewish Society* and Rubenstein's *Talmudic Stories.*

31. b. Sot 25a and 45a; b. Sanh 16a, 86b, 87a, and 88b (two occurrences).

32. y. Shab 1:4, 3d (‖ y. AZ 2:9, 41d); y. Yev 10:5, 11a (‖ y. Git 8:7, 49c); y. Sanh 8:6, 26b, y. Sanh 11:3, 30a.

33. See Rubenstein, *Talmudic Stories,* 34–63, 275–277.

tradition into the famous story we now know as the "oven of Akhnai" (b. BM 59a–b), as well as others such as that of Honi the Circle-Drawer (b. Taan 23a) and R. Kahana (b. BQ 117a–b), the Bavli redactors emphasized the protagonists' feelings of shame or disgrace. To Rubenstein, this emphasis on shame is directly related to the Bavli editors' emphasis on the sharp give-and-take of dialectical argumentation in their academies and the intense, public shame that a scholar could suffer if he failed to hold his own in such encounters. B. Avodah Zarah's imputation of such "embarrassment" to Rav at b. AZ 36a could thus be a conscious revision of y. Avodah Zarah to make the older source conform to the cultural norms of the redactors responsible for fixing the sugya into its place.

The fourth difference between the Talmuds' accounts of the Rav/ Shmuel dispute is that whereas y. Avodah Zarah's Rav yields to Shmuel and eats the Gentile oil, b. Avodah Zarah's Rav offers an interpretation of Dan 1:8 that justifies his continued avoidance of the oil. Rav's refusal to yield to Shmuel in b. Avodah Zarah certainly makes sense in light of the greater decentralization of the Babylonian amoraic movement and the differences between Babylonia and Palestine on the issue of the diversity of practice and/or opinion. As Richard Kalmin has pointed out, Babylonian rabbis "presided over their own 'fiefdoms,'" and on the rare occasions when dominant rabbis encountered each other and their different views, conflict and confusion tended to result.[34]

Finally, b. Avodah Zarah reworks and eliminates the pro-Patriarchal polemic we had noted in our discussion of y. Shabbat. I pointed out earlier that the Palestinian sugya, particularly in the y. Shabbat version, presented a polemic against the prohibition of Gentile oil that emphasized the Patriarch's authority to rescind the prohibition. One Babylonian sage (Shmuel) willingly acquiesced in the Patriarch's action, while the other (Rav) did so unwillingly. While b. Avodah Zarah does not dispute the validity of the rescission of the prohibition, there is clearly no polemic supporting the Patriarch's authority. In b. Avodah Zarah, Shmuel believed the prohibition to be merely of *rabbinic* origin. Therefore, he does not quite yield to the Patriarch's authority; rather, he assumes that the Patriarch had agreed with *him* about the source of the prohibition, which could then justify its abrogation. Whereas y. Avodah Zarah/y. Shabbat's Rav can be a "rebellious elder" for refusing to obey the Patriarch, b. Avodah Zarah's Rav does not eat the Gentile oil. B. Avodah Zarah's muting of the pro-Patriarchal polemic is clearly a conscious re-working of the older source

---

34. See Kalmin, *Sage in Jewish Society,* 11–12; idem, *Sages, Stories, Authors, and Editors,* 213–215.

that better reflects its own cultural environment, in which the Palestinian Patriarch played little if any direct role.[35]

I.c. B. Avodah Zarah 67a–b ∥ Y. Avodah Zarah 5:3, 44d ∥ Y. Orlah 2:6, 62b—The "Imparting of Taste"

There is a halakhic link between this example and the previous one. In the previous example, we noted that one of the ways b. Avodah Zarah reworked y. Avodah Zarah was by introducing into Shmuel's permissive argument regarding Gentile oil the notion that the Patriarch had permitted the oil because נותן טעם לפגם מותר, meaning, "if [a forbidden food item which falls into permitted food] imparts [a bad] taste [the effect of which is] to blemish [the permitted food into which it falls], it [that resulting mixture] is permitted." B. Avodah Zarah's interest in that halakhic principle is apparent in this example as well, where we see b. AZ 67a–b reaching into y. Orlah to find material that will support it. B. Avodah Zarah must reach out to another Yerushalmi tractate to find such material because the local parallel at y. AZ 5:3, 44d does not display an interest in this halakhah. B. Avodah Zarah has thus introduced new material from within the Yerushalmi itself to the inherited y. Avodah Zarah material in order to further a halakhic agenda it does not share with that tractate.

At b. AZ 67a–69a, the Bavli discusses a general principle set out in m. AZ 5:2:

A. . . . This is the general principle: every [forbidden food item which has fallen into a permitted item and] imparts taste [to the permitted item] in which there is pleasure [for the eater], is forbidden.

B. Every [forbidden food item which has fallen into a permitted item and] imparts taste [to the permitted item] in which there is no pleasure, is permitted—like the vinegar which fell onto the pounded grains.

At the risk of redundancy, let us note again that if the forbidden item imparts an enjoyable taste to the food, the resulting mixture is forbidden, while if the imparted taste is deleterious to the food, the resulting mixture is permitted.

As part of its overall discussion of "the imparting of taste," b. Avodah Zarah presents a sugya reminiscent of one found at y. Orl 2:6, 62b.

---

35. For fascinating evidence of the Bavli's negative attitude toward the Patriarchate, see b. Sanh 5a. There the Bavli makes clear that while rabbinic ordination by the Exilarch is effective in Palestine, ordination by the Patriarch is *ineffective* in Babylonia. See Isaiah Gafni's discussion of the Sanhedrin sugya in *The Jews of Babylonia in the Talmudic Era: A Social and Cultural History* (Jerusalem: Merkaz Zalman Shazar, 1990), 100–101 (Heb.).

B. Avodah Zarah 67a–b

A. Resh Laqish said: "[The] 'imparting of taste' of which they spoke—it is not that they say [of a pot of food into which a forbidden item fell], 'this pot lacks salt [or has] too much salt, lacks spices or has too many spices,' but rather [it is] any [pot of food] that lacks nothing but is not eaten because of this [the taste of the forbidden item that had fallen in]."

[Rashi points out that this is a strict understanding of "the imparting of taste as a blemish is permitted." Should a forbidden item have fallen into the pot, imparting a good taste, the cook cannot add salt or spices and then claim that the resulting bad taste is attributable to those and not to the forbidden item. Should the cook do that, the resulting mixture is forbidden. Rather, only if the bad taste is solely attributable to the forbidden item is the mixture permitted.]

B. *And there are those who say*: Resh Laqish said: "The 'imparting of taste' of which they spoke—they do not say, 'This pot lacks salt or has too much salt, lacks spices, or has too many spices,' rather, now, behold, [the forbidden item] damages [the taste of the food in the pot]."

[Rashi points out that this is a lenient understanding of the principle. Should a forbidden item have fallen into the pot, the cook cannot claim that the reason it is imparting a bad taste is because the pot still needs to be properly seasoned. Rather, since the taste of the forbidden item is bad right now, given the state of the pot as it is, we say its taste is ruined and permit it.]

C. R. Abbahu said in the name of R. Yohanan: "Every [forbidden food item] the taste of which [in a mixture] and its [physical] substance [even by itself, outside of a mixture] are forbidden, we lash [the person who ate this forbidden thing], and [the measurement of the minimum amount of the forbidden item which must be present in the pot in order for the eater to be lashed] is an olive's worth [of the forbidden item per] piece of bread[-sized amount of the food in the pot. If the forbidden item's] taste [is present in the mixture, but] its [physical] substance is not, it [the mixture] is forbidden, but we do not lash him. And if it [the forbidden item] added taste to the detriment of the mixture (טעם לפגם), it [the mixture] is permitted."

D. *And let it say, if it imparted* [נתן, rather than "added"] *taste to the detriment* [of the mixture], *it is permitted?*

E. *Behold, this* [the fact that R. Abbahu teaches "added" rather than "imparted"] *teaches us that even though there were other things that damaged* [the taste of the mixture] *along with it* [the forbidden item] [the mixture is nevertheless permitted. This is a lenient position. R. Abbahu is saying that even though the taste of the mixture had already been ruined by other means, so that the addition of the forbidden item really makes no difference to the taste, the mixture will still be permitted if the forbidden item added in some way to the bad taste].

F.   *And the law is in accordance with the latter statement of Resh Laqish* [in §B].

G.   R. Kahana said: "From the words of all of them, we learn that 'נותן טעם לפגם מותר.'"

H.   Abaye said to him: "As regards all [of the rest] of them, very well! But [as to] Resh Laqish, he said 'They said,' and he does not hold that way himself."

I.   *From this* [should we infer] *that there is one who holds* נותן טעם לפגם אסור? [B. Avodah Zarah goes on to explore R. Meir's isolated view, which is that נותן טעם לפגם אסור.]

Y. Orlah 2:6, 62b

A.   R. Abbahu in the name of R. Yohanan: "There are three 'impartations of taste.' Everything that [if a] nonspecialist tastes it and says: 'This pot lacks nothing,' and this [forbidden thing] fell in, this is [a case of] נותן טעם לשבח which is permitted."

[P'nei Moshe explains that in this case, since the forbidden item does not improve the taste, which was fine already, the food should be permitted.]

B.   [R. Abbahu continues]: "And even if he [the nonspecialist] says: 'Spice X is in the pot,' this is נותן טעם לפגם which is permitted."

[P'nei Moshe explains that if even a nonspecialist can distinguish the taste of a particular forbidden spice in the pot, and this spice is deleterious to the taste of the food, the nonspecialist should be believed and the food permitted.]

C.   [R. Abbahu continues]: "And everything which an expert tastes and says: 'Spice X is in the pot,' this is נותן טעם לפגם which is forbidden."

[Per P'nei Moshe, if only an expert was able to detect the deleterious effect of the forbidden spice, then the pot should be forbidden since a nonspecialist may err and come to consider use of that forbidden spice permitted.]

[.   .   .   .   ]³⁶

D.   R. Abbahu in the name of R. Yohanan: "All imparters of taste [meaning all forbidden foods which impart taste to permitted foods into which they were dropped]—we do not lash [those who ate them] on their account unless he [the eater] tastes the actual taste of the physical substance of the forbidden item" [meaning that the forbidden item had to have been physically present in some quantity].

E.   R. Hama b. R. Yose raised an objection before R. Yohanan: "Behold, meat in milk! Behold [even if the eater] did not taste the physical substance of

---

36. A sugya with no parallel at b. AZ 67a–b has been omitted.

the forbidden item, [but simply its taste, the milk having disappeared into the meat,] you say he should be lashed!"

F.   And he [R. Yohanan] accepted it.

G.   *And what is "he accepted it"?*

H.   [He accepted it] *like a man who heard the words of the man with whom he is litigating, and accepted them.*

[·]³⁷

The variant views presented by Resh Laqish concerning נותן טעם לפגם in b. Avodah Zarah (§§A and B), are attributed in y. Orlah to R. Abbahu in the name of R. Yohanan.³⁸

In y. Orlah, R. Abbahu presents three scenarios—two with nonspecialists and one with an expert—involving a pot into which forbidden food falls. The existence in Palestine of these multiple scenarios involving the pot may account for the existence of the variant versions of Resh Laqish in b. Avodah Zarah. Thus, this may be an example in which an "איכא דאמרי" ("there are those who say") is created in Babylonia because of the prior existence of multiple scenarios presented by an amora in Palestine.

Of greater importance is the fact that in b. Avodah Zarah, the Resh Laqish statements and that of R. Abbahu in the name of R. Yohanan concerning lashing for tasting a forbidden item (§§A–C) are juxtaposed. At y. Orl 2:6, 62b, these differing teachings are also presented in the same order (§§A–D), but with two other, unrelated sugyot placed between them. The first omitted sugya was perhaps deliberately excised by the b. Avodah Zarah redactors due to its irrelevance to the subject that interested them here—"the imparting of taste." The omitted sugya begins with another statement by R. Abbahu in the name of R. Yohanan, that

all forbidden [food] items [that were cooked with permitted items of the same variety such that the taste of the forbidden item cannot be distinguished]—we measure them [the forbidden items] as if they were the size of an onion or a leek [so that if an onion- or leek-sized amount of the forbidden item could impart taste to something else, then the whole mixture should be forbidden].

---

37. Material without parallel at b. AZ 67a–b is omitted.

38. A careful look at Resh Laqish's statement in b. AZ shows that he is not represented as speaking in his own name at all. Rather, he purports to be quoting someone else (§A), and Abaye himself later emphasizes this (§H). Thus b. AZ is perhaps representing Resh Laqish as being the tradent through whom the teaching of others—whom we know from y. Orl to be R. Abbahu in the name of R. Yohanan—was reported in Babylonia. Yet this hypothesis is problematic because there is only one instance in the two Talmuds (y. Bik 1:6, 64a) in which Resh Laqish appears to be quoting R. Yohanan.

Although omitted by b. Avodah Zarah, R. Abbahu's teaching about the "onion-" or "leek-sized" measure of forbidden items is found at b. Hul 97b, which shows that it was known in Babylonia. It may have been deliberately excised from *here.*

The second of the y. Orlah sugyot omitted by b. Avodah Zarah begins with yet another statement by R. Abbahu, this time about the "imparting of taste" in relation to a Nazirite's dietary restrictions. Y. Orlah's introduction of the Nazirite into the discussion is sufficiently beyond the scope of b. Avodah Zarah's exploration of m. AZ 5:2 that its omission is unsurprising.

What remains to be considered is how b. Avodah Zarah has actually used the material it has taken from y. Orl 2:6, 62b. B. Avodah Zarah 67a–b has inserted this material between two sources derived from y. AZ 5:3, 44d.

Y. Avodah Zarah 5:3, 44d

A. R. Yohanan said: "That which [the mishnah] said [that if the forbidden item does not impart an enjoyable taste to the permitted item, it is permitted] only applies [to the case of vinegar that fell on] boiling [pounded grains]. But with regard to cold [pounded grains], it is forbidden [because the resulting food item is edible]. For so do the people of Sepphoris make, and they call it 'cress-dish.'"

B. *If they* [the pounded grains] *were boiled and cooled?* [This is a question concerning the view of R. Yohanan. Are the cold, pounded grains forbidden only if they had never been hot, or even if the vinegar fell on them after they had cooled down from a boiling state?]

C. *From here* [i.e., on the basis of your question], *even if they are boiled they should be forbidden, since it is their nature to cool!*

D. *For it was taught in a baraita:* **All imparters of taste, whether for the benefit or detriment** [of the food into which they fell] **are forbidden—the words of R. Meir. But the Sages say: "For the benefit** [of the dish] **is forbidden, for the detriment** [of the dish] **is permitted, just like** [the case of] **vinegar that fell on pounded grains"** (t. Ter 8:9).

B. Avodah Zarah 67a–b

A. And R. Yehudah said in the name of Shmuel: "They [the mishnah] taught only [that if the forbidden item does not impart an enjoyable taste to the permitted item, it is permitted] only if [the vinegar] fell onto boiling grains. But if it fell onto cold grains and he heated them . . . forbidden."

B. And likewise when Rabin came, he said in the name of Rabbah b. Bar Hanna in the name of R. Yohanan: "They [the mishnah] taught only [with respect to the case in which the vinegar] fell onto boiling grains. But if it fell onto cold grains and he heated them . . . forbidden."

C. And likewise when R. Dimi came . . . And so do they make [a dish like this, consisting of vinegar and pounded grains] on Sabbath eves in Sepphoris, and call them "cress-dishes."

[B. Avodah Zarah 67a–b §§A–I, translated above (pp. 117–118), should be inserted here.]

D. *For was it not taught* [in a baraita]: "נותן טעם לשבח and נותן טעם לפגם are both forbidden"—the words of R. Meir. R. Shimon said: "לשבח is forbidden, but לפגם is permitted."

B. Avodah Zarah has thus placed the material it took from y. Orlah between the sugya and Toseftan baraita it inherited from y. AZ 5:3, 44d. The Orlah material helps b. Avodah Zarah fix the definition of נותן טעם לפגם מותר (the halakhic position it favors on 67b). While y. Avodah Zarah's Toseftan baraita (like t. Ter 8:9 itself) directly connects the tannaitic dispute to the situation of "vinegar that fell on the pounded grains," b. Avodah Zarah's Toseftan baraita raises the issue to a higher level of legal abstraction and specifically cites the legal concept נותן טעם לפגם and whether it is permitted or forbidden. Indeed, it is likely that b. Avodah Zarah consciously altered its text of the baraita so as to emphasize this abstract concept over and above the specific case of "vinegar that fell on pounded grains."[39] Indeed, b. Avodah Zarah's overall discussion at 67a–b—unlike y. Avodah Zarah's—is much more focused on this halakhic issue, thanks in large part to the use of y. Orl 2:6, 62b. And, as we saw in the previous example (b. AZ 35b–36a, 37a ‖ y. AZ 2:9, 41d), this halakhic issue is of demonstrable interest to b. Avodah Zarah, *not* to y. Avodah Zarah.

II
B. Avodah Zarah Tends to Eliminate Materials of Particular Relevance to the Land of Israel or Its Roman Cultural Context

There is a sense in which this type of Babylonian reworking of y. Avodah Zarah can be seen as simply the flip side of the previous: to the extent that b. Avodah Zarah adds a Babylonian cultural or halakhic perspective to a y. Avodah Zarah sugya, it stands to reason that this addition may replace a uniquely Palestinian cultural or halakhic reference. We have seen evidence of this in the examples we have already studied in this chapter: in b. AZ 6b ‖ y. AZ 1:1, 39b, the Bavli removed y. Avodah Zarah's references

---

39. See Friedman, "Ha-baraitot she-be-Talmud ha-Bavli ve-yahasan le-Tosefta" for evidence that the Bavli does consciously alter the texts of baraitot.

to the Dead Sea and to the *ducenarius,* a Roman official who was likely little known (if at all) to the Babylonian redactors; in b. AZ 8a ‖ y. AZ 1:2, 39c, the Bavli removed the Greek and Latin exclamation attributed to Adam in y. Avodah Zarah;[40] and in b. AZ 35b–36a ‖ y. AZ 2:9, 41d, the Bavli eliminated the unique Palestinian amoraic use of the "rebellious elder" epithet for an opponent, as well as the pro-Patriarchal polemic we observed in y. Avodah Zarah.

But there is more to b. Avodah Zarah's elimination of uniquely Palestinian cultural and halakhic perspectives than these adjustments to sugyot that b. Avodah Zarah appropriated from y. Avodah Zarah. B. Avodah Zarah *tends*—and again, "tends" does not imply an immutable rule—to excise aggadot that are of particular relevance to the Land of Israel or that reflect Greco-Roman myth or epic. This type of b. Avodah Zarah reworking of y. Avodah Zarah is admittedly more difficult to establish firmly than the others because one must argue that b. Avodah Zarah's complete elimination of a y. Avodah Zarah text, or its replacement of one text with a completely different one, is conscious and dispositive of b. Avodah Zarah's reliance on y. Avodah Zarah. Such a claim is difficult to establish convincingly, unlike the other cases in which we can observe b. Avodah Zarah's reworkings of what are demonstrably parallel y. Avodah Zarah texts. Nevertheless, despite its circumstantial nature, this evidence is important because of what it suggests when taken together with the other evidence, and also because of the promise it holds as an avenue of future research into the literary relationship between the Talmuds.

II.a. B. Avodah Zarah 2a–3b ‖ Y. Avodah Zarah 1:1, 39a–b— The Opening Aggadic Sequences of the Tractates

The Avodah Zarah tractates stand out from most others in that both open with lengthy sequences of aggadic materials. Although b. Avodah Zarah is faithful to this structural feature of y. Avodah Zarah, it reworks the content of the aggadot so as to better reflect its own religious and cultural concerns.

After a short interrogation of the three-day period of commercial abstention of m. AZ 1:1, y. Avodah Zarah moves into stories about the biblical King Jeroboam and his introduction of idolatry to the Northern Kingdom of Israel.[41] The Jeroboam materials are arranged in three large sec-

---

40. In this parallel pair of sources b. AZ also removed y. AZ's discussions of the "*taxes,*" or "offices of the civil governor," of Caesarea and Duqim.

41. Y. AZ effects a nice transition between these materials: it begins by having R. Hama b. Uqba ground the three-day prohibition of the mishnah in Amos 4:4. R. Yose objects to this derivation on the grounds that if that verse is really the

tions. According to the first, Jeroboam begins to entice Israel to idolatry immediately upon assuming the throne by insisting to them that the way of idolatry is easy and permissive, unlike the more demanding way of Torah. In the second section the tables are turned: the people try to entice a drunken Jeroboam into idolatry at his coronation celebration, but he puts them off until the next day. He also expresses fear of the Sanhedrin, which the people neutralize either through murder or (according to another opinion) by removing the members of the Sanhedrin from their position. In the third section, Jeroboam's revolt against Torah is the result of his anxiety about potential humiliation in Jerusalem in the presence of Solomon's successor Rehoboam. In order to keep his own people away from the Jerusalem Temple, he set up golden calves as border markers and even invented his own religious festivals to fill the cultic gap created by the prohibition of pilgrimages to Jerusalem.

Taken together, the Jeroboam aggadot explain that the pervasive presence of what we might call "state-sponsored idolatry" in the Land of Israel is originally attributable to the biblical-era revolt of an Israelite king. We cannot determine whether the Palestinian sages had paganism or Christianity in mind, but they were clearly focused on idolatry in the Land.

B. Avodah Zarah's opening aggadah is entirely different. B. Avodah Zarah opens with an immensely rich narrative about God's judgment of the nations, their attempts (particularly Rome and Persia) to justify their non-observance of Torah and alleged efforts on behalf of Israel, God's willingness to give them a "second chance," their inevitable failures, and God's laughter.[42] B. Avodah Zarah's focus is on the theological implications of the relationship between Israel and the nations, of God's relationship to the nations, and of where the other nations stand vis-à-vis divine revelation (the Noahide laws). These three themes recur throughout the tractate. Stories illustrating different perspectives on the relationship between Israel and the nations are found at, *inter alia*, 8b (the Roman Empire candidly admits its dependence on Israel in acquiring world mastery); 10a–11a (encounters between Rabbi and Antoninus, the Roman martyr

---

source of the prohibition then even the Diaspora should observe it, which t. AZ 1:1 shows is not the case. Y. AZ asks how R. Yose interprets the verse, and the response on R. Yose's behalf is that Amos 4:4 pertains to the reign of Jeroboam. The subject of Jeroboam having been raised, the Yerushalmi then moves into a lengthy sequence of Jeroboam materials. It is unclear whether the response attributed to R. Yose is simply the assertion that the verse refers to Jeroboam, or whether we are to assume as well that R. Yose is also the source of the first of the Jeroboam aggadot.

42. See Jeffrey L. Rubenstein, *Talmudic Stories*, 212–242.

Qetia b. Shalom and the convert Onqelos b. Qalonymos);[43] 16b–17a and 17b–18a (R. Eliezer's and R. Hanina b. Teradyon's encounters—the latter a martyrdom—with Rome); 54b–55a (polemics against idolatry); and 65a (Rava's encounter with the Gentile hegemon Bar Shishaq). With one exception, these stories do not appear in y. Avodah Zarah.[44]

The interest in the Noahide laws we observe in this aggadah (2b–3a) also appears at 5b–6a, 24b (b. Avodah Zarah makes the biblical character Aravnah the Jebusite a *ger toshav,* unlike y. Avodah Zarah), 51a, and 65a. Taken together, all of this evidence strongly suggests that the absence from b. Avodah Zarah of an opening aggadah that explains the coming of idolatry to the Land of Israel, and the replacement of this material with texts that touch on broader themes b. Avodah Zarah develops throughout the tractate, was a deliberate choice of the redactors. In sum, b. Avodah Zarah remained faithful at the macro level to y. Avodah Zarah's placement of aggadah at the beginning of the tractate, while feeling free to rework it in accordance with its own interests.

II.b. Greco-Roman Mythical Allusions Are Missing from B. Avodah Zarah

At y. AZ 1:2, 39c, R. Yohanan explains the origins of Kalends as resulting from the contest between the Egyptian general and the Roman general Yanobris (=Januarius), who agrees to kill himself so that Rome can attain world mastery.[45] Yanobris' sacrifice prompted the cry "Qalendas Yanobris!" and the day of mourning on the second day of Kalends, which y. Avodah Zarah notes is known as the "black day" (Greek: *melani 'imera*[46]). The Romans considered the "black day" unlucky for warfare, and in y. Avodah Zarah R. Yudan Antodria observes that lentils planted on that day will not flourish.[47] This particularly Roman cultural and religious allusion is missing from b. Avodah Zarah.

Later on the same page, R. Levi reports that when the biblical king Solomon married Pharaoh's daughter, the angel Gabriel planted a reed in the sea onto which sediment piled, eventually becoming the foundation of

---

43. See my "The Power Conferred by Distance From Power."

44. The exception is the story of R. Yehudah Nesiah's encounter with the *min* at b. AZ 6b, which has a parallel at y. AZ 1:1, 39b and interesting intertexts in b. AZ at 10b and 65a.

45. See the translation and discussion above, on pp. 43–50 and 149–151.

46. My transliteration of this phrase follows Peter Schäfer, "Jews and Gentiles in Yerushalmi Avodah Zarah," 340.

47. For the Roman references to the contest of Yanobris and the Egyptian general and the perception of the "black day," see Peter Schäfer, "Jews and Gentiles in Yerushalmi Avodah Zarah," 340 and sources cited.

the "great city" of Rome. Rome's urban development was enhanced when Jeroboam set up his golden calves, at which time "Romulus and Remus" built two huts there. These traditions are found juxtaposed at b. Shab 56b (and not at all in b. Avodah Zarah), where the particularly Roman reference to "Romulus and Remus" is missing.

Lastly, at y. AZ 3:1, 42c, R. Yonah reports that "Alexander the Macedonian" (Alexander the Great) wished to ascend high into the sky, and he saw the earth as a sphere and the sea as a dish (therefore his statues represent him as holding a sphere). This Alexander the Great legend, well known in the Roman cultural context, is not found in the Bavli.[48]

III
At Times B. Avodah Zarah Organizes Materials in a More Sensible Order Than Y. Avodah Zarah

At times b. Avodah Zarah demonstrably improves upon the order of presentation of materials found in y. Avodah Zarah, either by excising materials from a given sugya or sequence of sugyot and placing them elsewhere in a more appropriate context, or by re-arranging materials within the context of the same sequence of sugyot. We have already seen examples of this at b. AZ 6b ‖ y. AZ 1:1, 39b; b. AZ 35b–36a, 37a ‖ y. AZ 2:9, 41d; and b. AZ 67a–b ‖ y. AZ 5:3, 44d ‖ y. Orl 2:6, 62b, which we had analyzed for other purposes. What follows are four additional examples of this b. Avodah Zarah tendency.

III.a. B. Avodah Zarah 2a ‖ Y. Avodah Zarah 1:2, 39c— אידיהן *Versus* עידיהן

Y. Avodah Zarah opens its treatment of m. AZ 1:3 ("and these are the festivals [אידיהן] . . .") with a short sugya containing Rav's and Shmuel's variant readings of three words in the Mishnah that are spelled with either "א" or "ע."

---

48. For a discussion of this legend, see Karin Luck-Huyse, *Der Traum vom Fliegen in der Antike* (Palingenesia LXII; Stuttgart: Franz Steiner, 1997). But see b. Ned 9b, in which the Bavli presents an aggadah which is clearly a version of the Narcissus legend. One explanation for the different treatment of the Narcissus-type myth is that both y. Ned 1:1, 36b and tannaitic sources thoroughly "judaized" it as an aggadah about an anonymous young man and the venerable Shimon ha-Tsadiq. Thus, the myth is not readily recognizable as such, unlike the cases of the "black day," "Romulus and Remus," and "Alexander the Great," which were not—and perhaps could not be—so thoroughly judaized. The issue requires further research.

Y. Avodah Zarah 1:2, 39c

A. [From the mishnah:] **And these are the festivals (אידיהן) of the nations.**

B. Rav said: "[The mishnah should read] 'עידיהן,'" and Shmuel said: "[The mishnah should read] 'אידיהן.'"

C. [The rationale of] *the one who said* [that the mishnah should read] "עידיהן" [is that it is found in Isa 44:9]—"and they are their witnesses (ועידיהם המה)." [The rationale of] *the one who said* [that the mishnah should read] "אידיהן" [is that it is found in Deut 32:35]—"for their day of disaster is near (כי קרוב יום אידם)."

D. Rav said: "[M. Eruv 5:1 should read] 'מאברין,'" and Shmuel said: "[M. Eruv 5:1 should read] 'מעברין.'"

E. [The rationale of] *the one who said* [that the mishnah should read] "מאברין" [is that] *we are adding a limb* (אבר) *to it.* [That is, we are extending the boundary of the city from which we wish to measure and mark out the Sabbath boundary. First, we add areas to the city, and then measure the Sabbath boundary from those newly added areas.] [The rationale of] *the one who said* [that the mishnah should read] "מעברין" [is that the city] *is like a pregnant woman* [whose belly extends out farther than it usually does, although it is still a part of her. Thus, per m. Eruv 5:1, we are extending the usual boundary of the city, although the extension is still to be considered part of it].

F. Rav said: "[M. Ber 8:6 should read] 'יאותו,'" and Shmuel said: ["M. Ber 8:6 should read] 'יעותו.'" [The rationale of] *the one who said* [that the mishnah should read] "יאותו" [is that it is consistent with Gen 34:15]—"only on this condition will we agree with you (אך בזאת נאות לכם)." [The rationale of] *the one who said* [that the mishnah should read] "יעותו" [is that it is consistent with Isa 50:4]—"to know the word that sustains the tired (לדעת לעות את יעף דבר)."

There are parallels to this sugya at y. Ber 8:7, 12c and y. Eruv 5:1, 22b. In both parallels, the sugya begins by first presenting Rav's and Shmuel's divergent readings of the local mishnah, and introduces the other two differences with "We learned there in a mishnah." In addition, both parallels include a question about Rav's and Shmuel's different readings of the Avodah Zarah mishnah which is missing from y. AZ 1:2, 39c: "And how does Shmuel interpret Rav's verse 'and they are their witnesses (ועידיהם המה)'? [Shmuel interprets the verse as meaning] that they [the idols worshiped by the nations] will in the future embarrass their worshipers at the day of judgment."

B. Avodah Zarah's version of this sugya is attached to the very first mishnah at 2a ("three days before the festivals of idolaters . . ."):

B. Avodah Zarah 2a

A. Rav and Shmuel: One teaches [that the mishnah should read] "אידיהן,"
and one teaches [that the mishnah should read] "עידיהן." *The one who*
teaches "אידיהן" is not mistaken, and the one who teaches "עידיהן" is not mis-
taken.

B. *The one who teaches "אידיהן" is not mistaken, for it is written* (Deut 32:35), *"For*
their day of disaster is near (כי קרוב יום אידם)." And the one who teaches "עידיהן"
is not mistaken, for it is written (Isa 43:9), *"Let them bring their witnesses to*
justify them (יתנו עידיהם ויצדקו)."

C. *And the one who teaches "אידיהן," what is the reason he does not teach "עידיהן"?*
He will say to you: "Disaster is preferable [as the notion that should be expressed in the mishnah]." *And the one who teaches "עידיהן," what is the rea-*
son he does not teach "אידיהן"? He will say to you: "What is it that will lead to
their disaster? The testimony that they will give about themselves. Therefore,
'testimony' (עדות) is preferable [as the notion that should be expressed in the
mishnah]."

D. *And this "let them bring their witnesses to justify them," is it written about idol-*
aters? [No!] *It is written about Israel! As R. Yehoshua b. Levi said:* "In the
world to come, all the commandments that Israel fulfilled in this world
will come and testify about them, as it is said (Isa 43:9): 'Let them bring
their witnesses to justify them'—these are Israel; 'Let them hear and say,
"It is true"' (Isa 43:9)—these are the idolaters."

E. *Rather, R. Huna b. de-Rav Yehoshua said:* "The one who said 'עידיהן' [is deriving that version] from here: 'All who make idols—all of them are nothing, and the things they value cannot help, and they [the idols] are their
witnesses (Isa 44:9).'"

Both y. AZ 1:2, 39c and b. AZ 2a present Rav's and Shmuel's disagreement over whether to teach "איד" or "עיד" and provide scriptural justifica-
tions for their respective positions. Yet the Talmuds associate their respective sugyot with different mishnayot: y. Avodah Zarah uses its sugya to
launch its discussion of m. AZ 1:2, while b. Avodah Zarah places its sugya
right at the beginning of the tractate. Is this different placement the result
of b. Avodah Zarah's conscious decision to move the sugya, or is it simply
the result of b. Avodah Zarah's having received the sugya attached to a
different mishnah than y. Avodah Zarah?

Looking more closely at this and other differences between the y. and
b. Avodah Zarah sugyot, we can observe a pattern of difference that
points to b. Avodah Zarah's conscious intervention in moving the sugya.
First, b. Avodah Zarah's linkage of the Rav and Shmuel dispute to the first
mishnah of the tractate is logical since that is the first time the problematic
word "אידיהן" appears. By linking the dispute to the first mishnah, therefore, b. Avodah Zarah has improved upon y. Avodah Zarah's linkage of
this dispute to the tractate's second mishnah. Second, b. Avodah Zarah

omits the references—found at y. AZ 1:2, 39c and the two Yerushalmi parallels—to Rav's and Shmuel's disagreements about m. Ber 8:6 and m. Eruv 5:1. B. Avodah Zarah's omission of this part of the y. Avodah Zarah sugya makes sense since it is irrelevant to the Avodah Zarah mishnah. We have already observed b. Avodah Zarah's tendency to excise materials irrelevant to a main issue or context in our analysis of the Talmuds' treatments of Gentile oil at b. AZ 35b–36a, 37a ‖ y. AZ 2:9, 41d, where b. Avodah Zarah excised y. Avodah Zarah's discussion of Rabbi's conflict with his colleagues about divorce in order to allow the sugya on oil to flow more smoothly. We will examine other instances of this tendency shortly.

Of greater importance are the differences between the sugyot that result in b. Avodah Zarah's serving as a smooth introduction to the long sequence of aggadic materials stretching from b. AZ 2a to 5b. As Jeffrey Rubenstein has pointed out, b. Avodah Zarah initially points to Isa 43:9 as the source for "עידיהן," and, after a bit of dialectic, settles on the "correct" (or, the "original") scriptural source at Isa 44:9.[49] The choice of Isa 43:9 as the verse that was destined to be rejected was probably due (as Rubenstein suggests) to its pivotal role in the eschatological aggadah at 2a–3b, and by quoting it early "the redactors create a neat segue to the story [about the judgment of the Gentile nations at 2a–3b]."[50] Thus, the presence of Isa 43:9 in b. Avodah Zarah alone is not due to b. Avodah Zarah's having received a sugya similar to, yet different from, that of y. AZ 1:2, 39c as part of a shared stratum of early talmud. Rather, b. Avodah Zarah deliberately introduced the verse in furtherance of a literary purpose particular to itself: creating a segue to the sequence of aggadic materials at the beginning of the tractate. Moreover, b. Avodah Zarah's proposal of a verse that is ultimately rejected in favor of the "correct" verse is, as Rubenstein and Shamma Friedman have pointed out, a characteristic feature of Bavli sugyot generally.[51] It thus seems reasonable to conclude that b. Avodah Zarah consciously chose to place this sugya at the beginning of the tractate.

III.b. B. Avodah Zarah 11b ‖ Y. Avodah Zarah 1:2, 39c— Rearranging Lists of Idolatrous Festivals

M. Avodah Zarah 1:3, it will be recalled, listed the Gentile festivals subject to the three-day restrictions of m. AZ 1:1. These festivals were Kalends, Saturnalia, Kratesis, the coronation-days of emperors, their birthdays, and the anniversaries of their deaths. After discussion of Kalends and Saturna-

---

49. Rubenstein, *Talmudic Stories,* 235–237.
50. Ibid., 236.
51. Ibid. See also Friedman, *"Yevamot X,"* in *Texts and Studies,* 324–325.

lia, y. Avodah Zarah discusses Gentile festivals other than those mentioned in m. AZ 1:1:

A. R. Ba in the name of Rav: "There are three times [i.e., idolatrous festivals] in Babylonia, and three times in Medea. The three times in Babylonia: *Muharin, Kanony,* and *Kanvatta.* The three in Medea: *Nosradey,* and *Turyaski,* and *Muharneki.*"

B. R. Huna in the name of R. Nahman b. Yaaqov: "*Naroz* falls on the second of Adar in Persia, and on the twentieth of Adar in Medea."

C. "Saturnalia" [means] "hidden hatred" (שנאה טמונה). [It is also an acrostic:] "He hates" (שונא); "he avenges" (נוקם); "he holds a grudge" (נוטר). This is just as you say: "And Esau held a grudge against Jacob" (Gen 27:41).[52]

D. R. Yitshaq b. R. Lazar said: "In Rome, they [the Israelites] call [Saturnalia] '[the time of] the hidden hatred of Esau.'"

E. And Kratesis . . . [further discussion in y. Avodah Zarah omitted].

Y. Avodah Zarah had been discussing Kalends and Saturnalia immediately prior to listing Babylonian and Medean holidays. Y. Avodah Zarah interrupts that discussion to list these holidays in §§A–B, and then returns in §C to Saturnalia, moving on to Kratesis in §E and in what follows. The odd point about y. Avodah Zarah's list of the Babylonian and Medean holidays is that it interrupts an ongoing discussion of the Roman festivals mentioned in m. AZ 1:3. By contrast, b. Avodah Zarah puts off its own list of the Persian and Babylonian festivals until after it has concluded its discussion of the Roman holidays of m. AZ 1:3.

> *These* [the festivals just discussed] *are* [the festivals] *of the Romans. And what are those of the Persians? Mutardi, Turyaski, Muharneki, and Muharin, these are* [the holidays of] *the Persians and the Romans. And what are those of the Babylonians? Muharneki, and Aknaya, Bahnani, and the tenth of Adar.*[53]

Once again, b. Avodah Zarah has improved upon the presentation of materials found in the earlier Talmud.

III.c. B. Avodah Zarah 22b–23a ‖ Y. Avodah Zarah 2:1, 40c— Leaving Animals in the Custody of Gentiles

The pertinent part of m. AZ 2:1 rules that "We do not house beasts in the inns of idolaters because they are suspected of bestiality." Both Talmuds place the following similar sugyot early in their treatments of this mishnah.

---

52. It is unclear whether §C is a continuation of R. Huna, or whether it belongs to the editorial voice of the Yerushalmi.

53. These transliterations follow Jacob Neusner, *A History of the Jews in Babylonia* (5 vols.; Leiden: E. J. Brill, 1965–1970), 2:88, and the sources cited at 2:89n1.

As we will see, b. Avodah Zarah reworks y. Avodah Zarah's sugya to eliminate a logical problem and thereby create a much smoother sugya.

Y. Avodah Zarah 2:1, 40c

A. R. Zeirah, R. Abbahu in the name of R. Yose b. R. Hanina; R. Ba, R. Yonah [said]: "Resolve [that m. AZ 2:1, which says that Israelites must not leave their animals in Gentile inns, is] like [the view of] R. Liezer[54] [in m. Parah 2:1, where he forbids all animal purchases from Gentiles. The Sages in Parah permit it. R. Liezer is seen as being concerned about Gentile bestiality, while the Sages are apparently unconcerned about it]. For R. Liezer said: **'It** [a beast] **is not** [to be] **bought from Gentiles'** (m. Par 2:1)."

B. R. Yonah asked: "And why do we not resolve [the mishnah as reflecting] the views of everyone [R. Liezer and the Sages who disagree with him]? As R. Lazar[55] said in the name of Rav: 'And even according to the one who said that it is permitted to sell [a beast to Gentiles], it is forbidden to leave [animals] alone with them.' [Thus m. AZ 2:1 represents the views of both R. Liezer, who forbids animal sales to Gentiles, and the Sages who permit it, since neither permits leaving animals alone with Gentiles.]

C. "If [the Israelite] transgressed [and] left [his beast] alone [with a Gentile], all agree[56] [that we must be concerned about the possibility of bestiality]." [Thus, neither R. Liezer nor the Sages makes a distinction between behavior that is ideally preferred (לכתחילה) and that which is acceptable only after the fact (בדיעבד). R. Yirmiyah will implicitly challenge the assumption that the Sages make no such distinction.]

D. R. Yirmiyah said: "Let's derive [whether we are supposed to make distinctions between לכתחילה -and בדיעבד-thinking] from this: **The woman who was trapped in the hands of Gentiles: for purposes of** [collecting] **money—she is permitted to her husband; for purposes of life and death** [the kidnappers threaten to kill her]—**she is forbidden to her husband** (m. Ket 2:9)." [This example shows that we do distinguish between לכתחילה -and בדיעבד-thinking. Although m. AZ 2:1 says, "A woman must not be alone with them," we see from m. Ket 2:9 that if she is trapped alone with Gentiles for purposes of money, she is nevertheless permitted to her husband.]

---

54. This is the tanna R. Eliezer.

55. This is the amora R. Eleazar b. Pedat.

56. R. Yonah is explaining his view that the mishnah represents the views of both R. Liezer and the Sages by refuting an implicit argument against that view. That implicit argument is that perhaps m. AZ 2:1 represents R. Liezer's view, but only represents the Sages' view "לכתחילה," that is, in the first or ideal instance. By contrast, m. Par 2:1 would represent the Sages' view "בדיעבד," that is, after the fact. Were this argument to be accepted, then it could not be claimed—as R. Yonah wishes to do—that m. AZ 2:1 in fact represents the views of both R. Liezer and the Sages in their entirety.

E.   R. Yose said: "A woman is different, because it is her way to scream."
[That is, m. Ket 2:9 has nothing to tell us about לכתחילה -and בדיעבד-
thinking. The woman of m. Ketubbot is permitted to her husband because she will scream if attacked; fearing this, the Gentile will stay away
from her so as not to jeopardize his collection of the ransom money,
which is his real goal.]

F.   *Tell yourself that she was a deaf-mute* [who cannot scream. On this assumption, R. Yirmiyah's reading that m. Ket 2:9 is dealing with לכתחילה and
בדיעבד must be correct].

G.   [If so,] *it is her way to hint!* [I.e., with hand gestures; thus R. Yose's objection to R. Yirmiyah still stands.]

H.   *What is the result? Resolve* [that m. AZ 2:1 is] *like* [the view of] *R. Liezer, for
R. Liezer said:* **"It** [a beast] **is not** [to be] **bought from Gentiles"** (m. Par
2:1).

Y. Avodah Zarah develops its argument to this point in the following
steps:

1.   M. Avodah Zarah 2:1 reflects the view of R. Liezer (=Eliezer) in
m. Parah 2:1 (§A).

2.   R. Yonah challenges this and proposes that m. AZ 2:1 may actually reflect the views of both R. Liezer *and* the Sages. R. Yonah points out that neither R. Liezer nor the Sages makes a distinction between behavior that is "ideally" (לכתחילה) forbidden
but nevertheless permitted after the fact (בדיעבד) (§§B–C).

3.   R. Yirmiyah points out on the basis of m. Ket 2:9 that the Sages
do, in fact, make a distinction between לכתחילה and בדיעבד, *contra* R. Yonah (§D).

4.   This issue is discussed through §G. R. Yose ultimately objects
without refutation to R. Yirmiyah, which vindicates R. Yonah's
conclusion in §C. Logically, then, the Talmud's conclusion
should be that m. AZ 2:1 reflects the views of both R. Liezer
and the Sages.

5.   Y. Avodah Zarah concludes that m. AZ 2:1 reflects only the
view of R. Liezer as seen in m. Parah 2:1 (§H)—which is unexpected in light of step 4.

B. Avodah Zarah 22b–23a

A.   *They raised an objection* [to m. AZ 2:1 from t. AZ 2:1]: **We buy from them
beasts for sacrifice and are not concerned about male or female bestiality, nor are we concerned about "setting aside"** [the possibility that the
beast had been set aside prior to sale as a future idolatrous offering], **nor
about worship** [the possibility that the animal had been worshiped].

B. *It works well* [not to be concerned about] *"setting aside" and "worshiped," for if he* [the Gentile] *had set it aside or if he had worshiped it, he would not sell it! Rather, let us be concerned about male and female bestiality.*

[·]⁵⁷

C. Ravina said: "There is no conflict [between m. AZ 2:1, which forbids leaving beasts alone with Gentiles, and t. AZ 2:1, which permits purchasing beasts from them]. This one [m. AZ 2:1] refers to ideally preferred behavior (לכתחילה), while this one [t. AZ 2:1] refers to action after the fact (בדיעבד)."

D. *And from where do you derive that there is a distinction between* לכתחילה *and* בדיעבד? *From that which was taught in a* mishnah [m. AZ 2:1]: **A woman must not be sequestered with them, because they are suspected of sexual immorality.** *And they raised an objection* [from m. Ket 2:9]: **A woman who was trapped in the hands of idolaters: for purposes of** [collecting] **money—she is permitted to her husband; for purposes of life and death—she is forbidden to her husband.**

E. *Rather, no—learn from this that we do make a distinction between* לכתחילה *and* בדיעבד.

F. *From where? Perhaps I will truly say to you that even after the fact* (בדיעבד) [a beast bought from Gentiles is] *also not* [permitted]. *And here, this is the reason that she* [the woman of m. Ket 2:9] *is* [nevertheless permitted to her husband]: *for* [the Gentile kidnapper] *is fearful for the loss of his money. Know this, from that which it teaches at the end* [of m. Ket 2:9]: **For purposes of life and death—she is forbidden to her husband.** [Thus, the only reason she could be permitted to him is if her kidnapping was only for purposes of collecting ransom money.] *And there is nothing more to say about this.*

G. R. Pedat said: "There is no difficulty [between m. AZ 2:1 and t. AZ 2:1]: this one, [m. AZ 2:1, reflects the view of] R. Eliezer, and this one, [t. AZ 2:1, reflects the view of] the Rabbis. As it was taught in a mishnah about the red heifer [m. Par 2:1]: **R. Eliezer says: 'It is not bought from idolaters, and the Sages permit.'**"

B. Avodah Zarah develops its argument as follows:

1. Ravina draws a contrast between m. AZ 2:1's לכתחילה orientation as contrasted with t. AZ 2:1's בדיעבד orientation (§C).

2. The anonymous voice continues the discussion of לכתחילה and בדיעבד in §§D–F, comparing m. AZ 2:1 to m. Ket 2:9.

---

57. Further discussion of this baraita, as well as a lengthy digression on the subject of Gentile bestiality, has been omitted.

3. R. Pedat claims that m. AZ 2:1 reflects the view of R. Eliezer (§G).

Before analyzing how b. Avodah Zarah has reworked y. Avodah Zarah, we must establish that it is, in fact, a version of y. Avodah Zarah and not independently based on m. AZ 2:1, on other tannaitic sources, or on early talmud. Although m. AZ 2:1 raises the suspicion of Gentile bestiality, it alone does not call for the similar sugyot in the two Talmuds. Nothing in the mishnah calls for the common citation of m. Par 2:1, which says nothing at all about bestiality. Nor does m. AZ 2:1 call for any discussion about whether it reflects the view of R. Eliezer and/or the Sages. That discussion is, in fact, called for neither by m. AZ 2:1 nor by m. Parah 2:1, but reflects an exegetical move made by the Talmuds themselves as they pondered the two mishnayot in relation to each other. Nothing in m. AZ 2:1 requires an excursus into לכתחילה- and בדייעבד-thinking, and nothing in the mishnah requires that this examination be conducted with reference to m. Ket 2:9.

Nor do the similarities between the sugyot stem from the other tannaitic sources cited. First, they are drawn from different places—m. Ketubbot, m. Parah, and (in b. Avodah Zarah) t. Avodah Zarah—and so do not form a sequence of related tannaitic sources on which both Talmuds may have drawn independently. Second, these tannaitic sources are well-integrated into the discussions in which they appear; the common list of tannaitic sources is more likely a result, rather than the cause, of the overall similarity in the sugyot.

Finally, the hypothesis of early talmud fails to persuade because there is no evidence that amoraim either juxtaposed all these materials or were aware of the juxtaposition. Moreover, when we focus specifically on both Talmuds' concern with לכתחילה and בדייעבד, we find this concern only in the Talmuds—none of the tannaitic sources cited deal with this issue. It strains credulity therefore to imagine that there was some other early talmud source that also discussed this issue, and which left its mark only in the two Talmuds and nowhere else. The more reasonable inference is that b. Avodah Zarah is derived from y. Avodah Zarah.

Armed with that inference, we are now ready to study just how it is that b. Avodah Zarah reworked the y. Avodah Zarah sugya. Looking back on y. Avodah Zarah and on the outline of its argument, we notice an oddity: R. Yose objects without refutation to R. Yirmiyah (§G), which has the effect of vindicating R. Yonah's conclusion in §C that neither R. Liezer nor the Sages distinguish between לכתחילה- and בדייעבד-thinking. This means that m. AZ 2:1 should be understood to represent the views of both. Yet, inexplicably, y. Avodah Zarah asserts in §H that m. AZ 2:1 only represents R. Liezer's view!

B. Avodah Zarah, on the other hand, creates a smoother sugya by quoting t. AZ 2:1 and conducting its discussion of לכתחילה and בדיעבד on the basis of a comparison between m. AZ 2:1, t. AZ 2:1, and m. Ket 2:9—*without reference* to m. Parah 2:1, R. Eliezer, and the Sages. B. Avodah Zarah concludes its discussion of לכתחילה and בדיעבד in §F just as y. AZ did in §G—there is no distinction between לכתחילה and בדיעבד. And just as y. Avodah Zarah had asserted in §H that m. AZ 2:1 represented R. Liezer's view, b. Avodah Zarah asserts the same in §G. But the critical difference between the Talmuds is that while y. Avodah Zarah's conclusion in §H was unexpected and problematic after its conclusion in §G, b. Avodah Zarah's is not. By separating the treatment of לכתחילה and בדיעבד from the question of which tanna(im)'s view lies behind m. AZ 2:1, b. Avodah Zarah can have its cake and eat it too—it can assert that there is no distinction between לכתחילה and בדיעבד *and* that m. AZ 2:1 represents the view of R. Eliezer—as b. Avodah Zarah demonstrates by a comparison with m. Parah 2:1. Once again, b. Avodah Zarah has improved upon the presentation of materials in the earlier Talmud.

III.d. B. Avodah Zarah 27b–28b ‖ Y. Avodah Zarah 2:2, 40d–41a— Israelites, Gentiles, and Medicine

In chapter 2 we analyzed y. and b. Avodah Zarah's versions of the story of the hapless Eleazar b. Dama, who died of snakebite because R. Yishmael did not allow him to be healed by a *min*. We saw there that b. Avodah Zarah's version of the story is more similar to y. Avodah Zarah's than to t. Hullin's. Our task now is to consider y. Avodah Zarah in its larger context and assess how b. Avodah Zarah sensibly reworked that context in order to better adapt the story for its own use.

In y. AZ 2:2, 40d–41a, the Eleazar b. Dama story is the fourth in a sequence of four sugyot. The sequence opens with R. Yaaqov's declaration in the name of R. Yohanan that "We may heal ourselves by means of everything except for idolatry, sexual immorality, and bloodshed." That is, medicines derived from idolatry, sexual immorality, or bloodshed are forbidden for use. The Yerushalmi unpacks this list by taking up the issues of idolatry, sexual immorality, and bloodshed in order. It opens its consideration of medicines derived from idolatry by considering the issue of leaves derived from an *asherah*-tree (which is worshiped), and R. Aha's and R. Yonah's possibly differing attitudes toward healing waters derived from the "source" (lit. the "maleness") of Duhi (which was presumably an idol in Palestine). This sugya is followed by R. Huna's declaration that he will quote a source that prohibits healing by means of sexual immorality, and a lengthy sugya exploring the intersection of healing and sexual immorality. A third sugya follows which opens with R. Hanina's declaration that he is about to quote a source that interdicts healing by means of bloodshed, and an equally lengthy sugya that builds on m. Ohal 7:6 (which explores when the life of either a mother or a fetus should take precedence). The story of Eleazar b. Dama is the fourth sugya in this sequence.

This perusal of the sequence of sugyot shows that the first and fourth sugyot (both dealing with idolatry) are the only ones directly relevant to the Avodah Zarah tractates. B. Avodah Zarah logically eliminates the second sugya (sexual immorality) and the third (murder), which the Bavli places elsewhere in thematically more appropriate places: b. Pes 25a–b, b. Yoma 82a–b, and b. Sanh 74a–75a. B. Avodah Zarah also logically eliminates the first sugya which, although it deals with idolatry, includes the Palestinocentric reference to R. Aha's and R. Yonah's encounters with the waters of Duhi. As we have seen, such Palestinocentric references are a type of source that b. Avodah Zarah tends to omit.[58]

B. Avodah Zarah places its reworked version of the Ben Dama story (27b) immediately following a baraita that forbids a person to have dealings with or accept healing from a *min* even if only temporarily to stave off an inevitable death. B. Avodah Zarah thus juxtaposes the Ben Dama story—which is about *minut*—and a source that has already called the student's attention to that theme. Further, b. Avodah Zarah added to y. Avodah Zarah the unattributed observation that "heresy is different because it pulls, and he [the one who falls in with heresy] will come to be pulled after them [the heretics]." This addition is unsurprising in light of b. Avodah Zarah's greater interest in the theme of *minut*. B. Avodah Zarah continues to develop the *minut* theme at 28a, where R. Abbahu is described as taking violent exception to the medical ministrations of a certain "Yaaqov *mina*."

Moreover, let us consider b. Avodah Zarah's ending to the Ben Dama story, which it added to the y. Avodah Zarah version:

> *And* [according] *to R. Yishmael, these words* [Lev 18:5] *apply in private* [a person may choose transgression over death if the transgression will take place in private], *but in public, no. As it was taught in a baraita:* **R. Yishmael would say: "From where do we know that if they say to a person 'Serve idols and do not be killed' that he may serve and not be killed? The verse teaches 'and he shall live by them'—and not die by them. Is that true even in public? The verse teaches 'And do not desecrate My holy Name [in public]'"** (Lev 22:32) (Sifra to Leviticus, *Aharei Mot, pereq* 13).

---

58. Even at b. Pes 25a, where the Bavli deals with R. Yohanan's tradition about healing, it eliminates the Palestinocentric story about the "source" of the waters of Duhi.

This additional passage introduces the issue of sanctifying versus desecrating God's Name. The Dying rather than worshiping idols publicly sanctifies God's Name; choosing public worship over death is a desecration. The concern about public desecration of God's Name in this passage presages the redactors' mention of this concern at 28a in the context of R. Yohanan's public disclosure—without permission—of a Gentile woman healer's remedy for a gum ailment.

B. Avodah Zarah has thus eliminated material found in y. Avodah Zarah that was not directly connected to the subject matter of the tractate, placed the material it did take from y. Avodah Zarah (the Ben Dama story) in a context that highlighted the theme of that material (*minut*), and continued even after the Ben Dama story (28a) to develop the two themes of *minut* and desecration of God's Name which it highlighted in its reworking of y. Avodah Zarah's story. B. Avodah Zarah thus not only improved upon y. Avodah Zarah's original contextualization of the Ben Dama material, but worked to connect its reworked version tightly into its new b. Avodah Zarah context.

IV

B. Avodah Zarah Views a Source in Connection with an Amoraic Concern That Y. Avodah Zarah Had Viewed in Connection with the Mishnah

IV.a. B. Avodah Zarah 11b–12a ‖ Y. Avodah Zarah 1:4, 39d— Israelites and Idolatrous Fairs

M. Avodah Zarah 1:4 rules that even if an idolatrous festival is going on within a city, Israelites may do business with Gentiles outside the city and vice-versa. In its second clause, the mishnah rules that traveling to a city in which there is an idolatrous festival is forbidden if there is only one road leading to the city (for then people might think that the Israelite is going there in order to celebrate), but is permitted if there are multiple roads. Finally, the mishnah rules on the basis of a case in Bet Shean that an Israelite may only do business during festival time with "unwreathed" stores. Let us now examine the relevant texts:

Y. Avodah Zarah 1:4, 39d

A. *Behold, is the "interior of it"* (תוכה) [i.e., of the city in which there is an idol,] *forbidden* [for Israelite commercial interaction with Gentiles]? [Just] *because there is one image in it, should the interior of* [the city] *be forbidden* [in its entirety to Israelite business]?

B. Resh Laqish said: "They [the sages of the mishnah] taught [that **a city in which there is an idol, the outside is permitted**—implying that the interior is forbidden] only with respect to a fair [in honor of the idol]. [He goes on:]

C. "And what is the difference between 'the interior of it' and 'outside of it'? [The city-dwellers in] 'the interior of it' benefit from the tax [imposed by the city in honor of the idol and thus commerce with them is] forbidden; 'outside of it,' which does not benefit from the tax, is permitted.' And if 'outside of it' benefits from the tax, even [that] is forbidden."

D. *And was it not taught in a baraita* [t. AZ 1:8[59]]: **We go to a fair, and buy from there male and female slaves and beasts.** Resh Laqish said: "Not just Israelite slaves, but even Gentile slaves, for [the Israelite buyer] brings them close under the wings of the Divine Presence."

E. *And was it not taught in a baraita:* If [an Israelite] **bought from there** [the idolatrous fair] **clothing—it should be burned; a beast—it should be hamstrung; monies—he should bring them to the Dead Sea**?! [This contradicts t. AZ 1:8.]

F. [This latter baraita] *goes well with* [t. AZ 1:8 with respect to] **clothing—it should be burned; monies—he should bring them to the Dead Sea** [there is no conflict between the baraitot on these points because t. AZ 1:8 does not discuss these things. But] **a beast—it should be hamstrung**?! [This contradicts t. AZ 1:8,] *for was it not taught in the baraita:* **We go to a fair and buy from there male and female slaves and beasts?** [Didn't] *Resh Laqish say,* "Not just Israelite slaves, but even Gentile slaves, since [the Israelite buyer] brings them close under the wings of Heaven"?

G. *You may resolve* [the conflict by assuming that the purchaser of t. AZ 1:8 was an] *Israelite* [buying a beast from an] *Israelite* [and thus there is no need to hamstring].

The key point to note here is that y. Avodah Zarah uses t. AZ 1:8 as part of its explication of the mishnah. The mishnah rules that Israelites may not do business with Gentiles in a place in which there is an idol, and, typically, y. Avodah Zarah quotes a baraita in connection with that mishnah which is inconsistent with it.[60] T. Avodah Zarah 1:8's inconsistency with the mishnah lies in its assumption that Israelites may attend fairs, which were presumably somehow connected to idolatry. Before examining how b. Avodah Zarah uses t. AZ 1:8, there is more y. Avodah Zarah material we must set out. This material does not follow immediately in the text, but is separated from the preceding by material without parallel in b. Avodah Zarah.

---

59. Zuckermandel, 461.

60. See, e.g., m. AZ 1:1 and the discussion of that mishnah beginning at y. AZ 1:1, 39b.

H. *With what were they* [the stores mentioned in m. AZ 1:4] *wreathed* (מעוטרות, a word in the mishnah)?

I. R. Yohanan said, "With myrtle." R. Shimon b. Laqish said, "With all other species."

J. *On the view of R. Yohanan, all of them* [all stores wreathed with myrtle] *are forbidden* [since it is presumed that the wreathing is in honor of the idol]. *On the view of Resh Laqish, all that is forbidden is the addition* [that is, any additional species added to what already adorned the store. The addition is presumed to be in honor of the idol].

K. *How does he* [the Israelite] *act* [on the view of Resh Laqish]? *If* [the store-keeper] *was accustomed to bring out five baskets* [of decorative fruit to fix up the store for the idol] *and he brought out ten—if it is said* [that the extra five are for the sake of] *"wreathing,"* [then they are forbidden]; *if it is said they are for business* [additional decorations to attract customers], *then those fruits are permitted.*

Now, let us examine b. AZ 12b–13a:

A. R. Shimon b. Laqish said: "They [the sages of the mishnah] only taught [that wreathed stores are forbidden if they are] wreathed with roses and myrtle *which give pleasure with their smell,*[61] but [if they are] wreathed with fruits, these are permitted" [the Israelite may buy from them even though the sale will indirectly benefit idolatry].

B. *What is the reason* [that Resh Laqish allows the Israelite to buy]? *For the verse says:* "And not one bit of the condemned [property] will stick to your hand (Deut 13:18)." *It is benefiting from* [idolatry] *which is forbidden, but causing benefit* [to idolatry] *is permitted.*

C. And R. Yohanan said: "Even if [the stores] are wreathed with fruits, it is also forbidden [for the Israelite to buy from them]." *Inference from minor to major. If benefiting from the idolatry is forbidden, isn't causing benefit to the idolatry that much more forbidden?*

D. *They raised an objection:* **R. Natan says: "On the day that idolatry provides tax relief, they** [the local authorities] **announce and say: 'Whoever picks up a wreath and places it on his head and on the head of his ass in honor of the idol—the tax will be forgiven him. And if not—the tax will not be forgiven him.' An Israelite who happens to be there, what does he do? If he places** [the wreath on his head], **he will benefit** [from the tax relief];[62] **if he does not place** [a wreath on his head], **he will be**

---

61. I consider this part of Resh Laqish's statement to be an anonymous interpolation for two reasons: (1) it is missing from the y. AZ parallel; and (2) this interpolation is in Aramaic, while the rest of Resh Laqish's statement is in Hebrew. See Shamma Friedman, *"Yevamot X,"* 277–321, wherein he lists criteria for determining whether or not a Talmudic statement is in fact "attributable" to the Talmud's anonymous voice.

62. Further, by benefiting from the tax relief granted in honor of the idol the Israelite is impermissibly deriving benefit from an idol.

benefiting [the idol by paying the tax]. **From here they said: '[The Israel-ite who] buys and sells in the marketplace of idolatry**—[if he bought] a **beast, it should be hamstrung; fruits, clothing, and vessels must be al-lowed to rot; monies and metal vessels must be taken to the Dead Sea.' And what is hamstringing? Cutting the tendons of its hoofs beneath the ankle."** *It is nevertheless taught:* **If the Israelite places the wreath, he turns out to be benefiting from the idolatry; if he does not, he is caus-ing benefit to the idolatry.** [This conflicts with Resh Laqish's view, which is that there exists a situation in which the Israelite can buy, although that will indirectly benefit the idolatry].

E. R. Mesharshya b. de-R. Idi said: "R. Shimon b. Laqish holds: 'The Rabbis argue with R. Natan, and I agree with the Rabbis who argue with him.' And R. Yohanan holds: '[The Rabbis] do not argue [with R. Natan].'"

F. *And they do not argue? But was it not taught in a baraita:* **We go to a fair of idolaters, and buy beasts, male and female slaves, houses, fields, and vineyards from them . . .** (t. AZ 1:8; Sem 4:25); *and R. Yohanan says:* "The law is like R. Yose."

[By emphasizing that the law is like R. Yose, R. Yohanan implies that the law is not like the Rabbis, who disagree with R. Yose. So if R. Yohanan disagrees with the Rabbis here and agrees with R. Natan earlier, then the Rabbis and R. Natan must themselves disagree.]

G. *Consequently they* [the Rabbis and R. Natan] *argue!*

H. *R. Yohanan says to you:* "*In reality they do not argue, and there is no difficulty* [between R. Natan's baraita and t. AZ 1:8]. *Here,* [R. Natan's baraita, which forbids buying at the fairs, deals with an Israelite] *who buys from a traveling vendor from whom the city exacts the tax. Here,* [t. AZ 1:8, which permits the purchases, deals with an Israelite] *who buys from a private householder from whom they do not exact the tax.*

Unlike y. Avodah Zarah, b. Avodah Zarah explicates t. AZ 1:8 in con-nection with the amoraic dispute about what the mishnaic term "wreath-ing" means. We therefore see y. Avodah Zarah using the baraita in direct connection with the mishnah, and b. Avodah Zarah using it in connection with an amoraic dispute *about* the mishnah.

Baruch Bokser analyzed another example of this phenomenon in con-nection with b. Ber 47b–48a ‖ y. Ber 7:2, 11b, where y. Berakhot deployed a teaching of Shmuel in connection with m. Ber 7:2, while b. Berakhot deployed it in connection with the Palestinian amoraic dispute about whether a minor child could be an "adjunct" to a *zimmun* for recitation of the Grace after Meals.[63] As in the case studied by Bokser, b. Avodah Za-rah's deployment of t. AZ 1:8 in connection with an amoraic dispute likely

---

63. See Baruch Bokser, "A Minor for *Zimmun*," and my "A Bavli Sugya and Its Two Yerushalmi Parallels."

marks its sugya as a diachronic development beyond the y. Avodah Zarah sugya.

We must also consider the presence in both Talmuds of the R. Yohanan/Resh Laqish dispute. The mishnah clearly calls for discussion of what "wreathing" means, which both Talmuds provide. But nothing in the mishnah, nor in other tannaitic sources, requires that both Talmuds discuss wreathing in connection with this particular amoraic dispute.

The hypothesis that b. Avodah Zarah's recourse to this amoraic dispute is due to a shared stratum of early talmud is appealing in this case because b. Avodah Zarah presents the fifth-generation R. Mesharshya b. de-R. Idi's comment (§E) on how the older amoraic dispute relates to the baraitot the Bavli quotes in §D. It thus certainly looks as though R. Mesharshya was familiar with the R. Yohanan/Resh Laqish dispute and with non-Toseftan baraitot that bear upon the interpretation of that dispute. But a closer look at y. Avodah Zarah §§H–K and b. Avodah Zarah §§A–E casts doubt on the reliability of the attribution to R. Mesharshya and, by extension, on the identification as early talmud of the shared R. Yohanan/Resh Laqish dispute. B. Avodah Zarah altered the presentation of Resh Laqish's view in §A to refer to the "pleasure" the plants used for wreathing provide. The anonymous voice in §B questions Resh Laqish's ruling that an Israelite may buy from a store adorned with a non-fragrant wreath, but concludes on his behalf that while benefiting *from* idolatry is forbidden, causing benefit *to* it is not. B. Avodah Zarah also altered R. Yohanan's view in §C to include a *qal va-homer* argument that mentions "benefiting from" idols and "causing benefit to" idols. The language of "benefiting" appears as well in R. Natan's non-Toseftan baraita in §D, which also, interestingly, refers to wreaths. These non-Toseftan baraitot are missing from y. Avodah Zarah, with the exception of the middle portion that discusses how an Israelite should destroy items he purchased at an idolatrous fair. Putting all these data together, it seems that Bavli editors working with y. Avodah Zarah's versions of the R. Yohanan/Resh Laqish dispute added the references to "benefiting" and also emended (or perhaps even created) the non-Toseftan baraitot attributed to R. Natan that also mention "benefiting" idolatry and wreathing. The question is: Who were these editors? Was R. Mesharshya one of them? Were they amoraim who preceded or followed him, or perhaps post-amoraic redactors? The sugya itself yields no evidence that the scholars responsible for altering the older dispute were amoraim who preceded or followed R. Mesharshya, let alone that he himself was responsible for it.

Reading b. Avodah Zarah over carefully, we see that an editorial hand has reworked the old R. Yohanan/Resh Laqish dispute about wreathing into a dispute about something else. That "something else" is a dispute at a higher level of abstraction: a dispute about receiving benefit from, or conferring benefit on, idolatry. This reworking of the amoraic dispute is carried right through §§A–H, and is the agenda at stake in the unfolding of the sugya. This concern about receiving benefit from or causing benefit to idolatry is also a thematic concern we see elsewhere in b. Avodah Zarah: at 6a, the Bavli suggests that a reason for m. AZ 1:1's prohibitions is to prevent an idolater from profiting, and at 6b, R. Yehudah Nesiah worries about the consequences (which in his case are the psychic benefits conferred) of accepting a *min*'s gift. All this being so, the likely source for the reworking of y. Avodah Zarah in b. Avodah Zarah is the post-amoraic redactors, who alone have the sort of view of the whole that accounts for this consistency of theme.

Nor can the hypothesis that early talmud is responsible for the Talmuds' common deployment of the R. Yohanan/Resh Laqish dispute derive support from the fact that the fifth-generation R. Mesharshya appears to know and respond to it. R. Mesharshya is represented as knowing the *emended* amoraic dispute, and, as we have concluded, the emendations are likely the work of the redactors. This leaves us with two possibilities: (1) The attribution to R. Mesharshya is pseudepigraphic; or (2) R. Mesharshya was aware of the R. Yohanan/Resh Laqish dispute more or less as it appeared in y. Avodah Zarah, but the b. Avodah Zarah redactors altered the entire sugya, thus making it appear that R. Mesharshya knew the emended older amoraic dispute. Whichever possibility is correct, it is clear that R. Mesharshya's presence in b. Avodah Zarah's sugya is no impediment to the logical conclusion that the b. Avodah Zarah redactors reworked y. Avodah Zarah, yielding the sugya we now have.

Another important point—which forms a nice segue to section V, below—is that b. Avodah Zarah reworked y. Avodah Zarah so as to highlight a legal concept of interest to it, and unknown to y. Avodah Zarah. Y. Avodah Zarah's R. Yohanan held that the storekeeper's wreathing of his store with myrtle (presumably in any amount) renders his store off-limits to Israelites, while Resh Laqish held that the particular species used is not as important as the fact that the storekeeper added flora to the outside of his store. We may presume that the additional flora were placed in honor of the idol. In y. Avodah Zarah, then, the dispute was over whether it is the species of plant (R. Yohanan) or the motivation for the placement of any plant or fruit (Resh Laqish) that matters. By contrast, b. Avodah Zarah's anonymous voice explains that stores wreathed with roses and myrtle are prohibited to Israelites because they will benefit from the nice smell—a benefit that comes about because of the decoration in honor of idolatry. This explanation implicates this Palestinian amoraic dispute in the larger Bavli dispute (b. Pes 76b; b. AZ 66b) as to whether or not "smell

is consequential" (ריחא מילתא היא or ריחא לאו מילתא היא). If smell *is* consequential, then a person may be punished for enjoying a forbidden smell; if
not, he will not be. This discussion of smell is directly related to b. Avodah
Zarah's larger concern here at 12b–13a: the issue of benefiting from, or
conferring benefit upon, idolatry. By smelling the fragrant wreath placed
in honor of the idol, the Israelite benefits from idolatry, according to
b. Avodah Zarah's reworking of Resh Laqish. The Israelite thus may not
purchase from stores bearing fragrant wreaths, but may purchase from
stores that do not, even though he may nevertheless be indirectly conferring a benefit on idolatry. According to b. Avodah Zarah's reworking of
R. Yohanan, the Israelite may not buy from any store bearing a wreath—
fragrant or otherwise—for if benefiting from an idol is forbidden, isn't
conferring a benefit all the more forbidden? B. Avodah Zarah's introduction of a legal concept of interest to it elsewhere in this and another Bavli
tractate and its recasting of the amoraic dispute in light of that concept are
additional evidence of the b. Avodah Zarah redactors' reworking of the
older y. Avodah Zarah sugya.

V

B. Avodah Zarah Reworks Y. Avodah Zarah Sugyot in Order to Raise Legal Issues to a Higher Level of Abstraction

Scholars have long recognized that the Bavli exhibits a greater interest in
abstract legal conceptualization than the Yerushalmi.[64] That is, the Bavli
tends to rework legal concepts to express them as abstract notions not directly tied to the casuistic, case-specific contexts in which the concepts
may have originated. There are a number of examples in the Avodah Zarah tractates of b. Avodah Zarah reworking y. Avodah Zarah sugyot in order to highlight legal issues raised in the older sugyot and reformulate
them at a higher level of abstraction. We will begin with a fairly simple example in which b. Avodah Zarah, faced with a y. Avodah Zarah sugya
that seems unrelated to the local mishnah, searches for a higher level of legal conceptualization that includes both the mishnah and the ill-fitting
y. Avodah Zarah sugya accompanying it. In this case, b. Avodah Zarah
employs legal conceptualization as a tool to rework the y. Avodah Zarah
sugya and make it fit better with the local mishnah.

---

64. See Leib Moscovitz, *Talmudic Reasoning: From Casuistics to Conceptualization*
(Tübingen: Mohr Siebeck, 2002), 14 and sources cited. Moscovitz himself cites the
example of b. AZ 48b, which employs the principle *zeh ve-zeh gorem*; see 6, 331–333.

V.a. B. Avodah Zarah 20b ‖ Y. Avodah Zarah 1:8, 40a

Y. Avodah Zarah 1:8, 40a

A. R. Bun b. Hiyya asked: "Is even a large beast in dispute? [Can the Israelite] sell [it] to [the Gentile] on the condition that he slaughter it?"

B. *It was found* [to have been] *taught* [in a baraita] *that even a large beast is in dispute.* **R. Yehudah says: "He sells to him on the condition that he slaughter it"** [compare t. AZ 2:1[65]].

B. Avodah Zarah 20b

A. They asked: "[If an Israelite sold a Gentile] a beast on the condition that he slaughter it, what [is the law]?"

B. *There* [in the mishnah] *what is the reason that R. Yehudah permits* [the conditional sale]*?* [Is it] *because* [the trees or other items attached to the land] *are not in* [the Gentile's] *domain and he cannot delay* [fulfilling the condition to cut] *them* [down], *but* [as to] *an animal, since it is in the domain of the idolater, he can delay* [fulfilling the condition to slaughter] *it? Or perhaps there is no difference* [between the two cases]*?*

C. *Come and hear that which was taught in a baraita:* [An Israelite may sell to a Gentile] **an animal on the condition that he slaughter it and he** [the Gentile] **slaughters, the words of R. Yehudah. R. Meir says: "We only sell** [to Gentiles that which is already] **slaughtered"** [compare t. AZ 2:1].

The pertinent part of the mishnah (m. AZ 1:8) provides that Israelites may not sell to Gentiles crops that are attached to the ground, but may do so once they have been cut. R. Yehudah dissents, and rules that an Israelite may sell attached crops to a Gentile on the condition that the latter cut them.

The mishnah is talking about crops; it does not call for a sugya such as the one we find here in both Talmuds, which discuss whether or not an Israelite can sell an animal to a Gentile on the condition that he slaughter it. Nor does the Talmuds' shared Toseftan baraita, t. AZ 2:1, call for the sugya. The baraita is not the starting-point of the discussion; rather, it is cited as the answer to the question attributed either to R. Bun b. Hiyya (y. Avodah Zarah) or the anonymous voice (b. Avodah Zarah). The similar form of the question and answer in both Talmuds points to b. Avodah Zarah's having adopted the question and answer raised earlier in y. Avodah Zarah.

Y. Avodah Zarah does not explain how the mishnah, which deals with land and crops, calls for a question about the sale of a beast. B. Avodah Zarah, by contrast, supplies the conceptual missing link between the

---

65. Zuckermandel, 462.

mishnah's "crops" and the Talmudic question about beasts by looking for a higher level of abstraction that encompasses both. B. Avodah Zarah does this by raising the larger issue of whether or not the Gentile's purchased property is in his own domain. Will R. Yehudah rule the same way in both cases, despite the fact that the purchased trees or crops are not in the Gentile's domain but the animal is? Or will this difference cause R. Yehudah to rule differently? B. Avodah Zarah thus clarified a difficulty it did not create and forged a link between the sugya and the mishnah for which it was an ill-fit.

V.b. B. Avodah Zarah 32a ∥ Y. Avodah Zarah 2:3, 41b— Desiring the Existence of a Forbidden Item

Y. Avodah Zarah 2:3, 41b

A. *And Hadrianic pottery?* R. Zeirah in the name of R. Yirmiyah: "The law is like R. Meir, as it was taught (t. AZ 5:8[66]): **Hadrianic pottery is forbidden, and its prohibition is a prohibition of benefit—the words of R. Meir. But the Sages say, "Its prohibition is not a prohibition of benefit."**

B. R. Yirmiya asked R. Zeirah: "We learned in the mishnah (m. Orl 3:1) that a garment [which was sewn with forbidden *orlah* materials must be burned]. Here [with respect to Hadrianic pottery], what [is the law]?"[67]

C. And [R. Zeirah] was angry before him [R. Yirmiyah]. He [R. Zeirah] said to him: "Even according to the one who says there [that Hadrianic pottery] is permitted [i.e., the Sages, would agree that] here [the garment] is forbidden. There [with Hadrianic pottery], the forbidden item is not recognizable [because the libation-wine has soaked into the clay], but here [with the garment], the forbidden item is recognizable."

D. *And what about* [using Hadrianic pottery] *to support a bed?* R. Lazar said: "Permitted," and R. Yohanan said: "Forbidden."

B. Avodah Zarah 32a

A. *What is Hadrianic* [pottery]? R. Yehudah said in the name of Shmuel: "Pottery of Hadrian Caesar." When R. Dimi came, he said: "There was virgin soil that no man had ever cultivated. He [Hadrian] cultivated it, planted it [with grapes], and put the [resulting] wine into white earthenware vessels that would absorb the wine. They [the soldiers] would break them

---

66. Zuckermandel, 466.

67. According to that mishnah, a garment sewn with forbidden *orlah* materials must be burned. Comparing that case to the case of Hadrianic pottery, which is a matter of forbidden idolatrous materials, how can the Sages allow an Israelite to benefit from Hadrianic pottery?

into potsherds and carry [the pieces] with them. [In whatever place] they would come to, they would dissolve [the pieces in water] and drink."

B. R. Yehoshua b. Levi said: "Our first [mixing of wine with water, which is quite strong,] is like their third [mixing]."

C. *They asked: What about* [using the Hadrianic pottery] *to support the legs of a bed? Is it permitted to desire the* [continued] *existence* [of a forbidden item] *by means of something else, or not?* [That is, if the forbidden item will be used for something other than its intended purpose, as with Hadrianic pottery being used to support a bed.] *Come and hear, for* [this is a dispute of] *R. Eleazar and R. Yohanan. One forbids, and one permits.*

Our focus is on y. Avodah Zarah §D and b. Avodah Zarah §C. B. Avodah Zarah has taken the simple question and (disputed) answer about whether or not Hadrianic pottery can be used to support a bed, and has interpolated the legal concept it sees as underlying the question: Is an Israelite permitted to desire the continued existence of a forbidden item (and allow it to exist), if he intends that forbidden item to be used for a purpose other than its normally intended use? By recasting y. Avodah Zarah's question in this way, b. Avodah Zarah makes it appear as if the Palestinian amoraim R. Eleazar and R. Yohanan disputed this larger issue, which we know from y. Avodah Zarah they did not.

The Bavli deploys this notion of "desiring the [continued] existence of a forbidden item" later at 63b and again at 64a. In both cases we can see clearly how the b. Avodah Zarah redactors reworked the simpler y. Avodah Zarah sugyot to reflect the legal concept they saw implicit therein:

Y. Avodah Zarah 5:1, 44c

R. Yirmiyah asked: "What about [if] his wage is for smashing barrels of libation-wine?" [Is it then permitted?] *Even so* [i.e., even though the worker is being paid to destroy the offending wine], *his wage is forbidden.*

B. Avodah Zarah 63b

R. Nahman, Ulla, and Abimi b. Papi were sitting together, and R. Hiyya b. Ami was sitting with them. They sat and asked: "What about [if] his wage is for smashing [barrels of] libation-wine?" *Do we say that since he* [the worker] *desires its* [the wine's] *continued existence* [for a period long enough for him to destroy it and be paid for doing so], *it is forbidden, or is anything the purpose of which is to diminish nonsense acceptable?*[68] [Meaning that permitting the continued existence of the prohibited wine is permit-

___

68. I am assuming that this part of the question is anonymous by comparison with y. AZ, in which this part of the question does not exist.

ted if the ultimate purpose is to destroy it, the "nonsense."] R. Nahman said: "Let him smash, and may a blessing come upon him."

In this case, the concept "desiring the [continued] existence of a forbidden item" was deployed in order to explore the case of an Israelite who was owed a wage for smashing barrels of libation-wine. The Israelite clearly would desire the continued existence of the barrels for as long as it would take for him to smash them and earn his wage, and ultimately R. Nahman permits him to do so. The final deployment of this concept appears shortly after this one, at 64a.

Y. Avodah Zarah 5:1, 44c–d

A. Asi said: "The monies [obtained through the sale] of libation-wine in the hands of a Gentile are forbidden. The monies [obtained through the sale] of an idol in the hands of a Gentile—R. Yonatan said 'Permitted,' and R. Yohanan said 'Forbidden.'"

B. *A baraita supports this one and a baraita supports that one. The baraita that supports R. Yohanan:* **A Gentile that owed money to an Israelite—he** [the Gentile] **should not say, "Wait** [for payment] **until I sell libation-wine, wait until I sell an idol, and I will give you** [what is owed]**." I say** [that were the Gentile to do so the monies would be forbidden,] **lest he have exchanged** [the libation-wine or idol directly for the monies with which he repaid the Israelite] (t. AZ 8:16[69]).

C. *The baraita that supports R. Yonatan:* **A Gentile who owed money to an Israelite—behold, this one** [the Gentile] **may sell libation-wine and give** [the proceeds] **to him; an idol and give** [the proceeds] **to him.**

B. Avodah Zarah 64a

A. *They were again sitting and asking:*[70] "What about the monies of a Gentile [obtained through the sale of] an idol?" *Does it* [the idol] *hold its monies in the hands of the Gentile or not?*[71]

B. R. Nahman said to them: "It makes sense that the monies [obtained through the sale of an idol] in the hands of a Gentile are permitted . . ." [An initial unsuccessful attempt to derive this conclusion is here omitted.]

C. *Rather, derive it from here:* **An Israelite who was owed a *maneh* by an idolater, and** [the Gentile] **sold an idol and brought him** [the money, or sold] **libation-wine and brought him** [the money], **it is permitted. But if he** [the Gentile] **said to him: "Wait until I sell an idol and I will bring you**

---

69. Zuckermandel, 472.

70. The reference is to the same amoraim who were "sitting and asking" at 63b.

71. I am assuming that this part of the question is anonymous by comparison with the parallel question in y. AZ. Another point in favor of the anonymity is that the issue of "holding its monies" is raised anonymously at b. AZ 62a.

[the money, or sell] **libation-wine and I will bring you** [the money], **it is forbidden"** (t. AZ 8:16).

D. *What is the difference between the beginning and the end* [of the baraita]? R. Sheshet said: "[The wage is forbidden at] the end because he [the Israelite creditor] is like one who desires its [the idol's or libation-wine's] continued existence" [and thus is penalized for so desiring].

[Further discussion of the concept is omitted].

In all three cases—32a, 63b, and 64a—b. Avodah Zarah reworked the parallel y. Avodah Zarah sugyot to include the legal concept "desiring the [continued] existence of a forbidden item." B. Avodah Zarah's introduction of a higher level of legal conceptualization to capture what it saw as being at stake in the Yerushalmi is the fruit of its reflection upon the work of the Yerushalmi.

VI
Conclusion

In this chapter we studied examples that show how the b. Avodah Zarah redactors reworked materials they appropriated from the earlier Talmud. These examples show that b. Avodah Zarah parallels to y. Avodah Zarah sugyot are often secondary reworkings of y. Avodah Zarah, and that these reworkings can be categorized under five principal headings:

1. Adding characerically Babylonian cultural, linguistic, or other features to y. Avodah Zarah sugyot;

2. Excising materials that are of specific relevance to the Land of Israel and/or the Greco-Roman cultural context of the Land of Israel;

3. Re-arranging materials in a more sensible order, including the creation of segues between materials that lacked such transitions in y. Avodah Zarah;

4. Deploying sources that y. Avodah Zarah had utilized to explore tannaitic issues in the exploration of amoraic issues; and

5. Making greater use of abstract legal conceptualization in reworking y. Avodah Zarah sugyot.

The evidence of this chapter shows that the differences between y. and b. Avodah Zarah sugyot should not be attributed to the Talmuds' having somehow received similar, yet different, versions of these sugyot as part of a shared pool of early talmud. Rather, it is more likely in these cases that b. Avodah Zarah worked with and emended the y. Avodah Zarah source.

4

B. Avodah Zarah's Awareness of Y. Avodah Zarah's Editing (Micro Analysis II)

In this chapter, we will move a step beyond our just-completed exploration of how b. Avodah Zarah sugyot are often the secondary reworkings of parallel y. Avodah Zarah sugyot by probing examples that show that b. Avodah Zarah was at times cognizant of how y. Avodah Zarah had been edited. In these examples, the b. Avodah Zarah redactors are aware of how y. Avodah Zarah ended its discussion of a particular point or how it left an issue unresolved; they, in turn, commence their discussion at that point or begin by taking up the unresolved issue. We will also examine a related example in which b. Avodah Zarah delves into the same halakhic context as y. Avodah Zarah in order to draw out a cited source, although the actual source cited in both Talmuds is itself different.

I
B. Avodah Zarah Begins at the Point at Which Y. Avodah Zarah Leaves Off

I.a. B. Avodah Zarah 8b ǁ Y. Avodah Zarah 1:2, 39c—
Rome's Struggle for Hegemony

Immediately following its account of the primordial origin of Kalends in the days of Adam, y. Avodah Zarah points out that R. Yohanan disagreed with it. R. Yohanan explained the origin of Kalends as a holiday

149

established to celebrate Rome's success in obtaining world-mastery over its archrival, Egypt. R. Yohanan recounts that Rome and Egypt had been engaged in a long-running and futile struggle to defeat each other. Wearying at last of the endless wars, the two sides decide to resolve the conflict with much less mutual bloodletting; whichever empire's general would commit suicide first on command would leave his empire the victor and master of the world. The Egyptian general did not listen to the command, but the Roman general—an old man named Yanobris—did, after being promised that his twelve sons would be raised to high positions of honor after his death. For this reason (according to R. Yohanan), the day marking this suicide and Rome's elevation in the world is called "Kalends Yanobris."

Later on, the Yerushalmi presents what appears to be a baraita-fragment with a question and answer about it:

Y. Avodah Zarah 1:2, 39c

A. **"And Kratesis—the day that Rome seized the monarchy** [over the world]."

B. *And was that not already taught?* [Did not R. Yohanan's story already establish Kalends as the day that Rome seized control over the world?]

C. R. Yose b. R. Bun said: "A second time" [that is, R. Yohanan's story about Kalends marked only the first time that Rome seized power over the world. Kratesis marks a second occasion on which they did it, in order to finally consolidate their power].

It is apparent from §B that the Yerushalmi editor is aware that R. Yohanan's earlier story about Kalends is, in fact a story that *appears earlier* in the text. Of greater importance is the fact that y. Avodah Zarah does not expand on R. Yose b. R. Bun's resolution in §C. It does not tell us anything about this alleged second seizure of world sovereignty by Rome.

Now let us examine the parallel at b. AZ 8b, the very beginning of b. Avodah Zarah's sugya about the meaning of "Kratesis."

B. Avodah Zarah 8b

A. *What is Kratesis?*

B. R. Yehudah said in the name of Shmuel: "The day that Rome seized sovereignty [over the world]."

C. *And was it not taught in a baraita:* **"Kratesis and the day that Rome seized sovereignty"?**

D. R. Yosef said: "Rome seized [power on] two occasions; once in the days of Queen Cleopatra, and once in the days of the Greeks."

From the story that follows, recounting Rome's outmaneuvering of the Greeks for world-mastery, we can conclude that the victory over Cleopatra was the first, interim victory. Kratesis, then, celebrates the final victory over the Greeks. Significantly, b. Avodah Zarah then takes a good deal of space on 8b to discuss Rome's second, and final, victory over the Greeks. Comparing y. and b. Avodah Zarah, we thus see that the former moved in two steps: (1) recounting the initial victory over the Egyptians; and (2) establishing that Kratesis commemorates the second and final Roman victory (over whom?). Yet y. Avodah Zarah did not expand on the second point. B. Avodah Zarah, on the other hand, simply *asserts* that Rome had an initial victory over the Egyptians—the details of which it does not elaborate—and then goes on to expand on Rome's second and final victory, forever celebrated as Kratesis. B. Avodah Zarah thus expanded on that as to which y. Avodah Zarah kept silent, and only hinted at that about which y. Avodah Zarah had more to say.

The fact that y. Avodah Zarah presents Rome's initial victory over Egypt as a rationale for Kalends, while b. Avodah Zarah sees it in relation to Kratesis, is not that important. The key is that y. Avodah Zarah *ends* on the note that Kratesis marks Rome's second victory and fails to elaborate on that, while b. Avodah Zarah *opens* its Kratesis sugya on this very note—with a lengthy, narrative elaboration of that second victory. Let us examine some other examples.

I.b. B. Avodah Zarah 35b ‖ Y. Avodah Zarah 2:9, 41d— The Prohibition of Gentile Milk

The Yerushalmi opens its consideration of this issue with a question: "The milk of a Gentile—why is it forbidden?" It goes on to answer this initially in terms suggested by R. Ba b. R. Yehudah in the name of R. Shimon in the name of R. Yehoshua b. Levi: the reason for the prohibition is the fear that the milk had been exposed, as a result of which some venomous creature may have deposited poison in it. After some discussion of this issue, y. Avodah Zarah presents the alternative view of R. Yirmiyah: "The milk of a Gentile—why is it forbidden? Because of the mixing-in [of the milk of an] unclean animal." The Yerushalmi supports R. Yirmiyah's view with a baraita (t. AZ 5:11) that rules that if a Gentile is milking a cow in the presence of an Israelite, the Israelite need have no concerns about that milk; presumably, the Israelite's presence is sufficient to deter the Gentile from mixing the milk of an unclean animal into the permitted milk. Thus, the baraita shows that the concern about "Gentile milk" is the fear of a possible mixing-in of unclean milk, not a concern about exposure to poison. At this point, y. Avodah Zarah leaves the topic of milk altogether and goes on to discuss Gentile bread.

The Bavli on 35b never considers that the prohibition of Gentile milk may be due to "exposure" concerns. B. Avodah Zarah opens its sugya by quickly assuming that the fear of the mixing of "unclean" with "clean" milk is the rationale for the prohibition, and its discussion proceeds on that basis.

> *Milk—why be concerned about it? If it is because of substituting* [unclean for clean milk]—*clean milk is white, unclean milk is green!* [Thus there is no need for concern, since the two can be easily distinguished.] *If it is because of* [a concern about] *mixing* [unclean with clean milk]—*let it* [the milk] *stand! For the Master said: "Clean milk stands* [hardens]; *unclean milk does not stand."*

The rest of b. Avodah Zarah's short discussion proceeds on the assumption that the rationale for the prohibition is the concern about the mixing of unclean with clean milk. Once again, b. Avodah Zarah has opened its sugya with the last-stated assumption of the parallel y. Avodah Zarah sugya.

I.c. B. Avodah Zarah 38a ‖ Y. Avodah Zarah 2:9, 41d— Roasted Locusts

Both Talmuds place versions of this sugya after their lengthy treatments of Gentile oil (discussed earlier in chapter 3). Let us examine the sugyot:

Y. Avodah Zarah 2:9, 41d

A. *Their* [Gentiles'] *roasted egg: Bar Qappara permitted* [it for Israelite consumption] *and Hezekiah forbade it. Up to this point* [that is, Bar Qappara's and Hezekiah's dispute concerns an egg that was] *intentionally roasted* [by a Gentile for preparation as a food item]. *If it was unintentionally roasted?* [What then? May an Israelite eat it, since the Gentile did not intend to cook it as food?]

B. *Let us derive from this:* It once happened that a blaze erupted in a thicket of reeds and an uncleared plot of date palms, and there were locusts there that were roasted. The matter came before R. Mana, who forbade [Israelites to eat the unintentionally roasted locusts].

C. R. Abbahu said: "[The reason for R. Mana's stringency was] because of the intermixing of [clean locusts with] unclean locusts."

D. R. Yose b. R. Bun said: "This is one of the stringencies of Rav. Rav went down there [to Babylonia] and saw them being [too lenient], and was strict with them."

B. Avodah Zarah 38a

A. R. Beruna said in the name of Rav: "An idolater who lit a fire in an uncleared piece of land—all the locusts on the land are forbidden."

B. *How is this? If it is said that he* [the Israelite] *does not know which is pure* [i.e., permitted] *and which is impure, why does it matter* [whether an] *idolater* [lit the fire]? [The same concern applies] *even with an Israelite* [if an Israelite had lit the fire]! *Rather*, [the reason for Rav's prohibition is] *because of the* [prohibition of] *cooked food of Gentiles.* [By lighting the fire, the Gentile has—whether intentionally or not—"cooked" the locusts, which renders them forbidden for Israelite consumption.]

C. *Did he* [Rav] *prohibit* [consumption of the locusts if they were cooked] *in this manner? For did not R. Hanan b. Ami say in the name of R. Pedat in the name of R. Yohanan:* "[As to an] idolater who singed the hair off an animal's head [in preparation for eating it], it is permissible [for an Israelite] to eat of it, even [if the hair was singed off] the top of [the animal's] ear." [We may derive from this that the Gentile] *intended* [only to] *remove hair* [but not to cook; thus the animal may be eaten by an Israelite.] *Similarly here* [in the locust case, the Gentile only] *intended to clear the plot of land* [and thus the locusts should be permitted].

D. *Really,* [Rav had prohibited the locusts] *because he did not know which were pure and which were impure. And the incident that occurred involved a Gentile.*

On the subject of the roasted eggs of Gentiles, y. Avodah Zarah wonders whether there is a legal distinction between intentional roasting, which renders the food forbidden, and unintentional roasting. If the latter occurred, may an Israelite eat the eggs? Although a ruling by R. Mana forbidding some unintentionally roasted locusts is initially seen as responsive to this question, R. Abbahu asserts that R. Mana's ruling was based on other concerns. Y. Avodah Zarah closes with R. Yose b. R. Bun's view that the prohibition of the roasted locusts was a stringency of Rav; essentially, the locusts should have been permitted, but Rav forbade them in order to reverse what he perceived to be a trend toward religious laxity.

B. Avodah Zarah separates the issue of the roasted egg from that of the roasted locusts, dealing with the former later at 38b. It opens its consideration of the roasted locusts just where y. Avodah Zarah left off, with a reference to Rav's prohibition of them, and then moves on in §B to raise a question about what we can recognize as R. Abbahu's interpretation of R. Mana's stringency in y. Avodah Zarah §C. B. Avodah Zarah discusses this interpretation in its own §§B and C with reference to intentionality and the "cooked food of Gentiles," ultimately concluding in §D that the locusts had indeed been prohibited because of the difficulty of distinguishing the pure from the impure. Once again, b. Avodah Zarah has opened its consideration of a question taken up in the earlier Talmud with the views with which y. Avodah Zarah had concluded.

I.d. B. Avodah Zarah 41a–b ‖ Y. Avodah Zarah 3:2, 42c—
The Shards of Idolatrous Objects

Examining both Talmuds' treatments of m. AZ 3:2, we see that b. Avodah Zarah has taken into account the last-stated proposition presented by

y. Avodah Zarah about this mishnah, and that this, in turn, accounts for the way b. Avodah Zarah proceeds.

M. Avodah Zarah 3:2

A. The one who finds the shards of images,[1] behold, these are permitted.

B. If he found the form of a hand or the form of a foot, behold, these are forbidden, because the likes of them are worshiped.

Y. Avodah Zarah 3:1, 42c

A. R. Yose in the name of R. Yohanan: "[The reason that the shards of vessels are permitted is because] most of them come from the *delphicae* [three-legged tables used by waiters]."[2]

B. *From this* [that is, "if this is so"], *even the "form of hand" and "form of foot"!* [If the reason for the permission of the shards is because most come from the statuary made for the *delphicae*, then why should this not suffice as a reason to permit the forms of hands and feet, most of which could also come from there?]

C. *It* [the case of the "form of hand or foot"] *is different,* **because their likes are worshiped.** *As it is written . . .*

At this point, y. Avodah Zarah's understanding of the mishnah is clear. The mishnah had taught that different legal consequences attach to the "shards of vessels," which are permitted, and the "form of hand or foot," which are not. The Yerushalmi explains this difference straightforwardly: most "shards of vessels" are shards of statuary made for strictly decorative purposes as attachments to the *delphicae*, and are therefore permitted, while, as per the mishnah, most "forms of hand or foot" are worshiped, and must therefore be forbidden. At the very end of its treatment of this mishnah, the Yerushalmi places the following statement:

R. Abin in the name of R. Shimon: "That which it says [that the "forms of hand or foot" are forbidden] applies to a situation in which they are lacking a base. But if they have a base, I say that they have come from the shards (שברים) [and thus should be permitted]."

Reading R. Abin's statement very carefully, one can see that he is proceeding on a different assumption than R. Yose in the name of R. Yohanan. The latter had explained the mishnah's distinction between the permitted "shards of vessels" and the forbidden "form of hand or foot" by positing that the "shards of vessels" come from objects that *had not been worshiped,*

---

1. In y. AZ's mishnah, the reading is "shards of vessels" (כלים).

2. See Jastrow, *Dictionary,* 311.

such as the *delphicae*. The anonymous voice even clarified that a "form of hand or foot" that came from *delphicae* would be forbidden "because their likes are worshiped." Thus, at this point in the sugya, we see that the only permitted "shards of vessels" are those that come from vessels that *had not* been worshiped, and are not of a type *ordinarily worshiped*, such as the "form of hand or foot." R. Abin, by contrast, assumes that the mishnah's "shards of vessels" (שברי כלים) *can* include shards of idolatrous objects. We can reconstruct his assumption by working through his argument about the "form of hand or foot." To R. Abin, if the "form of hand or foot" are standing alone and not on a base, this indicates that they were made in order to stand alone, and hence, as per the mishnah, they must have been made that way in order to be worshiped.[3] On the other hand, if the "forms of hand or foot" *are* standing on a base, this indicates that they have broken off from a larger statue (and presumably lack sanctity) and thus, in his own words, "they have come from the shards" and should be permitted. R. Abin does not seem concerned that the "form of hand or foot" standing *on* the base may have been part of a statue that had at one time been worshiped; nor does he seem concerned about permitting some "forms of hand and foot" although "the likes of them are worshiped." Indeed, R. Abin appears to be saying that if an object is broken, it is permitted—regardless of what its function had been prior to its destruction.[4] This is distinct from the position of R. Yose in the name of R. Yohanan quoted earlier. It is also the note on which y. Avodah Zarah's treatment of this mishnah ends.

B. Avodah Zarah 41a–b

A. Shmuel said: "[The mishnah's permission of the 'shards of images' includes] even the shards of idols."

B. *And did we not teach in the mishnah:* **Shards of images** [which implies that the images are non-idolatrous]?

C. *It is the case that even shards of idols* [are included in the mishnaic phrase "shards of images"].

D. *And the reason that the mishnah taught* **"shards of images"** *is because it wished to teach at the end:* **If he found the form of a hand or the form of a foot, behold these are forbidden, because the likes of them are**

---

3. Admittedly, the notion that a hand could be found resting on a base seems odd. This rendering of R. Abin's position follows P'nei Moshe to y. AZ 3:1, s.v. הדא אמרה.

4. Compare P'nei Moshe, s.v. הדא אמרה. It is possible that the reason for R. Abin's different understanding of the mishnah is that his mishnah-text was like the one we now have in the Bavli (שברי צלמים).

worshiped. [That is, had the mishnah read "shards of idols" instead of the way it reads, one might have thought that the only "forms of hand or foot" that are forbidden are those that come from idols, but not those that were decorative. So, by teaching "shards of images," we learn that all images of hand and foot are forbidden—even those that may not have been worshiped.]

E. *It was taught in the mishnah:* **If he found the form of a hand or the form of a foot, behold these are forbidden, because the likes of them are worshiped.**

F. *Why? Are they not* **"shards"** [which should be permitted, as per the the first clause of the mishnah]?

G. Shmuel interpreted it (תרגמה) [meaning that Shmuel interpreted the prohibition of the form of hand or foot in the mishnah] as relating to a situation in which they are standing on their bases.

Shmuel and b. Avodah Zarah's anonymous voice in §§A–D understand the phrase "shards of images" to include shards of idols. The anonymous voice does not seriously entertain even the possibility that it refers only to shards of non-idolatrous images. Thus, b. Avodah Zarah has opted for R. Abin's view rather than R. Yose's: "shards" includes idols, and once again a b. Avodah Zarah sugya opens on the note with which the y. Avodah Zarah treatment ended.

I.e. B. Avodah Zarah 44b ‖ Y. Avodah Zarah 3:4, 42d— R. Gamliel's Response

M. Avodah Zarah 3:4 recounts the well-known story about R. Gamliel's presence in the bath-house of Aphrodite and the pagan Proclus' challenge to him about his behavior.[5] Proclus cites Deut 13:18 ("and do not let any of the spoils stick to your hand") as proof that the Rabbi should not be bathing in Aphrodite's bath-house. According to the mishnah, R. Gamliel responds with different answers: Aphrodite entered R. Gamliel's domain, and not vice-versa; Aphrodite is clearly intended as a decoration for the bath-house, while the bath-house was not built for Aphrodite; and finally, Aphrodite is not being treated with the reverence due a deity since men are standing around her nude and not showing her divine honors.

---

5. For a recent discussion of this mishnah which explores it as an example of rabbinic accommodation to living in a world dominated by idolatry, see Seth Schwartz, "Gamaliel in Aphrodite's Bath: Palestinian Judaism and Urban Culture in the Third and Fourth Centuries," in *The Talmud Yerushalmi and Graeco-Roman Culture,* vol. 1 (ed. Peter Schäfer; Tübingen: Mohr Siebeck, 1999), 203–217.

Y. Avodah Zarah 3:4, 42d

A. The Scholars,[6] R. Hama b. Yose in the name of R. Hoshaya; R. Zeirah in the name of R. Yehoshua b. Levi: "[R. Gamliel] responded to him [Proclus] with an evasive answer [that for all the money in the world, Proclus would not enter the house of his god naked, while in the bathhouse, men were standing around naked and were not embarrassed to urinate into the drain under the statue]. For if it were not so [if the answer were meant to be responsive], [Proclus] should have [further] responded to him from [the case of] Baal Peor, the worship of which is only by means of uncovering [one's body]."

B. *What is the result? That* [deity] *as to which a person behaves* [disrespectfully] *because of divinity* [like Peor, for whom disrespectful behavior is worship]—*it is forbidden* [for an Israelite to participate in a disrespectful activity in its presence]. *And that* [deity] *as to which a person does not behave* [disrespectfully] *because of divinity* [like Aphrodite, for whom such behavior is not worship]—*it is permitted* [for an Israelite to participate in a disrespectful activity in its presence].

Y. Avodah Zarah begins this sugya by citing amoraim who held that R. Gamliel's answer to Proclus was an evasive answer. R. Gamliel answered Proclus's challenge by pointing out that, whereas no amount of money in the world could convince a worshiper to dishonor his god, Proclus and the other men were standing in the bathhouse naked, urinating, and in a state of impurity caused by seminal emissions. This answer had to be evasive, claim these amoraim, because had it been meant as a serious debating point, Proclus should have responded from the case of the god Baal Peor, whose worship consists precisely of such seemingly disrespectful behavior. Responding to this suggestion, y. Avodah Zarah's anonymous voice asks: What is the result? That is, the Yerushalmi sees the challenge that could have been made to R. Gamliel from Baal Peor as a real one, and offers a response to it as if the challenge had in fact been raised. The response (drawn from the mishnah) is that an Israelite would be forbidden to bathe in a bathhouse built with a statue of Peor (since his worship is in this fashion), but permitted in a bathhouse built with a statue of Aphrodite (since her worship is not in this fashion).

Thus, having begun with an amoraic suggestion that R. Gamliel answered Proclus evasively, y. Avodah Zarah ends on the note that R. Gamliel's last answer to Proclus was in fact a real answer—when understood in light of the case of Peor, which y. Avodah Zarah, not R. Gamliel, raised.

---

6. The word translated above as "The Scholars" is חברייא. Sokoloff, *Dictionary*, 185, offers "friend" and "colleague" as possible meanings of the root ח־ב־ר, but also points to Palestinian sources in which it means "scholar" or "student."

Now, we can see how b. Avodah Zarah builds on this Yerushalmi
conclusion.

B. Avodah Zarah 44b

A. R. Hama b. Yosef said in the name of R. Oshaya: "R. Gamliel responded
to that *hegemon* (general) with a deceptive answer, but I say it was not deceptive."

B. *What was its deceptiveness? In that he* [R. Gamliel] *said to him,* **"This one**
[Aphrodite] **stands on the drain, and everyone urinates in front of her."**

C. *And if he urinates in front of her, what difference does it make? For did not Rava
say,* "Peor proves [that disrespectful behavior toward an idol does not
necessarily nullify it] for they [his worshipers] expose themselves before
him every day, and he is not nullified."

D. [Continuing the explication of A:] "And I say it was not deceptive. This
one's [Peor's] worship is in this fashion, and this one's [Aphrodite's]
worship is not in this fashion." [Thus, R. Gamliel's answer in §B was not
deceptive, since it stems from the fundamental difference between the
worship of these two gods.]

Y. Avodah Zarah had opened with the unequivocal view that R. Gamliel's answer to Proclus was evasive, claiming that were it not, Proclus
should have raised the issue of Peor. A bit later, y. Avodah Zarah responded to Proclus' hypothetical Peor challenge, and then concluded that
R. Gamliel's last-recorded answer to Proclus was not evasive after all.

In crafting the Bavli sugya, the b. Avodah Zarah redactors have taken
account of the conclusion that R. Gamliel's answer is ultimately determined not to be deceptive. In §§A and D of the Bavli sugya, the redactors
have modified the amoraic statement to include y. Avodah Zarah's conclusion that R. Gamliel's answer is not evasive, and that an Israelite may
derive benefit from a deity in an Aphrodite-like situation, but not in a
Peor-like situation. Moreover, in its §C, b. Avodah Zarah fills in a lacuna
in y. Avodah Zarah's mention of disrespectful behavior toward Peor—
what is it exactly about the worship of Peor that distinguishes the situation of that god from that of Aphrodite? Once again, we see the b. Avodah
Zarah redactors crafting their own sugya in order to take account of the
conclusions reached by the earlier Talmud.

I.f. Y. Sheviit 8:6, 38b ‖ B. Avodah Zarah 62a–b ‖ Y. Avodah
Zarah 5:1, 44c—Libation-Wine and the Sabbatical Year

We explored these sugyot in chapter 2 as part of our analysis of how
b. Avodah Zarah sugyot tend to resemble y. Avodah Zarah parallels more
closely than they do parallels in other Yerushalmi tractates. These sugyot

also illustrate the tendency under examination in this section: b. Avodah Zarah sugyot that commence their deliberations at the point at which y. Avodah Zarah had left off. I will not repeat the entire analysis here in detail, but simply highlight those parts of the sugyot that illustrate this point.

Y. Sheviit 8:6, 38b

D. R. Hila said: "Our baraita is dealing with those who carry fruits of transgression. And what does 'their wage is שביעית' mean? [It is interpreted] in accordance with what R. Abbahu said in the name of R. Yohanan: '[As to] libation wine, [the Sages] penalized him [the person who unlawfully transacts business in libation wine] with a penalty [in that he cannot retain his wage].'"

As I pointed out earlier, the y. Sheviit passage ends with R. Hila's restrictive reading of the baraita in t. Shevi 6:26, which he finds confirmed in R. Abbahu's tradition about the penalty the Sages imposed on an Israelite who transacts business in libation wine. Now let us look again at y. AZ 5:1, 44c:

A. *And is it not his* [the worker's] *wage he* [the master] *is giving him?* [So why should the wage be forbidden?]

B. R. Abbahu in the name of R. Yohanan: "[The Sages] penalized him with a penalty [for working with an item, libation wine, that is forbidden in benefit]."

[·]

E. R. Yeli said: "The baraita is dealing with fruits of transgression.[7] As R. Abbahu said in the name of R. Yohanan concerning libation wine: '[The Sages] penalized [the worker] with a penalty.'"

As we noted earlier, the y. Avodah Zarah redactors saw R. Hila as the conclusion of the y. Sheviit sugya, lifted out R. Abbahu's tradition about libation wine and placed it early in their own sugya, formulated a question to which it would be the answer, and only then incorporated the rest of the y. Sheviit sugya that had led to that result.

Now let us recall how b. AZ 62a–b worked with this material:

A. *What is the reason his* [the worker's] *wage is forbidden?* . . .

[·]

---

7. As we pointed out earlier, R. Yeli's statement is rendered according to the y. Shevi parallel, which is superior to y. AZ.

D.   R. Abbahu said in the name of R. Yohanan: "It is a penalty that the Sages imposed with respect to donkey-drivers and libation wine."

B. and y. Avodah Zarah's shared early placement of R. Abbahu in their parallel sugyot is a telling indicator of b. Avodah Zarah's closer relationship to y. Avodah Zarah than to y. Sheviit. But what is especially significant for our analysis in this chapter is that R. Abbahu's statement early in y. AZ 5:1, 44c (§B) only referred to libation wine; it was R. Yeli who first made the connection at the *end of the sugya* between the penalty for transactions in libation wine and the penalty for the donkey-drivers of t. Shevi 6:26. B. Avodah Zarah thus not only presupposes y. Avodah Zarah in general terms, but even emends R. Abbahu's statement in its own §D to take account of R. Yeli's deployment of that statement at the very end of the y. Avodah Zarah sugya.

II

B. Avodah Zarah Answers a Question Left Virtually Unanswered in Y. Avodah Zarah

II.a.   B. Avodah Zarah 11b–12a ∥ Y. Avodah Zarah 1:4, 39d— The Fair of Aza

In its treatment of m. AZ 1:4 at 39d, y. Avodah Zarah raises four questions. Three of these are answered within the Yerushalmi itself, while the fourth is not. The fourth question alone is taken up for discussion at b. AZ 11b–12a.

The first question is attributed to R. Zeirah, and concerns his doubt about a ruling of R. Yohanan. The latter had apparently ruled that an Israelite may buy items and services from a Gentile innkeeper (פונדק) during a fair established for idolatry. R. Zeirah asks: "It is forbidden [to buy] from a fair, but permitted from an inn?" R. Zeirah himself suggests an answer to his question, and this answer is later confirmed by R. Ba b. Hiyya b. Ba in the name of R. Yohanan.

The second question is attributed to R. Hisda, and also concerns the proper interpretation of a view of R. Yohanan. The latter had ruled that if one exchanges an animal for an idol, the animal is forbidden to an Israelite. R. Hisda is puzzled by this: bowing to the animal would not even render it forbidden, so why should the exchange? R. Hisda too suggests an answer to his own question, which he finds to be confirmed in the name of R. Yohanan.

The third question is sent from R. Shimon b. Yohanan to R. Shimon b. Yotsadaq, asking about whether the "fair of Tyre" is idolatrous in origin or not. The question is answered in the affirmative.

The discussion of the fourth question unfolds as follows:

Y. Avodah Zarah 1:4, 39d

A. R. Yitshaq b. Nahman asked R. Hanina: "What about the fair of Aza?"

B. He said to him: "Have you never gone to Aza before and seen an Israelite and Gentile who are sharing a pot? [The Israelite] is not concerned whether the Gentile stirs the pot!" [Normally, stirring the pot might be considered an act of cooking by the Gentile, which would render the pot's contents forbidden to the Israelite as "the cooked food of Gentiles"].

C. *And this* [alleged answer] *is difficult! He asks him this, and he answers him this!*

D. *Rather, since R. Hanina never said a word that he had never heard in his days* [from his own master], *for this reason, he* [R. Yitshaq b. Nahman] *asked him this, and he* [R. Hanina] *answered him this.*

Even without y. Avodah Zarah's expression of surprise in §C, it is easy to see the unresponsiveness of R. Hanina's answer. Although y. Avodah Zarah goes on to give an answer of its own in §D, this answer is more of an evasion than an answer, especially by comparison with the three preceding questions, to which much more direct answers were proffered. Interestingly, this—and only this—question is taken up by b. Avodah Zarah, which attempts to erect a sturdier bridge between the question and the answer.

B. Avodah Zarah 11b–12a

A. *What is "outside of it"* (חוצה לה) *[a term in m. AZ 1:4]?*

B. R. Shimon b. Laqish said in the name of R. Hanina: "'Outside' [is] like [the distance of] the fair of Aza [from the city of Aza itself]."

C. *And there are those who say:* R. Shimon b. Laqish asked R. Hanina: "What about the fair of Aza?"

D. He said to him: "Have you never gone to Tyre before, and seen an Israelite and an idolater who placed two cooking-pots on one stove, and the Sages were not concerned about them?"

E. *What does "the Sages were not concerned about them" mean?*

F. Abaye said: "[The Sages were not concerned] about carrion- meat. We do not say that perhaps the Israelite turned his face aside, and the idolater threw carrion into the [Israelite's] pot." *Similarly, the Sages were not concerned about monies obtained through idolatry.*

[That is, just as the Sages were not concerned that the Gentile would throw a piece of carrion into the Israelite's pot *from outside,* so were they not concerned about an Israelite making profit and holding monies that were acquired through a sale to a Gentile *outside* the city in which there was an idolatrous festival.]

G. Rava said: "What is 'the Sages were not concerned?' [The Sages were not concerned] about the cooked food of Gentiles." *Similarly, the Sages were not concerned about their festival-days.*

[Just as the Sages were not concerned that the close cooking-quarters would result in the Israelite eating Gentile food, so were they not concerned that the Israelite's proximity to a city in which an idolatrous festival was taking place would result in his obtaining monies made through that festival directly.]

H. Rabbah b. Ulla said: "The Sages were not concerned about a pipe." [That is, the Sages were not concerned that the Gentile would connect his pot to the Israelite's with a pipe and transmit non-kosher food into it.] *Similarly, the Sages were not concerned about* [the prohibition of commerce with Gentiles] *before their festivals.*

[Just as the Sages were not worried about this unlikely culinary possibility—so were they not concerned that Israelite commerce with merchants outside the city of Aza itself would cause them to financially benefit the city in the three days leading up to the festival.]

The amoraim in §§F–H do not discuss the unresponsiveness of §D to the question in §C. Rather, they appear to be answering the anonymous question in §E: what is the meaning of the enigmatic phrase "the Sages were not concerned about them"? The redactors take this concern one step further and try to make R. Hanina's statement not simply comprehensible by itself, but also responsive to R. Shimon b. Laqish's initial question about the fair of Aza. The redactors' decision to take up this question, then, is due to the same puzzlement that motivated y. Avodah Zarah's outburst in its own §C: the sense that the question and answer simply do not correspond.

Now, did b. Avodah Zarah take up the question *because* of the earlier Talmud's puzzlement, or on the basis of its own, independent confusion? The absence from b. Avodah Zarah of y. Avodah Zarah's outburst and evasive answer, as well as the inherent strangeness of this question and answer, suggest that b. Avodah Zarah may have acted independently. Yet the fact that this question is the poorly answered fourth of four questions—three of which were answered definitively—in y. Avodah Zarah, as well as b. Avodah Zarah's three attempts to prove that the answer *is directly* responsive to the question, indicate instead that b. Avodah Zarah is attempting to do better what it knows to have been partially and incompletely done before. Rather than provide answers to questions that y. Avodah Zarah had answered completely and definitively, b. Avodah Zarah chose to go over ground that it sensed y. Avodah Zarah had left unsettled, even confused.

III

B. Avodah Zarah Moves in the Same Direction as Y. Avodah Zarah, But Uses Different Sources

In this case, b. Avodah Zarah illustrates a point by citing a text from the same overall literary context as the text cited by y. Avodah Zarah to illustrate the same point. Due to a halakhic difference between the Talmuds the illustrative texts cited are not themselves the same. But b. Avodah Zarah is aware of the context from which the earlier Talmud drew, and it returns to that same context to find its own text.

III.a. *B. Avodah Zarah 20a ‖ Y. Avodah Zarah 1:9, 40a— Giving a Free Gift to a Gentile*

Y. Avodah Zarah 1:9, 40a

A. R. Zeirah in the name of R. Yose b. Hanina; R. Abba, R. Hiyya in the name of R. Yohanan: "'Do not show them mercy' (לא תחנם, Deut 7:2) [means] do not give them grace (חן). לא תחנם—do not give them a free gift (חנם). לא תחנם—do not give them settlement (חניה) in the Land [of Israel]."

[•]⁸

B. לא תחנם—do not give them a free gift. *But was it not taught in a baraita* [t. Pes 2:15⁹]:

C. **It once happened that R. Gamliel was traveling along the way, and he saw a loaf of fine bread (קלוסקין) cast aside on the road. He said to his slave Tavi: "Pick up this loaf."** He [R. Gamliel] **saw a Gentile coming towards him. He said: "Mabgai** [presumably the name of that Gentile], **take this loaf." R. Ilai ran after him** [the Gentile Mabgai]. **He said to him: "What is your name?" He said to him: "Mabgai." "And from where are you?" He said to him: "I am one of the station-guards** [of the stations leading to royal vineyards]**." "And had you ever met R. Gamliel before?" He said to him: "No." R. Gamliel had discerned this** [that the Gentile's name was Mabgai] **with the holy spirit. And we learned from him three things: We learned that we do not pass by** [abandoned] **foods, and that the leaven of a Gentile is permitted immediately after Passover, and that we assume that most passers-by are Gentile."**

---

8. R. Yose's view that houses may be rented to Gentiles in Palestine and R. Yose b. R. Bun's view that Gentiles may not be buried there have been omitted since they have no parallel in b. AZ.

9. Lieberman, 146–147.

Y. Avodah Zarah questioned the apparent scriptural prohibition against giving a free gift to a Gentile by citing the case of R. Gamliel at t. Pes 2:15, who had given a loaf of fine bread to a Gentile (whom he did not even know). B. Avodah Zarah takes a different approach to the issue of the "free gift."

B. Avodah Zarah 20a

A. *Another interpretation:* לא תחנם—*do not give them a free gift.*

B. *And the* [prohibition against giving a free gift to a Gentile is] *a tannaitic dispute. As we learn in a baraita:*

C. **Do not eat anything that dies by itself. Give it to the stranger (גר)** [i.e., the Gentile who adheres to the Noahide laws] **in your gates and he will eat it, or sell it to the Gentile (נכרי)** (Deut 14:21). **This teaches only that** [the animal that dies by itself] **is to be "given" to the stranger and "sold" to the Gentile** [idolater]. **From where do we know that it can be "sold" to the stranger?—Scripture says, "Give it" or "sell." From where do we know that it can be "given" to the Gentile?—Scripture says, "Give it and he will eat it," or "sell to the Gentile." It turns out that you can say that the stranger and the Gentile are the same in that both "giving" and "selling" apply to each—the words of R. Meir. R. Yehudah says: "The matters are as written. To the stranger by 'giving,' and to the idolater by 'selling.'"**

Even without moving into b. Avodah Zarah's analysis of this baraita, we can see that the two Talmuds have used different sources in approaching the issue of the "free gift" to the Gentile. Yet a truly thorough analysis must take us deeper into the context of b. Avodah Zarah's choice about how to deal with the issue. And that context shows us an affinity between the y. and b. Avodah Zarah approaches that is otherwise invisible.

The baraita cited by b. Avodah Zarah appears also at b. Pes 21b. M. Pesahim 2:1 establishes that as long as an Israelite is permitted to eat leaven before Passover, he may also use it for various purposes, including "selling it to a Gentile (נכרי)." The baraita cited at b. AZ 20a appears at b. Pes 21b as part of a lengthy sugya that begins with a teaching of Hezekiah: "From where do we know that it is forbidden to derive benefit from leaven on Passover? Scripture teaches (Exod 13:3), 'Leaven *shall not be eaten'*—there should not be a permission [regarding the leaven that could bring] about eating." The Bavli infers from this that had the Torah not written it "shall not be eaten," one could only have derived a prohibition against *eating* leaven, but not one against deriving other benefit from it.

The Bavli then points out that this inference conflicts with a view of R. Abbahu, according to whom the root א־כ־ל implies a prohibition against both eating and benefit, "unless the verse distinguishes between them for you just as it distinguished with regard to the animal that died by itself."

The Bavli then goes on to cite and discuss the baraita that also appears at b. AZ 20a. This entire sugya in Pesahim has a Palestinian parallel at y. Pes 2:1, 28c, where the baraita discussing Deut 14:21 is cited in a more expansive form and discussed at greater length.

Thus although b. AZ 20a and y. AZ 1:9, 40a deal with the issue of the "free gift" to the Gentile differently, they do so by drawing on source-materials that pertain to the same halakhic context—the issue of transferring ownership of leaven to Gentiles. Y. Avodah Zarah had dealt with the issue by citing t. Pes 2:15, in which R. Gamliel *gives* leaven to a Gentile. Rather than citing t. Pes 2:15, b. Avodah Zarah cited a baraita about carrion-meat that was part of a sugya attached to m. Pes 2:1 that discusses *selling* leaven to a Gentile. B. Avodah Zarah 20a thus cited a tannaitic source that preserved (however obliquely) the Yerushalmi's nexus of "Gentile" and "leaven" while also highlighting—as the Yerushalmi did not—the tension between "giving" and "selling" to a Gentile.

B. Avodah Zarah's awareness of the overall literary context from which y. Avodah Zarah drew is thus apparent, but a closer examination of the sugyot reveals that b. Avodah Zarah's choice of a different baraita was likely done intentionally in order to highlight a halakhic difference with y. Avodah Zarah.[10] While y. Avodah Zarah permits an Israelite to give foodstuffs to an idolater, b. Avodah Zarah does not—an Israelite may only give foodstuffs to the "resident alien," who observes the Noahide laws. This halakhic difference reflects the Bavli's greater interest in and attention to the Noahide laws and to Jews' obligations to Noahides. For example, the Bavli, unlike the Yerushalmi, devotes extensive space to a discussion and elaboration of these laws (b. Sanh 56b–57b).[11] Further, the later amoraic strata of the Bavli expand the application of Lev 19:14's command "do not place a stumbling-block before the blind" to include a prohibition against doing anything that would cause a Noahide to violate one of his seven Noahide laws (e.g., b. AZ 6a; b. Ned 62b). The Bavli leaves open the issue of whether the obligation to die for the sanctification of God's Name (martyrdom) extends to Noahides as well as to Israelites—unlike the Yerushalmi, which clearly restricts martyrdom to Israelites alone (b. Sanh 74b–75a; compare y. Shevi 4:2, 35a). Although the matter certainly requires further research, the Bavli's overall greater interest in Noahides and the Noahide laws likely underlies the halakhic difference between the

---

10. See the earlier discussion of b. AZ's tendency to introduce uniquely Babylonian halakhic perspectives into its reworkings of y. AZ sugyot, at pp. 101–121.

11. But see Menahem Katz, "Yerushalmi, End of Tractate *Avoda Zara*—The 'Missing Yerushalmi' Revisited," *Sidrah* 12 (1996): 79–111 (Heb.), who argues that y. AZ once included discussion of the Noahide laws but that the material, known to the rishonim, is now lost to us.

Bavli's and Yerushalmi's attitudes toward giving free food to Gentiles at b. AZ 20a and y. AZ 1:9, 40a. The Bavli's greater interest in the Noahide laws and in Israelite respect for Noahides' observance of their laws likely explains why b. Avodah Zarah limits the permission to give free gifts to Gentiles only to those Gentiles who have eschewed idolatry and observe the Noahide laws.

III.b. B. Avodah Zarah 73a–b ‖ Y. Avodah Zarah 5:11, 45a— Mixtures of Permitted and Forbidden Liquids

This example is of interest because b. Avodah Zarah substitutes Babylonian amoraic argumentation that does the identical conceptual work attributed to a Palestinian amora in y. Avodah Zarah. The developmental path of the b. Avodah Zarah sugya is thus the same as that of the y. Avodah Zarah sugya, but b. Avodah Zarah has, as it were, "updated" the argumentational steps along that path.

M. Avodah Zarah 5:8

A. Libation-wine is forbidden and renders [other liquids into which it may have been poured] forbidden in any amount.

[. . . .][12]

B. This is the general rule: [If a forbidden] type [of liquid, such as libation-wine, falls] into [a permitted version of] its type [such as permitted wine], [the forbidden liquid renders the resulting mixture forbidden] in any [even the smallest] amount. [If the forbidden liquid falls into another liquid] not of its type [such as libation-wine into water; it renders the mixture forbidden only if it fell in an amount] that "imparts taste."

Y. Avodah Zarah 5:11, 45a

A. *We learned there in a mishnah* (m. AZ 5:8): **Libation-wine is forbidden and renders forbidden in any amount.**

B. Hezekiah said: "A cup [the contents of which] were mixed of a forbidden [substance] and of a permitted [substance], if the forbidden [substance] fell in at the end [i.e., after the permitted substance], it [the entire mixture] is forbidden; if the permitted [substance] fell [in] at the end, it [the entire mixture] is permitted."[13]

---

12. Material not relevant to these sugyot is omitted.

13. This sugya has a parallel at y. Orl 2:7, 62b upon which we will rely. In y. AZ the initial presentation of Hezekiah's view is that . . . ונפל איסור בתוך איסור והיתר בתוך היתר. This text does not make sense in light of the continuation of the sugya, in which the discussion clearly revolves around whether the forbidden substance or

[In the first scenario, water was mixed with permitted wine, after which forbidden wine fell in. In the second scenario, water was mixed initially with forbidden wine, after which permitted wine fell in.[14]]

C.   R. Shmuel b. R. Yitshaq said: "This is the opinion of R. Liezer. For R. Liezer said, 'After the last, I come.'" [That is, R. Liezer also determines the legal status of the mixture by whether the forbidden or permitted substance fell in last.]

D.   R. Yirmiyah said: "It is a stringency in relation to [the laws of] libation-wine." [Meaning that the reason Hezekiah forbade a mixture into which the forbidden substance had fallen last was not because he agrees with R. Liezer, but because he wished to be especially strict about libation-wine.]

E.   R. Yose asked: "If it is a stringency in relation to [the laws of] libation-wine, then even if the permitted [substance] fell in at the end, let it [the mixture overall] be forbidden!"

F.   R. Yasa said in the name of R. Yohanan: "A cup [the contents of which] were combined of a forbidden [substance] and a permitted [substance], you consider [lit., 'see,' רואה] the permitted [substance] as if it is not. That forbidden [substance], if there is in it enough so that it 'imparts taste' (נותן טעם), [the mixture is] forbidden, and if not, it [the mixture] is permitted."

[That is, water, permitted wine, and forbidden wine were mixed together in a cup. In order to assess the status of the mixture, we consider the permitted wine as if it does not exist. If there is enough forbidden wine to impart taste to the water, the mixture is forbidden; if not, it is permitted.[15]]

G.   R. Hoshaya said: "And that is [only] the case if the permitted [substance] fell in at the end."

H.   R. Imi said in the name of R. Yohanan: "It makes no difference whether the forbidden [substance] fell in at the beginning and the permitted [substance] at the end, or whether the permitted [substance] fell in at the beginning and the forbidden [substance] at the end. Even [a mixture of] water and wine, even if [the mixture was made by means of permitted wine, after which forbidden wine fell in], you consider (רואה) the permitted [substance] as if it does not exist. That forbidden [substance], if there is in it enough so that it 'imparts taste' (נותן טעם), it [the mixture is] forbidden, and if not, it [the mixture] is permitted."

---

the permitted substance fell "at the end" (בסוף, not בתוך). Consequently, we have relied upon the y. Orl text.

   14. See P'nei Moshe, s.v. חזקיה אמר כוס שמזגו.

   15. See P'nei Moshe, s.v. רבי אסי בשם ר' יוחנן.

I.   R. Zeirah said: "[As to] all that was said [above], and all of the teachings [stated in the name of R. Yohanan], how is it done?" [I.e., how do we apply the teaching of R. Yohanan?]

J.   R. Yose b. R. Bun, R. Abbahu in the name of R. Yohanan: "A flask of liba- tion- wine that fell into a jug of [permitted] wine which then fell in turn into a cistern of water: you consider (רואה) the permitted [wine] as if it is not. That forbidden [wine]—if there is in it enough so that it 'imparts taste' [the mixture is] forbidden, and if not, it [the mixture] is permitted."

Despite the length of this sugya, it may be divided into sections that show us a clearly discernible pattern of development.

1. Initial statement of Hezekiah's position [§B].

2. R. Shmuel b. R. Yitshaq's attempt to ground Hezekiah's posi- tion in R. Liezer's view that "אחר אחרון אני בא" [§C].

3. R. Yirmiyah's rejection of this attempt [§D].

4. R. Yose challenges the premise of R. Yirmiyah's rejection of R. Shmuel b. R. Yitshaq [§E].

5. The Yerushalmi introduces R. Yohanan's "רואה" rationale, and proceeds to cite sages who discuss it [§§F–H].

6. R. Zeirah is puzzled about how to interpret and apply R. Yohanan's "רואה" rationale [§I].

7. The sugya ends with a concrete illustration of how to do just that [§J].

The Yerushalmi sugya is an editorial construction in which the state- ments of the amoraim are integrated into a dialectical framework not of their own making. Looking closely at §§A–E, we see that R. Yirmiyah's al- ternative understanding of Hezekiah in §D and R. Yose's challenge to that alternative understanding in §E are comments on Hezekiah's view *alone*. Nothing in the exchange between these two sages indicates that either was aware that R. Shmuel b. R. Yitshaq had connected Hezekiah's view in §C to the view of R. Liezer. Thus, the presence of R. Yirmiyah and R. Yose in the sugya at the points at which we find them is due to their placement there by editors who are using all these statements in order to craft a sugya. Further, nothing in §§A–E would have prepared the reader for the shift to the "רואה" rationale in §§F–H. Rather, it is the Yerushalmi editors who move in §§F–H to introduce sages who discuss R. Yohanan's concept of "רואה," and to close on the note that R. Yohanan used this concept to re- solve a particular case. Now let us see if this editorial craft is reflected in the b. Avodah Zarah parallel.

B. *Avodah Zarah* 73a–b

A. It was said: [As to] libation-wine that fell into a cistern, and a ladle-full of water fell there [too]: Hezekiah said: "If it [the water] expanded by means of the forbidden [substance], it [the entire cistern] is forbidden; if it expanded by means of the permitted [substance], it [the entire cistern] is permitted." R. Yohanan said: "Even if it expanded [meaning, the last liquid to fall in] was the forbidden [substance], it [the entire cistern] is permitted.'"

B. R. Yirmiyah said to R. Zera: "Let us say that Hezekiah and R. Yohanan are disputing as to the same disagreement between R. Eliezer and the Rabbis. For it was taught in a mishnah (m. Orl 2:11): [As to] **ordinary leaven and terumah-leaven that fell into dough, if there is not enough of this one to cause fermentation, or of that one to cause fermentation, and they combine and cause fermentation: R. Eliezer says: 'After the last one, I come' (אחר אחרון אני בא), and the Sages say: 'Whether the forbidden** [substance] **fell in at the beginning or the end,** [the total mixture] **is only forbidden when there is in it enough** [forbidden matter] **to cause fermentation.'** "

C. *And does this make sense* [i.e., to attribute the Hezekiah/R. Yohanan dispute to the earlier tannaitic dispute]*? For didn't Abaye say:* "They [R. Eliezer and the Rabbis] taught [their positions] only [in the situation in which] he pre-emptively removed the forbidden [substance from the receptacle into which it had fallen]. But if he had not preemptively removed the forbidden [substance], [all presumably agree that the mixture is] forbidden"?

D. *Hezekiah says like whom?* [In the latter situation, in which the forbidden substance was not removed, R. Eliezer would opine that even if the permitted substance were the last to fall in, the mixture would still be forbidden. This is unlike Hezekiah's initial position, and thus he cannot be said to agree with R. Eliezer. On the other hand, even in the original tannaitic scenario in which the forbidden substance was removed, the Rabbis opine that even if the forbidden substance falls in last, the resulting mixture could still be permitted, which also contradicts Hezekiah's initial position. Thus, he cannot be said to agree with the Rabbis either. As a result, the Hezekiah/R. Yohanan dispute is not understandable in light of the tannaitic dispute.]

E. *Rather, here they* [Hezekiah and R. Yohanan] *are disputing about "considering"* (רואין)*. Hezekiah does not accept "רואין," and R. Yohanan does.*

F. *And does R. Yohanan accept "רואין"? For didn't R. Asi ask R. Yohanan:* "As to two cups, one of ordinary [wine] and one of *terumah*[-wine], that he mixed and combined one with the other—what [is the law]?" *And he* [R. Yohanan] *did not solve it for him!*

G. *At the beginning he did not solve it for him. At the end, he solved it for him.*

H. It was also said: R. Ami said in the name of R. Yohanan, and some say R. Asi said in the name of R. Yohanan: "As to two cups, one of ordinary

[wine] and one of *terumah* [wine] that he mixed and combined one with
the other, we consider (רואין) the permitted [wine] as if it does not exist.
And as to the rest [i.e., the forbidden *terumah*-wine], water overwhelms it
and nullifies it."

Once again, we will first examine the similarities that show the
b. Avodah Zarah sugya to be a version of the y. Avodah Zarah sugya, and
then we will study the differences and evaluate their significance. B. Avodah Zarah develops along a path similar to that of the Yerushalmi sugya,
as the following outline illustrates:

1. Initial statement of Hezekiah's (and R. Yohanan's) position
   (§A).

2. R. Yirmiyah's attempt to ground the positions in m. Orl 2:11.
   Hezekiah's view obviously seems analogous to that of R. Eliezer (§B).

3. Anonymous voice rejects this attempt because of Abaye's understanding that had there been no preemptive removal of the
   forbidden item from the mix, both R. Eliezer and the Rabbis
   would agree that the mixture is forbidden. This leaves Hezekiah with no tannaitic precedent for his view (§§C–D).

4. Anonymous voice attempts to ground the Hezekiah/R. Yohanan dispute in a dispute about "רואין" (§E).

5. Anonymous voice questions whether "רואין" is really R. Yohanan's view in light of the fact that he did not use that rationale
   in order to answer a question put to him (§F).

6. Assurance that ultimately R. Yohanan did use "רואין" to answer a question in a concrete case (§§G–H).

Comparison of the two sugya outlines shows the similarities between
their constituent materials and flow of argument. To facilitate a closer examination, Chart 4.1 sets the common features of the sugyot side-by-side.

Examination of the chart shows that b. Avodah Zarah was guided by
the earlier editing in steps 2 (bringing in R. Eliezer in relation to Heze-
kiah/R. Yohanan), 3 (discussing the rejection of an exegetical move before
proceeding on to רואין), and 4–6 (רואין, the question about it, and its concrete application). The chart also shows some differences that are worthy
of comment. First, y. Avodah Zarah opens with a statement of Hezekiah,
while b. Avodah Zarah opens with a dispute between Hezekiah and
R. Yohanan. Reading y. Avodah Zarah carefully, one can see that, although it never actually juxtaposes the two views in a dispute format, Hezekiah and R. Yohanan are in fact presenting two distinct views. If one

Chart 4.1

Yerushalmi	*Bavli*
1. Opens with view of Hezekiah.	1. Opens with dispute of Hezekiah and R. Yohanan.
2. R. Shmuel b. R. Yitshaq grounds Hezekiah's view in R. Liezer's.	2. R. Yirmiyah grounds the dispute in that of R. Eliezer and the Sages.
3. R. Yirmiyah rejects this attempt, arguing that Hezekiah's view is attributable to the stringency of the prohibition of libation-wine. R. Yose points out the flaw in R. Yirmiyah.	3. No parallel; editor rejects R. Yirmiyah's attempt on the basis of Abaye's understanding of the R. Eliezer/Sages dispute.
4. R. Yasa in the name of R. Yohanan introduces the "רואה" rationale, which then is the subject of discussion.	4. Anonymous voice introduces the "רואין" rationale, which then becomes the subject of discussion.
5. R. Zeirah wonders how to apply "רואין."	5. Anonymous voice questions whether or not "רואין" is really R. Yohanan's view.
6. R. Yose b. R. Bun and R. Abbahu in the name of R. Yohanan illustrate its application.	6. R. Ami or R. Asi in the name of R. Yohanan illustrate its application.

accepts R. Yohanan's "רואה" rationale, then there may well be situations in which a mixture would be permitted even though the forbidden substance fell in last—*contra* Hezekiah. The Bavli redactors, then, correctly read the obvious implication of the Yerushalmi sugya, and opened their sugya with a presentation of their dispute.

A second major difference is that b. Avodah Zarah has no parallel to R. Yirmiyah's claim that Hezekiah's view is attributable to the "stringency of the law pertaining to libation-wine," nor to R. Yose's challenge to that claim. The Bavli instead substitutes Abaye's claim that R. Eliezer and the Rabbis only dispute in one particular case, but agree in another that the mixture would be forbidden. The result of Abaye's reading of the tannaitic dispute is that Hezekiah is left without a tannaitic precedent.

Although the Bavli has substituted objections, it reaches the same exegetical result as the Yerushalmi in a different way. The Yerushalmi's assumption had been that Hezekiah's view was that of R. Liezer—until R. Yirmiyah's objection. R. Yirmiya maintained that Hezekiah was of the view that "איסור בסוף אסור" not because of R. Liezer, but because of the stringency of libation-wine. To this, R. Yose protests that were R. Yirmiyah correct, then Hezekiah's view would have to be "היתר בסוף אסור"—which it is not. Hence, R. Yirmiyah must be wrong. In the Bavli, R. Yirmiyah, like R. Shmuel b. Yitshaq, juxtaposed the Hezekiah/R. Yohanan dispute and the tannaitic one. Abaye is then introduced into the sugya to say that if the forbidden substance was not removed from the mix, then R. Eliezer's view—and Hezekiah's, who allegedly agrees with him—would have be "הגדילו בהיתר אסור." But Hezekiah's view is *not* that "הגדילו בהיתר אסור." R. Yose's objection to R. Yirmiyah in y. Avodah Zarah and the anonymous voice's application of Abaye in b. Avodah Zarah are thus doing the identical conceptual work—showing that the preceding view would have to result in a representation of Hezekiah's view that is contrary to what we know it to be. Thus, that preceding view has to be rejected, be it R. Yirmiyah's in y. Avodah Zarah, or R. Yirmiyah's(!) in b. Avodah Zarah.

This analysis illustrates an important source of textual difference between the Talmuds. Despite using the same building-blocks (Hezekiah, the mishnah from Orlah, רואין), and despite arriving at the same conceptual point, the Bavli did not follow the identical path the Yerushalmi took to get there. The *destination* was the same, but the *path* was different.[16]

IV
Conclusion

In this chapter we studied examples that show that the b. Avodah Zarah redactors were sometimes aware of some aspects of the editing of the Yerushalmi. The Bavli redactors either commenced their own sugya with the last-stated point in the related Yerushalmi treatment (b. AZ 8b ‖ y. AZ 1:2, 39c; b. AZ 35b ‖ y. AZ 2:9, 41d), or, in a related vein, ignored questions that the Yerushalmi asked and answered, while taking up one question to which the Yerushalmi provided an answer its own editors found unsatisfactory (b. AZ 11b–12a ‖ y. AZ 1:4, 39d). We also saw that the b. Avodah Zarah redactors took y. Avodah Zarah's final conclusion into account in crafting their own sugya overall (b. AZ 41a–b ‖ y. AZ 3:2, 42c; b. AZ

---

16. This example raises the interesting question of whether there are any patterns in the Bavli's substitution of exegetical means for arriving at the same end, and suggests that the Bavli may wish to substitute later Babylonian traditions for earlier ones (both Palestinian and early Babylonian).

44b ‖ y. AZ 3:4, 42d; y. Shevi 8:6, 38b ‖ b. AZ 62a–b ‖ y. AZ 5:1, 44c). In another example, the b. Avodah Zarah redactors reached the same conclusion as y. Avodah Zarah but with different argumentation (b. AZ 73a–b ‖ y. AZ 5:11, 45a and the parallel at y. Orl 2:7, 62b). Finally, on account of a halakhic difference between the Talmuds, b. Avodah Zarah cited a source different from that cited by y. Avodah Zarah in discussing the same issue, though from the same halakhic context (b. AZ 20a ‖ y. AZ 1:9, 40a).

With these findings in hand, we can refine the earlier observations about b. Avodah Zarah's awareness of y. Avodah Zarah. These findings provide additional support for the theory that the b. Avodah Zarah redactors were looking at "talmud"—not simply citing various Palestinian oral traditions from different places and/or time-periods. Only redactors examining an earlier edited work would be able to do what we have shown b. Avodah Zarah to have done in this chapter. Not only did the b. Avodah Zarah redactors appropriate y. Avodah Zarah sugyot and clusters of sugyot (chapters 2 and 3) in whole or in part into their own Talmud, but they were also aware of aspects of the earlier redactors' trains of thought and the conclusions they had reached in Palestine with those materials. This latter point is a good segue to the third major body of evidence we will examine—the Palestinian nature of many of the anonymous statements we find in the Bavli.

5

The Provenance of Anonymous Material in the Bavli and the Role of Anonymous Material in B. Avodah Zarah's Appropriation of Y. Avodah Zarah (Micro Analysis III)

O ver the past seventy years or so (and, with the addition of Isaac Halevy, even longer), scholars have labored hard to understand the provenance, function(s), and possible agenda(s) of the Bavli's unattributed material. The study of the Bavli's anonymous voice (hereinafter "anonymous Bavli") has not yielded a scholarly consensus about its provenance, agenda (or lack thereof), or role in the redaction of the Bavli itself.[1] A definitive resolution of the questions pertaining to the anonymous Bavli is beyond the scope of this book. But the unattributed material in

---

1. See, e.g., David Halivni, *Sources and Traditions* (New York: Jewish Theological Seminary, 1968–1982; Jerusalem: Magnes, 1993–2003) (Heb.). Naturally, other scholars who have studied the redaction of the Bavli have of necessity considered the question as well. See Julius Kaplan, *The Redaction of the Babylonian Talmud* (Jerusalem: Makor, 1933); Kalmin, *Redaction of the Babylonian Talmud*; idem, *Sages, Stories, Authors, and Editors*; Dor, *Teachings of Eretz Israel*. More recently, scholars have begun to investigate the intellectual and spiritual worldviews of the anonymous Bavli. See Yaakov Elman, "Righteousness as Its Own Reward: An Inquiry into the Theologies of the Stam," *PAAJR* 57 (1990–91): 36–67; Rubenstein, *Talmudic Stories*; idem, *Culture of the Babylonian Talmud*.

b. Avodah Zarah nevertheless merits our attention because, to the extent that this material is determined to be a contribution of the Bavli redactors, it may shed light on b. Avodah Zarah's appropriation of y. Avodah Zarah.

We will begin with a brief survey of earlier scholars who considered the question of the anonymous Bavli either in relation to Palestinian learning (Isaac Halevy and Zwi Moshe Dor) or in relation to the redaction of the Bavli itself (David Halivni). We will then move on to a preliminary classification of anonymous material in the Bavli that will enable us to identify anonymous material that most likely represents the contribution of the redactors. This in turn will enable us to venture some tentative hypotheses as to how the anonymous material sheds light on b. Avodah Zarah's appropriation of y. Avodah Zarah.

I
Precursors in the Study of the Anonymous Bavli in Relation to Palestinian Learning: Isaac Halevy and Zwi Moshe Dor

Isaac Halevy (1847–1914) responded to the *Wissenschaft des Judentums* in his monumental work of Orthodox *Wissenschaft* entitled *Dorot ha-Rishonim*. Apropos of the Bavli's anonymous voice, Halevy purported to demonstrate that it was aware of its anonymous Yerushalmi counterpart, and that it incorporated conclusions from Yerushalmi sugyot into the parallel Bavli sugyot.[2]

Like Isaac Halevy, Zwi Moshe Dor, in his posthumously-published *The Teachings of Eretz Israel in Babylon*, recognized that the Bavli's anonymous voice often drew on Palestinian traditions.[3] Dor examined several issues related to the broader theme reflected in the title of the book: the special relationship of Rava to the teachings of R. Yohanan, the Palestinian traditions in R. Papa's learning, as well as his relationship to the teachings of R. Yohanan and Resh Laqish, and the Bavli's adaptation and use of Palestinian amoraic teachings and sugyot. He also studied the differences between the Babylonian and Palestinian versions of what are allegedly the same amoraic traditions, and found that the Bavli may consciously rework Palestinian traditions in order to prevent a conflict with a divergent Babylonian halakhah, or to present the logical end-result of an amora's position as being already an explicit part of his statement.[4] Dor thus correctly saw that differences between the Talmuds' presentations of the

---

2. Isaac Halevy, *Dorot ha-Rishonim*, 8:128–130.
3. Dor, *Teachings of Eretz Israel*, 71, 75–78, 86–94.
4. Ibid., 97, 101, 116.

same materials need not be interpreted as stemming from different sources or the vagaries of oral transmission; rather, they could be the result of the Bavli's conscious and creative appropriation of the Palestinian material into its new intellectual environment.

II
David Halivni's Contribution to the Study of the Anonymous Bavli

David Halivni's original formulation of his theory suggested that the anonymous Bavli is the literary product of scholars he termed *stammaim*, who allegedly flourished from approximately 430 CE (the date of R. Ashi's death) until nearly 500, the traditional date of the start of the saboraic period.[5] They completed and expanded the traditions they received, added rhetorical questions and answers, related different sugyot to each other, and, in short, created the Talmudic sugya as it exists in the Bavli.[6] Halivni also introduced into the study of the Bavli the sense that to know the source of the anonymous Bavli is, in effect, to know who "wrote the Talmud." He has now advanced the theory that the *stammaim* were active "at the end of the era of the last sages mentioned in the gemara . . . of whom the last, apparently, was Rabai de-min Rov . . . who lived approximately fifty years after Ravina II, which is at the mid-point of the sixth century."[7] According to Halivni's revised view, then, the redaction of the Bavli began in the latter half of the sixth century and likely continued into the seventh.

In a recent volume of *Sources and Traditions*,[8] Halivni distinguished four categories of anonymous Bavli, not all of which are considered to be the products of scholars who lived and worked in the post-amoraic period. Halivni posited the existence of early *stammaim* whom he calls "juxtaposing *stammaim*" and "repeater-*stammaim*" (סתמאים תנאים), as well as other *stammaim* whose job it was to place appropriate (anonymous) questions before amoraic "answers." The "juxtaposing *stammaim*" worked with amoraic statements. They either juxtaposed differing amoraic statements into a dispute-form (e.g., "R. Yohanan said 'X,' Hezekiah said 'Y'"), or combined identical amoraic views into one statement. Similarly, the "repeater-*stammaim*" worked with the statements of tannaim and amoraim within two or more generations after the tradent's death, expanding or re-wording a statement.

---

5. See his *Sources and Traditions*.
6. Halivni, *Sources and Traditions*: Shabbath, 6.
7. Halivni, *Sources and Traditions*: Baba Mezia, 11–12.
8. Halivni, *Sources and Traditions*: Baba Kama.

Halivni's recent start in trying to distinguish early from late anonymous material is necessary, but inadequate because it is based on *a priori*
assumptions about what is "early" or "late" "stammaitic" activity. As we
saw in chapters 3 and 4, b. Avodah Zarah reworked some amoraic statements in order to take account of exegetical results in the parallel y. Avodah Zarah sugya. Unless we suppose that "repeater-*stammaim*" who
worked on tractate b. Avodah Zarah had a version of y. Avodah Zarah at
their disposal already in the amoraic period—unlikely since the amoraim
themselves are unaware of the selections and sequences of topics characteristic of the Yerushalmi—these sorts of "stammaitic" activities are more
likely post-amoraic.

Halivni has also not sufficiently taken into account one other important factor in his study of the anonymous Bavli, the *geographical* factor. We
can distinguish between anonymous Bavli that is attributed elsewhere—
either in the Yerushalmi or elsewhere in the Bavli—to Palestinian amoraim, anonymous Bavli that is also anonymous in the Yerushalmi, and
anonymous Bavli that has no Palestinian counterpart. Having identified anonymous Bavli that is attributable to Palestinian amoraim, we will
be able to look for patterns: is the "Palestinian" anonymous Bavli regu-
larly attributable to a particular set of Palestinian amoraim? Are there differences between Palestinian and non-Palestinian anonymous Bavli? And,
of greatest importance for our purpose: Is the "author" of the anonymous
Bavli responsible for the correspondences between the two Talmuds? Is all
of the anonymous Bavli the work of the redactors of the tractate?

III
Anonymous Statements in the Bavli Can Be Attributed to Palestinian Amoraim

In this section, we will first set out five examples of this phenomenon in
b. Avodah Zarah as well as one from another tractate. We will first set out
the anonymous statement, followed by the Palestinian source to which it
can be attributed. We will then move on to an analysis of what these examples show.

III.a. B. Avodah Zarah 7a (Anonymous Bavli)

פשיטא דמחלוקת ואחר כך סתם הלכה כסתם

---

9. How can we be certain that this statement was made by the anonymous
Bavli? The statement is integrated within a dialectical context in which positions

It is obvious: [When] *a dispute* [in a mishnah is] *followed by* [the same matter decided unequivocally in an] *anonymous* [mishnah], *the law is like the anonymous* [mishnah].[9]

Y. Yevamot 4:11, 6b

רבי מנא בעא קומי ר' יודן תמן אמר ר' חזקיה רבי אבהו בשם ר' לעזר כל
מקום ששנה רבי מחלוקת וחזר ושנה סתם הלכה כסתם משנה

R. Mana asked R. Yudan: "There R. Hezekiah said [in the name of] R. Abbahu who said in the name of R. Lazar: 'Every place in which Rabbi taught a dispute, and then went back and taught [the matter unequivocally in] anonymous [form], the law is like the anonymous mishnah'"?[10]

III.b. B. Avodah Zarah 7a (Anonymous Bavli)

ורב הונא משום דאין סדר למשנה

And Rav Huna [holds the position he does because he also claims] *that there is no order to the Mishnah.*

Y. Demai 5:1, 24c

רבי יוסי בשם רבי זעירא אין משנה אמורה על סדר

R. Yose [said] in the name of R. Zeirah: "The Mishnah is not stated in order."

III.c. B. Avodah Zarah 38a (Anonymous Bavli)

אמר רב ברונא אמר רב עובד כוכבים שהצית את האור באגם כל החגבים
שבאגם אסורין היכי דמי אילימא דלא ידע הי טהור והי טמא . . .

R. Beruna said in the name of Rav: "An idolater who lit a fire in an uncleared piece of land—all of the locusts on the land are forbidden." *How is this? If it is said that he* [the Israelite] *does not know which is pure* [i.e., permitted] *and which is impure . . .*

---

are being attributed to R. Huna, with whom R. Yosef disagreed (. . . ורב הונא) and to R. Yosef (. . . ורב יוסף). Since these amoraim are not represented as speaking for themselves, but as having positions attributed *to* them, this statement about deriving law from the mishnah is most likely the work of the anonymous Bavli.

10. See also b. Yev 42b, where the same tradition is attributed initially to either R. Papa or R. Yohanan, and then is stated by R. Abbahu in answer to a question from his assistant R. Nahum.

[The anonymous voice first takes up the possibility that the reason for the prohibition is that there is an indistinguishable blending of permitted and forbidden locusts.]

Y. Avodah Zarah 2:9, 41d

מעשה שנפלה דליקה באשת קנים ובאגם תמרים והיו שם חגבים ונצלו אתא
עובדא קומי ר' מנא ואסר א"ר אבהו משום תערובת חגבין טמאים

It once happened that a blaze erupted in a thicket of reeds and an uncleared plot of date-palms, and there were locusts there which were roasted. The matter came before R. Mana, who forbade [Israelites to eat the unintentionally-roasted locusts]. R. Abbahu said: "[The reason for R. Mana's stringency was] because of the intermixing of [clean locusts with] unclean locusts."

[The anonymous Bavli has commenced its discussion of the prohibition at 38a with the one and only explanation for it offered in the Yerushalmi.]

III.d. B. Avodah Zarah 50a (Anonymous Bavli)

רבי ישמעאל סבר עושין מרקוליס קטן בצד מרקוליס גדול

R. Yishmael opines that they make a small Mercurius by the side of a large Mercurius.

Y. Avodah Zarah 4:1, 43c

א"ר אמי טעמא דר' ישמעאל משום מרקוליס גדול אצל מרקוליס קטן . . .

R. Ami said: "The reasoning of R. Yishmael [who in the mishnah said that three stones found lying side-by-side next to a Mercurius statue are forbidden, while two lying together are permitted] is that [he asserts that idolaters build] a large Mercurius [statue] next to a small Mercurius [statue]."

III.e. B. Avodah Zarah 62a (Anonymous Bavli)

אלא הואיל ותופס את דמיו כעבודת כוכבים

Rather, [the reason the wage of the worker is forbidden is that] since it [libation-wine] *"holds its monies" like idolatry.* [That is, just as money obtained through selling an idol never loses its status as idolatry, so does money obtained through selling libation-wine never lose its status as libation-wine.]

Y. Avodah Zarah 5:1, 44c

אסי אמר דמי יין נסך ביד גוי אסור דמי ע"ז ביד גוי . . . ר' יוחנן אמ' אסור

Asi said: "The monies of wine poured out as a libation which are in the hands of a Gentile are forbidden; the monies of idolatry in the hands of a Gentile . . . R. Yohanan says: 'Forbidden.'"

III.f. B. Sukkah 31b (Anonymous Bavli)

ואלא לרבי יהודה הא כתיב הדר ההוא הדר באילנו משנה לשנה

But according to R. Yehudah, is it not written "goodly"? [How could R. Yehudah not agree that the citron must be "goodly" in form? Does not Scripture expressly require that?] *That* [i.e., the scriptural reference to "goodly"] *means "that which lives* ['הˉדר' as opposed to 'הדר'] *in its tree from year to year."*

B. Sukkah 35a

ר' אבהו אמר אל תיקרי הדר אלא הדר דבר שדר באילנו משנה לשנה

R. Abbahu said: "Do not read הדר (goodly), but rather הˉדר (that which lives). [The citron is that] which lives in its tree from year to year."[11]

*   *   *

While six examples are admittedly a very small sample, they yield an interesting pattern. Of the six examples, three of the anonymous Bavli traditions are attributable to R. Abbahu, one to R. Zeirah, and one each to R. Ami and R. Yohanan. Aside from R. Yohanan, whose image looms large in the Bavli, these are all Palestinian amoraim of the third generation. Thus, most of these traditions date from the latter part of the third century CE. The traditions represent the rabbinic centers of Caesarea (R. Abbahu) and Tiberias (R. Yohanan and R. Ami), while R. Zeirah (and R. Abbahu as well, for that matter) also falls within the scholarly orbit of R. Yohanan and Tiberias. These examples of the attributable type of "Palestinian" anonymous Bavli, then, consist of Palestinian amoraic material dating from the latter part of the third century CE, largely from the schools of R. Yohanan and/or his major disciples. This suggests that R. Yohanan's

---

11. For another example of Palestinian anonymous Bavli that is attributed to R. Abbahu in the Yerushalmi, see b. Sanh 6a and y. Sanh 1:1, 18a. At 6a the anonymous Bavli raises a question and draws conclusions in connection with a discussion by R. Abbahu of m. Bekh 4:4 that in the Yerushalmi are attributed to R. Abbahu himself.

pre-eminence in the Bavli may be discernible not merely from his ubiquitous attributed statements, but from examination of this concise type of attributable "Palestinian" anonymous Bavli as well.

Examination of these examples also shows that "Palestinian" anonymous Bavli attributable to Palestinian amoraim tends to be concise and
non-argumentative; in other words, it is essentially anonymous amoraic
material. We may infer, then, that "Palestinian" anonymous Bavli attributable to Palestinian amoraim is material that dates from the amoraic period
itself and may be distinguished as such by its characteristic brevity and
similarity to attributed amoraic activity. Moreover, given that this type of
anonymous Bavli is essentially an amoraic voice, we see that we should
neither look to it as the source of the structural similarities between the
Talmuds we studied in chapter 2, nor as the voice of whichever editors incorporated y. Avodah Zarah sugyot into b. Avodah Zarah. *The "Palestinian" anonymous Bavli attributable to Palestinian amoraim does not function in
an editorial capacity. It transmits traditions; it does not order and arrange materials within b. Avodah Zarah.* The anonymous transmission within Babylonia
of Palestinian amoraic traditions is an interesting phenomenon that requires more research; at the very least, it shows a high degree of assimila-
tion of Palestinian amoraic traditions within rabbinic Babylonia.

IV
Anonymous Material in B. Avodah Zarah That Is Also Anonymous in Y. Avodah Zarah

Not all of the Palestinian anonymous Bavli is attributable—some is anonymous in the Yerushalmi as well. We will now analyze this doubly anonymous material to see whether there might be a distinction in function between this sort of material and that studied in the previous section.
Perhaps, rather than simply conveying Palestinian amoraic traditions
anonymously, this sort of Palestinian anonymous Bavli also conveys the
viewpoints of the earlier Talmud's editorship.

IV.a. B. Avodah Zarah 40b ‖ Y. Avodah Zarah 3:1, 42b
‖ Y. Demai 2:1, 22b–c

M. Avodah Zarah 3:1 records a dispute between R. Meir and the Sages.
The former asserts that all images are prohibited because they are worshiped once a year, while the Sages counter that only certain images are
forbidden—those in which a human figure is holding a staff, bird, or ball.

R. Shimon b. Gamliel extends this prohibition to include human figures holding any sort of object at all.

B. Avodah Zarah 40b

A. *If they are worshiped once a year, what is the reason of the Sages?*

[According to the Sages, many images are permitted, since they do not portray figures holding the halakhically problematic objects. Yet, the Talmud asks, if those figures are nevertheless worshiped once a year, how can the Sages hold them to be permitted?]

B. R. Yitshaq b. Yosef said in the name of R. Yohanan: "In R. Meir's location, they would worship [them] once a year." *And R. Meir, who concerns himself even about a minority of situations (דחייש למיעוטא) decreed* [a prohibition as to] *other places because of that place* [even though the images were not being worshiped once a year anywhere else]. *And the Sages, who are not concerned about a minority of situations, did not decree* [a prohibition concerning] *other places because of that place.*[12]

Y. Avodah Zarah 3:1, 42b

A. R. Hiyya b. Ba said: "[All images are forbidden] because they are worshiped in the great city of Rome twice in a Sabbatical cycle [twice every seven years]."

B. *From this* [i.e., based on R. Hiyya's statement], *let them be forbidden in a place in which they are worshiped, and permitted in a place in which they are not worshiped!*

C. R. Yose said: "Since they are forbidden in one place, they are forbidden in every place."

D. *What view do we hold? If it is clear that the images are of kings, all agree that they are forbidden . . . rather, we maintain that* [the images] *are* [set up with] *no determinable purpose. R. Meir says* [that images set up with] *no determinable purpose are* [considered to be] *of kings.*

Although it is the traveler (נחותא) R. Yitshaq b. Yosef who conveys R. Yohanan's interpretation of R. Meir in b. Avodah Zarah, he presents a view that is similar, although hardly identical, to both §§A and C in y. Avodah Zarah. Further, the explanation attached to his interpretation is not found in y. Avodah Zarah. We should not consider that explanation to be part of R. Yitshaq b. Yosef's statement for two reasons: first, it is in Aramaic, while his statement is in Hebrew; and second, it provides an explanation provided in y. Demai by the Yerushalmi's own anonymous voice.

---

12. We will explain shortly why the material marked as anonymous is assumed to be so.

Y. Demai 2:1, 22b–c

M. Demai 2:1 begins by setting out a list of fruits and crops that are always and everywhere to be tithed as if they are *demai* (produce as to which there is doubt as to whether it had been tithed). In the course of the Yerushalmi's discussion, a dispute between R. Lazar and R. Yohanan is presented in which R. Lazar maintains that the mishnah is talking only about one who buys from a Gentile (since perhaps the latter bought from an Israelite and tithing really is required); one who buys from an Israelite must tithe as if the produce had definitely not been tithed. R. Yohanan, on the other hand, asserts that the mishnah is saying that regardless of who the seller is, the purchaser must tithe as if the produce is *demai*. After this, the Yerushalmi goes on:

A.   *R. Lazar is of the view that most of the Land of Israel is in the hands of Gentiles.*

B.   *R. Yohanan is of the view that most of the Land of Israel is in the hands of Israelites.*

C.   *And even if R. Lazar agrees with R. Yohanan that most of the Land of Israel is in the hands of Israelites, R. Lazar is concerned about the minority of cases (* חש
למיעוט).

As the anonymous Yerushalmi interprets R. Lazar, the mishnah's unspecific reference to the need to tithe as if for *demai* must only refer to produce bought from Gentiles, since they own most of the Land of Israel. Yet, maintains the Yerushalmi, even if R. Lazar agreed with R. Yohanan's demographic assessment, he would still maintain his position that only produce bought from Gentiles is to be tithed as *demai* since he worries about even a minority of situations—in this case, the speculative situation that even in a Land of Israel owned mostly by Israelites, the Israelite buyer bought from a Gentile who had himself bought from an Israelite.

The anonymous Yerushalmi has utilized the notion of חש למיעוט to explain R. Lazar, just as the anonymous Bavli did at b. AZ 40b in order to explain R. Meir. This idea of חש למיעוט appears nowhere else in the Yerushalmi, and, significantly, the concept is cited in y. Demai in order to explain an amoraic dispute pertaining to Israelites *and* Gentiles. The anonymous Bavli uses this concept in only one other place, b. Hul 6a, again in connection with R. Meir and again in connection with issues involving Israelites and outsiders (in this case, Samaritans). The *only* place at which the concept seems attributed to amoraim (b. Hul 86a) is one in which the context does *not* deal in some way with Gentiles. This suggests that the anonymous Bavli has taken over from the anonymous Yerushalmi not only the concept, but also the overall context—Israelites and Gentiles—in which חש למיעוט is deemed applicable.

IV.b. B. Avodah Zarah 47a ‖ Y. Bikkurim 1:2, 63d

B. Avodah Zarah 47a

A. Resh Laqish asked: "One who bows down to a palm-tree—can its branch (לולב) be used for the commandment?"[13]

B. *A tree that was planted from the beginning for that purpose should not be a question for you, for that would be forbidden even for a private person* [using the branch for a non-sacred purpose]. *A tree that was planted and then at the end* [sometime after it was planted] *was worshiped should be a question for you. And you should not have a question based on the view of R. Yose b. R. Yehudah, for* [according to him] *it would be forbidden even for a private person. Based on the view of the Sages, you should have a question: What is the law about* [using this branch to fulfill] *a commandment? Is it disgusting in the view of the High One (*מאיס כלפי גבוה*)* [meaning that God would not desire service with this idolatrous object], *or not?*

C. *When R. Dimi came, he said:* "[Resh Laqish] was troubled by [the case of] the *asherah*-tree, which has been invalidated [from being an idolatrous object and hence is permitted for use by an Israelite]." *Is there disqualification with regard to commandments, or is there not disqualification with regard to commandments?*

[If there is "disqualification" (דיחוי), then since the palm-branch once could not have been used for the commandment, it can never be used, even if it later was "invalidated" from its previous status as an idolatrous object.]

[The sugya continues with a discussion of דיחוי.]

Sections B and C present two distinct explanations of what is actually troubling Resh Laqish. According to the anonymous Bavli in §B, Resh Laqish is troubled by how the Sages' view affects his case. Is the detached palm-branch "disgusting" (מאיס) or not? If so, it cannot be used; if not, it can be. Implicit in this explanation is the idea that being an idolatrous object *per se* does not disqualify the object for Israelite ritual use. Once detached from a worshiped tree, the branch might still be considered "not 'disgusting'" and hence fit for use,[14] even if it had not formally been invalidated as an idolatrous object.

---

13. The Torah commands at Lev 23:40 that Jews should "take" the "fruit of a beautiful tree" along with three other plants during the festival of Sukkot. The rabbis understood from this that Jews should celebrate the festival by waving a palm branch surrounded by willow and myrtle, along with a citron (*etrog*) for seven days. It is this palm branch to which Resh Laqish refers in §A.

14. Appropriately, Tosafot (to b. AZ 47a, s.v. מי) immediately points out that one of the options entertained by Resh Laqish in §B is the same as that of Rava at

Section C, by contrast, opens with R. Dimi's tradition that Resh Laqish was, in fact, concerned about the "*asherah* that had been invalidated [from being worshiped]." According to this interpretation of Resh Laqish, he is concerned about disqualification: having once been unfit for use, is it always unfit (despite invalidation)? Or, having once been unfit for use, does its later invalidation render it fit? The Bavli editor has used R. Dimi's statement as the opening remark of §C and the second way to understand Resh Laqish. We must now look to a partial parallel to this sugya at y. Bik 1:2, 63d in order to compare the anonymous Bavli and the Bavli editing overall to what we find in this earlier version of the same sugya.

M. Bikkurim 1:2 makes the point that one who steals (גזלן) land may not bring first-fruits and recite the appropriate verses because Scripture explicitly commands that these acts be performed with fruits of *your* land—the stolen land is not the property of the robber.

Y. Bikkurim 1:2, 63d

A. *Up to now* [the mishnah is talking about] *one who stole land. If he* [the robber] *stole a branch and planted it, does he not owe* [the owner] *money?* [Hence, having paid the compensatory damages he owes, the robber should then be able to bring first-fruits from the tree that grows from that branch.]

B. *But it is necessary* [to raise a question about the latter case of the stolen branch] *according to the Rabbis. Are ritual objects like the High One (* מצוות הן כגבוה*)? Or are they not like the High One? If they are like the High One, he* [the robber of the branch] *does not bring* [first-fruits from the tree that grows from the branch], *and if you say they are not like the High One, he does bring.*

C. *Everyone agrees with respect to the* asherah-*tree that has been invalidated that he* [an Israelite now receiving benefit from it] *does not bring lumber* [from it to the Temple] *for the altar.*

D. R. Shimon b. Laqish asked: "Can he bring from it [the invalidated *asherah*-tree] a palm-branch [to fulfill the commandment on Sukkot]?" *Are ritual objects like the High One? Or are they not like the High One? If you say that they are like the High One, he cannot bring; if you say that they are not like the High One, he can bring. It is obvious that he can bring a palm-branch from it* [the invalidated *asherah*-tree] *since ritual objects are not like the High One.*

Sections B in both Talmuds are very similar. Both the anonymous Bavli and anonymous Yerushalmi resolve that an issue is presented according to the Sages' view, and that the legal bottom-line will depend, in turn, on whether using an idolatrous object is "disgusting to God" (מאיס כלפי גבוה)

---

b. Suk 31b; to wit, that a לולב של אשירה (a palm branch detached from an *asherah* tree) can be used to fulfill a commandment.

or whether ritual objects are (or must be) like the High One (מצוות כגבוה הן), i.e., whether they must be as fit as objects used in the Temple in order to be suitable for ritual purposes. Moreover, unlike the Palestinian anonymous Bavli studied earlier, which was concise, brief, and declarative, the anonymous material here in both Talmuds' §B is dialectical and argumentative. Thus, brevity is not necessarily a reliable criterion by itself for distinguishing Palestinian from non-Palestinian anonymous Bavli; *all anonymous Bavli material must always be checked for possible Palestinian parallels.*

Another point is that the juxtaposition in the Yerushalmi of Resh Laqish and the anonymous material is done by the redactors; Resh Laqish himself asks only about the palm-branch. The proof that this is so is that while Resh Laqish asks about the palm-branch in both Talmuds, the continuation of his statement differs in both (although largely similar in content). This supports the conclusion that the material following his question about the palm-branch was added by both Talmuds' anonymous editorial voices. This editorial juxtaposition of the amora and the anonymous material is carried over into the Bavli sugya where Resh Laqish's question about the palm-branch is also followed by strikingly similar anonymous material. Thus, in this case, the anonymous Yerushalmi that is carried over as anonymous Bavli *does* represent a Babylonian editorial adoption of an editorial decision made by the Yerushalmi.

Yet, although this largely similar anonymous material is present in the same point in the argument in both Talmuds, the Talmuds use the material differently. The Yerushalmi applies this material directly to Resh Laqish in its §D and unequivocally answers his question—the palm-branch can be used, since the "ritual objects are not like the High One." The Bavli leaves this anonymous material as an unresolved question in §B, then moves on in §C to cite R. Dimi and takes the sugya in a different direction—ultimately leaving Resh Laqish's question unanswered.

In the Bavli's §C, R. Dimi observes that Resh Laqish's question pertained to the invalidated *asherah*-tree. There was no way R. Dimi could have known this from the way Resh Laqish's question was presented at b. AZ 47a, since Resh Laqish asked only about a tree to which a person had bowed, and had not identified the tree as an *asherah*. Whoever is presenting R. Dimi's observation is bringing a Palestinian tradition to bear on the interpretation of Resh Laqish, and this Palestinian tradition is found at §§C–D of the y. Bikkurim sugya. Examining R. Dimi's statement in light of these sections, we see that the version of R. Dimi's statement that is presented in the Bavli takes account of the material that is anonymous in the Yerushalmi. This suggests both that the Bavli editors were making use of already-existing anonymous material found in the Yerushalmi, and that the anonymous Yerushalmi includes material that dates from the amoraic period, and should not necessarily be presumed to be the voice of post-amoraic editors.[15] The Bavli used R. Dimi as the pivot on which the sugya would turn from being a discussion about מאיס כלפי גבוה to one about דיחוי, for which there is no precedent in the older sugya.

Considering the Bavli editors' work in this sugya overall, we see that they worked in b. AZ 47a with a sugya remarkably similar to that at y. Bik 1:2, 63d. They presented as anonymous, material that was also anonymous in the Yerushalmi, but it is not in this anonymous material *itself* that we see their editorial hand, but in *how they worked with it*. Whereas the anonymous Yerushalmi definitively resolved Resh Laqish's question, the Bavli editors dropped that resolution. Instead, they used R. Dimi as the basis to begin a discussion of "disqualification in regard to commandments"[16] and thus created a sugya that deviates completely from the older Palestinian one.

What we have learned thus far is that the anonymous material in the Bavli may not necessarily represent the voice of the Bavli redactors. If the anonymous material is attributable to a Palestinian amora, then this anonymous Bavli may be early and unrepresentative of the voice of the post-amoraic Bavli redactors. If the anonymous Bavli is also present in the Yerushalmi as anonymous material, then further examination of how the material is used in the two Talmuds may show that the Bavli is adopting some of the Yerushalmi's editorial decisions, or it may not.

V

Anonymous Material in the Bavli That Cannot Be Shown to Be Palestinian

Not all anonymous Bavli can be attributed to a Palestinian amora. Nor is it necessarily present in the Yerushalmi as anonymous material. For ease of

---

15. See also b. AZ 51b and y. AZ 4:3, 43d (Abaye interprets a mishnah just as the anonymous Yerushalmi did); b. AZ 75a and y. AZ 5:14, 45b (y. AZ presents an anonymous statement that is attributed to R. Shmuel b. Yitshaq in the Bavli); and b. AZ 76a and y. AZ 5:15, 45b (m. Zev 11:7 is invoked anonymously in the Yerushalmi, while it is cited by R. Amram and R. Sheshet in the Bavli). Taken together, these four examples suggest that the anonymous Yerushalmi may be an amoraic voice. But there are also examples that suggest that the voice is post-amoraic. See, for example, y. Ber 7:1, 11a, in which the anonymous Yerushalmi explicitly anticipates a reader's objection to using a source from the Order Teharot in order to derive laws pertaining to blessings, and responds to it. We see that the anonymous Yerushalmi, like its Babylonian relative, can be assumed neither to be uniformly early nor uniformly late.

16. See also the related sugyot at b. Suk 33a and b. Hul 87a.

reference, this material will be referred to herein as "Babylonian anonymous Bavli." Such "Babylonian" anonymous Bavli may be a significant factor in tracing b. Avodah Zarah's reliance on, and appropriation of materials from, y. Avodah Zarah. The following examples will make this clear.

V.a. Babylonian Anonymous Bavli Links Palestinian Materials Together

(1) B. Avodah Zarah 67a–b ‖ Y. Avodah Zarah 5:3, 44d

This sugya was discussed at great length at pp. 116–121, above. We did not emphasize there, however, how the Babylonian anonymous Bavli on 67b links together Palestinian materials found adjacent to each other at y. AZ 5:3, 44d but which had become separated in b. Avodah Zarah because of b. Avodah Zarah's introduction of material from y. Orlah. At 67a, b. Avodah Zarah presents a Palestinian sugya explaining the mishnah's clause, "This is the general principle: Every [forbidden food item which has fallen into a permitted item and] imparts taste [to the permitted item] in which there is pleasure [for the eater], is forbidden." The sugya ends on the note that the people of Sepphoris used to prepare a dish called שחליים, in which wine was poured into cold, pounded grains and then heated.

At this point, the Yerushalmi moves right into a dispute between R. Meir and the Sages about the principle of "imparting taste," while b. Avodah Zarah moves from the culinary tastes of Sepphoris into the material it drew from y. Orl 2:7, 62b. On 67b, after the conclusion of its borrowing from y. Orlah and some apparently amoraic commentary upon it, the anonymous Bavli points out: "*From all of this,* [may we infer] *that there is* [support] *for the one who holds that the imparting of taste to the detriment* [of the dish] *is forbidden? Yes!*" At this point, b. Avodah Zarah cites the dispute between R. Meir and R. Shimon, which, but for the name of R. Meir's partner in dispute, is the same as that in the Yerushalmi. Although this particular anonymous Bavli is itself nowhere attested in Palestinian literature, it provides the segue by means of which the Bavli will resume the interrupted structural similarity to the parallel Yerushalmi treatment of the mishnah.

(2) B. Avodah Zarah 6b ‖ Y. Avodah Zarah 1:1, 39b

We studied this example exhaustively at the beginning of chapter 3, but must return to it briefly to point out the presence in b. Avodah Zarah of what I am here calling "Babylonian anonymous Bavli," the "glue" that holds together portions of the older Palestinian sugya (better than y. Avodah Zarah had).

Y. Avodah Zarah 1:1, 39b

A. *It is understandable* [that there be a prohibition] *against lending* [items to Gentiles three days before their festivals].

B. *But not to borrow* [items] *from them?*

C. [The prohibition of borrowing makes sense *because* [the Israelite] *is like one who raises up a name for* [the Gentile. By borrowing from him, the Israelite shows him honor in which the Gentile will rejoice on his festival].

D. *It is understandable* [that there be a prohibition] *against lending him money* [three days before his idolatrous festival].

E. *But not to borrow* [money] *from them?*

F. *Because* [the Israelite] *is like one who raises up a name for him.*

G. *It is understandable* [that there be a prohibition] *against repaying them* [three days prior to their festivals].

H. *But not to be repaid by them* [for a loan]?

I. *It is in order that* [the Gentile] *not say that his idolatry assisted it* [the repayment].

J. R. Ba b. Tablai said in the name of Rav: "If it was a lost [unsecured] loan, it is permitted [to receive repayment three days prior to, or on, the Gentile's festival]."

K. *And so it was taught:* **A lost** [unsecured] **loan** [is one made] **with witnesses; a loan is not lost** [if made] **with a document. Even a loan with a document may be lost, since a person does not always merit** [being able] **to pay off his debt.**

L. *What is the result?* [What is the definition of a "lost," or unsecured, loan?]

M. *An unsecured loan is a loan without collateral; a loan is not unsecured with collateral.*

N. *Then he found it* [the meaning of "lost loan"] *taught as in the first* [baraita in §K]: **A loan is lost if made with witnesses, a loan is not lost with a document.**

O. *It was taught there in a mishnah:* **R. Yehudah says: "A woman should not put on cosmetic paint, because it is a disgrace for her"** (m. MQ 1:7). [While she has the paint on, she looks unattractive; the cosmetic benefits of the paint will only be apparent when she removes it. Thus R. Yehudah holds that she should not put it on during the intermediate days of a Festival, since she will look unattractive during the Festival.]

P. R. Hanina and R. Mana [disagreed about what R. Yehudah and his opponents, the Sages, really meant]. One said: "They were arguing about a cosmetic paint that she removes during the Festival, but a cosmetic paint that she removes after the Festival is forbidden." [As to the first, since she will obtain some of the cosmetic benefit during the Festival, the Sages permit it. Yet the Sages and R. Yehudah both agree that if she will in no way benefit from the paint during the Festival, she is forbidden to apply it.] And the other said: "They were arguing about a cosmetic paint that she removes after the Festival, but a cosmetic paint that she removes during the Festival is permitted."

Q. *And they did not know which said which and which said which* [unnamed sages did not know which statement was attributable to R. Hanina and which to R. Mana].

R. *From what R. Hanina said in the name of R. Yose in the name of R. Yohanan:* "R. Yehudah is consistent with his own opinion. Just as he said there [m. MQ 1:7] that temporary disgrace is considered disgrace, so he says here [m. AZ 1:1] that temporary pain is pain." *So it is* [R. Hanina] *who says that they were arguing about a cosmetic paint that she removes during the Festival, but a cosmetic paint that she removes after the Festival is forbidden.*

The Yerushalmi moves from questioning m. AZ 1:1's pairing of prohibitions (no lending or borrowing items, no lending or borrowing money, no repaying debts or being repaid) in §§A–I to a discussion of what type of loan an Israelite is permitted to collect from a Gentile in §§J–N, to a consideration of whether an Israelite can put herself through unpleasantness during the Festival in order to derive a benefit after it is over in §§O–S. B. Avodah Zarah follows the same basic structure, but with the addition of anonymous Bavli not found in y. Avodah Zarah.

B. Avodah Zarah 6b

A. *It is understandable* [that it be forbidden] *to lend* [items] *to them, since* [then the Israelite] *is enriching them.*

B. *But by borrowing from them he is diminishing them!* [so why the prohibition?]

C. Abaye said: "There was a decree [prohibiting] borrowing from them lest he lend to them."

D. Rava said: "All of [the prohibitions of m. AZ 1:1] are on the grounds that [the Gentile] will 'go and thank' [his god]."

E. *It is understandable* [that it be forbidden] *to lend them money, since* [the Israelite] *is then enriching them.*

F. *But borrowing* [money] *from them, why* [should it be forbidden]?

G. Abaye said: "There was a decree [prohibiting] borrowing money from them lest he lend to them."

H. Rava said: "All of it is on the grounds that he will 'go and thank.'"

I. *It is understandable* [that it be forbidden] *to repay them, since he is then enriching them.*

J. *But by being repaid by them* [the Israelite] *is diminishing them!*

K. Abaye said: "There was a decree [prohibiting] being repaid by them lest he repay [a loan he borrowed from] them."

L. Rava said: "All of it is on the grounds that he will 'go and thank.'"

M. *And they* [the prohibitions of m. AZ 1:1] *are all necessary. For had the tanna taught only* [that it was forbidden] *to transact business with them on the grounds that he would be enriching* [the Gentile, who would then] *go and give thanks, one then would have thought that* [he is permitted to] *borrow from them, since he thereby diminishes them!*

N. *And had the tanna taught* [the prohibition against] *borrowing from them,* [that would have been on the grounds that borrowing from the Gentile] *is important to him* [it makes the Gentile feel important], *and he would "go and thank." But borrowing money from them should be permitted since it would be a cause of sorrow. He would say: "The money will not return to me."*

O. *And had the tanna taught that it was forbidden to borrow* [money] *from them because he would say: "Against his* [the Israelite borrower's] *will I will exact repayment," and nevertheless now go and thank, but* [then I might have thought that it would be permitted] *to be repaid by them, since the money would not return to them. I would say: "He is in pain, and will not go and thank"*—[so all the statements in m. AZ 1:1 are] *necessary.*

P. *And R. Yehudah disagrees* [with the principle that] *"even though* [the Gentile] *is upset now, he will be happy later"?* [In m. AZ 1:1 R. Yehudah permits an Israelite to accept repayment from a Gentile prior to the festival because this will upset the Gentile prior to the festival. The Sages forbid the repayment because even though the Gentile is "upset now," he will be "happy later."]

Q. *And was it not taught in a baraita:* **R. Yehudah says: "A woman should not put on cosmetics during the Festival, since it is a disgrace for her." And R. Yehudah agrees that she can apply a cosmetic paint during the Festival that she can remove during the Festival; even though she is upset now, she will be happy later.**

R. R. Nahman b. Yitshaq said: "Leave aside the laws of the intermediate days of a Festival, for all of them [are based on the principle of] 'upset now, happy later' [thus, they are not to be compared to the laws against doing business with idolaters]."

S. Ravina said: "When it comes to loan repayment, an idolater is always upset."

T. *Our mishnah* [which prohibits accepting repayment from a Gentile in every case] *is inconsistent with R. Yehoshua b. Qorha. For it was taught in a baraita:* **R. Yehoshua b. Qorha said: "We do not collect from them a loan evidenced by a document, but we do collect from them a loan made orally, because** [the Israelite collecting] **is like 'one who saves** [Israelite property] **from their hands'"** (t. AZ 1:1).

Sections M–P are "Babylonian anonymous Bavli" not attested in y. Avodah Zarah. In chapter 3, it was explained that §§M and N deal with two issues not taken up in the preceding Palestinian sugya: the relationship between the mishnah's initial prohibition of buying and selling and the other prohibitions of the mishnah, and the apparent redundancy of forbidding the borrowing of items from Gentiles, and (in a distinct prohibition) the borrowing of money. The redundant §O was designed to introduce the idea of the Gentile's being "in pain" now. Section O's introduction of this idea, in turn, was meant to pave the way to the introduction of R. Yehudah's view on being "in pain now, but happy later" in §P and thus to the dispute over women's application of face-paint during the Festival.

The important point to note is that §§M–O are Babylonian anonymous Bavli not attested in y. Avodah Zarah. The author(s) of this Babylonian anonymous Bavli, as we pointed out, had to have known both the older Palestinian sugya (y. §§A–I, above) reproduced in the Bavli (which they supplemented at b. §§M and N), and the already-existing juxtaposition of that sugya with the discussion of the mishnah from Moed Qatan—to which they segued by means of §O after their digression. Moreover, by inserting such a segue into this pre-existing Palestinian order, the Babylonian anonymous Bavli improves upon the presentation of these materials in y. Avodah Zarah, which had no such transition at all. Once again, we see that Babylonian anonymous Bavli is the means by which the b. Avodah Zarah editors connect Palestinian materials together (better than y. Avodah Zarah itself had).[17]

V.b. The Babylonian Anonymous Bavli Re-Casts an Older Palestinian Sugya into a More Expansive, Dialectical Construction

(1) B. Avodah Zarah 20b ‖ Y. Avodah Zarah 1:8, 40a— Selling to Gentiles With a Condition

The first clause of m. AZ 1:8 says that an Israelite may not sell items attached to land in Palestine—such as trees or crops—to a Gentile while they are so attached. Even though the Israelite is presumed to retain ownership of the land itself, he has through this sale given the Gentile some form of rootedness in the land, which is impermissible. R. Yehudah sees no such difficulty, and allows the sale on the condition that the Gentile cut the attached items off the land.

Y. Avodah Zarah 1:8, 40a

A. R. Bun b. Hiyya asked: "Is even a large beast in dispute? [Can the Israelite] sell [it] to [the Gentile] on the condition that he slaughter it?"

---

17. Another point is that, although the content of this Babylonian anonymous Bavli is not itself Palestinian, its author(s) used a Palestinian dialectical vehicle, the "צריכא" construction, with which to present it. This construction justifies seemingly redundant statements in a tannaitic source by pointing out the erroneous conclusions the student would reach but for the presence of the apparently-redundant materials. The "צריכא" is by no means an invention of the Bavli; examples of it are found in the Yerushalmi as well. See, for example, y. Peah 1:5, 16c and y. AZ 1:5, 39d.

B. *It was found* [to have been] *taught* [in a baraita] *that even a large beast is in dispute.* R. Yehudah says: "He sells to him on the condition that he slaughter it" [compare t. AZ 2:1].

In this sugya, the third-generation Palestinian amora R. Bun b. Hiyya asks if the mishnah's dispute concerning land and items attached to it applies as well to the sale of a large beast. This question is not called for by the mishnah itself, which is concerned about Gentile settlement in the land of Israel. On the face of it, it seems difficult to see the connection between this mishnah and a question about the sale to a Gentile of a large beast.[18] Despite this oddity, b. Avodah Zarah places a version of the same sugya in connection with this mishnah.[19]

B. Avodah Zarah 20b

A. They asked: "[If an Israelite sold a Gentile] a beast on the condition that he slaughter it, what [is the law]?"
B. *There* [in the mishnah] *what is the reason that R. Yehudah permits* [the conditional sale]*? [Is it] because* [the trees or other items attached to the land] *are not in* [the Gentile's] *domain and he cannot delay* [fulfilling the condition to cut] *them* [down]*, but* [as to] *an animal, since it is in the domain of the idolater, he can delay* [fulfilling the condition to slaughter] *it? Or perhaps there is no difference* [between the two cases]*?*
C. *Come and hear that which was taught in a baraita:* [An Israelite may sell to a Gentile] **an animal on the condition that he slaughter it and he** [the Gentile] **slaughters, the words of R. Yehudah. R. Meir says: "We only sell** [to Gentiles that which is already] **slaughtered"** [compare t. AZ 2:1].

The author of the anonymous §B seems troubled by the same question we asked earlier about y. AZ 1:8, 40a: How does a question about the sale to a Gentile of a large animal have any connection to m. AZ 1:8? As we discussed earlier, §B responds to this skillfully by looking for a higher level of conceptualization that will encompass both the mishnah and the animal query. That higher level is the issue of whether or not the Gentile's purchased property is considered to be a part of his domain. Will R. Yehudah rule the same way in both cases, despite the fact that the purchased trees or crops are not in the Gentile's domain but the purchased animal is? Or

---

18. Once again, we must caution that a distinction must be made between that which is called for by the mishnah and typical Talmudic dialectic to which students of the literature are accustomed. There is nothing about this mishnah—taken on its own terms—that calls for consideration of the question about the beast. The fact that y. AZ does this is because of that Talmud's own intellectual predilections.

19. For a more expansive discussion of this sugya and of b. AZ's typically Babylonian predilection for a higher degree of legal conceptualization than we see in the Yerushalmi, see chapter 3, pp. 142–147.

will the difference in domain mean that R. Yehudah will rule differently in the two cases? The anonymous editor is thus expanding and trying to clarify an older Palestinian sugya that he himself did not create, trying to find a way to link it to the mishnah to which it belongs but from which it seems distinct. Having inherited both a sugya and a context, the anonymous b. Avodah Zarah editors have added to the sugya in order to better explain its place in that context.

VI
Conclusion

On the basis of an admittedly small sample, we have suggested that it is useful to categorize anonymous Bavli into two large geographical groups: Palestinian or Babylonian. Palestinian anonymous Bavli may be further subdivided into material that is attributable to Palestinian amoraim, and that which is also anonymous in the Yerushalmi. The former is essentially amoraic material that is anonymous; it is brief, declarative, and does not do editorial work such as expanding or further elucidating prior sources, or linking together different sugyot. The latter type of Palestinian anonymous Bavli is more likely to convey the editorial decisions of the Yerushalmi to the Bavli, but may not always do so. Finally, simply because some anonymous Bavli is exclusively "Babylonian" in provenance does not mean that it has no awareness of the prior Talmud. Babylonian anonymous Bavli can provide the "glue" that joins together in the Bavli materials that were already joined in the Yerushalmi, as well as create a more dialectical sugya out of a simpler Palestinian source. Yet Babylonian anonymous Bavli can also introduce a Babylonian halakhic agenda into a discussion that seems opposed to it.

The scholar is therefore well advised to approach the study of the anonymous Bavli with as few *a priori* assumptions as possible. Merely identifying anonymous Bavli as anonymous tells us very little about the authorship of that material, let alone of the Bavli as a whole. The key is to identify its geographical provenance and function within a given sugya. Only by assessing its relationship (or lack thereof) to the constituent sugyot that comprise a given mishnah-treatment can we arrive at any firm conclusions about the anonymous Bavli.

Appendix

The Babylonian Anonymous Bavli Shows the Influence of a Babylonian Halakhic Agenda

Among the unresolved issues pertaining to the Bavli's anonymous voice is whether it inserts a Babylonian halakhic perspective or whether its concerns are primarily exegetical. While we cannot hope to resolve this issue with one example, the following may contribute at least a small part to the ongoing discussion. At b. AZ 69b, the Babylonian anonymous Bavli asks a question about a particular halakhic position vis-à-vis m. AZ 5:3–4. In these mishnayot, the anonymous tanna rules that if an Israelite and a Gentile are transporting wine together, and the Israelite informs the Gentile that he will be absent for a while, the wine is forbidden if the Israelite was absent for a period of time sufficient for the Gentile to have drilled a hole in the wine-barrel and patched it up again. R. Shimon b. Gamliel, by contrast, allows for a longer period of absence: the wine is forbidden only if the Jew was gone long enough for the Gentile to have completely opened the barrel, replaced the top with a new one, and for the seal of the new top to have dried.

At 69b, the Bavli records Rava's view that the law follows R. Shimon b. Gamliel. Following some anonymous discussion of Rava, the anonymous Bavli wonders:

> Since our view is that of R. Shimon b. Gamliel who does not worry about piercing [a hole in the barrel], and [since] the halakhah is like R. Eliezer, who does not worry about counterfeiting [R. Eliezer's view is that we do not worry that a Gentile would go to the trouble of breaking a Jew's seal to open a wine-barrel and then counterfeiting his seal to cover his deed], then what is the reason we do not leave wine in the hands of idolaters?

196

The answer provided is "because of attachment" [the concern that the Gentile would make a small opening in the barrel with an attached covering, big enough to smell and possibly even taste the wine]. The Babylonian anonymous Bavli is puzzled: since "our view" represents two lenient positions, why is contemporary practice not lenient? The anonymous Bavli's reference to what "our view" is and the question's focus on normative practice shows that we are dealing with someone's *halakhic* agenda, not an exegetical one.

6

The Historical Context of B. Avodah Zarah's Appropriation of Y. Avodah Zarah

This book illustrates that the study of a Bavli tractate's relationship to its Yerushalmi parallel must be methodologically eclectic. A macro approach is necessary but not sufficient, and the same goes for a micro approach. By combining the textual breadth characteristic of Neusner and Jaffee, detailed sugya analysis like that of Friedman, and comparative studies of the two rabbinic communities and their literatures like those of Kalmin and Friedman, we are able to see much more clearly than most earlier scholars how y. Avodah Zarah influenced b. Avodah Zarah. Our understanding of b. Avodah Zarah's deep roots in y. Avodah Zarah also has an important implication for the study of the Bavli overall. *The Bavli should not be studied without reference to the Yerushalmi.* A scholar wishing to study the formation of Bavli sugyot, Bavli hermeneutics, or the redaction-history of a Bavli tractate must seek out any Yerushalmi parallels—be they parallel sugyot, sugya-clusters, or a whole tractate—and exhaustively compare them to the Bavli text(s) under consideration. Unless our hypothetical scholar does so, she will have only a partial understanding of whatever it is she is trying to study.

Our conclusion that y. Avodah Zarah influenced the formation and structure of b. Avodah Zarah has an important implication as well for any historical conclusions we might be inclined to draw from specific Bavli passages. Even without a complete study of all Bavli tractates and their Yerushalmi parallels, the fact that in this case y. Avodah Zarah was a critical factor in the formation of b. Avodah Zarah should give us methodological pause: In deciding what is truly "Babylonian" in the Bavli for purposes of reconstructing Babylonian Jewish social or intellectual history, we must not assume that the mere presence of a passage in the Bavli guarantees that it represents the views and/or culture of the Bavli's redactors. Rather, we must first seek out any extant parallel(s) to that passage in the Yerushalmi. Only what is *new and different* in the Bavli passage represents the Babylonian contribution; we must recognize, even more than previously, the extent to which the Bavli is beholden to the Palestinian amoraic heritage.[1]

What remains for us to do in this chapter is to examine how the conclusion we have developed on the basis of a purely textual analysis of the tractates—that y. Avodah Zarah influenced b. Avodah Zarah—makes sense in terms of the historical context *outside* of the Talmuds. This examination will require us to look at the historical circumstances of Palestinian Jewry in the fifth, sixth, and early seventh centuries, the issue of which Babylonian rabbinic generation was likely to have received and utilized y. Avodah Zarah, and issues pertaining to orality and literacy, specifically what the redacted y. Avodah Zarah would have looked like and how it would have been transmitted to Babylonia. In brief, our analysis will support the conclusion that the fifth-century y. Avodah Zarah was likely transmitted to Babylonia by Palestinian scholars—most likely a very small group—in the sixth or possibly early seventh century. Babylonian scholars of the sixth century or later were aware of y. Avodah Zarah and utilized it in the formation of what became b. Avodah Zarah.

It may be objected that the historical examination we are about to undertake is not necessary because, given the history of contacts between the rabbinic communities, the time it would have taken in the fifth century for y. Avodah Zarah to have "jelled" as a redacted text, and the inevitable time lag attendant upon the difficulties of travel between the two centers, one could reasonably hypothesize that y. Avodah Zarah would have reached Babylonia in the sixth or seventh centuries even without the other

---

1. See also Shamma Friedman, "La-aggadah ha-historit," 119–122; Rubenstein, *Talmudic Stories.* Comparative study of the Talmuds may also show that, at times, the Bavli preserves more authentic versions of Palestinian sugyot than are currently found in printed editions of the Yerushalmi. For example, at b. AZ 53a, the Bavli presents a dispute about whether delivery of an idol to a Jewish or to a Gentile smelter (צורף) constitutes nullification (ביטול) of the idol. At y. AZ 4:5, 44a, both the Venice and Kratoschin editions read "for need" (לצורך), rather than "to a smelter" (לצורף), which is how the Bavli and the Leiden manuscript of the Yerushalmi read. The reading of the Bavli and Leiden make more sense, since it is difficult to make sense of a sale "for need." The Bavli thus preserves a version of the Palestinian sugya that is more authentic than that of the printed editions, and also provides added support to the reading in Leiden.

factors we will adduce. This objection is not without merit, especially given the impossibility of proving that this or that historical event caused a Palestinian scholar or scholars to go to Babylonia. But without such an external historical analysis, we are left to draw a major historical conclusion—that y. Avodah Zarah influenced the formation of b. Avodah Zarah—on the basis of a purely textual analysis. The strength of the conclusion that y. Avodah Zarah influenced b. Avodah Zarah is enhanced by external historical evidence which buttresses the conclusion we may sensibly draw from the texts.

I
Palestine in the Sixth and Seventh Centuries

The period stretching from the fourth through the seventh centuries was pivotal for Palestinian Jewry. Archaeological and literary remains from this period show the emergence of a distinctive Late Antique Jewish culture and the rabbinization of non-rabbinic Palestinian Jewry.[2] Yet, beginning in the late fifth century and continuing into the early seventh, there is also evidence of increasing imperial hostility toward the Jews and a growing Christian population in Palestine and religio-cultural Christianization of the area. Further, there is internal Jewish literary evidence of the misery these trends caused the Jews. The unrest of the sixth-century Samaritan revolt (ca. 550) was succeeded by the violent upheavals of the early seventh-century Byzantine/Persian and Byzantine/Arab wars and the end of Byzantine sovereignty over Palestine. Unsurprisingly, these trends caused a decline in the Jewish population of Palestine, with many Jews seeking refuge in the Diaspora. We will examine each of these four trends separately—growing Imperial hostility, Christianization of Palestine, Jewish literary evidence of growing misery, and political/military upheaval. Finally, we will explain how these trends support the notion of the exportation of y. Avodah Zarah from Palestine to Babylonia. But first, we will review the evidence showing the spread of rabbinic Judaism in Palestine and the strengthening of Judaism there generally in the fifth and sixth centuries. This evidence does not contradict evidence of increasing Jewish misery in the fifth through the seventh centuries. To begin with, human phenomena are quite complex, and it is not impossible that positive and negative trends can coexist—as we will clearly see that they do. Second, it is logical to assume that only a strong rabbinic Judaism, deeply-rooted

2. See, generally, Seth Schwartz, *Imperialism and Jewish Society, 200 B.C.E. to 640 C.E.* (Princeton: Princeton University Press, 2001).

among the people by the sixth century, could have been preserved amid the tumult of the late sixth and early seventh centuries.

I.a. The Rabbinization of Palestinian Jewry in the Fifth and Sixth Centuries

Seth Schwartz has persuasively traced the crystallization (by the second century BCE), collapse (in 70 CE) and reemergence (between the fourth and sixth centuries) in altered form of what he calls the "ideological complex" of God-Temple-Torah. For our purposes, we will focus on the fourth- to sixth-century period, in which Palestinian Jewry underwent a process which Schwartz labels "judaization." The seventh-century decoration of the Rehov synagogue with a mosaic inscription dealing with tithes and the Sabbatical year is one interesting example of judaization.[3] Schwartz points out that the Rehov synagogue had been decorated with friezes of lions in the fifth century.[4] The replacement of these pictorial friezes with a geometric mosaic—not to mention the halakhic one—indicates that something has changed in Palestinian Jewry. Whereas pre-sixth-century synagogues display iconography, those of the sixth and early seventh centuries show evidence of an aniconic tendency, typified by the growing evidence of geometric mosaics or the disfigurement of human or divine figures. With respect to the Rehov inscription (which is arguably derived from the Yerushalmi), Schwartz comments that "iconophobia complemented rabbinization."[5]

In the fourth to sixth centuries, the institution of the synagogue itself was "reaching its maximal diffusion"[6] in Palestine, with pride of place accorded to the niche in which the Torah scroll would be kept, and a greater sense of the numinous nature of the Torah.[7] The shift away from iconography and toward an architectural emphasis on the Torah's place in the synagogue shows the growing influence of a rabbinic conception of what makes a synagogue holy, as opposed to the older non-rabbinic sense that the synagogue's very structure conveys its sanctity.[8] This period also witnesses the emergence of the *piyyut* genre and the performance of these complex, rabbinically inspired poetic compositions in synagogues.[9] What

---

3. This example will be discussed more fully below (see pp. 221–224).

4. Schwartz, *Imperialism*, 260.

5. Seth Schwartz, "Rabbinization in the Sixth Century," in Schäfer, *The Talmud Yerushalmi In Graeco-Roman Culture III*, 58.

6. Schwartz, *Imperialism*, 241.

7. Ibid., 242.

8. Ibid., 261.

9. Ibid., 263–274.

then has changed in Palestinian Jewry? Schwartz is undoubtedly correct to point to rabbinic influence, or to "the same complex of factors that favored the growth of rabbinic influence."[10] As he puts it:

> . . . by about 500 almost all Jewish villages, though they regarded themselves as religiously discrete, participated in a common ideology; all utilized surplus capital to build and maintain synagogues, all had placed the Torah at the physical and perhaps symbolic centers of their world, and all regarded themselves as constituting "Israel," or rather an agglomeration of discrete Israels.[11]

If in the fourth to sixth centuries the synagogue was spreading, rabbinization was well underway, and rabbinic literary production was at its height—as exemplified by the redactions of the Yerushalmi and the major midrash-collections—then external pressures on the Jews, although always unwelcome and unpleasant, cannot have been so harsh as to have prevented these developments from occurring. As we move deeper into the sixth and then into the seventh centuries, however, the picture begins to change drastically.

I.b. *Deterioration of the Status of the Jews in Roman Imperial Legislation in the Fourth to Sixth Centuries*

Examination of the Roman imperial legislation concerning the Jews[12] shows evidence of deterioration in the perception of the Jews of the Empire. Before describing this evidence, a word is in order about what it does and does not show. It is too much to claim that the prohibitions or privileges provided by a given piece of legislation were immediately put into practice as enacted. Given the vastness of the Empire, its later division into Eastern and Western suzerainties, and difficulties in oversight and communications, such an immediate translation from enactment to reality is highly unlikely. Rather, what is significant for our purposes is the changing *attitude* toward the Jews reflected in the imperial legislation. While not a direct indicator of what was happening to the Jews "on the ground" at any given time, the legislation reflects the existence and deepening of hostile attitudes toward the Jews in an increasingly Christian Roman world.

---

10. Ibid.

11. Ibid., 240.

12. This material has been collected, translated, and annotated by Amnon Linder in *The Jews in Roman Imperial Legislation* (Detroit: Wayne State University Press/Israel Academy of Arts and Sciences, 1987). All references to and quotations from this legislation will be drawn from Linder's compilation.

The first of these trends is that, as a general matter, the emperors begin to classify the Jews along with pagans and heretics beginning in 383 CE.[13] This trend becomes particularly pronounced in the fifth century. In 408, Honorius, along with Theodosius II, condemned "[t]he audacity of the Donatists, the heretics and the Jews" who "want to throw the sacraments of the Catholic faith into disorder," and called for "a just and retributive chastisement" to be imposed on those "who shall attempt to do anything that is contrary and adverse to the Catholic sect."[14] More legislation against harassment of the Catholic Church by Donatists, heretics, Jews, and pagans was enacted in 409, in the wake of attacks on Catholic clergy in Africa.[15] In 423, Honorius, with Theodosius II, enacted legislation in which they indicated their desire that "the Jews . . . know . . . that we take with pleasure the occasion of the repetition of the law" [by which they had previously, in their own terms, "suppressed the arrogance and the audacity of the abominable pagans, as well as of the Jews and the heretics"], although Christians were to abstain from inflicting damage on Jews and from destroying and despoiling synagogues. This protection of synagogues is important because Jews, unlike pagans and heretics, retained the right to have holy places and practice their rituals. Jews, however, would be subject to confiscation of property and exile for circumcising a Christian.[16] Later in 423, these two emperors issued a confirmation of the policy against destroying synagogues,[17] in which the Jews were classified together with pagans and heretics. In 425, Theodosius II and Valentinian III barred Jews and pagans from the practice of law and the service of the State.[18] More elaborate clarification of imperial policy toward Jews, Samaritans, pagans, and heretics was provided in 438 by another decree of the same emperors.[19]

The significance of this fifth-century trend of classifying the Jews along with pagans and heretics[20] is that the practice of Judaism is now

---

13. See *CTh* 16:7:3 (Linder, *The Jews*, 168–174).

14. *CTh* 16:5:44 (Linder, *The Jews*, 239–241).

15. *Sirm* No. 14 and partially preserved at *CTh* 16:2:31 and 16:5:46 (Linder, *The Jews*, 241–255).

16. *CTh* 16:8:26 (Linder, *The Jews*, 289–295).

17. *CTh* 16:8:27 and 16:10:24, as well as at *CJ* 1:11:6 (Linder, *The Jews*, 295–300).

18. *Sirm* No. 6 (Linder, *The Jews*, 305–337).

19. *Theodosius II, Novella 3* (Linder, *The Jews*, 323–337).

20. Although, as Seth Schwartz points out, there is a key distinction between Jews on the one hand, and pagans and heretics on the other: Jews always retained the right to maintain their holy places and observe their rituals, unlike pagans and heretics.

considered to be a religious deviation from Christianity, rather than the perpetuation of ancient national customs as the pagan Empire had conceived it. Jewish religion is, at bottom, simply not a welcome part of a Christian society.

The Jews were pushed out of the imperial service entirely in the fifth and sixth centuries. In 418, Honorius, together with Theodosius II, declared participation in "the State service" off-limits to men "living in the Jewish superstition," while allowing that those already serving should be allowed to complete their terms of service. "Jews educated in the liberal studies" were specifically permitted to continue "practicing as advocates" as well as "to enjoy the honour of the curial liturgies."[21] However, in 425, Theodosius II and Valentinian III declared that the practice of law and participation in the State service were closed to Jews and pagans, basing this decision on the ground that "we do not wish people of the Christian Law to serve them, lest they substitute, because of this mastery, the venerable religion by a sect."[22] A similar point was made with greater rhetorical ferocity by Justin and Justinian in 527, who declared that "we order that those who are heretics, and above all the pagans, Jews, Samaritans, and those similar to them, if they take part in any of all those [municipal honors] we have already recalled . . . they shall be thrown out on the spot from participating in these."[23] The ultimate purpose of these harsh measures was stated earlier in the same piece of legislation:

> As for the other heretics . . . as well as . . . the Jews and the Samaritans, we intend not only that what was already laid down in the laws shall be recalled and made firmer through this present law, but also that more shall be declared; through which greater security, also honour and esteem shall envelope [sic] those sharing in our pure faith. *It shall then be possible for all to perceive, as we said, that even what pertains to the human advantages is withheld from those who do not worship God rightly.* (emphasis added)

In this edict, Justin and Justinian also declared Jews (among others) to have an inferior status to Orthodox Christians in litigation, while in 531, Justinian declared that Jews and heretics could no longer serve as witnesses against Orthodox Christians.[24]

In the fifth century, we see the beginning of an imperial tendency to interfere with the practice of Judaism. In 408, Theodosius II and Honorius prohibited the Jews from engaging in Purim festivities which appeared to

---

21. *CTh* 16:8:24 (Linder, *The Jews*, 280–283).
22. *Sirm* No. 6 (Linder, *The Jews*, 305–313).
23. *CJ* 1:5:12 (Linder, *The Jews*, 356–367).
24. *CJ* 1:5:21 (Linder, *The Jews*, 371–375).

mock Christianity,[25] a provision carried over into the Justinian Code.[26] The most glaring evidence of imperial willingness to interfere in Jewish religious practice is Justinian's enigmatic *Novella* No. 146 of 553,[27] in which, *inter alia*, he declares that

> what they call *deuterosis* . . . we prohibit entirely, for it is not included among the Holy Books, nor was it handed down from above by the prophets, but it is an invention of men in their chatter, exclusively of earthly origin and having in it nothing of the divine.[28]

Schwartz suggests that the *deuterosis* might refer to sermons or *qerovot* (types of *piyyutim*), which are literary compositions influenced by the rabbinic liturgical guidance in tractates Berakhot and Megillah.[29] If Schwartz is correct, then Justinian's *Novella* No. 146 evidences both the increasing sixth-century rabbinization of the Palestinian Jewish community as well as the imperial desire to remove any impediments to the successful conversion of the Jews.

Of all the legislation we have reviewed, the sixth-century legislation of Justinian seems the most driven by the theologically-based desire to isolate the Jews and make their continued existence as Jews ever more unpleasant, although it is the culmination of trends that had been developing in the fifth century as well. "What pertains to the human advantages is withheld from those who do not worship God rightly"—with such an imperial watchword, Palestinian Jewry was certainly on notice that it had no friends in the imperial government of the Empire in the sixth century.

I.c. The Growing Christianization of Palestine in the Fifth and Sixth Centuries and Its Effect on the Jews

Much archaeological evidence suggests that the Christian population of Palestine grew, and that Christianity became a pervasive feature of the Palestinian landscape in the fifth to sixth centuries. Based upon the study of over three hundred remains of churches, Ze'ev Safrai concluded that church construction spread from classical sacred sites and urban and village settings in the first half of the fifth century to even rural areas in the later fifth and sixth centuries. Safrai dates most of the Palestinian

---

25. *CTh* 16:8:18 (Linder, *The Jews*, 236–238).

26. *CJ* 1:9:11 (ibid.).

27. Linder, *The Jews*, 402–411.

28. The meaning of *"deuterosis"* is unclear, but it is unlikely that it refers to the Mishnah, as some have claimed. See Jean Juster, *Les Juifs dans l'Empire Romain* (2 vols.; Paris: Librairie Paul Genthner, 1914), 1:369–377.

29. Schwartz, "Rabbinization," 68.

churches, as well as Christian archaeological remains overall, to this late fifth- to sixth-century period. From the sixth century until the Arab conquest, "the churches became a central feature in the urban and rural landscape in most regions of Palestine."[30] Churches were also built over destroyed or abandoned pagan temples beginning in the mid-fourth century. Churches were built over temples in Bethlehem and Mamre, while there was an attempt to build one over the abandoned temple of Hadrian in Tiberias. At the beginning of the fifth century, the temple in Gaza was turned into a church, and even the Samaritan shrine on Mt. Gerizim was "converted" in the late fifth century.[31] This spurt in church construction, and especially the spread of church construction into rural areas, indicates an increased Christian population meant to be served by those churches. Safrai concludes—on a rather ideologically charged note—that "the movement of conversion to Christianity apparently began to assume significant dimensions only in the sixth century, mainly among the pagan population."[32]

Studies of Christian appropriation of Jewish burial places also point to a growing Christian presence in Palestine in the fifth to sixth centuries, as well as to the fact that, *contra* Safrai, conversion to Christianity in this period was a trend not only among pagans. Based on their study of a cemetery at Beth Guvrin containing both Jewish and Christian iconography, Jodi Magness and Gideon Avni concluded that

> the evidence from the Menorah Cave and the distribution of clearly Jewish and Christian symbols on lamps from the other caves is suggestive of a change over time in the religious orientation of the cemetery's occupants. It seems that the initial (late second to fourth century) burials in these caves were Jewish. The first evidence for Christian presence dates to the fourth or fifth century, and is most common during the late sixth to early eighth centuries.[33]

Magness and Avni point out that there is support (albeit indirect) from historical sources for the demographic conclusions drawn from the cemetery, noting that "by the sixth century, [Beth Guvrin] was clearly Christian in character."[34] Nor was this phenomenon of Christian reuse of Jewish

---

30. Ze'ev Safrai, *The Missing Century; Palestine in the Fifth Century: Growth and Decline* (Leuven: Peeters, 1998), 71.

31. Ibid., 72–73.

32. Ibid., 130.

33. Jodi Magness and Gideon Avni, "Jews and Christians in a Late Roman Cemetery at Beth Guvrin," in Lapin, *Religious and Ethnic Communities in Later Roman Palestine*, 111.

34. Magness and Avni, "Jews and Christians," 113.

burial places limited to Beth Guvrin; Christians also reused other Jewish tombs, dating to the Second Temple, between the fifth and seventh centuries.[35]

While the Jewish population of Palestine was still relatively large at the end of the fourth century through the early fifth, the rise of Christianity and its growing hold on the country exerted a negative effect on the Jewish population, and set it on a course of decline in the fifth century.[36] The Jewish population continued to decline in the fifth and sixth centuries,[37] although the discovery of synagogue remains dating from this period[38] and ongoing literary production should make one cautious about too-pessimistic assessments of the size of the Jewish population. Yet Yaron Dan is correct that "the self-preservation of Palestinian Jewry in the new circumstances was made more and more difficult."[39]

I.d. The Witness of the Piyyutim to Jewish Attitudes About Life Under Rome and Byzantium

As noted previously, Jewish literary production and innovation continued in the late fifth century and on into the sixth, despite the worsening conditions of life under Christian Rome. The earliest extant *piyyutim* are creations of the fifth-century liturgical poet Yose b. Yose,[40] and this new genre gained practitioners in the succeeding centuries. In this period, Palestinian Jewry also produced a post-Yerushalmi halakhic literature consisting of responsa and books of halakhot—presaging literary developments in the Middle Ages.[41]

---

35. Ibid., 112–113. See also Gideon Avni, "Christian Secondary Use of Jewish Burial Caves in Jerusalem in the Light of New Excavations at the Aceldama Tombs," in *Early Christianity in Context: Monuments and Documents* (ed. F. Manns and E. Alliata; Jerusalem: Studium Biblicum Franciscanum, 1993), 265–276.

36. Yaron Dan, "Erets Yisra'el ba-me'ot ha-hamishit veha-shishit," in *The Land of Israel From the Destruction of the Second Temple to the Muslim Conquest* (ed. Zvi Baras et al.; 2 vols.; Jerusalem: Yad Ben Zvi, 1982), 1:267 (Heb.).

37. Dan, "Erets Yisra'el," 267; Simha Assaf, *Tequfat ha-Geonim ve-sifrutah* (Jerusalem: Mossad HaRav Kook, 1967), 92 ("there was also an exodus [from the Land] that was caused by the difficult conditions, the pressure and the want, the endless revolts and upheavals. The number of emigrants exceeded the number of immigrants").

38. For example, the famous Bet Alpha synagogue. See Dan, "Erets Yisra'el," 293–294.

39. Dan, "Erets Yisra'el," 267.

40. See Aharon Mirsky, *Yosse Ben Yosse: Poems* (Jerusalem: Mossad Bialik, 1977) (Heb.).

41. For more on these developments, see Mordecai Margaliot, *Hilkhot Erets Yisra'el min ha-Genizah* (Jerusalem: Mossad HaRav Kook, 1973).

Examination of these literary works (especially the *piyyutim*) discloses evidence of bitter unhappiness at the conditions of Jewish life under Christian Rome at this time. However, given the ubiquity of Israel's enemies in the Hebrew Bible and the pervasiveness of "exile" as a Jewish theme, care must be taken to distinguish clear poetic references to Rome from more general references to persecution, troubles, and exile. We will therefore utilize only specific references to persecutions and/or hardships brought about by *Rome* (under any of its rabbinic names) as evidence relevant to the evaluation of the condition of Palestinian Jewry under Byzantium.

After describing the tenth plague to befall the Egyptians in biblical times, the great sixth-century poet Yannai wishes the same on Christian Rome (poetically equated with "Edom")[42] as he prays: "May it be heard about Edom as it was heard about Egypt / [May the] 'burden of Dumah'[43] be like the 'burden of Egypt.'"[44] Moving on, Yannai wishes that "the firstborn of the kingdom of their nation . . . exterminate them with anger."[45] Yannai expresses similar sentiments in a poem wherein he compares the four kingdoms that have ruled the people Israel to four types of skin-ailments. Although most of the line pertaining directly to the "hand of Edom" is missing, Yannai follows his reference to Rome (by means of which "our honor has fallen") with the following poignant plea: "We are dead in life / Resurrect us / For You are our life."[46] Yannai's point seems to be that the four kingdoms are dangerous skin ailments that cause the afflicted person (the people Israel) to be considered leprous, further causing him, in turn, to be effectively viewed as "dead."[47]

Writing poetically about the destruction of Sodom and Gomorrah, the poet Shimon bar Megas asks, "Let us see You attired in red / God, make Edom / Like the overturning of Sodom / May it be time for [Edom] to be

---

42. For a study of the Late Antique/early medieval Jewish equation of Rome with Esau, see Gerson Cohen, "Esau as Symbol in Early Medieval Thought," in *Jewish Medieval and Renaissance Studies* (ed. Alexander Altmann; Cambridge: Harvard University Press, 1967), 19–48.

43. The "burden of Dumah" is a prophecy of Isaiah recorded at Isa 21:11–12, understood early as a reference to Rome.

44. See Menahem Zulay, *Piyyute Yannai* (Berlin: Schocken, 1938), 90.

45. Ibid.

46. Ibid., 135–136.

47. See b. AZ 5a, where the leper is one of four considered to be dead while living. Interestingly, this aggadah appears in b. AZ toward the end of the long aggadic composition pertaining to the fate of Israel and the other nations at the end of history. Whether or not Yannai intended to introduce all these intertextual hints is an interesting question, but one that goes beyond the scope of this work.

destroyed and made desolate."[48] Like Yannai, Shimon bar Megas calls
down on Rome the tenth plague of Egypt, asking, "May the Edomites be
uprooted [by means of] the plague of 'the strengths' [firstborn; called
'strengths' by reference to Gen 49:3, where Jacob calls Reuben the 'beginning of my strength (אוני)']."[49]

The poet Yehudah is extremely interesting because in his poems, he
points to a specific impact that persecution had on Jewish worship, and
also locates himself geographically as a probable Palestinian living *outside*
Palestine.[50] First, in a typical plaint of the time, he asks, "Until when will
the End be lengthened over Israel?"[51] meaning, How long will it be until
divine deliverance? In a poem based on Deut 29:9, Yehudah again asks,
"Until when will Your people all be scattered / To the four corners of the
earth, on them was the earth / And they [Rome] prevented me from seeking You and from unifying You, King of the World / In my integrity up-
hold me and set me in Your presence forever (Ps 41:13)."[52]

Yehudah's allusion to a possible liturgical change brought about because of Rome is consistent with the Roman imperial attitude we identified earlier as being that of the sixth-century emperor Justinian. My claim
is not that Yehudah is pointing to a piece of now-lost legislation promul-
gated by Justinian; rather, it is that given what we do know of the sixth-
century imperial willingness to interfere in the synagogue (Justinian's *Novella* No. 146 of 553), it seems more likely than not that the earliest time at
which the "prevention" mentioned by Yehudah may have occurred was
in the sixth century.

---

48. Joseph Yahalom, *Liturgical Poems of Šim'on Bar Megas* (Jerusalem: The Israel
National Academy of Sciences, 1984), 133 (Heb.).

49. Ibid., 190.

50. Wout Jac. Van Bekkum, *Hebrew Poetry From Late Antiquity; Liturgical Poems of
Yehudah: Critical Edition With Introduction and Commentary* (Leiden: E. J. Brill, 1998).

51. Ibid., 25.

52. Ibid., 89. The interesting reference to the inability to engage in "unifying
You" may well be a reference to the recitation of the *Shema,* by which God's unity is
proclaimed. Yehudah may be referring to the same change in Palestinian liturgy
referred to by the late eighth-century opponent of Palestinian learning Pirqoi b.
Baboi, who noted, "And so did Mar R. Yehudai (Gaon Baghdad, ca. 750) say, that
they [Rome] had decreed a persecution on the people of the Land of Israel; that
they should not recite the *Shema* nor pray," as a result of which the Palestinians,
among other changes, recited the *Shema* in the additional *"musaf"* prayer on the
Sabbath—an innovation disliked by the Babylonians. The epistle of Pirqoi b. Baboi
has been published in pieces in a number of places. The most complete version is
that published by Jacob Mann in *REJ* 70 (1920): 129–148. My translation is of a portion found on p. 133. See also Jacob Mann, "Changes in the Divine Service of the
Synagogue Due to Religious Persecutions," *HUCA* 4 (1927): 241–310.

Finally, Yehudah asks: "Until when will we live outside of the Land / And the Prince of the Kingdom of Edom be exalted up to the heavens / Bring him low, and bring him down to the depths of the earth / And let the heavens rejoice and the earth be glad."[53] As Van Bekkum notes, "The geographical hint 'outside the Land' is of great interest, and may be a direct indication that the community to which Yehudah belonged lay somewhere outside the Land of Israel."[54]

I.e. Palestinian Jewry and the Byzantine Conflicts with Sassanian Persia in the Sixth and Seventh Centuries

Another fascinating, albeit disturbing, set of references is found in a late (probably early seventh century) fragment of a dirge initially published by Simcha Assaf and subsequently studied by Mordecai A. Friedman.[55] The partially preserved poem mentions the slaughter of Jews—including sages (who may or may not have been rabbinic sages)—that occurred in Kefar Hebronah, Ono, Jaffa, Lod, Huseifah, and Haifa. "Great ones and scribes" were murdered in Kefar Hebronah, while "they trampled and slaughtered the חבורה (scholarly fellowship) of Ono."[56] Mention is made of "Your honored elders (זקנים)" in Jaffa, while in Haifa, "they slaughtered elders" and "the elders of the circle (עגולה) have ceased" (probably a reference to m. Sanh 4:3).[57] The poet also mentions the destruction of synagogues in these places. The sad events described in this dirge are testimony to the dangerous position of Palestinian Jewry in the Late Byzantine period, and to what may have led some, especially scholars, to leave the country.

---

53. Van Bekkum, *Hebrew Poetry*, 104.

54. Ibid., xvi.

55. Simha Assaf, "Qinah qedumah 'al hurban ha-qehillot be-Erets Yisra'el," in *Texts and Studies in Jewish History* (Jerusalem: Mossad HaRav Kook, 1946), 9–16 (Heb.); Mordecai Akiva Friedman, "Ono—yedi'ot hadashot mi-kitvei ha-Genizah ha-Qahirit," in *Between Yarkon and Ayalon: Studies on the Tel Aviv Metropolitan Area and the Lod Valley* (ed. David Grossman; Ramat-Gan: Bar Ilan University, 1983), 73–85 (Heb.). The dating of this dirge has been a matter of dispute. Assaf maintained that the dirge was written during the First Crusade, while acknowledging the force of arguments supporting a Late Byzantine (late sixth-/early seventh-century) date. Friedman consulted Ezra Fleischer and S. D. Goitein about dating the dirge, and the former proposed an early seventh-century date. Based on the absence of references to Islam, Friedman proposes that the poem was written during the years 600–634, probably around 629, when the Emperor Heraclius exacted vengeance on Palestinian Jewry after his reconquest of Palestine from the Persians.

56. Friedman, "Ono," 74.

57. Ibid.

I.f. Conclusion

Conclusions drawn from archaeological finds and the internal evidence of
Jewish literary sources all point to the conclusion that the situation of the
Jews in Palestine seriously deteriorated in the sixth and early seventh centuries. The growing religious-based imperial hostility discernible in imperial legislation concerning the Jews is also a factor to be considered, although it is difficult to draw direct connections between specific imperial
laws and the concrete situations in which Jews may have found themselves. The Christianization of the population and the face of Palestine itself led to a decline in the Jewish population of Palestine. While Palestine
was not at all *emptied* of Jews—in fact, synagogues continued to be built
and decorated, and literature continued to be produced—Simhah Assaf
and Yaron Dan have both noted that the sixth century was a time of noticeable decrease in the Jewish population of Palestine. Gedaliah Alon
agreed,[58] although he hastened to add that "in spite of the diminution of
the Jewish population in the country . . . I do not think that they dropped
below the level of a rather considerable proportion of the total."[59] This
conclusion is buttressed by the interesting implication of the poet Yehudah that he and others are living outside the Land and praying for the fall
of Edom so that they may return.

   There is no evidence of a *mass* migration of scholars to Babylonia in
the sixth to seventh centuries. But two factors suggest that there likely was
a migration of a small number of scholars. First, given the history of scholarly movement between the two rabbinic centers, the increasing pressures
in Palestine that we have described may well have caused at least a few
scholars to emigrate.[60] Among these may have been some who brought

---

58. Gedaliah Alon, *The Jews in Their Land in the Talmudic Age (70–640 C.E.)* (Cambridge, MA: Harvard University Press, 1989), 755.

59. Alon, *The Jews*, 757.

60. Nevertheless, there is evidence of at least one notable immigrant *to* Palestine
in the sixth century. *Seder Olam Zuta* contains a tradition that after the execution in
Persia of the rebellious exilarch Mar Zutra in the sixth century, his young son (also
named Mar Zutra) went to Palestine and was appointed *"resh pirqei."* See *Seder
Olam Zuta* (ed. Manasseh Grossberg; London: n.p., 1910), 53–54. See also H. Z.
Hirschberg, "Joseph, King of Himyar, and the Coming of Mar Zutra to Tiberias,"
in *All the Land of Naphtali* (ed. H. Z. Hirschberg and Y. Abiram; Jerusalem: ha-
Hevrah le-Haqirat Erets-Yisra'el ve-Atiqoteha, 1967), 139–146 (Heb.), and idem,
"Mar Zutra, the Head of the Sanhedrin at Tiberias," in *All the Land of Naphtali*, 147–
153 (Heb.). Most recently, see Ze'ev Safrai and Aren M. Maeir, "אתא אגרתא ממערבא
('An Epistle Came From the West'): Historical and Archaeological Evidence for the
Ties Between the Jewish Communities in the Land of Israel and Babylonia During

y. Avodah Zarah to Babylonia. Second, we must view rabbinic peregrinations in light of the larger Roman cultural context, in which geographical mobility was a notable characteristic of the elite.[61] Christian ascetics and missionaries, and pagan philosophers, crossed the frontier between the often-warring Sassanian Persia and Byzantium without much impediment; a Christian bishop named Milles is alleged to have traveled from Susiana in Persia to Jerusalem and Alexandria to tour famous monasteries.[62] In light of these larger cultural factors, it is hardly unreasonable to assume that a small movement of scholars from Palestine to Babylonia occurred, and that these scholars were the conduit by which y. Avodah Zarah reached Babylonia.

II
What Babylonian Generation Is Aware of
Y. Avodah Zarah?

Palestinian scholars brought y. Avodah Zarah to Babylonia, and I have hypothesized that this transmission occurred in the sixth or early seventh centuries. But in order to put that dating on a firmer footing, we need to consider who the likely Babylonian recipients were. Clarifying the issue of which Babylonian scholars likely received y. Avodah Zarah and when will help lay to rest two alternative suggestions for how y. Avodah Zarah came to Babylonia: that it came (1) as early talmud during the amoraic period; or (2) immediately following the Yerushalmi's redaction in the early fifth century.

II.a. Amoraim Are Unaware of Y. Avodah Zarah

Our analyses in chapters 2 through 5 showed that Babylonian amoraim were not aware of the structural similarities between the redactional

---

the Talmudic Period," *JQR* 93:3–4 (Jan–Apr 2003): 497–531. It is unlikely that Mar Zutra played much of a role in the transmission of the Yerushalmi to Babylonia since there is no tradition that he ever returned there.

61. See, e..g., A. H. M. Jones, *The Later Roman Empire 284–602: A Social, Economic, and Administrative Survey* (2 vols.; Oxford: Basil Blackwell, 1964), 2:1021–1024.

62. See Samuel N. C. Lieu, "Captives, Refugees and Exiles: A Study of Cross-Frontier Civilian Movements and Contacts Between Rome and Persia From Valerian to Jovian," in *The Defence of the Roman and Byzantine East* (ed. Philip Freeman and David Kennedy; 2 vols.; Oxford: BAR International Series, 1986), 2:475–505.

contexts of their traditions in b. and y. Avodah Zarah. *The Babylonian amoraim do not know y. Avodah Zarah; nor, for that matter, do they know that they are part of a "Talmud."*[63]

Two examples will remind us of this point. At y. AZ 2:3, 41a, both R. Yitshaq b. Nahman and R. Shimon are represented as quoting R. Yehoshua b. Levi's tradition that there is no concern about "exposure" in relation to "sweet," "bitter," or "sharp" wine. This is followed by a story about the exposure of R. Yehoshua b. Zeidel's "boiled" wine, and the resolution of the status of that wine by reference to a Resh Laqish tradition about "sweet" wine similar to that of R. Yehoshua b. Levi. A story then follows about a group discussion of exposure that took place in the presence of the ill R. Yannai son of R. Yishmael, more cases of exposure involving R. Ami and Bar Yudanah, a question to R. Abbahu about exposed boiled wine that he answers by reference to R. Yohanan's ruling about *qarenum*, a case of exposed water, and consideration of the psychology of snakes. A close reading of this cluster of sugyot reveals that the Palestinian amoraim are aware only of their own traditions, not of the fact that these traditions were arranged in this particular order. No amora is aware of the traditions that precede or follow his own. A key proof of this is the story about the group discussion in the presence of R. Yannai son of R. Yishmael; nothing in the story indicates that the amoraim involved were aware of the larger redactional context in which the story is now found.

Turning now to the structurally similar parallel at b. AZ 30a, we see that the cluster of sugyot opens with Rabbah and R. Yosef's shared tradition that there is no concern about exposure in relation to "boiled" wine, followed by b. Avodah Zarah's version of the group discussion about exposure in the presence of the sick R. Yannai b. Yishmael. There then follows a story about Shmuel and Ablat (a Gentile) that proves that there is no concern about libation-wine in connection with boiled wine, and then stories about exposed boiled wine involving the maidservant of R. Hiyya and the attendant of R. Ada b. Ahavah. Stories about the psychology of snakes then follow, to be succeeded by stories and traditions about exposed water. Finally, near the end of this cluster of materials, we see R. Yehoshua b. Levi's tradition about "sweet," "bitter," and "sharp" wine, and traditions about *qarenum* in the names of Resh Laqish and R. Abbahu.

Examining the constituent sugyot in this cluster, we see once again that not one of the amoraim mentioned and/or quoted demonstrates any awareness of a context for his tradition larger than the tradition itself.

---

63. For a similar conclusion based on a comparative study of b. and y. Hor, see Jaffee, "The Babylonian Appropriation of the Talmud Yerushalmi."

Looking at b. Avodah Zarah's version of the story about R. Yannai b. Yishmael, nothing at all in the story reveals any awareness that the story is integrated into a larger context about exposed wine and water, and the psychology of snakes.

If the amoraim quoted in these parallel sugya-clusters in the Talmuds were not aware of the selection and sequence of their traditions, then they cannot be responsible for the particular arrangement that now exists. Rather, a *post*-amoraic editorial hand must have collected these constituent sugyot and created the sequences of materials we now find.

The shared sugya found at y. AZ 5:14, 45b and b. AZ 75a also nicely illustrates this point about amoraic unawareness of the redactional context of their traditions. Both sugyot open with concrete questions: about a "papyrus vessel plastered by a Gentile" in y. Avodah Zarah, and "grape-cluster wraps of Arameans" in b. Avodah Zarah. The path taken by both sugyot after their quotations of t. AZ 9:3 was probably not known to either R. Yose b. R. Bun or R. Abbahu, the amoraim who were allegedly asked the initial questions. After quoting from t. AZ 9:3, both sugyot present the anonymous question "What is 'עונה'?" and present similar traditions with similar attributions to answer that question. Although these traditions are apparently in conflict, both Talmuds give the identical resolution to the conflict: anonymously in y. Avodah Zarah, and in the name of R. Shmuel b. Yitshaq in b. Avodah Zarah.

It is clear that beginning with the anonymous question "What is 'עונה'?" both sugyot move off in a new direction that could not have been contemplated by the amoraim who originally cited t. AZ 9:3 in response to the questions posed to them. This "new direction" is editorially constructed as a continuation of the sugya. The amoraim are not aware of the switch in the sugya's direction. That switch was most likely the work of post-amoraic redactors.

Now that we have reminded ourselves that the amoraim mentioned in b. Avodah Zarah are not aware that their traditions are integrated within a selection and sequence of sugyot like that of y. Avodah Zarah, and that this awareness is more likely a characteristic of post-amoraic redactors, we must investigate whether it is possible to date (relatively) this new awareness. When does amoraic activity in Babylonia cease and editorial activity—characterized in b. Avodah Zarah by reception of y. Avodah Zarah—begin?

II.b. *The Latest Amoraic Activity Recorded in B. Avodah Zarah*

In his *Redaction of the Babylonian Talmud*, Richard Kalmin presented his conclusions as to the identities of "the Amoraim who were active during the seventy-four to ninety-three years between the death of Rav Ashi in

427 CE and the beginning of the Saboraic period in 501 or 520 CE."[64] The occurrence of any of these names in b. Avodah Zarah will give us a clue as to the relative date of the latest amoraic activity recorded there.

At b. AZ 26b (and the parallel at b. Hor 11a), Rav Aha is juxtaposed in a dispute format (איתמר . . . פליגי . . . חד אמר . . . חד אמר . . .) with Ravina, whom Kalmin, following Meshulam Behr, Chanoch Albeck, and David Halivni, identifies as the "later" Ravina, who died ca. 501.[65] The later Ravina also appears at 69a, where his statement is placed after that of R. Ashi, and is the basis of an objection by Rav Tahlifa bar Giza. R. Sama b. de-R. Ashi is found at 50b, and at 63b, R. Yemar raises an objection to R. Ashi. Finally, Mar bar R. Ashi appears at b. AZ 75b. Of all these "post-Rav Ashi amoraim,"[66] the latest is the "later" Ravina, thus indicating that the *terminus ad quem* for the amoraic activity recorded in b. Avodah Zarah is ca. 500.[67] Kalmin is thus undoubtedly correct when he writes: "It should be noted . . . that the Yerushalmi, completed shortly before the death of Rav Ashi, appears to have exerted virtually no influence on the final generations of Amoraim." Moreover, "There seems to have been only minimal contact between Palestine and Bavel at this time."[68] The Babylonians, then, could have become aware of the early fifth-century y. Avodah Zarah in the sixth century at the earliest, after the amoraic period in Babylonia had come to an end.[69]

---

64. Kalmin, *Redaction of the Babylonian Talmud*, 12. The identities of the so-called saboraim and the nature of their activities has been, and in some circles continues to be, a source of scholarly controversy. For our purposes, it is unimportant whether the post-amoraic editors are called saboraim or something else; what is of most importance is that these post-amoraic scholars differ from their predecessors in their awareness and use of the Yerushalmi.

65. Ibid., 23.

66. The term is Richard Kalmin's. See his "The Post-Rav Ashi Amoraim: Transition or Continuity? A Study of the Role of the Final Generations of Amoraim in the Redaction of the Talmud" (Ph.D. diss., Jewish Theological Seminary, 1985).

67. See also Avinoam Cohen, *Ravina and Contemporary Sages: Studies in the Chronology of Late Babylonian Amoraim* (Ramat-Gan: Bar-Ilan University Press, 2001), 214n153 (Heb.), in which he cites b. AZ 69a as one of a list of sugyot in which "Ravina" is claimed to be the "later Ravina" rather than the Ravina who had been a student of Rava.

68. Kalmin, *Redaction of the Babylonian Talmud*, 168n102. In that note, Kalmin sets out a few examples of later amoraim transmitting Palestinian traditions. The key common denominator of these examples is that the amoraim transmit only isolated traditions and interpretations, and show no awareness of the larger redactional contexts of those traditions.

69. In this we agree with David Halivni's contention that "as long as the amoraim functioned, even just a few of them, this is still the amoraic period." See Halivni, *Sources and Traditions*: Baba Mezia, 12 (Heb.). As long as amoraim exist

We will now turn to the question of the form in which the Babylonian scholars may have received y. Avodah Zarah, and what it may have looked like.

III
In What Form(s) Did the Redacted Yerushalmi Exist?

The question of whether rabbinic literature was formulated and transmitted orally or in writing is not a new one. Saul Lieberman posited the theory of the oral publication of the Mishnah in "The Publication of the Mishnah."[70] Twenty-five years later, Jacob Neusner carefully studied the composition of the Mishnah and also concluded that it was oral,[71] although his account of the process of composition differs from that offered by earlier scholarship. The recent emergence of orality and literacy studies as a body of scholarship to be reckoned with by scholars of rabbinics has led to further reconsideration of this interesting (and ultimately insoluble) question. Our discussion of this scholarship in this section is not intended to settle the question of oral or written composition for all the rabbinic compilations once and for all, but to see what light this scholarship sheds on the movement of y. Avodah Zarah to Babylonia in the sixth or seventh centuries. Was that Yerushalmi tractate likely written, or was it transmitted orally? If written, what materials were employed? Did it take the form of a scroll or codex? If written, was each tractate written separately, or was the entire Talmud written all together in one scroll or codex? What evidence exists to suggest that one or another possibility is more likely? We will begin in III.a with a discussion of the recent scholarship about whether the Mishnah and Tosefta were composed in writing or orally. In III.b we will move on to consider the question of the Yerushalmi directly, and in III.c we will consider the likely cultural impact on the receptive group—the post-amoraic Babylonian scholars—of a written Yerushalmi tractate.[72]

---

and continue to function as amoraim, tractate-wide redactional activity cannot have begun.

70. Saul Lieberman, "The Publication of the Mishnah," in *Hellenism in Jewish Palestine* (New York: Jewish Theological Seminary, 1950), 83–99.

71. Jacob Neusner, *Oral Tradition in Judaism: The Case of the* Mishnah (New York: Garland, 1987), 61.

72. Although this book deals only with y. AZ and its influence on b. AZ, this section will at times refer to "the Yerushalmi." The reason for this is that, with the exception of the Yerushalmi Bavot tractates (the "Talmud of Caesarea"), the remainder of the Tiberian Yerushalmi was probably redacted in more or less the same time and place. Since there is no reason to think that y. AZ was redacted in a

III.a. Literacy, Orality, and Literary Composition Prior to the Redaction of the Yerushalmi

Rabbinic traditions such as the famous "words transmitted by mouth you may not write" (b. Git 60a) have traditionally been cited as evidence of the exclusively oral composition and transmission of rabbinic traditions during the tannaitic and amoraic periods. But the Palestinian rabbinic community does not seem to have been quite that allergic to writing down its legal traditions. At y. Kil 1:1, 27a, we are told that "R. Yose in the name of R. Hiyya b. Va found written in the notebook of R. Hillel b. R. Valens"[73] and that "R. Yonah in the name of R. Hiyya b. Va found written on the wall of R. Hillel b. R. Valens." In this case, what was "found written" was a list of vegetables; this, along with the tradition of R. Yonah that this list was written on a wall, is interestingly reminiscent of the Sabbatical year inscription found in the synagogue at Rehov (to be discussed below). Another reference to writing, at y. Maas 2:4, 49d, is perhaps of greater interest because of the light it sheds on the use of a written rabbinic source (a Toseftan parallel) to raise a question about an oral one. In this case, R. Yonah mentioned a tradition "found written in the notebook of Hilfai (a proper name)."[74] In a similar case at y. AZ 4:8, 44a–b, Shimon b. Hiyya is said to have been reciting to Hiyya b. Rav: "A Gentile—from when does he make libation wine?" (That is, from what age does his touch render wine libation wine?) Hiyya b. Rav's answer was "When [the Gentile] knows the meaning of idolatry." At this point, R. Yoshiah is said to have "taken out a *mekhilta* (collection)"[75] from which he corrected Hiyya b. Rav's response. As in y. Maaserot, then, we see an amora consulting a written text for a version of a tannaitic tradition that he uses to challenge a tannaitic tradition presented orally. And at y. Shab 16:1, 15c, R. Yehoshua b. Levi mentions consulting (just once!) a "book of aggadah."

These examples show only that certain amoraim consulted written sources on certain occasions, not that the accumulated legal and aggadic

---

different time or place than the rest of the Yerushalmi, conclusions with respect to the oral or literary nature of the redacted Yerushalmi are valid for y. AZ as well, and certainly vice versa.

73. This rendering of the name as "Valens" follows Catherine Hezser, *Jewish Literacy in Roman Palestine* (Tübingen: Mohr Siebeck, 2001), 96n284.

74. Ibid., 97. For a fuller discussion of this text, see Martin Jaffee, *Torah in the Mouth: Writing and Oral Tradition in Palestinian Judaism, 200 BCE–400 CE* (New York: Oxford University Press, 2001), 141.

75. Most likely this refers neither to the Mekhilta of R. Yishmael nor to that of R. Shimon b. Yohai, but, by analogy to the case in y. Maas, to a scroll containing some rabbinic traditions. There is no basis for assuming that this is "the" Mekhilta.

heritage of the Palestinian amoraim was received by them in writing. Moreover, the small number of examples suggests that consultation of written materials was likely the notable exception rather than the rule—otherwise why draw attention to the fact that in y. Maaserot and y. Avodah Zarah the tradition quoted as a challenge was drawn from a written source? Nevertheless, these examples do show two things: (1) some amoraim did have access to some tannaitic traditions in written form; and (2) at least some Palestinian amoraim were not averse to putting legal traditions into written form.

Despite these traditions, the consensus of scholars who have most recently studied this issue—Jacob Neusner, Yaakov Elman, and Catherine Hezser—is that the Mishnah and Tosefta as whole compilations most likely circulated orally during the tannaitic and amoraic periods.[76] Martin Jaffee, however, has recently argued that the composition of the tannaitic compilations was done in writing, and that the Mishnah and Tosefta even show evidence of reworking that was most likely done on the basis of written texts.[77] Jaffee's claim is quite clear:

> It is important to realize . . . that within the Tannaitic corpus itself these claims about the oral origins and primordial transmission of the tradition refer only to discrete halakhic teachings . . . or to isolated halakhic themes. . . . we find no assertion, for example, that various compilations of Tannaitic teachings—such as the Mishnah—were themselves unwritten or constituted some part of the primordial oral revelation.
>
> We are under no compulsion, therefore, from either logic or the testimony of the sources, to imagine that compilations such as the Mishnah were composed and edited solely through the mnemonically managed organization and manipulation of unwritten materials.[78]

Rather than accept the model of exclusive literacy or orality, we shall follow Jaffee in exploring "the model of interpenetration or interdependence of oral and written textual formations."[79] Hezser has rejected Jaffee's view of the largely written nature of rabbinic tradition, opting for the cautious conclusion that "we do not know for sure whether the entire Mishnah existed in written form in amoraic times."[80] Elman does not deny the pos-

---

76. See Neusner, *Oral Tradition in Judaism*; Elman, *Authority and Tradition*, 74 and idem, "Orality and the Redaction of the Babylonian Talmud," *Oral Tradition* 14(1) (1999): 52–99, esp. 55; Hezser, *Jewish Literacy*, 427. But see ibid., 422, where Hezser describes the Mishnah as one of several "written collections."

77. See Jaffee, *Torah in the Mouth*, especially 100–125, where he defends this claim through a detailed analysis of mishnayot from various tractates.

78. Ibid., 100.

79. Ibid., 101.

80. Hezser, *Jewish Literacy*, 203, 430. The quotation is on 430.

sibility that these tannaitic compilations existed in writing, although he insists on the exclusively oral transmission of these materials during the tannaitic and amoraic periods.[81]

None of these scholars entirely rules out the possibility of written versions of tannaitic materials, although Neusner and Hezser are skeptical that written transmission played much of a role at all. At the very least, Hezser, Jaffee, and Elman share the recognition that the Palestinian rabbis were not entirely averse to putting legal traditions into written form.

Shlomo Naeh's recent work on the Sifra to Leviticus advances the bold thesis that the nine "*megillot*" of which the Sifra was traditionally thought to be composed were nine actual *megillot* (scrolls).[82] He reached this conclusion by reconstructing, on the basis of manuscript evidence, what the nine *megillot* likely included. Naeh's finding that the *megillot* covered disparate subjects and were roughly equivalent in size led him to conclude that the traditional references to the "*megillot*" of which the Sifra is composed were no mere figure of speech. In fact, asserts Naeh, the Sifra *was* composed of nine *megillot,* which, for ease of use, were roughly equivalent in length (and, to ensure that equivalence, each *megillah* had to include material relevant to different topics; what was important was the size of the scroll). Naeh's insight that these nine *megillot* had to be scrolls, and not, say, a codex, was due to the observation that the concern about size is only relevant if one is producing a scroll—the page-flipping of a codex is unaffected by its size.[83] Naeh further noted that his own finding that the topics covered by the *megillot* fall into three groups of three supports the Talmudic references to the Sifra as falling into three groups of three. He concluded,

> It therefore makes sense that the division hinted at in the Talmud is the very division that underlies the manuscripts—and the one who would disagree bears the burden of proof. If so, one must also accept the conclusion that flows from that: the Sifra before the amoraim was already written and reduced to scrolls.[84]

Naeh also pointed out that the Talmudic name "Sifra" (book) itself indicates the likelihood that the work existed in writing.[85]

Like Jaffee, Naeh sees an interpenetration of oral and written modes of transmission, with the oral being preferred. But "this [oral] tradition of

---

81. Elman, *Authority and Tradition,* 74, 278–281.

82. Shlomo Naeh, "The Structure and Division of *Torat Kohanim* (A): Scrolls," *Tarbiz* 66 (1996–1997): 483–515 (Heb.).

83. We will defer until later a longer discussion about the issue of scroll versus codex.

84. Naeh, "Structure and Division," 504.

85. Ibid.

study and preservation, and also the oral nature imprinted in the style and techniques of the literature of the Oral Law, do not constitute an obstacle in principle to certain compositions of this literature being presented in a written form."[86]

III.b. The Redaction of the Yerushalmi—Written or Oral?

The scholars discussed in III.a have uncovered evidence and made arguments on the basis of tannaitic literature that strongly suggest that the Yerushalmi could have been redacted in writing, or at the very least could have circulated in some written form as well as orally. None of these scholars—with the possible exception of Hezser—extends these arguments to the Yerushalmi. But if the Mishnah was (Jaffee) or could have been (Hezser) in writing, if the Tosefta was written although its constituent baraitot circulated orally (Elman), if the Sifra was written on nine scrolls (Naeh), and if the Palestinian rabbis were not averse to writing down some legal traditions and occasionally referring to them, then there seems to be no obstacle to suggesting that the Yerushalmi could have existed (at least partially) in writing.[87] But it is obviously insufficient to base an opinion as important as one about the redacted form of the Yerushalmi on a "why not?" question. Nor, for that matter, should an opinion be formed solely on the basis of a simplistic reading of the rabbis' alleged preference for exclusive orality. We will therefore begin below with a discussion of the mosaic inscription unearthed in the Rehov synagogue, which is arguably derived from the Yerushalmi. We will then go on to discuss the redacted y. Avodah Zarah in light of recent research on the intellectual impact of literacy and orality. Finally, we will consider the question of whether y. Avodah Zarah would have appeared in Babylonia through oral presentation, on scrolls, or in a codex (or codices).

(1) The Inscription in the Synagogue at Rehov

Among the remains of the ancient synagogue at Rehov, near Bet-Shean,[88] is a large mosaic inscription found in the north narthex. One surprise of

---

86. Ibid., 508.

87. Catherine Hezser strongly maintains that the Yerushalmi was in fact written, although she is skeptical that written sources preserved throughout the amoraic period were important elements in its redaction. See Hezser, *Jewish Literacy*, 435.

88. See Yaacov Sussman, "A Halakhic Inscription from the Beth-Shean Valley," *Tarbiz* 43 (1973–1974): 88–158 (Heb.); idem, "Additional Notes to 'A Halakhic Inscription from the Beth-Shean Valley,'" *Tarbiz* 44 (1974–1975): 193–195 (Heb.); idem, "The Inscription in the Synagogue at Rehov," in *Ancient Synagogues Revealed* (ed. Lee I. Levine; Jerusalem: The Israel Exploration Society/Wayne State University

the inscription is its content—which is entirely halakhah, but without any connection to halakhot that would be considered of importance in a synagogue, such as prayers, blessings, etc. Rather, the halakhah of the inscription deals with produce forbidden in the Sabbatical year, tithes, and the fixing of precise boundaries relevant to those halakhot. Another surprise of the inscription is its exceedingly close relationship to material in our extant Yerushalmi.[89]

Yaacov Sussman, and to a lesser extent Ze'ev Safrai, has studied the relationship of this halakhic inscription to the Yerushalmi. Sussman has pointed out that all of the material in the inscription has parallels in Palestinian rabbinic literature, some in tannaitic and amoraic literature, and some only in amoraic literature.[90] These parallels are found at t. Shevi 4:8–11, Sifre Deut 51, y. Dem 2:1, 22c–d, and y. Shevi 6:1, 36c.[91] There is also a not inconsiderable number of variants—substantive and not—between the text of the inscription and the Yerushalmi, but in Sussman's words

> there is no doubt that the inscription as a whole is exceedingly close to the Yerushalmi. We have seen that everything found in the inscription is found in the Yerushalmi, and the one new paragraph . . . is apparently explicitly cited as an addition. And the opposite—everything that appears in the Yerushalmi on these subjects appears in the inscription.[92]

A bit later, Sussman is even more emphatic: "The complete text . . . flows from the Yerushalmi precisely."[93]

But if the text of the inscription is Yerushalmi, we must account for the variants in spelling, order of topics, and expression. Sussman notes a pattern of changes that indicates that the composer shifted materials around in order to adapt them better to their new context as a publicly available text of practical law. The composer put the list of forbidden produce and other matters pertaining to Bet-Shean first, and dwelled on Bet-Shean at some length. Materials of less pressing local relevance appear later in the inscription.[94] Conscious of the requirements of a practical legal guide, the

---

Press, 1988), 146–153; Ze'ev Safrai, "Marginal Notes on the Rehob Inscription," *Zion* 42 (1977): 1–23 (Heb.); idem, "The Rehov Inscription," *Immanuel* 8 (Spring 1978): 48–57. See also the discussions by Catherine Hezser in *Jewish Literacy*, 410–412, and Seth Schwartz in *Imperialism*, 260–261.

89. As noted earlier, this inscription is reminiscent of y. Kil 1:1, 27a's reference to the halakhic information that "they found written on the wall of R. Hillel b. R. Valens."

90. Sussman, "A Halakhic Inscription."

91. Ibid., 103, 107.

92. Ibid., 139.

93. Ibid., 141.

94. Sussman, "A Halakhic Inscription," 104.

composer eliminated the names of sages and their legal disputations, producing instead an anonymous, smoothly-flowing text. But Sussman acknowledged other differences that could not be explained as conscious adaptations of a Talmudic text to the form of a code, such as differences in the texts of baraitot and omissions, additions, and changes to the list of produce. These probably unconscious variants between the inscription and the Yerushalmi led him to claim that the composer of the inscription was probably working with a Yerushalmi not identical to our own. But Sussman also offered the explanation that since the seventh-century inscription is later than the Yerushalmi, it might reflect the accumulated changes to the Yerushalmi resulting from another two hundred or so years of transmission.[95] Ze'ev Safrai later also suggested that the composer of the inscription used a different text of the Yerushalmi,[96] although he acknowledged that "the inscription shows that the version of the Palestinian Talmud which we have, is reliable enough, and the sum total of changes is much less than expected."[97]

Both scholars seem to be assuming the existence of an "original" Yerushalmi, which subsequently underwent conscious and unconscious changes. But there was no such thing as an "original" in Late Antique book production. As Catherine Hezser has most recently pointed out,[98] "publication" meant that an author allowed the book to be released for reading and further copying. Copying a text during an oral reading would result in various versions, as each copyist introduced his own errors and even interpretations (correct or otherwise) into the text. Oral performances ("recitations") based on earlier oral performances would certainly result in various versions, as would even copying from a written copy. The result is that we cannot assume the existence of an "original" Late Antique work. "Our" Yerushalmi is not the original any more than the Rehov inscription is. But the exceedingly close literary relationship between the Rehov inscription and our Yerushalmi gives us a justified confidence that our Yerushalmi is a good base text to which the inscription may be compared. The key is to assess the nature of the differences between versions. Substantive differences and differences in the order of materials should be examined to see if they may be accounted for by such factors as differences in the functions of the different versions. Differences in spelling, expression, etc. are more likely the result of different oral recitations of the text.

---

95. Ibid., 143.
96. Safrai, "The Rehov Inscription," 55.
97. Ibid.
98. Hezser, *Jewish Literacy*, 424.

When all is said and done, the lesson of the Rehov inscription is that in the seventh century—either shortly before or shortly after the Arab conquest—some Yerushalmi texts existed in writing. The seventh-century Rehov inscription indicates that post-Talmudic Palestinians did not object to reducing their Talmud to writing,[99] and its close literary relationship to the Yerushalmi as we now have it suggests that "our" y. Avodah Zarah is a reliable indicator of y. Avodah Zarah as it was around the time it made its way to Babylonia.

(2) Y. Avodah Zarah's Transmission to Babylonia: Did Writing Play a Role?

The evidence we have so far examined indicates that it is possible (or even likely) that the Yerushalmi (or portions of it) was reduced to writing either at the time of its redaction or at points thereafter. It must be emphasized again that "reduction to writing" must not be taken to imply that the Yerushalmi existed in a fixed, unchanging text, given the realities of oral performance and Late Antique book production. We will now probe the issue of literacy and orality more deeply, in relation to the Yerushalmi itself. Do the structure and rhetoric of y. Avodah Zarah suggest that it was more likely redacted orally or in writing? Moreover, would it have been more likely for a written or an oral y. Avodah Zarah to make its way to Babylonia? We will approach these questions by considering the Yerushalmi in light of scholarship on the cognitive, cultural, and intellectual consequences of literacy.

Beginning in the early 1960's, a number of publications in a number of disciplines heralded the appearance of what became known as the "literacy hypothesis."[100] The key early publications were Eric Havelock's *Preface to Plato,* Jack Goody and Ian Watt's "The Consequences of Literacy," and Walter J. Ong's influential *Orality and Literacy: The Technologizing of the Word.*[101] "Literacy," as defined by these scholars, meant the emergence of alphabetic writing and its various cognitive and larger cultural effects,

---

99. See Hezser, *Jewish Literacy,* 422, 435, for a strong statement that the Yerushalmi was *created* in writing.

100. Jens Brockmeier et al., eds., *Literacy, Narrative and Culture* (Richmond, UK: Curzon, 2002), 6.

101. Eric Havelock, *A Preface to Plato* (Cambridge, MA: Harvard University Press, 1963); Jack Goody and Ian P. Watt, "The Consequences of Literacy," *Comparative Studies in Society and History* 5 (1963): 304–345; Walter J. Ong, *Orality and Literacy: The Technologizing of the Word* (New York: Routledge, 1982). Subsequent relevant work by Havelock includes *The Greek Concept of Justice: From Its Shadow in Homer to Its Substance in Plato* (Cambridge, MA: Harvard University Press, 1978), *The Literate Revolution in Greece and Its Cultural Consequences* (Princeton: Princeton

and the early claims made for the cognitive effects of literacy were indeed far-reaching. To Eric Havelock, Greek philosophy—the ultimate analytic enterprise—was made possible by writing: "Nonliterate speech had favored discourse describing action; the postliterate altered the balance in favor of reflection."[102] To Walter J. Ong, writing creates a distance between the knower and the known. Writing thus "sets up conditions for 'objectivity,' in the sense of personal disengagement or distancing."[103] Ong listed and discussed nine salient characteristics of oral as opposed to literate cultures.[104] Among these is the tendency of oral cultures to be aggregative rather than analytic because "without a writing system, breaking up thought—that, is analysis—is a high-risk procedure."[105] Oral cultures are also "close to the human lifeworld" and "agonistically toned," as well as "minimally abstract."[106] We may interpret Ong to mean that literate cultures display the opposite characteristics: they do break up thought and engage in abstract, analytic work, and they are much less "agonistically toned." Ong even opined that "writing makes possible the great introspective religious traditions such as Buddhism, Judaism, Christianity, and Islam."[107]

But the literacy hypothesis and its grand claims began to come under fire even prior to the 1982 publication of Ong's *Orality and Literacy*. Sylvia Scribner and Michael Cole attacked what they described as a "theory based on simple technological determinism"[108] that made large claims about how writing promotes abstract thinking and analytic reasoning without demonstrating that people in literate societies really do process information differently from those in nonliterate societies.[109] Scribner and Cole's overall contribution to the debate over the literacy hypothesis is their insistence that the technology of writing alone is not a sufficient cata-

---

University Press, 1982), and *The Muse Learns to Write: Reflections on Orality and Literacy from Antiquity to the Present* (New Haven: Yale University Press, 1986).

102. Havelock, *Literate Revolution*, 8. But see Piotr Michalowski, "Writing and Literacy in Early States: A Mesopotamianist Perspective," in *Literacy: Interdisciplinary Conversations* (ed. Deborah Keller-Cohen; Cresskill, NJ: Hampton, 1994), 49–70, who disputes Havelock's specific claims about the intellectual impact of the emergence of alphabetic writing in ancient Greece.

103. Ong, *Orality and Literacy*, 45–46.

104. Ibid., 37–57.

105. Ibid., 39.

106. Ibid., 49, 43.

107. Ong, *Orality and Literacy*, 105.

108. Sylvia Scribner and Michael Cole, *The Psychology of Literacy* (Cambridge, MA: Harvard University Press, 1981), 240.

109. Ibid., 7.

lyst for fundamental cultural change; scholars must also pay attention to the multiplicity of causes that are involved in any social change.

Alongside the critique of the literacy hypothesis as positing an "autonomous model of literacy"[110] according to which literacy alone—independent of social circumstances—affects intellection, another critique developed: that the literacy hypothesis was ethnocentrically biased toward the cultures of the West. Brian V. Street, a key representative of this critical tendency, focused his attention closely on Ong, charging that Ong's assumptions that literacy enables the "distinction of myth from history, the growth of science, objectivity, critical thought and abstraction" are the very assumptions on which "claims regarding 'Western' superiority are founded."[111]

Ruth Finnegan, while also a critic of both the "autonomous model of literacy" and its perceived Western bias, demonstrated a more nuanced appreciation of the literacy hypothesis.[112] While pointing out that "the mere technical existence of writing cannot effect social change,"[113] she also acknowledged that "without writing, extensive and accurate communication over time and space is impossible,"[114] ultimately concluding cautiously that "it is *possible* that there is indeed some necessary connection between literacy and the ability to conceptualize abstractly and argue rationally"[115] and that literacy can be seen as an "enabling factor" in bringing about certain forms of cognitive development, but is certainly not their only cause.

Jack Goody and David R. Olson, two key scholars associated with the literacy hypothesis (Goody being one of the "founders" of the hypothesis), have reconsidered it in light of the critiques in current scholarship on the literacy hypothesis.[116] In *The Interface between the Written and the Oral*,

---

110. The phrase is Brian V. Street's. See his edited volume *Cross-Cultural Approaches to Literacy* (Cambridge, UK: Cambridge University Press, 1993), 5.

111. Brian V. Street, *Social Literacies: Critical Approaches to Literacy in Development, Ethnography, and Education* (London: Longman, 1995), 155.

112. See Ruth Finnegan, *Literacy and Orality: Studies in the Technology of Communication* (New York: Basil Blackwell, 1988).

113. Ibid., 41.

114. Ibid., 44.

115. Ibid., 151. Emphasis in the original.

116. David R. Olson insists that despite the critiques of the literacy hypothesis, literacy has very real implications that ought not to be ignored. He locates the weakness of the literacy hypothesis in its assumption that *writing* is the bearer of the cognitive effect, and now points instead to the ways of *reading* and the approaches to texts and language that come about as a result of encountering written texts. Olson's new approach to the literacy hypothesis leads to some truly fascinat-

Goody acknowledged the criticisms of the literacy hypothesis, but force-fully reasserted his claim that the introduction of literacy to a culture can (but does not inevitably!) make a cognitive difference: "Try . . . expressing ideas [orally] in the form of the syllogism. Try comparing versions of the same story and perceiving the diversity and contradictions. Try formulat-ing opposition and analogy, in which both opposition (across) and anal-ogy (down) exist in the same time-frame. . . . try all this *without* writing." (emphasis in original).[117] Goody also suggested a number of characteris-tics of written materials, notably their "need" to present complete infor-mation and make all assumptions explicit, their noticeable reliance on "a more deliberate method" of organizing ideas, and their elimination of rep-etitions, digressions, and redundancies. He also pointed out that written materials display a greater use of abstract terms than oral recitations, are elaborated more, and show greater formality and more reliance on "dead" languages.[118]

Despite the criticisms that have been leveled at the literacy hypothe-sis, Goody, Olson, and Finnegan seem to agree that writing certainly facil-itates the intellectual processes of abstraction and analysis, and that writ-ing can lead to greater concern for how materials are ordered. These reconsiderations of the literacy hypothesis suggest that the Yerushalmi was most likely redacted in writing,[119] but we should be cautious about leaping directly to that conclusion. First, we are dealing with Talmudic Palestine, in which there was an interpenetration of oral and written

---

ing insights into the transition from medieval to Renaissance culture and from thence to modernity—transitions marked by new approaches to reading the Bible and the "book of Nature." Olson's reformulation of the literacy hypothesis is sug-gestive. If indeed the b. AZ redactors were looking at some written recensions of y. AZ, their interpretive methods would have included reading, which would cer-tainly have set the redactors and their methods apart from the earlier Babylonian scholars who studied unwritten Palestinian materials. And their new methods of reading may well have, in turn, inspired a new synthetic, analytic method of study and learning, part of which we see in b. AZ. See David R. Olson, *The World on Pa-per: The Conceptual and Cognitive Implications of Writing and Reading* (Cambridge, UK: Cambridge University Press, 1994).

117. Jack Goody, *The Interface between the Written and the Oral* (Cambridge, UK: Cambridge University Press, 1987), 72.

118. Ibid., 264.

119. For applications of some of this scholarship to Bavli redaction, see Baruch M. Bokser, "Talmudic Studies," in *The State of Jewish Studies* (ed. Shaye J. D. Cohen and Edward L. Greenstein; Detroit: Wayne State University Press, 1990), 80–112; David Kraemer, *Mind of the Talmud*, 115. For a critique of this application, see Yaakov Elman, "Orality and the Redaction of the Babylonian Talmud," 58n16.

learning modalities.[120] But, as Goody has pointed out, the example of the Indian Rgvedas suggests that writing can play a role even with a literature that is otherwise orally recited and transmitted. [121] Goody also points out that writing can lead to the creation of certain literary forms that are thereafter studied and transmitted orally.[122] Thus, even a culture which typically used and even ideologically valorized orality, such as the rabbinic culture of Palestine in late antiquity, need not have exclusively relied on orality in the generation and presentation of its literature—which it did not, as we know from the Rehov inscription.

Second, it is by no means clear that societies cannot do analytic work orally. Carol Fleisher Feldman studied the Wana people of Indonesia, who employ an oral discursive practice called *kiyori*. A *kiyori* is a two-line stanza, each line of which is broken into half lines with eight syllables in each.[123] A speaker fixes the "text" of his *kiyori* through a specific oral pattern, after which the *kiyori* is "published" and open to interpretations by others. Significantly, the creator of a *kiyori* invites such interpretation by deliberately choosing ambiguous and multivalent terms and expressions. The entirely oral nature of this process of creating and interpreting *kiyori* leads Feldman to doubt that writing is an indispensable prerequisite for analysis:

> Reflection is assisted when a text is fixed in a manner that invites subsequent interpretation. What is involved in 'fixing a text' is making the locution itself salient. What is involved in inviting an interpretation is the evocation of known procedures that are part of the tool kit of the culture for unpacking, explaining, or discussing the locution.[124]

Feldman explains that the oral *kiyori* are, in effect, functionally equivalent to written texts:

> Oral *kiyori* . . . and the written forms share a similar genre-like structure: Both are marked forms, marked as different from the language of every-

---

120. Compare Elman, ibid.

121. Goody, *The Interface*, 82.

122. Ibid., 106.

123. Carol Fleisher Feldman, "Oral Metalanguage," in *Literacy and Orality* (ed. David R. Olson and Nancy Torrance; Cambridge, UK: Cambridge University Press, 1991), 52. Although I rely herein on Feldman's work, I note that scholars of rabbinics must be careful about relying on non-legal oral aspects of other cultures in reconstructing the nature of the rabbis' orality. Scholarship about folk-tales, epic poems, songs, or *kiyori* must not simply be presumed to be relevant to the largely legal world of the rabbis.

124. Ibid.

day conversation; both have distinctive linguistic (lexical and syntactic) patterns; and both are used for particular occasions.[125]

I suggest that Feldman and the strong proponents of the literacy hypothesis (Goody, Olson) are both correct. Feldman is correct that writing is not necessary to facilitate analysis when the unit of material is fairly small—like a *kiyori*. By analogy, *memrot* and sugyot could very well have circulated entirely orally during the amoraic period—and undoubtedly did. *Memrot* are short; amoraic-era sugyot, as we have seen, are also fairly short. But the proponents of the literacy hypothesis are correct that lengthy analytic undertakings are more likely tied to the use of writing. Similarly, we can say that the emergence as a text of a lengthy analytic undertaking like a Yerushalmi tractate is more likely tied to the use of writing in some capacity. As Catherine Hezser put it,

> The composition of the Yerushalmi must be considered an entirely new phenomenon of late antiquity. Only when a written discursive structure existed was it possible to view individual opinions in a larger context and from a broader perspective. . . . differences of opinion and contradictions would become obvious and elicit harmonizations.[126]

---

125. Ibid., 56.

126. Hezser, *Jewish Literacy,* 435. Feldman might be inclined to agree. She does point out that

> there are . . . differences between written and spoken texts. . . . written texts can be much longer. . . . the sequence of text and interpretations stops after two to four steps for *kiyori*—no one, perhaps interprets a *kiyori* with respect to a *kiyori* twenty steps back in its derivation. . . . greater derivational depth together with the more extended text made available by writing makes possible a variety of genres unavailable to oral culture. (Feldman, "Oral Metalanguage," 56–57)

This consideration of orality and literacy raises an interesting possibility: Could the sixth-century diffusion of rabbinic culture in Palestine that Seth Schwartz described be due to the increasing role of writing in that culture? Martin Jaffee has persuasively demonstrated the ideological function of orality in creating and preserving a Palestinian rabbinic sense of group identity. By emphasizing the importance of oral transmission, Palestinian scholars kept their learning mostly within the group of rabbinic masters and disciples. Our hypothesis is that as writing gained more of a foothold in rabbinic culture, that culture came more to the attention of non-rabbinic Jews, eventually achieving the "diffusion" that Schwartz speaks of. The seventh-century Rehov inscription is a prime example of this: rabbinic legal material appears in writing in a venue that was frequented by non-rabbis as well as rabbis. Now, it is unclear whether this diffusion of rabbinic culture led to the increase in written presentation of rabbinic material or vice versa, but it does seem that there is a connection between the two.

(3) Scroll or Codex? What Writing Surfaces?

If writing played some role in the Yerushalmi's redaction, and if it did exist (in whole or in part) in writing at times subsequent to its redaction, we must try to determine the form the written Yerushalmi most likely took. Most scholars who have considered the issue believe that Jews did not adopt the codex until around the middle of the eighth century.[127] Since y. Avodah Zarah could not have influenced the formation of b. Avodah Zarah as late as the eighth century, it must have been brought there earlier, thus increasing the likelihood that it was in scroll-form, not in a codex.[128] Papyrus or leather seems most likely as the writing surface.[129]

Would the entire Yerushalmi have been written on one scroll, or would each tractate have been written on its own scroll? Shlomo Naeh's recent work on the Sifra to Leviticus suggests that like the Sifra, the Yerushalmi's constituent tractates would probably have been reproduced on separate scrolls, with consideration given to making the scrolls easy to manage and study from. The fact that the standard papyrus roll in the relevant period[130] consisted of about twenty sheets also militates against the notion that the entire Yerushalmi would have been written on one scroll. To these two points a third must be added: the phenomenon of "transferred sugyot" in the Yerushalmi. There is a tendency in the Yerushalmi to reproduce sugyot (or even longer units of material) word-for-word in every context in which the material could be relevant, without any attempt

---

127. See Stefan C. Reif, "Aspects of Medieval Jewish Literacy," in *The Uses of Literacy in Early Medieval Europe* (ed. Rosamond McKitterick; Cambridge, UK: Cambridge University Press, 1990), 146; Malachi Beit-Arié, *Hebrew Codicology* (Jerusalem: The Israel Academy of Sciences and Humanities, 1981), 9; Colette Sirat, "Le livre hébreux dans les premiers siècles de notre ère: le témoignage des texts," in *Les Débuts du Codex* (ed. A. Blanchard; Turnhout: Brépols, 1989), 115–124. But see Meir Bar-Ilan, "Writing in Ancient Israel and Early Judaism, Part Two: Scribes and Books in the Late Second Commonwealth and Rabbinic Period," in *Mikra* (ed. Martin Jan Mulder; Assen/Maastrict: Van Gorcum and Philadelphia: Fortress, 1988), 21–38.

128. See, e.g, Marc Bregman, "An Early Fragment of *Avot de-Rabbi Natan* from a Scroll," *Tarbiz* 52 (1983): 201–222 (Heb.); Shamma Friedman, "An Ancient Scroll Fragment (B. Hullin 101a–105a) and the Rediscovery of the Babylonian Branch of Tannaitic Hebrew," *JQR* 86:1–2 (Jul–Oct 1995): 9–50. Although neither scholar is able to date the scroll fragments he studied with precision, each concludes that the fragments must date from a period prior to the Jewish adoption of the codex. These scroll-fragments are further support for the notion that a written Yerushalmi may have existed in scroll-form. See also Shlomo Naeh, "Structure and Division."

129. Hezser, *Jewish Literacy,* 130–133; Bregman, "An Early Fragment," 202.

130. See Hezser, *Jewish Literacy,* 133 and sources cited.

to link the material into its new context. The most comprehensive work on transferred sugyot is Moshe Assis's 1976 dissertation "Parallel Sugyot in the Jerusalem Talmud," in which he notes that this phenomenon is a "result of a systematic effort by sages, who in seeing the Yerushalmi's brevity, wished to expand it from within by means of 'additions,' 'completions,' and 'fillings-in' of sugyot from place to place." Assis saw the transfer of sugyot as an essentially mechanical process which shows the efforts of "these 'last editors' of the learning of the Land of Israel."[131] Recently, Moshe Benovitz has taken issue with Assis's assumption that the transfer of sugyot was a mechanical and even arbitrary process. Benovitz studied in detail a particular case of transfer from which he learned that, although the texts of the transferred sugyot were not altered very much in the transfer, the scholars who made the transfers were "more than mechanical scribes: they transfer sugyot in order to shed light on other sugyot."[132] Benovitz sees the phenomenon of transferred sugyot as a way to create meaning in the Yerushalmi.

I wish to suggest a third hypothesis about the phenomenon of transferred sugyot that sheds light on the issue of whether the Yerushalmi would have been written on one or more scrolls. By moving material from one tractate to another in which it would also illuminate relevant subject matter, the redactors rendered each tractate independent of the others. When all of the Talmudic material one would need to properly study a given tractate is present in that tractate, one need not examine all the others in order to locate such relevant material oneself. The scholars responsible for the transferred sugyot thus expected that each tractate would be studied by itself.[133] This increases the likelihood that each tractate was written on its own papyrus or leather scroll.

III.c. Conclusion

Palestinian rabbis were not averse to writing down rabbinic traditions, although as the evidence of the Yerushalmi shows, writing was not the norm. Yet the seventh-century Rehov inscription, the scroll-fragment of

---

131. Moshe Assis, "Parallel Sugyot in the Jerusalem Talmud" (Ph.D. diss., Hebrew University, 1976), 8 (Heb.).

132. Moshe Benovitz, "Transferred Sugyot in the Palestinian Talmud: The Case of Nedarim 3:2 and Shevuot 3:8," *PAAJR* 59 (1993): 53.

133. This hypothesis must be tested in light of Assis' observation that there are many sugyot that *could* have been transferred, but were not. The failure to transfer these sugyot may be due to the redactors' conclusion that these sugyot had nothing to add to the contexts to which they would have been transferred (à la Benovitz), but the matter requires further research.

Avot de-Rabbi Natan, and Shlomo Naeh's impressive evidence for the likelihood that the Sifra to Leviticus existed in writing in Talmudic times all point to the likelihood that the Palestinian amoraic (legal) magnum opus, the Yerushalmi, existed in writing in whole or in part, either at its redaction or at some later point. Most scholars who encountered it would likely have encountered it in oral performance; but the work itself likely also existed in writing to some extent.

This conclusion is buttressed by scholarship in the field of orality and literacy. Eric Havelock, Jack Goody, and Walter J. Ong believed that written composition was necessary for advanced analytic thought (a view shared by Baruch Bokser and David Kraemer with regard to the Bavli), and although their "literacy hypothesis" has been subjected to much criticism over the last forty years, Goody and Ruth Finnegan maintain that there is a plausible connection between writing and analytic thought. Carol Fleisher Feldman demurred, holding that analysis requires "fixing a text," but that fixing a text may be done orally as well as in writing. Yet Feldman makes another point crucial to the thesis of this book: "*Kiyori* cannot exist across great swaths of time and space, for memory is short and reconstructive, and texts uttered rather than written three hundred years ago or . . . far away are simply unavailable exactly as uttered to an oral culture."[134] Ruth Finnegan also observed that "without writing, extensive and accurate communication over time and space is impossible."[135] Feldman's and Finnegan's observation about the inability of oral materials to travel well across great distances in time and space deserves closer consideration. The Yerushalmi was redacted at the beginning of the fifth century; the Bavli probably during the seventh. Even if y. Avodah Zarah did not arrive in Babylonia until some point in the sixth or early seventh centuries, is it really likely that it made its journey entirely orally, with no written *aide-mémoire* at all? Moreover, as Shlomo Naeh has pointed out, oral texts and traditions thrive naturally in their place of origin, in which they are part of a living community of learners and interpreters. But to spread a complete literary compilation to a distant time and place

> requires a sort of exodus of bearers of the tradition and the building of a complicated structure of transmission from mouth to mouth. It makes sense that in a situation such as this the possibility of written transmission . . . will receive a strong uplift, at least as an aid alongside the oral transmission.[136]

---

134. Feldman, "Oral Metalanguage," 56–57.
135. Finnegan, *Literacy and Orality*, 44.
136. Naeh, "Structure and Division," 511.

Feldman's, Finnegan's, and Naeh's independent observations make a good deal of sense. The transmission of y. Avodah Zarah to Babylonia by a small group of scholars was likely aided by some sort of written *aide-mémoire*. Moreover, codicological scholarship, as well as observations about the Yerushalmi itself, enable us to reach a tentative conclusion about the shape this written y. Avodah Zarah took. It probably consisted of a scroll of leather or papyrus, since each scroll probably contained approximately one tractate, with adjustments being made to enable a scroll to be easy to manage and read.

Two additional points require emphasis. The likelihood that a written y. Avodah Zarah reached Babylonia means that the Babylonian rabbis who reworked materials from that tractate were reworking materials they may have encountered in writing, as well as orally. Thus, the differences between parallel texts in the two Talmuds may result not only from the vagaries of oral transmission, but from conscious reflection upon a written text—even if encountered normally through oral recitation. Second, the likelihood that Yerushalmi tractates were written on their own scrolls suggests that not every tractate may have had the same reception history outside the Land of Israel. Not every Yerushalmi tractate may have come to Babylonia, and not every one that came to Babylonia may have come at the same time. Therefore, if further research finds that some Bavli-Yerushalmi pairs are structurally similar and others not (as may well turn out to be the case), this may be explained by the hypothesis that Yerushalmi tractates were written on different scrolls which had different post-redaction fates in exile.

IV
Conclusion

In this chapter, we have attempted to sketch a historical context for our conclusions based on purely Talmudic analysis in chapters 2–5. Study of b. Avodah Zarah shows that no amoraic generation is aware of the structural and substantive similarities between the redactional contexts of their statements in the Bavli and Yerushalmi. Moreover, the latest amoraic activity discernible in b. Avodah Zarah is that of the later Ravina, who died ca. 500. Thus, the sixth century is the earliest time at which y. Avodah Zarah can have made the impact it did on rabbinic scholars in Babylonia.

Somehow, then, y. Avodah Zarah made its way from Palestine to Babylonia in the sixth or early seventh centuries. Our review of sources regarding Palestinian Jewry in this period reveals that, although there were still synagogues, literary production, and a not inconsiderable Jewish population, that population was experiencing decline. This was most likely due to the growing Christianization of the population and physical appearance of Palestine itself. The increasing religiously motivated imperial hostility toward the Jews is also a factor to be borne in mind, although its concrete effects cannot be easily demonstrated. Practitioners of the new literary genre of *piyyut* provide moving evidence of the misery of the Jews under Christian Rome. There is even evidence that one poet, Yehudah, may have been part of a Palestinian Jewish community living outside the country and longing for the fall of "Edom" so that it could return. All these data powerfully suggest that the exportation of y. Avodah Zarah to Babylonia in the sixth or early seventh centuries—which we earlier established through internal analysis—was accomplished by (a likely small group of) Palestinian scholars who left Palestine at this time,[137] carrying y. Avodah Zarah with them on a leather or papyrus scroll.

---

137. See p. 212n60 for sources pertaining to the Babylonian Mar Zutra's emigration to Palestine in the sixth century.

Appendix

The Alleged Geonic *Teshuvah* in the *Sefer ha-Eshkol*

In his edition of the medieval halakhic work *Sefer ha-Eshkol* of R. Abraham of Narbonne (1110–1179) based on the Carmoly manuscript, Zvi Benjamin Auerbach included a responsum attributed to R. Hai Gaon.[1] The questioner asked about the relative halakhic authority of the two Talmuds in situations in which they differ because either the Bavli is opaque as to a term or topic about which the Yerushalmi is clear or the Yerushalmi's text is simply more comprehensible than its Bavli parallel. R. Hai answers with a statement of the position attributed to him elsewhere, according to which, in the event of a conflict between the Talmuds, the Bavli is to be preferred to the Yerushalmi, while if the latter provides information or clarification missing from—but not in conflict with—the Bavli, then it may be consulted since the Yerushalmi "is not inferior to the commentaries of the former [scholars]."[2]

In the Carmoly manuscript relied on by Auerbach, there follows a lengthy text that is missing from the Paris manuscript used by Shalom Albeck in his own critical edition of the *Sefer ha-Eshkol*. This text reads as follows:

> And [the fact that] R. Zera fasted in order that he forget the Talmud
> of the Babylonians and [the fact that] R. Yirmiyah said, "'He has made me

---

1. R. Abraham of Narbonne, *Sefer ha-Eshkol* (ed. Zvi Benjamin Auerbach; New York: Makhon Kornitzer, 1962).

2. Responsum of R. Hai Gaon, in *Teshuvot ha-Geonim* (ed. Simha Assaf; Jerusalem: Darom, 1929), no. 21.

live in the darkness'—this is the Babylonian Gemara" [b. Sanh 24a]. He said: "Foolish Babylonians, who live in a land of darkness—you recite traditions that make [understanding] dark." [The explanation for why the Bavli is supreme despite these anti-Babylonian statements is that] in their time, the reasoning of the Mishnah was not as clear to them [as it was to] the sages of the Land of Israel, for the greatest of the Sages and the Sanhedrin were still in the Land of Israel, and there were many [persecutory] decrees in Babylonia . . . and furthermore, the Land of Israel is certainly sanctified above all other lands . . .

In the days of R. Ashi and Ravina there was peace in Babylonia and persecution became harsh in the Land of Israel, and instruction (הוראה) was greatly diminished there, and from among those [scholars] who were there [in Palestine] Rabin and R. Dimi descended [to Babylonia]. Most of the *nahote* who descended were sages of the Land of Israel. And they [the Bavli] said, "From the days of Rabbi until R. Ashi we have not found Torah and greatness in one place"—and the Torah grew ever stronger in his [R. Ashi's] days.

Certainly the atmosphere of the Land of Israel makes one wise—and they said (b. Ket 75a), "Indeed, of Zion it will be said, 'This one and this one were born in her' (Ps 87:5)—one of them [the Palestinian sages] is worth more than two of us." And these [the Palestinians?] also were there ["there" now meaning Babylonia?], and our Talmud [the Bavli] came forth from them; therefore it is to be preferred over the Talmud of the Land of Israel. And furthermore, there was before them [the Bavli's editors] the Talmud of the Land of Israel, and they knew the rationales of the predecessors, and where they did not agree with them [those rationales], they moved away from the reasons of those who were before them. The general principle is that the "law follows the latest [scholars]."

The text of the passage is confusing (and its chronology embarrassingly incorrect for a Gaon), but it makes the basic point that the Bavli is supreme not only because its editors had the Yerushalmi before them, but because the great scholars of the Land of Israel participated directly in its creation. These Palestinian scholars left Palestine for Babylonia due to increasingly severe persecution, and came to Babylonia during the time of R. Ashi. The serendipitous combination of peaceful conditions in Babylonia and the leadership of R. Ashi ensured the creation of the Bavli, in which these Palestinian scholars had a pivotal role. Since Palestinian scholars participated in the creation of the Bavli—so the argument implicitly goes—the Yerushalmi is obsolete, since by working on the Bavli, the Palestinians implicitly recognize the latter as the grand rabbinic synthesis, to which the principle of "הילכתא כבתראי" applies. The passage claims (through the clever use of Ps 87:5, drawn from b. Ket 75a) that the Bavli is the ultimate Palestinian product, while simultaneously using that claim to completely undermine the authority of the Yerushalmi. At first glance, this passage appears to be a startling geonic confirmation of this book's thesis, and thus we must carefully consider its reliability as an historical source.

First, the presence of this somewhat confusing passage in only one manuscript of the *Sefer ha-Eshkol* raises the issue of whether or not this is an authentic part of the responsum attributed to R. Hai. Is the Paris manuscript relied on by Albeck defective, or was there an interpolation into the Carmoly manuscript? Moreover, if this passage is an interpolation, was it written by R. Abraham of Narbonne, or had it been inserted into an otherwise authentic responsum of R. Hai prior to R. Abraham's composition of his own book? These questions bear directly on the ultimate question—whether, and to what extent, this passage may be relied upon as an historical source.[3]

In considering whether or not this passage is attributable to R. Hai, we must carefully analyze the polemic lying beneath the surface of the passage. The passage seems to be based on the view that a purely Babylonian Bavli, one with no connection to the Yerushalmi at all, cannot be said to supersede the latter on the grounds of הילכתא כבתראי. Such a view is most likely a Palestinian rabbinic view from the post-Talmudic period, probably one held prior to the tenth century, at which time the Bavli surpassed the Yerushalmi as a subject of study even within Palestine itself.[4] The author, despite his obvious pro-Bavli stance, does not take issue with this view. Rather, he accepts it by arguing that the Bavli is, in fact, not a purely Babylonian product at all. The author could have made the point of Bavli supremacy simply by arguing that the Bavli editors had the Yerushalmi before them as they did their work (as he does claim and as the Rif claimed at the end of his codification of b. Eruvin). Yet the author of the passage goes even further than he needs to by arguing (albeit on the basis of a faulty chronology) that *Palestinian scholars participated in the creation of the Bavli*. Why would a Bavli supremacist go so far as to stress Palestinian participation in the editing of the Bavli and to cite Ps 87:5, which implies that the Bavli is a product of Zion? One possibility is that he is taking on yet another Palestinian position and turning it to his own advantage. Just as he implicitly accepted a possibly Palestinian view that a purely Babylonian Talmud could not supersede their own on the basis of הילכתא כבתראי, so is he accepting—while turning on its head—a possibly Palestinian view about the origins of the Bavli.

---

3. See Chaim Tchernowitz (Rav Tzair), *History of the Jewish Codes* (3 vols.; New York: The Jubilee Committee, 1946), 1:32–34 (Heb.) for discussion of his own views as well as those of Louis Ginzberg and Isaac Halevy.

4. See Mordecai Margaliot, *Hilkhot Erets Yisra'el min ha-Genizah*, 14.

If this analysis is correct, then R. Hai Gaon was most likely not the author of this text. Moreover, if this passage *is* the work of R. Hai, then why does he not mention either the Bavli's use of the Yerushalmi or the participation of Palestinian scholars in its creation, in his unquestionably authentic responsum found at *Teshuvot Ha-Geonim* no. 21 (ed. S. Assaf)?[5] And of course the glaring chronological error in the passage was unlikely to have been made by R. Hai. As Louis Ginzberg uncharitably observed, "Even beginning students know that Rabin and R. Dimi had already been dead for many years when Rav Ashi and Ravina were born!"[6]

This passage, then, is most likely an interpolation of unknown authorship inserted into what appears to be a version of R. Hai's responsum as published by Assaf. Nevertheless, it is not entirely without historical significance. That significance lies in the implicit polemic, the point of view acknowledged by the author through his use of it for his own ends. As noted, the author accepts and utilizes the notion that only a Bavli that has some Palestinian contribution to it may be said to supersede the Yerushalmi, and argues more than he needs to by asserting that Palestinian scholars who emigrated to Babylonia participated in the creation of the Bavli. These two points—implicitly asserted in order to be twisted about—may well have been points of view held at some point by Jews who viewed the Yerushalmi as authoritative. Thus, the notion that Palestinian emigrants to Babylonia contributed their learning to the formation of the Bavli was indeed a notion held by some Jews after the redaction of the Bavli, although, unfortunately, more than this cannot be said.

---

5. See also Louis Ginzberg, *A Commentary on the Palestinian Talmud*, 1:85, for a similar observation about the relationship between the responsum published by Assaf and this passage in the *Sefer ha-Eshkol.* Ginzberg also observed that parts of this passage seem to be copied word-for-word from the *Iggeret Rav Sherira Gaon*, and that R. Hai is not known to have done so in any of his authentic writings.

6. Ibid., 1:84.

7

Conclusion

Y. Avodah Zarah Influenced the Formation of B. Avodah Zarah

I recently participated in a conference where I presented a paper related to the thesis of this book, although unrelated to y. and b. Avodah Zarah specifically. In the discussion period, a colleague to whose views I always pay careful attention asked me to spell out the larger significance of demonstrating literary dependency between the Talmuds. I think that my colleague's question is a suitable one to consider as this book draws to a close.

My response must begin with a reiterated caveat. This book has demonstrated only that y. Avodah Zarah influenced the formation of b. Avodah Zarah, not that the Yerushalmi as a whole influenced the formation of the Bavli as a whole. Thus it would be imprudent to do more than point to what this book *suggests* in the way of larger significance. That said, this book has much to suggest. First, our finding that y. Avodah Zarah influenced b. Avodah Zarah, especially if this finding is followed up by similar findings from other studies of tractate pairs, suggests that our understanding of the formation of the Bavli may have to change. Without a doubt, the Babylonian Talmud is a remarkable intellectual and cultural achievement, but we may have to stop viewing it as virtually an entirely Babylonian creation. As Martin Jaffee pointed out some years ago, "it is not self-evident . . . that independence of judgment and vision, such as that exercised by the Bavli in its exegesis of the Mishnah, is incompatible with immersion in traditional processes of learning . . . The Bavli can indeed be 'original' while at the same time being largely dependent . . . on an earlier work for its power of originality."[1] In a related vein, our understanding of the relationship between the two rabbinic centers in the fifth through the seventh centuries may require revision, as we see that large blocks of edited materials drawn from the amoraic learning of the Land of Israel exerted a profound influence on that of Babylonia as late as the sixth or seventh century.

Apropos of this last point, a methodological point is in order. A key finding of this book is that macro analysis—the comparison of each Talmud's *entire* treatment of *each* mishnah in the tractate under study—is indispensable to forming an accurate picture of the relationship between the tractates. We must begin *big*, noting the large-scale inter-Talmudic similarities and progressively checking off alternative explanations for them. Only then should we proceed to the step of micro analysis and analyze precisely how the Bavli has reworked specific textual parallels. By analogy, a scientist wishing to explain the apparent hand-in-glove shapes of South America and Africa would be well-advised to begin by studying the forms of the continents rather than by commencing with soil samples in Brazil and Liberia. The time for such soil studies will come; but without the macro analysis of the structures and contours of the continents, there may be no larger context in which to locate and assess the true significance of the findings of micro analysis.

This book also helps us to better understand the intellectual profile of the Bavli redactors. Our work in chapter 2 demonstrates that the redactors appropriated a great deal of material from y. Avodah Zarah, and that these appropriations exhibit five tendencies:

1. B. Avodah Zarah appropriated y. Avodah Zarah sugyot or sequences of two or more y. Avodah Zarah sugyot in the same order as y. Avodah Zarah and attached to the same mishnah;

2. B. Avodah Zarah built up a complex sugya using materials marked as relevant to the issue by y. Avodah Zarah;

3. B. Avodah Zarah sugyot tend to resemble their y. Avodah Zarah parallels more closely than parallels in other rabbinic compilations;

4. B. Avodah Zarah placed materials at points in the tractate similar to where y. Avodah Zarah placed them; and

---

1. Martin Jaffee, "The Babylonian Appropriation of the Talmud Yerushalmi," 3n3.

5. B. Avodah Zarah sometimes used the same mishnah as y. Avodah Zarah as the opportunity to present similar genres of material.

The common feature of these five tendencies is that b. Avodah Zarah is demonstrably closer to y. Avodah Zarah than to other rabbinic compilations. This suggests both that the b. Avodah Zarah redactors had the tractate in some form and that they felt it appropriate to build their own work upon it.

The redactors remained *close,* but did not subordinate their own tractate entirely to y. Avodah Zarah. In chapters 3 and 4 we learned more about them: they revised and reworked their prior sources in characteristic ways. They tended to add Babylonian linguistic, cultural, and/or halakhic features to y. Avodah Zarah sugyot, they tended to leave out of b. Avodah Zarah materials found in y. Avodah Zarah that were of particular relevance to the Land of Israel, they re-arranged prior materials in a more sensible order, and they reworked their sugyot to exhibit a higher level of legal conceptualization than we see in y. Avodah Zarah. The redactors' creative appropriation of y. Avodah Zarah shows that they viewed themselves as authorized to interject their own contributions into the received heritage, even to the extent of rewriting vigorously. Similarly, we saw in chapter 4 that these creative redactors sometimes answered questions left unresolved in y. Avodah Zarah, or took up their own deliberations at the point where y. Avodah Zarah left off. The redactors were thus creative and pro-active; they did not simply leave us with a thin layer of redactional "icing" on the "cake" baked by the amoraim. To continue this metaphor, the redactors of the Bavli "baked the cake" using a modified version of y. Avodah Zarah's "recipe"—they revised it in light of their own cultural and other concerns.

In chapter 5, we explored the anonymous material in b. Avodah Zarah to see if this material, generally understood to be a product of the redactors, sheds any light on b. Avodah Zarah's appropriation of y. Avodah Zarah. We found that the anonymous material is classifiable into different categories, of which only one—"Babylonian anonymous Bavli"—can reasonably be seen as a product of the redactors and a source of information about the appropriation of y. Avodah Zarah.

This book also suggests that we must think harder about the mechanics of transmission between the rabbinic centers, and that we must question the often-unstated assumption that such transmission "just happened." In chapter 6, we focused on *how* y. Avodah Zarah would have gotten to Babylonia, and *in what form.* We concluded that it is plausible to assume that a small exodus of scholars from Palestine to Babylonia in the sixth or seventh century is responsible for the arrival there of y. Avodah

Zarah. First, there was a history of such scholarly travel between the rabbinic centers, and this history is consistent with what we know about the frequency of travel of Roman elites. The intellectual and religious cross-fertilization that followed in the wake of rabbinic travel is similar to what other scholars have observed in connection with the journeys of Christian clergy and pagan philosophers between Byzantium and Sassanian Persia.

Second, Jewish life in Palestine was rendered increasingly difficult in the sixth and early seventh centuries, which increased the likelihood of emigration. Noting the writing-down of Yerushalmi material in the Rehov inscription and the growing body of scholarship (by rabbinics scholars and others) on orality and literacy studies, we hypothesized that although orality was undoubtedly a primary method of study and transmission, y. Avodah Zarah may have come to Babylonia on a scroll of leather or parchment.

For over 1,000 years, the Babylonian Talmud has been the focus of intense and devoted scrutiny as well as the fountainhead of the classical halakhah. The Yerushalmi, although never entirely neglected, was relegated by the jurisprudence of geonim and rishonim to a secondary and subordinate status. This book has demonstrated that, with regard to b. and y. Avodah Zarah, we can discern the fingerprints of y. Avodah Zarah—not simply Palestinian learning generally—in the formation of b. Avodah Zarah. Whoever the scholars were that brought y. Avodah Zarah to Babylonia, their contribution to the making of the Bavli, and, by extension, to the formation of Judaism in the Middle Ages, is at once shrouded in mystery and of inestimable value.

Appendix

Complete List of Sugyot Drawn from Y. Avodah Zarah by B. Avodah Zarah

What follows is a complete listing of the sugyot that b. Avodah Zarah drew from y. Avodah Zarah, organized according to the type of appropriation that each sugya represents. This listing constitutes the complete results of my macro analysis of the Avodah Zarah tractates, and is the basis of the detailed textual work presented in the book. Sugyot that fit within more than one category are listed within each applicable category.

I. B. Avodah Zarah Appropriates Y. Avodah Zarah Sugyot (or Sequences of Two or More Y. Avodah Zarah Sugyot in the Same Order as Y. Avodah Zarah) Attached to the Same Mishnah

b. AZ 6b ‖ y. AZ 1:1, 39b
b. AZ 8a–b, 11b ‖ y. AZ 1:2, 39c
b. AZ 11b–12a, 12b–13a, 13b ‖ y. AZ 1:4, 39c–d
b. AZ 15a ‖ y. AZ 1:6, 39d–40a
b. AZ 20b ‖ y. AZ 1:8, 40a
b. AZ 22b–23a ‖ y. AZ 2:1, 40c
b. AZ 24a–b ‖ y. AZ 2:1, 40c
b. AZ 25b ‖ y. AZ 2:1, 40c
b. AZ 27b, 28a, 28b ‖ y. AZ 2:2, 40d–41a
b. AZ 30a, 30b–31a, 32a, 32b, 33a–b ‖ y. AZ 2:3, 41a–b
b. AZ 35b–36b, 37a, 37b–38a, 38b ‖ y. AZ 2:9, 41d
b. AZ 40a ‖ y. AZ 2:10, 42a
b. AZ 41a–b ‖ y. AZ 3:2, 42c
b. AZ 43b–44a ‖ y. AZ 3:3, 42d
b. AZ 44b ‖ y. AZ 3:4, 42d

b. AZ 48b ‖ y. AZ 3:13, 43b
b. AZ 50a, 50b, 51a ‖ y. AZ 4:1, 43c–d
b. AZ 51b ‖ y. AZ 4:2, 43d
b. AZ 51b, 51b–52a, 52b ‖ y. AZ 4:3, 43d–44a
b. AZ 53a ‖ y. AZ 4:5, 44a
b. AZ 57a, 57b, 58b–59a ‖ y. AZ 4:8, 44a–b; 4:10, 44b
b. AZ 60b ‖ y. AZ 4:11, 44b; 4:12, 44b
b. AZ 61a, 61b ‖ y. AZ 4:13, 44b
b. AZ 62a–b, 63b, 64a ‖ y. AZ 5:1, 44c–d
b. AZ 67a, 67b, 68a ‖ y. AZ 5:3, 44d
b. AZ 70a–b ‖ y. AZ 5:5, 44d
b. AZ 70b ‖ y. AZ 5:6, 44d
b. AZ 72b ‖ y. AZ 5:10, 45a
b. AZ 73a–b ‖ y. AZ 5:11, 45a
b. AZ 74a ‖ y. AZ 5:12, 45b
b. AZ 75a ‖ y. AZ 5:14, 45b

II. B. Avodah Zarah Builds a Complex Sugya Using Some Materials Marked as Relevant by the Y. Avodah Zarah Redactors

b. AZ 41b–42b ‖ y. AZ 3:2, 41d; 4:1, 43d; 3:13, 43b–c

III. Material in B. Avodah Zarah for Which There Is a Parallel in Y. Avodah Zarah and in Another Rabbinic Compilation or Tractate, and B. Avodah Zarah More Closely Resembles Y. Avodah Zarah

b. AZ 27b ‖ t. Hul 2:22–23 ‖ y. AZ 2:2, 40d–41a
b. AZ 62a–b ‖ y. Shevi 8:6, 38b ‖ y. AZ 5:1, 44c
b. AZ 15a, 16a–b ‖ y. AZ 1:6, 39d–40a; 1:7, 40a ‖ y. Pes 4:3, 30d–31a

IV. B. Avodah Zarah and Y. Avodah Zarah Place Similar Materials at Comparable Places in the Tractate, Although Not Attached to the Same Mishnah

b. AZ 16a–b ‖ y. AZ 1:6, 40a; 1:7, 40a
b. AZ 19b–20a ‖ y. AZ 1:9, 40a–b

V. B. Avodah Zarah Uses the Same Mishnah as Y. Avodah Zarah as the Opportunity for the Placement of Aggadah

b. AZ 2a–5b ‖ y. AZ 1:1, 39a–b

b. AZ 8a ‖ y. AZ 1:2, 39c
b. AZ 24a–b ‖ y. AZ 2:1, 40c

VI. B. Avodah Zarah Uses the Same Mishnah as Y. Avodah Zarah as the Opportunity to Explore the Same Topic(s) or Present the Same Genres of Material Not Called for by the Mishnah or Other Tannaitic Sources (Even Though the Sugyot Might Be Different)

b. AZ 46a–47a ‖ y. AZ 3:6, 42d–43a
b. AZ 48b ‖ y. AZ 3:13, 43b
b. AZ 51b ‖ y. AZ 4:2, 43d
b. AZ 58b–59a ‖ y. AZ 4:10, 44b
b. AZ 70a–b ‖ y. AZ 5:5, 44d

Selected Bibliography

Editions

Shishah Sidre Mishnah: With New Commentary, Introductions, Additions, and Completions. Edited by Chanoch Albeck. Tel-Aviv: Dvir, 1978.

Tractate Avodah Zarah of the Babylonian Talmud: MS Jewish Theological Seminary of America. Edited by Shraga Abramson. New York: Jewish Theological Seminary, 1957.

Avot de-Rabbi Natan. Edited by S. Z. Schechter. Repr., New York: Jewish Theological Seminary, 1997.

Babylonian Talmud, Vilna ed. with commentaries. Repr., Jerusalem, 1975.

Bar-Ilan Responsa Project. Bar-Ilan University Version 9.0. 1972–2001.

Midrash Bereschit Rabba. Edited by Judah Theodor and Chanoch Albeck. Berlin and Jerusalem: Akademie für die Wissenschaft des Judentums, 1903–1936. Repr., Jerusalem: Shalem, 1996.

Rabbinovicz, Rafael. *Diqduqei Soferim.* 12 vols. Repr., New York, 1976.

Rosenthal, David. "*Mishna Aboda Zara*: A Critical Edition (with Introduction)." Ph.D. diss., Hebrew University, 1971 (Hebrew).

Seder Olam Zuta. Edited by Manasseh Grossberg. London: n.p., 1910.

Sefer ha-Eshkol. Edited by Zvi Binyamin Auerbach. New York: Makhon Kornitzer, 1962.

Talmud Yerushalmi, Kratoschin ed. with brief commentary. Repr., Jerusalem: Shiloh, 1969.

Talmud Yerushalmi, MS Leiden, Cod. Scal. 3. Jerusalem: Kedem, 1971.

Talmud Yerushalmi, Zhitomir ed. with commentaries. Repr., Israel, n.d.

Teshuvot ha-Geonim. Edited by Simha Assaf. Jerusalem: Darom, 1929.

The Tosefta: According to Codex Vienna, with Variants from Codex Erfurt, Genizah Mss. and Editio Princeps (Venice 1521), Together with References to Parallel Passages in Talmudic Literature and a Brief Commentary. Edited by Saul Lieberman. *The Orders of Zera'im, Mo'ed.* New York: Jewish Theological Seminary, 1955, 1962.

Tosephta: Based on the Erfurt and Vienna Codices, with Parallels and Variants.
Edited by M. S. Zuckermandel. Jerusalem: Wahrmann, 1975.

Secondary Literature, Dictionaries, Modern Commentaries

Akenson, Donald Harmon. *Saint Saul: A Skeleton Key To The Historical Jesus.* New York: Oxford University Press, 2000.

Albeck, Chanoch. *Introduction to the Talmud, Babli and Yerushalmi.* Tel-Aviv: Dvir, 1969 (Hebrew).

Alon, Gedaliah. *The Jews In Their Land In The Talmudic Age (70–640 C.E.).* Cambridge, MA: Harvard University Press, 1989.

Aminoah, Noah. "Qit'ei talmud mi-siddur qadum be-massekhet Rosh Hashanah." Pages 185–197 in *Studies in Rabbinic Literature, Bible and Jewish History.* Edited by Yitshaq D. Gilat. Ramat-Gan: Bar-Ilan University Press, 1982.

———. *The Redaction of the Tractate Betza, Rosh-Hashana, and Ta'anit in the Babilonian Talmud.* (*sic*) Tel-Aviv: Tel-Aviv University, 1986 (Hebrew).

———. *The Redaction of the Tractate Qiddushin in the Babilonian Talmud.* (*sic*) Tel-Aviv: Tel-Aviv University, 1977 (Hebrew).

———. *The Redaction of the Tractate Sukkah and Moed-Katan in the Babilonian Talmud.* (*sic*) Tel-Aviv: Tel-Aviv University, 1989 (Hebrew).

Assaf, Simha. "Qinah qedumah 'al hurban ha-qehillot be-Erets Yisra'el." Pages 9–16 in *Texts and Studies in Jewish History.* Edited by Simha Assaf. Jerusalem: Mossad ha-Rav Kook, 1946.

———. *Tequfat ha-Geonim ve-sifrutah.* Jerusalem: Mossad ha-Rav Kook, 1967.

Assis, Moshe. "Parallel Sugyot in the Jerusalem Talmud." Ph.D. diss., Hebrew University, 1976 (Hebrew).

Avni, Gideon. "Christian Secondary Use of Jewish Burial Caves in Jerusalem in the Light of New Excavations at the Aceldama Tombs." Pages 265–276 in *Early Christianity in Context: Monuments and Documents.* Edited by F. Manns and E. Alliata. Jerusalem: Studium Biblicum Franciscanum, 1993.

Bar-Ilan, Meir. "Writing in Ancient Israel and Early Judaism, Part Two: Scribes and Books in the Late Second Commonwealth and Rabbinic Period." Pages 21–38 in *Mikra.* Edited by Martin Jan Mulder. Assen/ Maastrict: Van Gorcum and Philadelphia: Fortress, 1988.

Becker, Hans-Jürgen. *Die grössen rabbinischen Sammelwerke Palästinas.* Tübingen: Mohr Siebeck, 1999.

Beit-Arié, Malachi. *Hebrew Codicology.* Jerusalem: The Israel Academy of Sciences and Humanities, 1981.

Benovitz, Moshe. "Transferred Sugyot in the Palestinian Talmud: The Case of Nedarim 3:2 and Shevuot 3:8." *Proceedings of the American Academy for Jewish Research* 59 (1993): 11–57.

Bokser, Baruch M. "A Minor for *Zimmun* (y. Ber 7:2, 11c) and Recensions of Yerushalmi." *Association for Jewish Studies Review* 4 (1979): 1–25.

———. "Talmudic Studies." Pages 80–112 in *The State of Jewish Studies*. Edited by Shaye J. D. Cohen and Edward L. Greenstein. Detroit: Wayne State University Press, 1990.

———. *Yerushalmi Pesachim*. Edited by Lawrence Schiffman. Vol. 13 of *The Talmud of the Land of Israel: A Preliminary Translation and Explanation*. Edited by Jacob Neusner. Chicago: University of Chicago Press, 1994.

Boyarin, Daniel. *Dying for God: Martyrdom and the Making of Christianity and Judaism*. Stanford: Stanford University Press, 1999.

Bregman, Marc. "An Early Fragment of *Avot de-Rabbi Natan* From A Scroll." *Tarbiz* 52 (1983): 201–222 (Hebrew).

Brockmeier, Jens, Min Wang, and David R. Olson, eds. *Literacy, Narrative and Culture*. Richmond, UK: Curzon Press, 2002.

Chajes, Zvi H. *Imrei Binah*. Pages 495–497 in vol. 2 of *Kol Sifrei Mohara"ts Chajot*. Jerusalem: Divrei Hakhamim, 1959. Repr. from *Responsa of Mohara"ts* (1849–1850) (Hebrew).

Cohen, Avinoam. *Ravina and Contemporary Sages: Studies in the Chronology of Late Babylonian Amoraim*. Ramat-Gan: Bar-Ilan University Press, 2001 (Hebrew).

Cohen, Gerson. "Esau as Symbol in Early Medieval Thought." Pages 19–48 in *Jewish Medieval and Renaissance Studies*. Edited by Alexander Altmann. Cambridge, MA: Harvard University Press, 1967.

Dan, Yaron. "Erets Yisra'el ba-me'ot ha-hamishit ve-ha-shishit." Pages 265–299 in vol. 2 of *The Land of Israel From the Destruction of the Second Temple Until the Muslim Conquest*. Edited by Zvi Baras, Shmuel Safrai, Yoram Tsafrir, and Menahem Stern. Jerusalem: Yad Ben Zvi, 1982 (Hebrew).

Dor, Zwi Moshe. *The Teachings of Eretz Israel in Babylon*. Tel-Aviv: Dvir, 1971 (Hebrew).

Elman, Yaakov. "Orality and the Transmission of Tosefta Pisha in Talmudic Literature." Pages 123–180 in *Introducing Tosefta: Textual, Intratextual, and Intertextual Studies*. Edited by Harry Fox and Tirzah Meacham. Hoboken, NJ: Ktav, 1999.

———. "Orality and the Redaction of the Babylonian Talmud." *Oral Tradition* 14(1) (1999): 52–99.

———. *Authority and Tradition: Toseftan Baraitot in Talmudic Babylonia*. New York: Ktav, 1994.

———. "Argument for the Sake of Heaven: *The Mind of the Talmud*." *Jewish Quarterly Review* 84:2–3 (1993–1994): 261–282.

————. "Righteousness as its Own Reward: An Inquiry Into the Theologies of the Stam." *Proceedings of the American Academy for Jewish Research* 57 (1990–1991): 35–67.

Epstein, J. N. *Introduction to Amoraitic Literature: Babylonian Talmud and Yerushalmi*. Tel-Aviv: Dvir, 1962 (Hebrew).

Feldman, Carol Fleisher. "Oral Metalanguage." Pages 47–65 in *Literacy and Orality*. Edited by David R. Olson and Nancy Torrance. Cambridge, UK: Cambridge University Press, 1991.

Finnegan, Ruth. *Literacy and Orality: Studies in the Technology of Communication*. New York: Basil Blackwell, 1988.

Florsheim, Joel. "Sugyot Bavliot ba-Yerushalmi Neziqin." *Sinai* 120:2 (1997): 53–85; 120:3 (1998): 161–181.

Fraenkel, Zechariah. *Mavo ha-Yerushalmi*. Breslau: n.p., 1870. Repr., Jerusalem: n.p., 1967.

Friedman, Mordecai Akiva. "Ono—yedi'ot hadashot mi-kitvei ha-Genizah ha-Qahirit." Pages 73–85 in *Between Yarkon and Ayalon: Studies on the Tel Aviv Metropolitan Area and the Lod Valley*. Edited by David Grossman. Ramat-Gan: Bar-Ilan University Press, 1983 (Hebrew).

Friedman, Shamma. "An Ancient Scroll Fragment (B. Hullin 101a–105a) and the Rediscovery of the Babylonian Branch of Tannaitic Hebrew." *Jewish Quarterly Review* 86:1–2 (Jul–Oct 1995): 9–50.

————. "Ha-baraitot she-be-Talmud ha-Bavli ve-yahasan le-Tosefta." Pages 103–201 in *Atara L'Haim: Studies in the Talmud and Medieval Rabbinic Literature in Honor of Professor Haim Zalman Dimitrovsky*. Edited by Daniel Boyarin, Marc Hirshman, Shamma Friedman, Menahem Schmelzer, and Israel M. Tashma. Jerusalem: Magnes Press, 2000 (Hebrew).

————. "A Critical Study of *Yevamot X* With A Methodological Introduction." Pages 275–441 in *Texts and Studies: Analecta Judaica*. Edited by H. Z. Dimitrovsky. New York: Jewish Theological Seminary, 1978 (Hebrew).

————. "La-aggadah ha-historit ba-Talmud ha-Bavli." Pages 119–164 in *Saul Lieberman Memorial Volume*. Edited by Shamma Friedman. New York: Jewish Theological Seminary, 1993 (Hebrew).

————. *Talmud Arukh: BT Bava Mezi'a VI*. 2 vols. New York: Jewish Theological Seminary, 1993, 1997.

————. "Uncovering Literary Dependencies in the Talmudic Corpus." Pages 35–57 in *The Synoptic Problem in Rabbinic Literature*. Edited by Shaye J. D. Cohen. Brown Judaic Studies 326. Providence, RI: Brown Judaic Studies, 2000.

Gafni, Isaiah. *The Jews of Babylonia in the Talmudic Era: A Social and Cultural History*. Jerusalem: Merkaz Zalman Shazar, 1990 (Hebrew).

Ginzberg, Louis. *A Commentary on the Palestinian Talmud.* 4 vols. New York: Jewish Theological Seminary, 1941 (Hebrew).

Goodacre, Mark. *The Case Against Q.* Harrisburg, PA: Trinity Press International, 2002.

Goodblatt, David. *Rabbinic Instruction in Sassanian Babylonia.* Leiden: E. J. Brill, 1975.

Goodman, Martin. "Kosher Olive Oil in Antiquity." Pages 227–245 in *A Tribute to Geza Vermes: Essays on Jewish and Christian Literature and History.* Edited by Philip R. Davies and Richard T. White. Sheffield, UK: JSOT Press, 1990.

Goody, Jack. *The Interface Between the Written and the Oral.* Cambridge, UK: Cambridge University Press, 1987.

Goody, Jack, and Ian P. Watt, "The Consequences of Literacy." *Comparative Studies in Society and History* 5 (1963): 304–345.

Goshen-Gottstein, Alon. *The Sinner and the Amnesiac: The Rabbinic Invention of Elisha ben Abuya and Eleazar ben Arach.* Stanford: Stanford University Press, 2000.

Gray, Alyssa. "A Bavli Sugya and Its Two Yerushalmi Parallels: Issues of Literary Relationship and Redaction." To be included in *New Methods in Reading Rabbinic Literature: Hermeneutical Limits and Possibilities* (ed. Matthew A. Kraus; Piscataway, NJ: Gorgias, forthcoming).

———. "A Contribution to the Study of Martyrdom and Identity in the Palestinian Talmud." *Journal of Jewish Studies* 54:2 (Nov 2003): 242–272.

———. "The Power Conferred by Distance from Power: Redaction and Meaning in bAZ 10a-11a." To be included in *Creation and Composition: The Contribution of the Bavli Redactors (Stammaim) to the Aggadah* (ed. Jeffrey L. Rubenstein; Tübingen: Mohr Siebeck, forthcoming [2005]).

———. "A Talmud in Exile: The Influence of PT Avodah Zarah on the Formation of BT Avodah Zarah." Ph.D. diss., Jewish Theological Seminary, 2001.

Greenwald, Leopold. *Ha-ra'u mesadrei ha-Bavli et ha-Yerushalmi?* New York: ha-Makhon le-Mehqar u-le-Mada ha-Yerushalmi, 1954.

Halevy, Isaac. *Dorot ha-Rishonim.* 6 vols. Berlin: n.p., 1897–1939. Repr. 6 vols. in 8, Israel: Mif'alei Sefarim le-Yitso, n.d.

Halivni, David. *Sources and Traditions*: Baba Mezia. Jerusalem: Magnes Press, 2003 (Hebrew).

———. *Sources and Traditions*: Baba Kama. Jerusalem: Magnes Press, 1993 (Hebrew).

———. *Sources and Traditions*: Erubin-Pesahim. New York: Jewish Theological Seminary, 1982 (Hebrew).

———. *Sources and Traditions*: Shabbath. Jerusalem: Jewish Theological Seminary, 1982 (Hebrew).

———. *Sources and Traditions*: Yoma-Hagigah. Jerusalem: Jewish Theological Seminary, 1975 (Hebrew).

Hauptman, Judith. *The Development of the Talmudic Sugya: Relationship Between Tannaitic and Amoraic Sources*. Lanham, MD: University Press of America, 1988.

Havelock, Eric. *The Greek Concept of Justice: From Its Shadow in Homer to Its Substance in Plato*. Cambridge, MA: Harvard University Press, 1978.

———. *The Literate Revolution in Greece and its Cultural Consequences*. Princeton: Princeton University Press, 1982.

———. *The Muse Learns to Write: Reflections on Orality and Literacy from Antiquity to the Present*. New Haven: Yale University Press, 1986.

———. *A Preface to Plato*. Cambridge, MA: Harvard University Press, 1963.

Hayes, Christine Elizabeth. *Between the Babylonian and Palestinian Talmuds: Accounting for Halakhic Difference in Selected Sugyot from Tractate Avodah Zarah*. New York: Oxford University Press, 1997.

Hezser, Catherine. *Jewish Literacy in Roman Palestine*. Tübingen: Mohr Siebeck, 2001.

Hirschberg, H. Z. "Joseph, King of Himyar, and the Coming of Mar Zutra to Tiberias." Pages 139–146 in *All the Land of Naphtali*. Edited by H. Z. Hirschberg and Y. Abiram. Jerusalem: Ha-Hevrah le-Haqirat Erets-Yisra'el ve-Atiqoteha, 1967 (Hebrew).

———. "Mar Zutra, the Head of the Sanhedrin at Tiberias." Pages 147–153 in *All the Land of Naphtali*. Edited by H. Z. Hirschberg and Y. Abiram. Jerusalem: Ha-Hevrah le-Haqirat Erets-Yisra'el va-Atiqoteha, 1967 (Hebrew).

Holum, Kenneth G. "Identity and the Late Antique City: The Case of Caesarea." Pages 157–177 in *Religious and Ethnic Communities in Later Roman Palestine*. Edited by Hayim Lapin. Bethesda, MD: University Press of Maryland, 1998.

Jaffee, Martin. "The Babylonian Appropriation of the Talmud Yerushalmi: Redactional Studies in the Horayot Tractates." Pages 3–27 in *The Literature of Early Rabbinic Judaism: Issues in Talmudic Redaction and Interpretation*. Edited by Alan J. Avery-Peck. Vol. 4 of *New Perspectives On Ancient Judaism*. Lanham, MD: University Press of America, 1989.

———. *Torah in the Mouth: Writing and Oral Tradition in Palestinian Judaism, 200 BCE–400 CE*. New York: Oxford University Press, 2001.

Jastrow, Marcus. *Dictionary of the Targumim, the Talmud Bavli and Yerushalmi, and the Midrashic Literature*. New York: Pardes, 1950.

Jawitz, Ze'ev Wolf. *Sefer Toldot Yisra'el*. 10 vols. Tel-Aviv: Ahi'ever, 1935.

Jones, A. H. M. *The Later Roman Empire, 284–602: A Social, Economic, and Administrative Survey*. 2 vols. Oxford: Basil Blackwell, 1986.

Juster, Jean. *Les Juifs dans l'Empire Romain.* 2 vols. Paris: Librairie Paul Genthner, 1914.

Kalmin, Richard. "Christians and Heretics in Rabbinic Literature of Late Antiquity." *Harvard Theological Review* 87:2 (1994): 155–169.

———. "The Post-Rav Ashi Amoraim: Transition or Continuity? A Study of the Role of the Final Generations of Amoraim in the Redaction of the Talmud." Ph.D. diss., Jewish Theological Seminary, 1985.

———. *The Redaction of the Babylonian Talmud: Amoraic or Saboraic?* New York: HUC Press, 1989.

———. Review of Jack N. Lightstone, *The Rhetoric of the Babylonian Talmud, Its Social Meaning and Context. Journal of the American Oriental Society* 116:3 (1996): 558–559.

———. *The Sage in Jewish Society of Late Antiquity.* London: Routledge, 1999.

———. *Sages, Stories, Authors, and Editors in Rabbinic Babylonia.* Brown Judaic Studies 300. Atlanta: Scholars Press, 1994.

Kaplan, Julius. *The Redaction of the Babylonian Talmud.* Jerusalem: Makor, 1933.

Katz, Menahem. "*Yerushalmi,* End of Tractate *Avoda Zara*—The 'Missing *Yerushalmi*' Revisited." *Sidrah* 12 (1996): 79–111 (Hebrew).

Kohut, Alexander. *Arukh ha-Shalem.* 8 vols. 1878–1892. Repr., Vienna: Menorah, 1926.

Kraemer, David. *The Meanings of Death in Rabbinic Judaism.* London: Routledge, 2000.

———. *The Mind of the Talmud.* New York: Oxford University Press, 1990.

———. *Reading the Rabbis: The Talmud as Literature.* New York: Oxford University Press, 1996.

———. "Stylistic Characteristics of Amoraic Literature." Ph.D. diss., Jewish Theological Seminary, 1984.

Levy, Jacob. *Neuhebräisches und Chaldäisches Wörterbuch über die Talmudim und Midraschim.* Rev. Lazarus Goldschmidt. 2nd ed. Berlin: Benjamin Harz, 1924.

Lieberman, Saul. "The Publication of the Mishnah." Pages 83–99 in *Hellenism in Jewish Palestine.* New York: Jewish Theological Seminary, 1950.

Lieu, Samuel N. C. "Captives, Refugees and Exiles: A Study of Cross-Frontier Movements and Contacts Between Rome and Persia From Valerian to Jovian." Pages 475–505 in vol. 2 of *The Defence of the Roman and Byzantine East.* Edited by Philip Freeman and David Kennedy. Oxford: BAR International Series, 1986.

Lightstone, Jack N. *The Rhetoric of the Babylonian Talmud: Its Social Meaning and Context.* Waterloo, Ontario: Canadian Corporation for Studies in Religion/Wilfrid Laurier University Press, 1994.

Linder, Amnon. *The Jews in Roman Imperial Legislation.* 3 vols. Detroit: Wayne State University Press and Israel Academy of Arts and Sciences, 1987.

Luck-Huyse, Karin. *Der Traum vom Fliegen in der Antike.* Palingenesia 62. Stuttgart: Franz Steiner, 1997.

MacMullen, Ramsay. *Paganism in the Roman Empire.* New Haven: Yale University Press, 1981.

Magness, Jodi and Gideon Avni, "Jews and Christians in a Late Roman Cemetery at Beth Guvrin." Pages 87–114 in *Religious and Ethnic Communities in Later Roman Palestine.* Edited by Hayim Lapin. Bethesda, MD: University Press of Maryland, 1998.

Mann, Jacob. "Changes in the Divine Service of the Synagogue Due to Religious Persecutions." *Hebrew Union College Annual* 4 (1927): 241–310.

Margaliot, Mordecai. *Hilkhot Erets Yisra'el min ha-Genizah.* Jerusalem: Mossad HaRav Kook, 1973.

Michalowski, Piotr. "Writing and Literacy in Early States: A Mesopotamianist Perspective." Pages 49–70 in *Literacy: Interdisciplinary Conversations.* Edited by Deborah Keller-Cohen. Cresskill, NJ: Hampton Press, Inc., 1994.

Mirsky, Aharon. *Yosse Ben Yosse: Poems.* Jerusalem: Mossad Bialik, 1977 (Hebrew).

Moscovitz, Leib. "Designation is Significant: An Analysis of the Conceptual Sugya in bSan 47b–48b." *Association for Jewish Studies Review* 27:2 (Nov 2003): 227–252.

———. *Talmudic Reasoning: From Casuistics to Conceptualization.* Tübingen: Mohr Siebeck, 2002.

Naeh, Shlomo. "The Structure and Division of *Torat Kohanim* (A): Scrolls." *Tarbiz* 66 (1996–1997): 483–515 (Hebrew).

Neusner, Jacob. *Are the Talmuds Interchangeable? Christine Hayes's Blunder.* South Florida Studies in the History of Judaism 122. Atlanta: Scholars Press, 1995.

———. *Are There Really Tannaitic Parallels to the Gospels? A Refutation of Morton Smith.* South Florida Studies in the History of Judaism 80. Atlanta: Scholars Press, 1993.

———. *The Bavli and its Sources: The Question of Tradition in the Case of Tractate Sukkah.* Brown Judaic Studies 85. Atlanta: Scholars Press, 1987.

———. *The Bavli's Unique Voice: A Systematic Comparison of the Talmud of Babylonia and the Talmud of the Land of Israel.* 7 vols. South Florida Studies in the History of Judaism 71–73, 76–79. Atlanta: Scholars Press, 1993.

———. *A History of the Jews in Babylonia.* 5 vols. Studia Post-Biblica 9, 11, 12, 14, 15. Leiden: E. J. Brill, 1965–1970.

———. *Judaism: The Classical Statement: The Evidence of the Bavli.* Chicago: University of Chicago Press, 1986.

———. *Making the Classics in Judaism: The Three States of Literary Formation.* Brown Judaic Studies 180. Atlanta: Scholars Press, 1989.

———. *Oral Tradition in Judaism: The Case of the Mishnah.* Garland Reference Library of the Humanities 764. New York: Garland, 1987.

———. *Sources and Traditions: Types of Compositions in the Talmud of Babylonia.* South Florida Studies in the History of Judaism 36. Atlanta: Scholars Press, 1992.

———. *Torah: From Scroll to Symbol in Formative Judaism.* Philadelphia: Fortress Press, 1985.

———. *The Two Talmuds Compared.* 13 vols. Atlanta: Scholars Press, 1996.

Olson, David R. *The World On Paper: The Conceptual and Cognitive Implications of Writing and Reading.* Cambridge, UK: Cambridge University Press, 1994.

Ong, Walter J. *Orality and Literacy: The Technologizing of the Word.* New York: Routledge, 1982.

Rappaport, Shlomo Yehudah. "Toldot Rabbenu Nissim." *Bikkurei ha-Ittim* (1831): 90–92.

Reif, Stefan C. "Aspects of Medieval Jewish Literacy." Pages 134–155 in *The Uses of Literacy in Early Medieval Europe.* Edited by Rosamond McKitterick. Cambridge, UK: Cambridge University Press, 1990.

Rosenthal, David. "Arikhot qedumot ha-meshuqa'ot ba-Talmud ha-Bavli." Pages 155–204 in *Mehqerei Talmud: Talmudic Studies I.* Edited by Yaacov Sussman and David Rosenthal. Jerusalem: Magnes Press, 1990.

Rovner, Jay. "Pseudepigraphic Invention and Diachronic Stratification in the Stammaitic Component of the Bavli: The Case of Sukka 28." *Hebrew Union College Annual* 68 (1997): 11–62.

Rubenstein, Jeffrey L. *The Culture of the Babylonian Talmud.* Baltimore: Johns Hopkins University Press, 2003.

———. "Some Structural Patterns of Yerushalmi Sugyot." Pages 303–313 in vol. 3 of *The Talmud Yerushalmi and Graeco-Roman Culture.* Edited by Peter Schäfer. Tübingen: Mohr Siebeck, 2003.

———. *Talmudic Stories: Narrative Art, Composition, and Culture.* Baltimore: Johns Hopkins University Press, 1999.

Safrai, Ze'ev. "Marginal Notes on the Rehob Inscription." *Zion* 42 (1977): 1–23 (Hebrew).

———. *The Missing Century; Palestine in the Fifth Century: Growth and Decline.* Leuven: Peeters, 1998.

———. "The Rehov Inscription." *Immanuel* 8 (Spring 1978): 48–57.

Safrai, Ze'ev, and Aren M. Maier. "אתא אגרתא ממערבא ('An Epistle Came From the West'): Historical and Archaeological Evidence For the Ties

Between the Jewish Communities in the Land of Israel and Babylonia During the Talmudic Period." *Jewish Quarterly Review* 93:3–4 (Jan–Apr 2003): 497–531.

Schäfer, Peter. "Jews and Gentiles in Yerushalmi Avodah Zarah." Pages 335–352 in vol. 3 of *The Talmud Yerushalmi and Graeco-Roman Culture*. Edited by Peter Schäfer. Tübingen: Mohr Siebeck, 2003.

Schwartz, Seth. "Gamaliel in Aphrodite's Bath: Palestinian Judaism and Urban Culture in the Third and Fourth Centuries." Pages 203–217 in vol. 1 of *The Talmud Yerushalmi and Graeco-Roman Culture*. Edited by Peter Schäfer and Catherine Hezser. Tübingen: Mohr Siebeck, 1999.

———. *Imperialism and Jewish Society, 200 B.C.E. To 640 C.E.* Princeton: Princeton University Press, 2001.

———. "Rabbinization in the Sixth Century." Pages 55–69 in vol. 3 of *The Talmud Yerushalmi and Graeco-Roman Culture*. Edited by Peter Schäfer. Tübingen: Mohr Siebeck, 2003.

Scribner, Sylvia, and Cole, Michael. *The Psychology of Literacy*. Cambridge, MA: Harvard University Press, 1981.

Sirat, Collette. "Le livre hébreux dans les premiers siècles de notre ère: le témoignage des textes." Pages 115–124 in *Les Débuts du Codex*. Edited by A. Blanchard. Turnhout: Brépols, 1989.

Sokoloff, Michael. *A Dictionary of Jewish Palestinian Aramaic of the Byzantine Period*. Ramat-Gan: Bar-Ilan University Press, 1990.

Sperber, Daniel. *A Dictionary of Greek and Latin Legal Terms in Rabbinic Literature*. Ramat-Gan: Bar-Ilan University Press, 1984.

Sternberg, Meir. *The Poetics of Biblical Narrative: Ideological Literature and the Drama of Reading*. Bloomington, IN: Indiana University Press, 1987.

Street, Brian V., ed. *Cross-Cultural Approaches to Literacy*. Cambridge, UK: Cambridge University Press, 1993.

———. *Social Literacies: Critical Approaches to Literacy in Development, Ethnography, and Education*. London: Longman, 1995.

Sussman, Yaacov. "Additional Notes to 'A Halakhic Inscription From Beth-Shean.'" *Tarbiz* 44 (1974–1975): 193–195 (Hebrew).

———. "Ve-shuv le-Yerushalmi Neziqin." Pages 55–133 in vol. 1 of *Mehqerei Talmud: Talmudic Studies*. Edited by Yaacov Sussman and David Rosenthal. Jerusalem: Magnes Press, 1990.

———. "Babylonian Sugiyot to the Orders Zera'im and Toharot." Ph.D. diss., Hebrew University, 1969 (Hebrew).

———. "A Halakhic Inscription From the Beth-Shean Valley." *Tarbiz* 43 (1973–1974): 88–158 (Hebrew).

———. "The Inscription in the Synagogue at Rehov." Pages 146–153 in *Ancient Synagogues Revealed*. Edited by Lee I. Levine. Jerusalem: The Israel Exploration Society; Detroit: Wayne State University Press, 1988.

Tchernowitz, Chaim (Rav Tzair). *History of the Jewish Codes.* 3 vols. New York: The Jubilee Committee, 1946 (Hebrew).

Tennenblatt, M. A. *Peraqim hadashim le-toldot Erets Yisra'el u-Bavel bi-tequfat ha-Talmud.* Tel-Aviv: Dvir, 1966.

Van Bekkum, Wout Jac. *Hebrew Poetry from Late Antiquity: Liturgical Poems of Yehudah: Critical Edition with Introduction and Commentary.* Leiden: E. J. Brill, 1998.

Weiss, Abraham. *Le-heqer ha-Talmud.* New York: Feldheim, 1954.

———. *'Al ha-yetsirah ha-sifrutit shel ha-amoraim.* New York: Horeb, 1962.

Wissowa, Georg, ed. *Paulys Real-Encyclopädie der Classischen Altertumwissenschaft.* 24 vols. Stuttgart: J. B. Metzler Buchhandlung, 1905.

Yahalom, Joseph. *Liturgical Poems of Šim'on Bar Megas.* Jerusalem: The Israel National Academy of Sciences, 1984 (Hebrew).

Zulay, Menahem. *Piyyute Yannai.* Berlin: Schocken, 1938.

General Index

Palestinian rabbis on *minut*,
  97n12
on Ravina's identity in b. AZ
  26b, 216
Kraemer, David, 6n19, 59n26, 232
Kratesis, 47, 128, 150–151
Kratoschin edition of Yerushalmi,
  50n16, 54n20

L

Lazar, R. (Eleazar), 130, 179, 184
Lazar b. R. Tsadoq, R. (Eleazar b.
  Tsadoq), 108–109, 112
Leiden manuscript of Talmud
  Yerushalmi, 50n16, 55n21,
  106n26, 200n1
Levy, Yisrael, 16
libation-wine
  anonymous Bavli, 179–181
  benefit from, 63–66, 159–160
  boiled wine and, 214
  contamination of, 166–167,
    166n13
  repayment of loans by Gentiles
    and, 146–147
  wages for, 145–146, 159, 180
Lieberman, Saul, 26n79, 37, 217
Liezer, R. *See* Eliezer, R.
linguistic differences between
  Bavli and Yerushalmi, 89,
  89n3, 97
literacy hypothesis, 224–227, 232

M

macro analysis
  aggadah in, 48
  b. Avodah Zarah appropriation
    of y. Avodah Zarah sugyot,
    94–95

baraitot in, 48–49
biblical history review in, 52–53
disputes of Rav and Shmuel,
  57–58
Eleazar b. Dama story and, 59–
  62, 61n29, 134–136
importance of, 20–21
methodology of, 33–34, 85–86
mishnayot in, 47–49, 51, 57, 69,
  73
structural correspondences in,
  14–17
sugyot arrangements in, 15–16,
  22–24, 52, 56–58
three-day abstention from activities with Gentiles, 89, 94, 96
Tosefta, 60, 62
y. Avodah Zarah appropriation
  of b. Avodah Zarah sugyot,
  77–81
See also "called for by the mishnah"; early talmud; Jaffee,
  Martin; Rappaport, Shlomo
  Yehudah
Magness, Jodi, 207
Mamre, churches in, 207
Mana, R., 89, 152–153, 179–180,
  190–191
Mani b. Patish, R., 2n5
Mar bar R. Ashi, 216
Matana, R., 46, 46n10, 105
Matanya, R., 54
Meir, R., 47, 72, 120–121, 143, 164,
  182–184, 189
memrot, 5, 11, 18, 28–30, 32–33, 229
Mercurius, 54–58, 180
Mesharshya b. de-R. Idi, R., 139–
  141
micro analysis
  abstract legal conceptualization
    by Bavli, 140–147

oral transmission of rabbinic literature, 217–218, 220–221
Oshaya, R., 158

P, Q

Palestinian amoraim
  anonymous Bavli attributed to, 179–181
  dating of, 2n4
  as editors, 2n4
  Palestinian anonymous Bavli, 181–188
  rabbinic centers of, 181
  traditions of, 214–215
Palestinian anonymous Bavli, 181–188
Palestinian Jews
  demographics of, 201, 208, 212
  halakhic works of, 208
  judaization of, 202
  liturgy, 209–210
  persecution of, 203–205
  rabbinization of, 201–203
Palestinian Talmud. *See* Yerushalmi
Papa, R., 31–33, 176
Paris manuscript (*Sefer ha-Eshkol,* Albeck), 235, 237
Patriarchal authority, 108–110, 115–116n35
Pedat, R., 132–133
Peor. *See* Baal Peor
Pirqoi b. Baboi, 210n52
piyyut/piyyutim, 202, 206, 208–210, 234
P'nei Moshe, 50n15, 55n21, 118, 155nn3–4
private holidays of Gentiles, 47–48
Q hypothesis, 14n53, 19–21, 20n68, 22

R

Rabba bar Hanna, 120
Rabbah, 76, 214
Rabbah b. Bar Hana, 82–85
Rabbah b. Ulla, 28, 162
rabbinic court
  bills of divorce, 107, 109, 112–113
  community acceptance of judgments of, 109–110
  Patriarchal authority in, 108–109
  permissiveness of, 107, 109–110, 113
Rabbi (Yehudah ha-Nasi, R.), 1, 52, 106n26, 107–110, 114–115, 116n35
Rabin, 5n15, 6, 32, 120, 236
Rami b. de-R. Yeba, 78, 80, 80n49
Rami b. Hama, 75
Rappaport, Shlomo Yehudah, 11, 14–15, 34, 73–74
Rashi, 106n26, 117
Rav, 51
  on Babylonian leniencies, 152
  on cooked foods of Gentiles, 153
  on Creation in Tishrei, 44, 102
  disputes of Rav and Shmuel, 108–109, 111–115, 125–128
  embarrassment of, 111, 114–115
  on festivals of Gentiles, 43–45, 100, 105
  on Gentile oil, 106n26, 108–109, 112, 115
  on idolatry, 50, 55, 179
  as zaqen mamre (rebellious elder), 108–110, 114
Rava, 176
  as Bavli's addition to Yerushalmi sugya, 93, 100n18
  on commerce with Gentiles, 92–93, 162, 191

Safrai, Ze'ev, 206–207, 222–223

Sama b. de-R. Ashi, R., 216

Samaritans, 45, 201, 205, 207

Saturnalia, 45, 47, 74, 101–102, 105, 128–129

Schwartz, Seth, 44n6, 202–203, 206, 229n126

Scribner, Sylvia, 225–226

Sefer ha-Eshkol (R. Abraham of Narbonne), 235, 237

Shammai, 108, 112

Shema, 210n52

Sherira Gaon, R., 5n15, 238n5

Sheshet, R., 83–84, 188n15

Shimi b. Hiyya, R., 28

Shimon, R., 121, 151, 189, 214

Shimon b. de-R. Yannai, R., 2n5

Shimon b. Gamliel, Rabban, 28, 70–72, 182, 196

Shimon b. Laqish, R. *See* Resh Laqish

Shimon b. Pazi, R., 32

Shimon b. Yohanan, R., 160

Shimon b. Yotsadaq, R., 160

Shimon bar Megas, 209–210

Shimon ben Laqish, R. *See* Resh Laqish

Shmuel, 106n26, 108–109, 111–115, 120, 125–128, 144, 155–156

Shmuel b. R. Yitshaq, R., 167–168

Shmuel b. Yehudah, R., 5n15

Shmuel b. Yitshaq, R., 188n15

Sifra (tannaitic midrash to Leviticus), 220–221, 230, 232

Simlai the Southerner, 107–109, 111, 114

solstice, 43–46, 48, 101–103

stam ha-Talmud, 18

stammaim, 10, 10n30, 91n5, 176–178

Street, Brian V., 226

sugyot

amoraim and, 26, 31–32, 31n88, 49–50, 85n54, 181–182

analysis of, 16, 18, 18n64, 199

arrangement shared by Talmuds, 24–26

Bavli v. Yerushalmi influences on, 33

circulation of, 31–32

complex sugyot in b. Avodah Zarah, 53–58

context of, 32–33

in macro analysis, 15–16, 22–24, 52, 56–58, 77–81, 94–95

in micro analysis, 91, 94

mishnayot associated with, 126–127, 133

Palestinian sugyot, 2n4, 100n18, 182

rearrangement of, 126–127

simplicity of, 31–32

transmission from Land of Israel to Babylonia, 16

See also "called for by the mishnah"

Sussman, Yaacov, 2n4, 15, 22, 26n79, 27–30, 33, 222–223

synagogues

destruction of, 211

in Palestine, 202–203

Rehov synagogue, 202, 218, 221–224, 229n126, 231

Rome and, 204

Synoptic Gospels, 19

T

Tahlifa bar Giza, R., 216

Talmud Bavli. *See* Bavli

Talmud of Caesarea, 26n79, 217n72

Bavli awareness of, 5–12, 6n18,
7n22, 34–35
Bavli reorganization of, 89–95,
112–116, 119–121, 125–129,
135–136
biblical history review in, 52–54
dating of, 2, 2n2, 2n4
inscription at Rehov synagogue,
222–224
manuscripts of, 50n16, 54n20,
106n26, 200n1
nahote, 5–7, 5nn15–16, 6nn17–18,
22, 27, 31, 183, 236
Palestinian amoraim, 2n4, 179–
182, 214–215
scholar migrations to Babylonia,
212–213, 236, 241–242
shared material with Bavli, 5,
7n22, 22–23, 176, 230–231
transmission form of, 217–219,
221, 230–232
as Western, 9–10, 10n28
writing as possible *aide-mémoire*
for, 232–233
See also anonymous Yerushalmi;
b. Avodah Zarah; dispute
headings; Gentile headings;
idolatry; Israel, Land of; Palestine headings; y. Avodah
Zarah
Yeshua b. Pantera (Jesus), 59
Yirmiya, R., 144
Yirmiyah, R.
on Gentile milk, 151
housing of beasts with Gentiles,
130
on idolatry, 50, 54
on libation-wine, 145, 167
on mixtures of ordinary and
terumah leavens, 169
R. Yose refutation of, 131, 133
R. Zeirah citation of, 144
Yirmiyah b. Abba, R., 51

Yishmael, R., 59–62, 95, 180, 214
Yitshaq b. Eleazar, R., 83
Yitshaq b. Matana, R., 82
Yitshaq b. Nahman, R., 161, 214
Yitshaq b. Shmuel b. Marta, 107,
109, 111
Yitshaq b. Yosef, R., 5n15, 183
Yitshaq Napha, R., 52
Yohanan, R.
R. Abbahu and, 63, 66–67, 117–
119, 171
on amoraic dispute-format,
85n54
anonymous Bavli attributed to,
181
on business transactions with
Gentiles, 36, 91–92, 96, 138,
146, 160
Hadrianic pottery, prohibition
of, 144
on idolatry, 53–54, 56, 82, 89,
144, 154, 183
on imparting of taste, 117, 120,
167
on Kalends, 44–45, 105, 124,
149–150
on laborers' wages, 63, 66
on Land of Israel, 184
R. Lazar (Eleazar) and, 184
on libation wine, 159–160
R. Meir interpreted by, 183
as Palestinian scholar, 10n29
R. Papa and, 176
on rabbinic court procedures,
108–109
ro'eh (רואה) concept of, 168–171
on Sabbatical year transactions,
63–64
on Saturnalia, 45
stones of a worshipped mountain, 75
on use of forbidden item for another purpose, 145